CORRESPONDENCE
AND OCCASIONAL WRITINGS

NATURAL LAW AND
ENLIGHTENMENT CLASSICS

Knud Haakonssen
General Editor

Francis Hutcheson

NATURAL LAW AND
ENLIGHTENMENT CLASSICS

Correspondence and Occasional Writings

Francis Hutcheson

Private Correspondence and Unpublished
Documents edited by M. A. Stewart

Public Correspondence and Occasional Writings
edited by James Moore

With an Introduction by James Moore

*The Collected Works and Correspondence
of Francis Hutcheson*

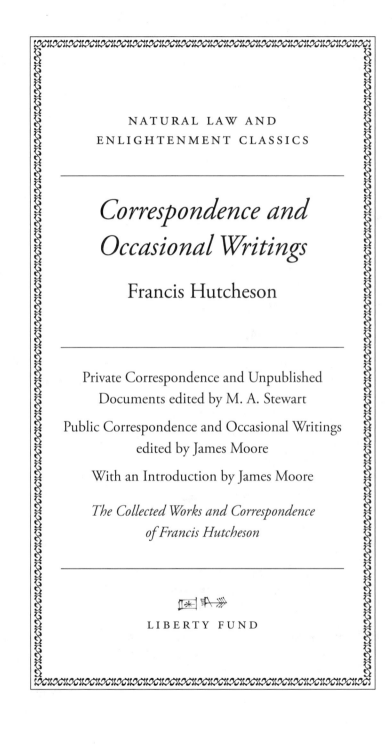

LIBERTY FUND

Introduction, editorial additions, and index © 2022 by Liberty Fund, Inc.
Frontispiece: Detail of a portrait of Francis Hutcheson by Allan Ramsay
(ca. 1740–45), oil on canvas, reproduced courtesy of the Hunterian Art
Gallery, University of Glasgow.

22 23 24 25 26 C 5 4 3 2 1
22 23 24 25 26 P 5 4 3 2 1

Library of Congress Cataloging-in-Publication Data
Names: Hutcheson, Francis, 1694–1746, author. | Stewart, M. A. (Michael Alexander),
1937- editor. | Moore, James, editor, writer of introduction.
Title: Correspondence and occasional writings / Francis Hutcheson ; private
correspondence and unpublished documents edited by M. A. Stewart ; public
correspondence and occasional writings edited by James Moore ; with an
introduction by James Moore.
Description: 1st. | Carmel, Indiana : Liberty Fund, Inc., 2022. |
Series: Natural law and Enlightenment classics | Includes bibliographical references
and index. | Summary: "Francis Hutcheson is often described as the father of the
Scottish Enlightenment, and in this modern edition, never-before-published
personal letters reveal the loyalty and lasting affection Hutcheson had for his friends,
and his published correspondence and speeches bring to light his polemical skills
in controversy and his preoccupation with religious and intellectual liberty"—
Provided by publisher.
Identifiers: LCCN 2021043604 | ISBN 9780865976276 (hardcover) |
ISBN 9780865976283 (paperback) | ISBN 9781614872894 (epub) |
ISBN 9781614876663 (kindle edition) | ISBN 9781614879367 (pdf)
Subjects: LCSH: Hutcheson, Francis, 1694–1746—Correspondence. |
Philosophy, Modern—Early works to 1800. | Philosophy, Modern—18th century.
Classification: LCC B1503 .A4 2022 | DDC 190.9/03—dc23/eng/20211027
LC record available at https://lccn.loc.gov/2021043604

LIBERTY FUND, INC.
11301 North Meridian Street
Carmel, Indiana 46032
libertyfund.org

CONTENTS

ACKNOWLEDGMENTS

The editors would like to express their gratitude to Laura Goetz and the editorial staff of Liberty Fund for their patience and continued support during the many years it has taken us to produce this edition. James Moore is grateful for the support of colleagues and the interlibrary loans staff of Concordia University.

We have also benefited from conversations with many colleagues and friends, among them Richard Sher, Luigi Turco, Ian McBride, John Wright, and Paul Wood.

And we are particularly indebted to Knud Haakonssen for advice, support, and collaboration on this volume.

GENERAL EDITOR'S PREFACE

The editorial work on Francis Hutcheson's private correspondence (part I of the present edition) was not entirely completed by the time the volume had to go into production. Professor M. A. Stewart was not at the time in a position to complete the remaining tasks. With his agreement I undertook some necessary supplementation of his annotations, cross-references, and the like. Furthermore, I added a previously printed letter (Letter 35) and annotated this. The transcription of the manuscript letters is entirely Professor Stewart's work. The bibliography has been established from the references in the annotations. I am indebted to Professor John Cairns for advice about two of the manuscripts.

Sadly, Professor Stewart passed away during the final production of this book.

Knud Haakonssen

On Professor Stewart's behalf, it is a pleasure to acknowledge the archives and collections that hold the documents transcribed here:

Aberdeen University Library
Edinburgh City Archives
Edinburgh University Library
Glasgow University Library
John Rylands University Library, Manchester
Magee University College, Londonderry
National Archives of Scotland
National Library of Scotland
Presbyterian Historical Society of Ireland
Public Record Office of Northern Ireland
Staatsbibliothek zu Berlin
Trinity College Dublin Library

INTRODUCTION

This edition of the correspondence and occasional writings of Francis Hutcheson marks the first attempt to gather the letters written by Hutcheson and the letters addressed to him. It is remarkable that no previous collection of his correspondence has been attempted. His writings had a pervasive influence upon other philosophers of the Scottish enlightenment. He appears to have been esteemed by many of his colleagues and students at the University of Glasgow, where he taught from 1730 until his death in August 1746. His correspondents included friends from his student years in Glasgow (1710–18). He also had friends in the Church of Scotland, the Church of Ireland, and the world of learned journalism in London, Dublin, and Amsterdam. His correspondence, private and public, consists very largely of letters written to and from this wide-ranging, often connected, circle of friends.

Private Correspondence

Hutcheson's personal correspondence is fragmentary. In almost every case, only one side of the correspondence has survived. There are thirteen letters from his cousin William Bruce (1702–55) in Dublin. Hutcheson would have met Bruce early in life, when he lived with Bruce's family (Hutcheson's aunt and uncle) from 1707 to 1710. The letters Hutcheson wrote to Bruce have not survived. There are nineteen letters from Hutcheson to the Reverend Thomas Drennan (1696–1768), who was Hutcheson's fellow student in Glasgow and who later assisted Hutcheson in his Dublin academy in the 1720s. Hutcheson's letters to Drennan are from the last nine years of Hutcheson's life (1737–46); those from Drennan to Hutcheson are no longer extant. The same one-way traffic applies

xiii

to Hutcheson's letters to his father, the Reverend John Hutcheson (d. 1729), to William Mace (d. 1767), and from David Hume (1711–1776).

After his student years in Glasgow, a period from which only one letter (Private Correspondence, Letter 1, below) survives, Hutcheson returned to Ireland, where he became occupied by the controversy surrounding Benjamin Hoadly, bishop of Bangor (Letter 2). In the years that followed, 1718–24, Hutcheson adopted the principles of Hoadly and his followers: ministers in the north of Ireland John Abernethy (1680–1740), James Kirkpatrick (1676–1743), and Samuel Haliday (1685–1739), who became his lifelong friends and allies. The publication of Hutcheson's *Inquiry* was advertised by Hoadly himself in *The London Journal* for October 31, 1724. In 1719–20, Hutcheson moved to Dublin, where he established a Dissenting academy at the corner of Dominick Street and Drumcondra Lane, later called Dorset Street. He conducted his Dublin academy through the 1720s, with the support of Thomas Drennan (Letter 15) and Presbyterian ministers in Dublin. And he would come to have other friends in Dublin, some of them highly placed in the established Church of Ireland (Letter 3).

The rumor that Francis Hutcheson might accept a living in the Church of Ireland alarmed his father, a defender of the catechisms and confessions of the Presbyterian Church. It was in response to the anxieties expressed by Reverend John Hutcheson that Francis Hutcheson wrote the remarkable letter (Letter 4) to his father of August 4, 1726, in which he expressed his opinions on the subject of church government but assured his father that he knew of no worldly consideration that would prompt him to conform. The Reverend John Hutcheson may have been relieved of his anxieties so far as his concern was the vocational intentions of his son. But there is no reason to suppose that he was persuaded by the considerations advanced in his son's letter.

Hutcheson's letter to William Mace of September 6, 1727 (Letter 5), is notable for its elaboration of a central theme in Hutcheson's metaphysics: his theory of concomitant ideas. In his Dissenting academy in Dublin in the 1720s, Hutcheson appears to have followed the general practice of teaching all parts of the arts curriculum: logic, metaphysics, and moral and natural philosophy. He later declared that he had read "Dr. Berkly's books" at that time (Letter 5). And he countered Mace's (Berkeleyan) skepticism by arguing that our acquaintance with objects in the external world can be explained by concomitant ideas of extension, figure, motion, rest, and solidity. He employed a similar line of reasoning to explain the ideas of self and consciousness of desire: everyone has an idea of self to which other perceptions are connected, and the perception of a desire (a concomitant idea) must be distinguished from the desire itself. It may be added that Hutcheson seems to have been acquainted with Berkeley in the 1720s when both were living in Dublin. Later he described Berkeley as "a man bursting almost with Vanity long ago" (Letter 16).

On December 19, 1729, Francis Hutcheson was elected professor of philosophy at the University of Glasgow to succeed Gershom Carmichael (1672–1729) (see "Documents Relating to Hutcheson's Appointment at the University of Glasgow": pp. 125–28). The election was closely contested: seven votes to five in favor of Hutcheson; the minority preferred Frederick Carmichael, the son of the previous occupant of the chair, because they judged him to be a more orthodox Presbyterian than Hutcheson. On the eve of the election, Robert Wodrow expressed a prescient apprehension: "Hou the principles he goes on agree with the truths generally received in this Church, and what influence his teaching them here may have, time will discover" (Wodrow, *Analecta*, 4:99). Hutcheson's arrival in Glasgow was delayed until October 1730; he "subscribed the Confession of Faith in presence of the presbytery of Glasgow" on October 29 and delivered his inaugural lecture on November 3 ("Documents," p. 127. Wodrow wrote of his lecture: "His character and carriage seems prudent and cautious, and that will be the best vidimus of him" (Wodrow, *Analecta*, 4:187).

On September 4, 1732, a letter (Letter 8) was sent to a professor at the University of Glasgow from "Your Most devoted Pupil, Patrick Lang." There are a number of reasons to believe that the letter was addressed to Francis Hutcheson. Patrick Lang would have taken Hutcheson's class in moral philosophy in the year immediately preceding the letter. The letter was found in a collection that contains other letters addressed to Hutcheson, notably those by William Bruce. The letter contains an extended reflection on Livy's *Early History of Rome*, which Lang was inspired to read by the lectures of his professor, and lists political writers who celebrated the advantages of the mixed constitution of the Roman Republic and whom Hutcheson cited on this and other subjects in *A System of Moral Philosophy* and *A Short Introduction to Moral Philosophy*. Moreover, the principles that the student drew from Livy's *History* are consistent with Hutcheson's moral philosophy.

The absence of the proper name of the professor from the letter can be readily explained by the subject of the opening paragraphs. Patrick Lang was eager to obtain his professor's approval for his controversial opinions on revealed religion. He had written to the same professor before on this subject and had been cautioned. Hutcheson typically exercised great discretion on the subject of revealed religion. As he told his father and as will be remarked in his Occasional Writings, he preferred to keep his views on the subject of Christian revelation and church government to himself. And Lang's beliefs were clearly inconsistent with Christian and trinitarian orthodoxy.

Hutcheson maintained close ties with family and friends in Ireland during his years in Glasgow, as we learn from the letters sent to him by his cousin William Bruce. The letters from Bruce typically express great affection and esteem for his cousin. There are frequent references to family: to Hutcheson's elder brother, Hans (Letter 7); to Hutcheson's half-sister, "Cousen Rhoda" (Letters 10, 32, and 41); and to John Trail, cousin of both Hutcheson and Bruce (Letter 10). Bruce was concerned about the morals of his nephews, James and Samuel Bruce (Letter 11), and was himself the beneficiary of Hutcheson's moral counsel (Letter 19).

It is clear that Hutcheson was, after all, contemplating an appointment in the established church (Letter 10). This appears to be the background to his wish to circulate the manuscript of *A System of Moral Philosophy* among his Irish connections. Notwithstanding Bruce's warning that the manuscript might be lost (Letter 19), it was sent to Ireland with instructions that it be shown to Edward Synge (1691–1762) and Thomas Rundle (1687/8–1743), bishops of Ferns and Leighlin, and Derry, in the Church of Ireland (see Letters 7, 21, and 38). In a later letter (Letter 25) Bruce returned to his opinion that Hutcheson might be better employed in the established church than at the University of Glasgow. Bruce had become alarmed by an attack on Hutcheson's orthodoxy in an open letter from a former student (see pp. 62–63 and 291–337). Hutcheson remembered Bruce in his will, and on Bruce's death, Gabriel Cornwall composed a memorial to the two men (see p. 131 and p. 20, note 25)

Hutcheson's acquaintance with the philosophy of David Hume dates from April 1739 when he thanked Henry Home for "the most obliging Present of your Friends Book" (Letter 26). *A Treatise of Human Nature*, volumes 1 and 2, had been published in January of that year. Hutcheson's response to these volumes on understanding and the passions was guarded, but Hume was prompted by this response to send Hutcheson a draft of the third volume of the *Treatise*, on morals. Hutcheson's "Reflections" on Hume's "Papers" and Hume's replies, both set out in Hume's letter to Hutcheson of September 17, 1739 (Letter 30), are notable for their disagreements on subjects of central importance in their moral philosophies which have been extensively discussed in the scholarly literature.

The most revealing account of Hutcheson's later years is contained in the letters he wrote to Thomas Drennan. The letters that have survived were written from 1737 to 1746, the last year of Hutcheson's life. In these letters Hutcheson gave Drennan news of his family and his students and wrote of the difficulty of electing professors who thought like himself to the University of Glasgow.

Hutcheson's later letters to Drennan express a recurrent concern about the affairs of a cousin, Alexander Young, son of his father's sister Mary ("Aunt Young") (Letters 53 and 56), and Hutcheson made provision in his will for Young (see p. 131). Hutcheson also advanced money to his students. He appears to have managed the finances of many of the students who studied with him (Letters 15, 28, and 42). He took responsibility for the moral life of his students and was pleased to be able to testify to their diligence and sobriety (Letters 29 and 45). The conduct of Robert Haliday, the son of his old friend and Drennan's colleague the Reverend Samuel Haliday, was a source of particular concern (Letters 37, 38, 39, 42, and 50). Irish students generally, especially boys from Trinity College, Dublin, had a pernicious influence on their classmates (Letters 21 and 37).

These letters are also an indispensable resource for Hutcheson's writing during this period: he told Drennan much of what he had been writing, emphasizing how important it was for Drennan to respect the confidentiality of what he had been told. It is characteristic of these letters, and of Hutcheson's disposition more generally, that he was reluctant to acknowledge authorship of writings that might alarm the more theologically orthodox among his contemporaries. This applied to manuscript materials that he circulated to friends (Letters 17 and 24) or published anonymously, namely the *Considerations on Patronages* and his and James Moor's translation and edition of *The Meditations of the Emperor Marcus Aurelius Antoninus* (see the Introduction in the edition by James Moore and Michael Silverthorne, Liberty Fund, 2008).

Hutcheson's reluctance to put his name on writings that challenged religious orthodoxy did not inhibit him from promoting "true religion" by supporting the appointment of men who thought like himself (or men who were at least not opposed to his thinking) to positions in the church and universities. His later letters to Drennan and others reveal his determination in such matters. He remained in Glasgow in failing health to cast a vote for James Moor on June 26, 1746, so that he might be elected professor of Greek (Letter 58). He made out his last will and testament on June 30, 1746, and died in Dublin a month later on August 8, 1746.

Public Correspondence and Occasional Writings

Hutcheson's public correspondence differs in a number of ways from his private and familiar letters. His letters printed in learned journals in England, Ireland, and the Netherlands are for the most part illustrative of his ability in controversy. In this respect they resemble and complement his publications.

The London Journal, 1724–25

Hutcheson's earliest publication was a letter to *The London Journal* of November 14 and 21, 1724. It was directed against "our Common Systems of Morality," the natural law treatises of Samuel Pufendorf assigned to students in universities and academies across Protestant Europe in the early eighteenth century. Hutcheson objected to Pufendorf's emphasis on fear of God and sovereign power as the most effective motives prompting men to live sociably and in peace. He deplored the absence of natural affection and kind passions in natural law treatises.

From April to December 1725, Hutcheson engaged in a friendly disagreement with Gilbert Burnet, who argued that reason, not benevolence or natural affections, should be considered the foundation of morality. In these letters, Hutcheson maintained that if men are moved "by the very frame of their nature" to feel natural affection for others, it is reasonable to consider virtuous conduct to be action motivated by benevolence. He argued that there is in human nature a "sixth sense," a moral sense, that brings to mind an idea of virtue whenever we perceive benevolence or kind affection in ourselves or in others. Burnet countered that the moral sense may be unfit, not right, unjust, or not conformable with truth; in such cases we must find a standard of reasonableness to judge the fitness or rectitude of the moral sense. Hutcheson appealed to Burnet to consider that terms such as "fit" and "right" beg the question; there must be an end to moral reasoning. And this end must be a sense that a particular quality of character is right or good.

Hutcheson concluded his argument with Burnet by observing (in the final paragraph of his letter of October 9, 1725) that there must also be "something in the *Divine Nature,* of a nobler kind, corresponding to our Kindness and sweetest Affections; by which the *Deity* desires universal Happiness as an *End.*" He would return to this argument in the third edition of *An Essay on the Nature and Conduct of the Passions and Affections with Illustrations on the Moral Sense,* pp. 151–53.

Letter to Samuel Card, October 1725

This letter was Hutcheson's defense against an accusation that in *An Inquiry into the Original of Our Ideas of Beauty and Virtue* (1725) he had plagiarized his definition of beauty from Jean-Pierre Crousaz. In his reply, Hutcheson acknowledged that he had read Crousaz's *Traité du Beau* "eight years before I began to write," but he had not seen the book since that time. He declared that he had drawn "all my ideas of any consequence on the subject from some of the ancients and from my Lord Shaftesbury."

The substantive point in Hutcheson's disagreement with Crousaz concerns the manner in which beauty is perceived. He declared of Crousaz that his "distinction between Beauty as Idea and Beauty as sentiment is one I have never favoured and have even formally attacked in my Book, although it is maintained strongly in his." Crousaz insisted on the distinction between ideas, which we can control intentionally, and sentiments, which are not in our power to control. It was Hutcheson's contention that we are so created that we are determined to bring an idea of beauty to mind by an internal sense; it cannot be brought to mind by an act of will. Similarly we are bound to feel pleasure whenever an idea of beauty comes to mind. This is part of the providence designed for us by a benevolent God. If we are misled in our judgments about beauty, it is not by our internal sensibility, it is by bad education, custom, and misleading associations of ideas. Once we cease to be imposed upon by philosophers who would convince us of the corruption of our sentiments and our fallen human nature, we cannot fail to apprehend the beauty of works of art and the universe itself.

The Dublin Weekly Journal, 1725

In June 1725, three letters from Hutcheson on the subject of laughter were published in *The Dublin Weekly Journal*. In these letters Hutcheson returned to the theme of his letter to *The London Journal* of November 1724, namely, the deficiency of the system of Pufendorf. He now reminded readers of Pufendorf's debt to Hobbes for his first principles; it would follow that if Hobbes's principles were unsound, this would have implications for the system of Pufendorf, for his system was also a selfish system; or so Hutcheson had represented it in 1724, as he would present it again in later writings.

Hobbes had discovered the cause of laughter in a man's sudden realization of his superiority over others. Hutcheson argued against this theory. If it were nothing but our imagined superiority to others that prompts us to laugh, we would be amused by poverty and illness. It must be something other than incapacity or inferiority that provokes laughter. Hutcheson discovered the source of laughter in the bringing together of ideas that bear a general resemblance to one another but are also opposed in some way. It is the juxtaposition of incongruous ideas in the description of a character, an action, or an event that provokes mirth. Hutcheson explained why a sense of the ridiculous was implanted in human nature that gives us not only pleasure but is also conducive to sociability. We perceive the person who prompts us to laugh in an amiable light, and we delight in company in which laughter is enjoyed. It is a sense, however, that should never be indulged in "weak company" or in the presence of "weak minds"—of persons who lack a just discernment of true greatness and dignity.

Hutcheson illustrated his theory with allusions to Homer and Horace, and, notably, the satirical writings of Samuel Butler (1613–80) and Archibald Pitcairne (1652–1713), both of whom found amusement in the excessive gravity of strict Presbyterians. But of all the writers who shaped his thinking on this subject none was more important than Joseph Addison (1672–1719). It was Addison's agreement, in part, with Hobbes in *The Spectator*, no. 47, that prompted Hutcheson to reflect on the subject of laughter, and he also professed a more general debt to Addison's essays on the pleasures of the imagination that would be developed more fully in *An Essay on the Nature and Conduct of the Passions and Affections*.

The Dublin Weekly Journal, 1726

In February 1726, *The Dublin Weekly Journal* published three letters from Hutcheson on Bernard Mandeville's *The Fable of the Bees; or, Private Vices, Public Benefits* (*Dublin Weekly Journal*, Letters 4, 5, and 6, below). Hutcheson had declared his opposition to "the Author of the *Fable of the Bees*" on the title page of the *Inquiry* (1725), but the engagement with Mandeville was more confined than this would suggest, and the reference was later removed. His principal antagonists in the *Inquiry* were again those "Moralists" who attempted to demonstrate that all moral action and approval must be motivated by self-interest or self-love: Pufendorf and his commentators and also Richard Cumberland (1632–1718). Hutcheson's discussion of Mandeville focused on *An Enquiry into the Origin of Moral Virtue*, prefaced to the second and third editions of the

Fable (1723 and 1724). In his *Inquiry* Hutcheson contested Mandeville's argument that virtue has its origin in artifice and education: in the honors and marks of commendation employed by rulers to encourage bravery and other useful qualities in subjects, and in the praise bestowed by parents on their children to motivate them to behave well. Hutcheson's more comprehensive case against Mandeville was made in the letters in *The Dublin Weekly Journal*.

In the first letter (*Dublin Weekly Journal*, Letter 4), Hutcheson countered Mandeville's proposition that the happiness and prosperity of individuals and societies require indulgence of the passions and desires by sketching the moral psychology he would later elaborate in *An Essay upon the Nature and Conduct of the Passions and Affections* (1728). Hutcheson distinguished between appetites (desires preceded by uneasiness) and affections or passions (desires that arise from a good opinion of their object). The former constitute the necessities of life and must be satisfied; the latter may be regulated and controlled by correcting erroneous opinions of imagined objects of desire. Once one has broken "foolish Associations of Ideas," one may enjoy the true or real pleasures of beauty and virtue.

In the second letter (*Dublin Weekly Journal*, Letter 5) he presented arguments to prove that private vices, such as intemperance, luxury, and pride, are not necessary for prosperity and general happiness. He acknowledged that such vices promote consumption, manufacturing, and trade. But he maintained that an equal prosperity may be achieved without these vices, and that private happiness will be enhanced by the recognition that virtue (kind affection for family, friends, and country; love of the Deity and trust in His Providence) affords a more probable prospect of happiness than indulgence of "a poor, selfish Pleasure."

In the third letter (*Dublin Weekly Journal*, Letter 6), Hutcheson reverted to a theme of his first letter: that *The Fable of the Bees* was written in a manner that made it impossible to answer. As in his letters on laughter, Hutcheson now drew upon the insights of Addison to demonstrate the strategies of authors who write in this style. They pretend to have deep knowledge and they write with "open Vanity": Mandeville's claim that he had "Anatomised" the passions was pretension of this sort. Mandeville gave his writing the appearance of invincibility by means of pedantry, contempt of the clergy, displays of erudition, inconsistencies, and dexterity in confuting opposing schemes. Hutcheson clearly hoped that by exposing Mandeville's "strengths" in this ironic manner he was also inviting the reader to recognize his adversary's weakness.

Many of the letters in *The Dublin Weekly Journal* were gathered in *A Collection of Letters and Essays on Several Subjects, Lately Publish'd in "The Dublin Journal"* (London, 1729). The printers (J. Darby and T. Browne) were also the printers and booksellers of Hutcheson's *Essay* (1728), and only Hutcheson's *Inquiry* and his *Essay* were advertised on the end page of volume 2 of *A Collection*.

On June 7, 14, and 21, 1729, *The London Journal* published three letters (not included in this volume) on *The Fable of the Bees*. The second and third letters consisted very largely of Hutcheson's letters to *The Dublin Weekly Journal* of February 12 and 19, 1726 (*Dublin Weekly Journal*, Letters 5 and 6). The occasion for the review of Mandeville's work in 1729 was the publication in that year of a second volume of *The Fable of the Bees*. The author of the letters to *The London Journal* declined comment on the second volume, "it being too low and mean to deserve one serious Thought." Instead of grappling with Mandeville's work on his own terms, the author in his second letter included in whole or in part paragraphs 2, 3, 7, 8, 9, 10, and 11 of Hutcheson's second letter. In his third letter, the author referred to Hutcheson not by name but as "a very Great Man" and as "This ingenious Gentleman (to whom we are obliged for a great many of the preceding Observations)." This letter reproduced Hutcheson's third letter almost verbatim, but among the slight changes was one in the final sentence: "Thus may thine enemies triumph, O Virtue! O Morality!"

Letter to William Smith on Robert Simson, 1735

Hutcheson's letter in the *Bibliothèque raisonnée des ouvrages des savants de l'Europe* for 1735 was a review or abstract of a book on conic sections by Robert Simson, professor of mathematics at the University of Glasgow. Simson protested against the use of algebra by modern mathematicians— Descartes, John Wallis, the Marquis de 'Hôpital, and others—to demonstrate the properties of parabolas, ellipses, hyperbolae, and other geometric forms. Simson defended the use of the analytic or synthetic method of ancient geometers—Euclid, Apollonius of Perga, Pappas of Alexandria—who provided simpler and more elegant demonstrations of the properties of curved or conical forms. In his review, Hutcheson declared that he had been able to write about Simson's work with greater ease because he had often talked with Simson about his scholarly work and Simson had told him things that were not included in his Preface. Hutcheson may also have been assisted by an abstract of Simson's book in Simson's handwriting. See below, pp. 267–71.

Considerations on Patronages, 1735

Considerations on Patronages Addressed to the Gentlemen of Scotland (1735) is another Hutcheson publication that has a complicated history. This is accounted for in detail in the notes, where it is also shown how the work complemented another pamphlet by William Grant (1700/1–64), the Clerk and Procurator General of the General Assembly of the Church of Scotland. Addressing different audiences, Hutcheson and Grant were writing in support of an Act of the General Assembly of the Church of Scotland in 1732, which proposed that "Heritors or Freeholders and elders" of the parish should be responsible for calling ministers. The act was intended to relieve the Church of Scotland of the grievance of patronage, the calling of ministers by the Crown and noble lords. Hutcheson also insisted that ministers should not be chosen by "the populace" or the congregation at large because the latter would most likely choose "weak zealots" for their ministers.

Shaftsbury's Ghost conjur'd: or, A Letter to Mr. Francis Hutcheson, 1738

The writer of this pamphlet attempted to demonstrate that Hutcheson's classroom teaching was utterly inconsistent with the Holy Scriptures and the received doctrines of the Presbyterian Church of Scotland as set out in *The Confession of Faith*. The letter was intended as a serious indictment of Hutcheson, inasmuch as the author knew that Hutcheson had taken an oath to teach nothing contrary to the *Confession*.

The writer was Hugh Heugh, who came from a family of strict evangelical Presbyterians. Heugh would have taken Hutcheson's class in moral philosophy in 1734–35, and he admitted that he was impressed by Hutcheson's lectures on first hearing: "my Fancy was tickled with your chimerical Ideas of Virtue and Moral Sense." But when he returned to the class a second time he "endeavoured to compare the Propositions I heard you advance with the Principles of our holy Religion, as contained in the Scriptures of Truth, and agreeably thereto summed up in our excellent *Confession of Faith*." He found that they did not match.

Hutcheson dismissed the pamphlet summarily in a letter to Drennan (Private Correspondence, Letter 27) as "some whimsical Buffoonry about my Heresy." Will Bruce took the matter more seriously, fearing that it might "destroy both your Satisfaction & Usefulness in your present Situation" and suggesting that Hutcheson might do well to return to Ireland to take up a position in the established church.

A Vindication of Mr. Hutcheson, 1738

Hutcheson's students and former students drafted a succinct response to the eleven propositions Heugh cited as evidence of Hutcheson's heresy. *A Vindication of Mr. Hutcheson from the Calumnious Aspersions of a Late Pamphlet* (1738) was published over the signatures of fourteen men, some of whom were very close to Hutcheson (the brothers Foulis and James Moor) and others who were ministers, preachers, elders, colleagues, and a merchant; and "we could have mentioned many more." They argued that the author frequently misrepresented Hutcheson; that he ascribed to Hutcheson positions he had cited only for purposes of disputation; that Hutcheson's reading of the Scriptures, on those occasions when he mentioned them, was consistent with interpretations offered by others, including Calvinists. In every case they argued that Hutcheson taught good philosophy.

The tension that existed in the Church of Scotland throughout the century is evident in this remarkable exchange between Hutcheson's

accuser and his defenders. There were defenders of Presbyterian orthodoxy as defined in *The Confession of Faith*; there were also supporters of
Hutcheson and others in the universities and the Church of Scotland
who considered 'true Religion' to be the promotion of piety and virtue.
Hutcheson clearly chose not to respond directly to the writer of *Shaftesbury's Ghost conjur'd*, but he may have advised his defenders in those
sections of the *Vindication* that report his opinions. No action was taken
against Hutcheson in the Glasgow Synod or in the General Assembly.
Hugh Heugh died while still a divinity student. His religious allies continued to secede from the Church of Scotland in ever increasing numbers
through the century.

Preface to *Divine Dialogues* by Henry More, 1743

Henry More (1614–1687), Fellow of Christ's College, Cambridge, combined Renaissance Platonism with the ideas of the later Stoics and the
Peripatetics. His *Divine Dialogues* were written in English for the general
reader. The *Dialogues* began with a brief discussion of "the preference of
virtue and assurance of an happy immortality before the pleasures and
grandeur of this present world." In the first dialogue, the participants
(who included a materialist, a Cartesian, a critic, a politician, and a wary
man, as well a "deeply-thoughtful" man and a "sincere lover of God and
Christ"—the last speaking for More) reviewed arguments for the existence of God and the attributes of divinity. In the second dialogue, the
order and design of the world were defended (against Lucretius) and the
beauties of the natural world were traced to a vital force in nature (against
Descartes and the mechanical system). The third dialogue defended the
goodness of the creation and the virtues of mankind, notwithstanding
the deformities found in certain religions and the barbarity of the morals
of many nations. In some earlier editions, a fourth and a fifth dialogue
were added; these were not included in the edition published in Glasgow
in 1743.

In his anonymous Preface, Hutcheson praised the agreeable manner of
More's demonstration of the being and attributes of God and his providence in this world. Despite "some little difficulties of metaphysics,"

Hutcheson was in no doubt about More's piety or his devotion to the cause of virtue. In a record of his own life, More declared that from his youth he had been antagonistic to Calvinism; he despised particularly the doctrine that some are predestined for eternal punishment, not because of rational insight but from "an internal Sensation" that also gave insight into divine justice and goodness. It is not surprising that Hutcheson found More's philosophy congenial; nor is it surprising, given More's declared hostility to Calvinism as many of Hutcheson's contemporaries understood it, that Hutcheson did not advertise his role as author of the Preface to the Glasgow edition of More's *Divine Dialogues.*

James Moore

EDITORIAL PRINCIPLES

The Private Correspondence and the Public Correspondence of Francis Hutcheson present different editorial challenges. In the Private Correspondence we have retained the original grammar, spelling, punctuation, italics, and capitalization wherever possible. There are many archaic spellings, and since many writers are represented, the spellings are also inconsistent. Similarly, the punctuation seems erratic by modern standards and the usage varies significantly from letter to letter. These features are part of the historical record for each of the writers, and modernization would amount to a rewriting of their texts. In cases where lack of punctuation or a missing letter is significantly disturbing, however, the characters have been supplied in <angle brackets>. This has been done as sparingly as possible. Contractions have been expanded only where they are unknown today.

The address, date, and source are indicated at the top of each letter. In cases where the "legal year" (beginning on March 25) is used or assumed, we indicate the "historical year" (beginning on January 1) in the conventional way after a backslash. Thus in Letter 7, William Bruce to Hutcheson, March 9, 1730/31, the writer had used a year that had begun on March 25 and thus had not ended by the time he wrote, but in our calendar (the one Hutcheson most often used) the year had begun on January 1 and was therefore already 1731. It is necessary to use slashes in Private Letters 7, 14, 19, 20, 27, 32, and 51, and in 4, 5, and 6 to *The Dublin Weekly Journal* in order to make the year clear. In the rest of the letters the year is in accordance with the modern calendar's "historical year." The difference in years is sometimes called "Old Style" versus "New Style," but it is not to be confused with the difference between the Julian and the Gregorian calendars; in all the letters here the monthly dates are still "Julian."

The Public Letters and Occasional Writings require particular attention to the arguments and the contexts of the publications. James Moore
is responsible for the presentation and annotation of the Public Letters
and Occasional Writings. With one exception, the text of the public letters reproduced in this edition follows the text of the first printing, supple-
mented by variant readings and by translations of the original, where this
is relevant. The exchange of letters between Hutcheson and Gilbert Burnet printed in *The London Journal* in 1725 was reprinted unrevised in 1735;
the only items printed for the first time in 1735 are the Preface and Postscript said to have been written by Gilbert Burnet "sometime before his
death" in August 1726. There is no evidence that Hutcheson was involved
in this publication. A more difficult editorial challenge was presented by
the letters first published in *The Dublin Weekly Journal* on June 5, 12, and
19, 1725, and February 4, 12, and 19, 1726. These letters were republished,
with many alterations, as *A Collection of Letters Lately Published in* The
Dublin Journal (London, 1729), and without further alterations as *Hibernicus's Letters* (London, 1734). Since Hutcheson clearly was involved in the
revisions for the 1729 edition, this is the text used in the present edition.
The variants from the first edition are recorded in the notes, except that
typographical changes of no significance for the meaning of the text have
not been noted. These are mainly variants in punctuation, capitalization,
and spelling, including the contractions common in early modern texts.

The letters published in French in the *Bibliothèque Angloise* in 1726
and in the *Bibliothèque raisonnée* in 1735 are followed by English translations by James Moore. The remaining items, *Considerations on Patronages*
(1735), *Shaftsbury's Ghost conjur'd* (1738), *A Vindication of Mr. Hutcheson*
(1738), and the Preface to *Divine Dialogues* by Henry More (1743), follow
the texts as they were first published.

In the Private Correspondence, <angle brackets> indicate a best guess
at the intended text of the original manuscript. In the Public Correspondence, page breaks are inserted in <angle brackets> or when there are no
page numbers in the original text. Original notes are indicated using the
standard sequence of symbols. Editorial additions to original notes are
indicated in square brackets following the original note. *The London Journal* and *The Dublin Weekly Journal* were printed in two or three columns,
and the column breaks are here indicated with a vertical bar: |.

ABBREVIATIONS

EUL: Edinburgh University Library

GUA: Glasgow University Archives

GUL: Glasgow University Library

NLS: National Library of Scotland

NRS: National Records of Scotland

ODNB: Oxford Dictionary of National Biography

PRONI: Public Record Office of Northern Ireland

LIST OF LETTERS, DOCUMENTS, AND OCCASIONAL WRITINGS

Private Correspondence, 1717–46

Letters

Public Correspondence and Occasional Writings

Letters to *The London Journal*, 1724–25

Private Correspondence and Unpublished Documents

Letters

1. To ANDREW ROSSE[1]

Address: To Mr Andrew Rosse, Professour in the University, Glasgow

MS: Staatsbibliothek zu Berlin, Preussischer Kulturbesitz, Handschriften-abteilung, Slg. Darmst. 2a 1755 (1): Hutcheson, Francis. Transcribed from photocopy.

Kilmarnock, June 13 1717

Sir

I had given you the trouble of a letter when I sent Plinys Panegyrick[2] had I known of the Carrier before the moment he went off. I was last night orderd by my Lady to write to you about Woodrow that you might prevent his engaging in any other business till my Lord Kilmarnock get some Post for Higgins, and to enquire upon what terms Mr Woodrow would be satisfied to serve my Lord Boyd.[3] I know this is all mere Sham and pretence to prevent your resenting it that such a fellow should be kept

---

1. Andrew Rosse (d. 1749), professor of humanity (Latin) at the University of Glasgow since 1706, and one of the first to adopt the vernacular language in his instruction. He demitted office in favor of his son, George Rosse, in November 1735.

2. Pliny the Younger, Roman lawyer and imperial administrator, flourished in the later part of the first century and the beginning of the second. His *Panegyricus* was a literary recasting of a speech to the Roman Senate in praise of the emperor Trajan.

3. William Boyd, third Earl of Kilmarnock ("my Lord Kilmarnock," 1683/4–1717), and his wife, Euphemia, Countess of Kilmarnock ("my Lady," b. 1684), were the parents of William Boyd ("my Lord Boyd," 1705–1746), who succeeded to the earldom in September of this year. Hutcheson had been employed as tutor to the younger Boyd in 1716–17, when the latter attended Rosse's Latin class at the University of Glasgow. The fourth Earl, as he became, joined the Jacobites in 1745, was captured after the battle of Culloden in 1746, and was taken to London, where he was tried and executed. John Wodrow ("Mr Woodrow") had entered the university as a member of Rosse's class in the 1709–10 session.

about my Lord notwithstanding your apearing against him; for I find my Lady's opinion of his profound merit in finding diversions for my Lord & teaching him to speak English is as high as ever. However I can not be so far carried with prejudice against him as not to be sensible that he is much less impertinent than formerly tho I would not make any such acknowledgement to my Lady. but for mr Woodrow I think no body could advise him upon such an uncertain expectation to neglect any opportunity of Setlement that offers.

My Lady would not allow my Lord to read any last week nor do I expect much good of him till Mr Gilmor return. We read out that Aeneid & a piece of Homer.

I never heard the least mention of any thing like the Paper you found nor can I imagine whose it could be. Give my most Humble Service to Mrs Rosse.

I am Sir
your most oblidged
and most obedient Servant
Franc. Hutcheson

2. To WILLIAM WRIGHT[4]

Address lacking

Copy: excerpt in William Wright to Robert Wodrow,[5] September 27, 1718: NLS, Wodrow Letters Quarto, vol. 20, no. 132.

[September 1718]

I find by the Conversation I have had with some Ministers and Comerades that ther is a perfect Hoadly mania[6] among our younger ministers In the North. and what is realie Ridiculous it does not serve them to be of his principles but the pulpits are ringing with them as if their hearers were all absolute princes going to Impose tests and confessions in their several territories,[7] and not a sett of people Entirely Excluded from the smallest hand in the Government any where and utterly Incapable of bearing any other part In persecution but the sufferers.[8]

4. Rev. William Wright (d. 1724), Church of Scotland minister. He entered Glasgow University in the 1689–90 session, proceeded to the divinity class 1693–94, where he was a fellow student with John Simson (later professor of divinity), and was ordained to the parish of Kilmarnock, Ayrshire, in 1700. He was the local parish minister when Hutcheson was tutor in the Earl of Kilmarnock's family.

5. Rev. Robert Wodrow (1679–1734), minister of Eastwood, Renfrewshire since 1703, and prominent Calvinist historian (*ODNB*).

6. Benjamin Hoadly, D.D. (1676–1761), at this time bishop of Bangor in Wales (*ODNB*). In *The Nature of the Kingdom, or Church, of Christ: A Sermon Preach'd before the King, at the Royal Chapel of St. James's, on Sunday March 31, 1717* (London, 1717), he had decried the use of ecclesiastical discipline to enforce political and civil ends.

7. Irish Dissenters were disadvantaged by the Test Act of 1703, which had required persons employed in public or military service to take communion in the Church of Ireland; and there had been debate in 1716–17 over the nature of the confessional subscription to which Presbyterians should be bound in negotiating with the government for a Toleration Act. Within Presbyterianism, a controversy arose in 1718 as to whether the General Synod had the authority to move a minister to a new posting without his, his congregation's, and his presbytery's consent, which might also be considered as falling broadly within Hoadly's strictures against unwarranted ecclesiastical controls. But only with the eruption of a pamphlet war in 1720 was there open debate on whether ministers could be required to subscribe to formularies of human devising such as the Westminster *Confession of Faith*.

8. This extract is embedded in a paragraph of a letter from Wright to Wodrow that begins "I had a Line this week from Ireland, from Mr Francis Hutchison which greatly afflicts me, His words are . . ." After the excerpted passage, Wright adds his

3. To WILLIAM KING[9]

Address: To his Grace The Arch Bishop of Dublin

MS: Trinity College Dublin Library, MSS 1995–2008, fol. 2125; small tear in the paper

Dublin, March 25th 1725

May it please your Grace

The Author of the book, which you will receive along with this letter,[10] thought it proper not to be known as the Author till he found how it would be recei<ved.> His diffidence of it's success hindered him from presenting a Coppy of it to your Grace sooner; but since he has found

---

own comment: "I have Reason Houever to aprehend that the Antipathie to confessions is upon some other grounds then a Neu spirit of Charitie. Dr. Clarks book I'm sufficiently Informed has made severals unfixed in their old principles, if not Intirely altered them. what sad Melacholie work is this<.> whither are we going. I smelt somewhat of the same sort from Mr Hallieday An<d> one Mr Pearse and several others of the English dissenters In may Last. pray provoke your professor Simson if you think him a fitt hand for it, to give some Antidote to this Venome for I knou he had thots about it some Time agoe." The reference to "Dr. Clarks book" is to the Church of England cleric Samuel Clarke's *Scripture-Doctrine of the Trinity* (London, 1712) (*ODNB*). Rev. James Peirce (1674–1726) was an English Dissenting minister and biblical scholar at Exeter, where he was drawn into controversy on the doctrine of the Trinity (*ODNB*). Samuel Haliday (1685–1739) was a prominent Irish Nonsubscribing Presbyterian minister educated at Glasgow under John Loudon and at Leiden, and ordained in Geneva. At his installation at the First Belfast Congregation in 1720, he refused to subscribe the Westminster Confession (*ODNB*). On John Simson, see below, Letters 12, 15, 24, 27, and 32.

9. Rev. William King (1650–1729), archbishop of Dublin from 1703 and previously bishop of Derry, was for a time the most polemical and powerful figure in the Church of Ireland and a strong force in Irish politics (*ODNB*). His philosophical study, *De origine mali*, was published in Latin in London and Dublin in 1702 but derived much of its reputation from the distortions of secondary sources; from a French précis in *Nouvelles de la république des lettres* (May–June 1703), which influenced a critique by Pierre Bayle; and from an English translation by Edmund Law, *On the Origin of Evil* (Cambridge, 1731; four further editions with updated commentary to 1781), whose annotations moved increasingly far from King's own intentions. A longtime opponent of the Dissenters, King became more accommodating after the limited Irish Toleration Act was passed in 1719. He lost power and effectiveness in the 1720s with the increasing anglicization of the Irish episcopate.

10. Hutcheson's *Inquiry into the Original of Our Ideas of Beauty and Virtue* (Dublin and London, 1725).

that it has pleased some persons of distinction, he begins to presume that it will not be dissagreeable to Your Grace; and would willingly hope that he shall make some small return in kind for that great pleasure he has very lately received, upon a subject that had long employed his thoughts, from the Author De Origine Mali. I am May it please your Grace

Your Graces Most obedient
humble Servant
Francis Hutcheson

4. To JOHN HUTCHESON[11]

Address: To The Revd Mr John Hutcheson at Ballyrea near Armagh

Copy: PRONI D971/34/G/1/1; a small amount of punctuation has been normalized, primarily in converting dashes to commas or periods, according to sense.

August 4th 1726

Honoured & Dear Sir,

I received Your letter by Mr Maconchy with the money you mention. I would not by any means delay giving you all possible Satisfaction upon the Subject you mention as giving you so much uneasiness; and that with the greatest freedom as to the best Friend I have in the World. I would sooner have wrote you on this Subject had I apprehended you uneasy about it.

I knew there was such a Rumour, but reports of that kind are so common and so industriously spread by those who are fond of Converts upon any Dissenters meeting with any Civility from Persons of Distinction

---

11. Rev. John Hutcheson (d. 1729), Presbyterian minister at Armagh, 1697–1729, and the father of Francis Hutcheson. He was the son of Rev. Alexander Hutcheson (d. 1711), minister at Saintfield, County Down. Educated at Edinburgh University, from which he graduated in 1675, he had by 1679 begun to conduct a Dissenting academy in Newtownards, County Down, which he continued for some years before being ordained to the ministry at Downpatrick, County Down, in 1690. He was the principal author of the posthumously published *Brief Review of a Paper Intituled A Letter from the Presbytery of Antrim, &c.* (Dublin, 1730).

that I did not imagine they would make any impressions upon my Friends.[12]

To have singular Principles on some points is incident I beleive to the best of Men, tho' the publishing them without necessity is too often a sign of Vanity<. T>his latter I have endeavoured always to avoid—the former is either innocent in many cases, or a pardonable weakness. As to the Seperation from the Church[13] I will own to you what I scarce ever own'd to any body else, that it seems to me wholly a point of Prudence—I do not imagine that either the Government or the Externals of Worship are so determined in the Gospel, as to oblige Men to one particular way in either. That all Societies may according to their own prudence choose a form of Government in the Church and agree upon such external order of Worship as they think will do most good to promote the true end of all, real Piety and Virtue—But without any Right of forcing others into it. Men may err & act incautiously in rashly choosing an inconvenient

12. The rumors in question seem to be given more specific content in "Sketches of the History of Presbyterians in Ireland, by William Campbell D.D. of Clonmel. 1803" (MS in the Presbyterian Historical Society of Ireland):

> Several members of the church of Ireland wished to have him invited to Dublin college, to reform it entirely, & to introduce a new system of education according to his own liberal, comprehensive views. Dr Domville, dean of Armagh, one of their most learned men, told this writer, their scheme was, to remove the provost to a bishoprick, & to bring Dr Hutcheson into his place, vested with the requisite authority to make all such changes as were necessary for improving the institution: which, it was obvious, must labour under very great radical defects; since from the foundation of the college, it had not produced more than two or three men, whose names were known in the learned world. But the evil genius of Ireland prevailed. A reform so much to be desired, did not take place. (p. 228)

Campbell was a northern Presbyterian minister of liberal tendencies who had entered Glasgow University in 1744 as a student in Hutcheson's class. He was a minister in Antrim and Armagh and finally at Clonmel, County Tipperary, where he died in 1805. The source of Campbell's information, Rev. Benjamin Domville, LL.D., a Dubliner (born Benjamin Barrington), entered Trinity College Dublin in January 1726, the year in which Hutcheson's father reported on the rumors. Barrington/Domville was rector and dean in Armagh during Campbell's time there. The provost of Trinity in 1726 was Richard Baldwin, who actually held office 1717–58 (*ODNB*).

13. That is, the separation of Dissenters from the established (episcopalian) Church of Ireland.

form, such as I really look upon the Established one to be. But when this is done by the Majority and yet neither Argument nor request will procure any Alteration, Provided the Essentials of Religion be preserved entire, it seems then, as to every particular Person a Question of Prudence, whether he will comply or not. That is to say, If in his circumstances He can propose to do more good by Seperation than by Conformity the former is His Duty, if not the latter.

To apply this closer to the present case, I think the Scotch Church had alwise a right to insist on their old way and resist Episcopacy; since it was never regularly introduced, but in a Tyrannical Manner, Contrary to the Consent of the People, and illegally & cruelly enforced by the most unjustifiable Methods, and was a less prudent Institution or Form than their own. But in King Charles the firsts Reign in England, had I lived then, I would only have enquired whether an Actual Separation would probably have done more good than the contrary, and practised accordingly. Before there was any considerable Body of Dissenters and while the Power of the opposite party was high it would not seem to me to have been any persons Duty to have openly Seperated or to have encouraged others to it to their Ruin. I cannot say that in such a case there was any Sin in conformity to all parts of the Worship Established at least for Laymen. After the Seperation was made and great Numbers agreed in different Forms from what was Established (and I am convinced more prudent ones) And Yet upon the Restoration the Episcopal Form turn'd into a Law and most unjustly enforced upon those who thought it absolutely Sinful, with the most cruel treatment of many of the best Subjects in the Nation; It was honourable and good and the Duty of every Man who was convinced of the goodness of the Cause, to continue their Dissent and not to Submit to these Religious Penal Laws which it seems to me no Magistrate can ever have a Right to make. I think the same reason for Dissent continues still that there is no obligation from the Command of the Magistrate in a matter beyond his province: But the same Reasons Justify Dissent which would Justify refusing Ship Money or any thing Commanded by the King in points not belonging to His Prerogative. The Dissenters have a right to continue as they are; and as I firmly beleive their Cause in most of the disputed points with the Church is the better, and their Method more expedient and conducive to the Ends of Religion than that which is Established, I should look upon it as my Duty, continually as far as my influence could go, to promote the Interest of that Cause. But as one who liked a Republic or Limited Monarchy better than an Absolute Monarchy might justly Swear Allegiance to an Absolute Monarch when there were no hopes of altering the Constitution, So I think much more might one receive from such a Monarch the largest Powers with a view to prevent worse coming into the place or to be more capable of recovering the Liberties of his Country from a Tyrant. So I would not blame any Man of my own Principles who for very important Purposes did Conform if the Ends proposed were such as would overballance the damage which the more just cause would Sustain by his leaving it, particularly if he had any prospect of getting an unjust Establishment altered. This prospect I see not the least probability of and Assure you as little Purpose have I of ever acting with other Intentions. After the Concern you have expressed on this head, I assure you I know not any worldly Consideration which I could propose or expect by Conformity, that I would not reject rather than give you the uneasiness I should apprehend from it.

I cannot however think you would have reason to be so much concern'd in this Affair were my resolutions different from what they really are. I am sensible of great corruption not so much in the Constitution of the Establishd Church (tho' it is not free of it) but in the general Practice of its Members. Yet it is certain they have some of the most valuable Men in this Age among them, And it is not every corruption in a Church which makes communion with it Sinful. Nay it is sometimes the more Mens Duty to continue to endeavour while there is any hope to make matters better. I often imagine that were it not for the offence which would be given on all sides by any Person who had not obtain'd already a most undisputed Character, it would be adviseable to hold Communion with all Protestants frequently, to show not only our good will & Charity but to shew our dislike of these little Divisions, occasioned sometimes by too much keenness on both sides about trifles; such things as are not determined by any command of God, which no man perhaps has a right to constrain those to practise who dislike them & which yet the bare doing of is not at all Sinful. The Reason why I imagine so much left in religious matters to human Prudence is this that I see no such particular distinct orders about the Government or Worship of the Christian Church in the New Testament as some do alledge. I am sure any of the Founders or Lawgivers of Human Societies are much more particular in all the orders of their Commonwealths & the several Powers of their Magistrates & the manner of proceeding in their several offices. From this I imagine no imperfection of the Holy Scriptures, but that much of these external things were left to Human Prudence. I wish you saw Sir James Harringtons treatise on Ordination against Hammond's Episcopal Form.[14] He seems to me to prove the same of the Presbyterian, that both Models were in different places practised by the Apostles, & consequently neither Necessary nor unlawful. When the whole body of the People agree in any of these Forms which are undetermined in Scripture, unless the corruption be very great Opposition or Seperation is Needless. When a Body is already seperated upon a more convenient Form, If they behave Charitably towards others their Seperation is no Sin but rather laudable and they are under no obligation to return. Things may be left to human Prudence to guide, when Men agree without Power to Compel. I have wrote with more freedom in this letter than I have ever used before with any body. The only Reason of these Rumours was My Lord Carteret's[15] talking publicly of His resolving to have me brought over to the Church to a good Living, & the Bishop of Elphins proffessing the same Intention.[16] They have both talk'd to me upon the subject of the Scruples of the Dissenters, & of my Sentiments of the Constitution of the Church. I generally evaded the Debate & spoke of the Church more charitably than they expected from whence They have concluded more than I ever intended. I had the like Discourse with the Bishop of Down where I was little pinched with

---

14. James Harrington (1611–1677), *The Prerogative of Popular Government. A Political Discourse in Two Books. The former containing the first Preliminary of* Oceana . . . *The second concerning Ordination, against Dr. H. Hammond, Dr. L. Seaman* . . . (London, 1658). Henry Hammond (1605–1660), Church of England clergyman (*ODNB*).

15. John, Lord Carteret (1690–1763), lord lieutenant of Ireland 1724–30 (*ODNB*).

16. Rev. Theophilus Bolton (1677/8–1744), a protégé of Archbishop William King, was bishop of Clonfert, 1722–24; of Elphin, 1724–29; and archbishop of Cashel from January 1730 (*ODNB*).

Argument.[17] He however I know spoke more positively then He had any ground for. If it were proper to tell you a Jest upon such a subject it would perhaps make you Laugh to hear His Opinion of all these Debates with Dissenters, Summed up thus "We (says He) would not sweep the House clean, & you stumbled at Straws." I own I look upon the matter of debate as of more consequence. The Ecclesiastic power in any Body Associated seems to me founded in the same manner as the Civil and to oblige all who have consented to it once, to obedience unless when the abuse of Power is so great as to overballance all the advantages of the Government, & to compensate all the disorders arising from an alteration of it. I imagine the Original of both to be in the same manner from God, who requires of us to do whatever may tend to the general Good and particularly to submit the ordinary debated Points either about Civil or Ecclesiastical matters, to the Cognizance of Arbitrators chosen by ourselves & limited according to our prudence. If in these points I am mistaken, I am sure I do no harm to others, since I have kept my Mind pretty much to myself in these matters & resolve to do so. I assure you if I should ever take contrary resolutions, of which I have no present presumption, I will let you know it, & consult you on every thing which appears difficult to me, & Pray, if you have leisure, let me know what you think faulty in what I wrote you. I am with Duty to my Mother Your most Dutiful Son

Franc: Hutcheson

Pray write me farther on this subject and assure yourself that there is no ground for your uneasiness. Were I disposed that way there is nothing to be got worth my Acceptance without some compliances to which I would not submit.

---

17. Francis Hutchinson (1660–1739), bishop of Down and Connor, 1721–39. Before settling in Ireland, he made his name with *An Historical Essay concerning Witchcraft* (London, 1718). He supported measures for the economic improvement of Ireland and later published *A Defence of the Antient Historians, with a Particular Application of It to the History of Ireland and Great-Britain and Other Northern Nations* (Dublin, 1734) (*ODNB*).

5. To WILLIAM MACE[18]

Address: To Mr. William Mace, at Mr. Osborn's, bookseller, Paternoster-Row

Copy: *European Magazine*, September, 1788, pp. 158–60

Dublin, Sept. 6, 1727

Sir,

I was very agreeably entertained this day se'nnight with your ingenious letter. The reason of my not answering you immediately was what you seem in the close of your letter to be apprized of, that the alterations you proposed would be unpopular, and not so fit for so inconsiderable a name as mine to venture upon in a treatise upon a subject equally concerning all mankind. I therefore sent you a letter by my old friend Mr. Mairs,[19] that I had some reasons requiring haste in the printing of those papers, and that I dared not venture upon publishing some alterations, according to your remarks, which agree with my own sentiments, and that in some others I differed from you, of which I would apprize you as soon as I had leisure: but as our distance makes correspondence very slow in its returns, I fear I cannot expect, in any tolerable time, to have your sentiments upon any doubtful points, so that I could make proper alterations according to them. I am extremely obliged to you for your kind offer of your good offices in this matter, and should be proud of having it in my power to make any grateful returns for it.

I was well apprized of the scheme of thinking you are fallen into, not only by our Dr. Berkly's books,[20] and by some of the old academics, but

18. William Mace (d. 1767), professor of law at Gresham College, London, from 1744. His correspondence with Hutcheson must date from early in his career, but information on this period is lacking.

19. Rev. John Mears (c. 1695–1767), Irish Presbyterian minister at Newtownards, County Down, who in 1725 joined with those who were formed into the Nonsubscribing Presbytery of Antrim. He later moved to Clonmell, County Tipperary, and then to Stafford Street, Dublin. Of Anglo-Irish extraction, he had studied natural philosophy at Glasgow University in the 1712–13 session before following Hutcheson into the divinity class (*ODNB*).

20. Rev. George Berkeley (1685–1753), absentee dean of Derry and former fellow of Trinity College, Dublin. He had published a partial account of his philosophy in *An Essay towards a New Theory of Vision* (Dublin, 1709), and his full-scale philosophy of

by frequent conversation with some few speculative friends in Dublin. As to your notion of our mind as only a system of perceptions, I imagine you'll find that every one has an immediate simple perception of *self*; to which all his other perceptions are some way connected, otherwise I cannot conceive how I could be any way affected with pleasure or pain from any past action, affection, or perception, or have any present uneasiness or concern about any future event or perception; or how there could be any unity of person, or any desire of future happiness or aversion to misery. My past perceptions or future ones are not my present, but would be as distinct as your perceptions are from mine: that it is otherwise I believe every one is conscious. As to material *substrata*, I own I am a sceptic; all the phaenomena might be as they are, were there nothing but perceptions, for the phaenomena are perceptions. And yet, were there external objects, I cannot imagine how we could be better informed of them than we are. I own I cannot see the force of the arguments against external objects, *i.e.* something like, or proportional, to our concomitant ideas, as I call extension, figure, motion, rest, solidity.

Figure and *bounded colour* are not to me the same. Figure accompanies bounded colour, but the same or perfectly like idea may arise by touch, without any idea of colour, along with the ideas of hard, cold, smooth. A man born blind might learn mathematics with a little more trouble than one who saw, had he figures artfully cut in wood. Messrs. Locke and Molyneux are both wrong about the cube and sphere proposed to a blind man restored to sight. He would not at first view know the sphere from a shaded plane surface by a view from above; but a side view would discover the equal uniform round relievo in one, and the cubic one in the other. We can all by touch, with our eyes shut, judge what the visible extension

---

immaterialism in *A Treatise concerning the Principles of Human Knowledge* (part 1 only, Dublin, 1710) and—in a more popular form, as a debate between the established new philosophy and his own—in *Three Dialogues between Hylas and Philonous* (London, 1713). He was at this time in London collecting funding for a missionary college in the Americas, which failed. He returned to Ireland as bishop of Cloyne in 1734. Berkeley and Hutcheson coincided as residents of Dublin between 1721 and 1724 and at least by the end of that period had a common friend in Edward Synge the Younger, but there is no evidence that they ever met (*ODNB*).

of a body felt shall be when we shall open our eyes; but cannot by feeling judge what the colour shall be when we shall see it; which shews visible and tangible extension to be really the same idea, or to have one idea common, viz. the extension; though the purely tangible and visible perceptions are quite disparate. If one should alledge that the two extensions, abstracted from the colours, are different ideas, but that by long observation we find what changes in the visible arise from any change of the tangible extension, and *vice versa*; and hence from groping a figure we know what its visible extension shall be; I think upon this scheme, it would be impossible that one who had only the idea of tangible extension could ever apprehend any reasonings formed by one who argued about the visible; whereas blind men may understand mathematics. To illustrate this, suppose a person paralytic and blind, with an acute smell, who had no idea of either extension; suppose there were a body whose smell continually altered with every change of its figure; one man seeing the several figures changing in a regular course foresees which shall come next, so the other knows the course of smells; he agrees with the blind man about names; the one noting by them the various figures, the other the various smells. The seer reasons about the figures, or forms one of Euclid's propositions concerning the proportion of the sides: is it possible the blind man could ever assent to this, or know his meaning from the smells? And yet men may so far agree, one of whom had only the idea of tangible extension. Or suppose a man had never seen sounding strings, but heard the several sounds, not knowing any thing of length or tension, that he was taught names for notes, such as dupla, sesquialtera; should one who saw the strings say, "the square of the cause of the octave was but a quarter of the square of the other cause," could the other ever apprehend him in this point from his ideas of sounds? And yet a man born blind could perceive this point, and agree with one who only had ideas of sight.

Duration and number seem to me as real perceptions as any; and I can have no other idea of your words for explaining duration, [viz. the order of our ideas]²¹ than this, a perception of the connexion or relation of our

21. Square brackets in the original.

several ideas to several parts of duration. What is order or succession of our ideas, unless duration be a real distinct idea accompanying them all? or how could the succession of ideas give us ideas of duration, if a part of duration were not connected with each of them? Number is also a real idea; the words are artificial symbols about which different nations differ, but agree in all their reasonings about the ideas of number, which are really the same. Numbers are the clearest ideas we have, and their relations are the most distinct, but often have nothing to do with wholes or parts, and are alike applicable to heterogeneous as homogeneous quantities.

I still cannot take *desire* to denote a complex idea. The Epicurean desire I am confident I should have myself as I mention it.

The prospect of interest is not desire, but something immediately preceding it, either *tempore* or *natura*, if you can bear such stuff: the prospect is an opinion or perception of relation, *i.e.* a judgment. The desire is as different from a judgment as sound from colour, as far as I can apprehend. One may wish he had *desire*, but you see I own a volition cannot directly raise desire. Volition is perhaps to be called the proper action, but I imagine we have volitions about ideas in compounding, comparing, attention, recalling, enlarging, diminishing, as well as about bodily motion; so that an universal palsy would not take away all volition: and beside, I am not fully convinced, though I have heard it alledged, that there can be no volition without effect, as well as desires which are not gratified. Desire and volition are distinct from each other, and both distinct from what we commonly call perceptions; though we have also an idea or consciousness of volition and desire. Quere, Is there not here plainly an idea, viz. that of desire or volition, and an object, viz. the desire or volition distinct from this perception of it? May there not be the same as to the ideas I call the concomitant?

As to the main point in your letter about our activity, we are very much of the same opinion. But you know how sacred a point human liberty and activity, in the common notions, are to the generality of men, and how prejudicial any singularity on these heads might be to one whose business depends upon a character of orthodoxy. I am very sensible that the truest ideas of human virtue and of the divine goodness may be given on your scheme; but how few are there whom we could convince on these points.

> *Vel quia turpe putant parere minoribus, et quae*
> *Imberbes didicere, senes perdenda fateri.*[22]

I have some nearer touches at these points in another set of papers, which I shall send over very soon to be joined with the other. But I am still on my guard in them.

I heartily wish you may find your new correspondent any way agreeable to you; I can only assure you of his hearty zeal for truth and virtue, and his particular regard and gratitude to you for your civilities.

I am, Sir,

Your most obliged humble servant,

Francis Hutcheson

---

6. From COLIN MacLAURIN[23]

Address lacking; endorsed by copyist "(To Dr Francis Hutcheson)"

Copy: NRS, RH1/2/497

Edinburgh, October 22. 1728

Dear Sir

Your letter did give me a very particular pleasure. The name agreeably surprized me when I looked at the end of it and I read the whole with some emotion and a pleasure of an uncommon sort Tho' I had often thought with esteem of the Author of the Inquiry into &c: Yet I had scarce before that moment considered him as my old acquaintance and joined these characters. Which I then did with too exquisite a Satisfaction to be understood by any but those who have a relish for or rather are

22. Horace, *Epistles*, II.i.84–85.

23. Colin MacLaurin (1698–1746), professor of mathematics, University of Edinburgh, from 1725. He had been a fellow student with Hutcheson at Glasgow before obtaining the chair of mathematics at Marischal College, Aberdeen, in 1719 (*ODNB*).

governed by these excellent principles you maintain in your Book. I have been always zealous for the moral sense and fond of improving it and must look on one that wants it if such a one there is, as less a man than if he wanted all the rest. As for those who would consider the humane state as a state of Misery Vanity and Wickedness whither they do it out of Compliment to the Vindictive Justice of their Deity or as some that refine farther that there might not be Exemples wanting to influence the other parts of the system of the world to a good behaviour or to shou their Beautys in a stronger light I oun I have so much Love and regard to Mankind as to wish that if there must be Exemples they may be as far from us as possible. It is most uncomfortable that We should be of no other use in the system but by a comparison to make others sensible of their bliss. God grant we may be of as little use this way as possible. No doubt the miserys of Men are many; yet many things we esteem evil very generally are found good without taking a larger vieu than of Mankind itself. The Uncertainty of human knowledge in the most important Questions of a future state the Deity the nature of the soul that men are forever disputing about has often appeared to me the greatest Evil of this state. Yet on further thoughts I have satisfyed myself besides the necessity there seems to be for all Beings to pass through an Infancy in knowledge had we had too plain discoverys of superior Beings and another life our humanity might have suffered by it & the mutual tyes & relations betwixt men been weakned by intercourse with them.

I sometimes please myself with thinking how agreeably some good men I know who do not believe a future state will be surprized to find themselves live after Death. The pleasure of finding ourselves exist after Death and the Wonderful manner of it will be an admirable Introduction into a new state.

But to leave our Philosophy to satisfy your Curiosity how it is nou with me. I have been settled here since the 1725 I had spent more than two years before in france & Loirain. I nou labour hard in the Winter having had sometimes 126 scholars at a time. I have five moneths Vacation in the summer which I either spend in England or in the Country at home. Besides my teaching I am obliged to mind other matters too because of my Character & situation. I am involved in a dispute with the forreign

Mathematicians about estimating the forces of Bodys in Motion and am going to publish a small treatise just nou on that subject wherein I endeavour to answer all they have said hitherto against our Doctrine. To make it of more use I make it a compleat treatise on the Motions arising from the Collision of Bodys and solve several new Problems in it I was led into this dispute by the R. Academy of Sciences giving their annual prize in 1724 to a paper I sent them in which I endeavoured to demonstrate our Doctrine. The celebrated Mr. Beinouilli had given in a piece which compeated with mine. Which he has since published; and by it I think myself obliged to answer.[24]

Thus I have endeavoured to shou you with what readiness I am willing to keep a correspondence with you<.> I shall have a particular regard to the young Gentlemen you have recommended to me; and indeed they deserve all the distinction I can pay them. On reading over my letter which I have writ with some liberty & in haste I find it is only to such as Mr. Hutcheson I ought to open my sentiments. I knou tho' I differed from you I would be safe. I shall have a particular pleasure in hearing from you and receiving your Commands and am

Dear Sir

your most Obedient

most Humble Servant

Colin MacLaurin

---

24. In 1724 both MacLaurin and the Swiss mathematician Jean Bernoulli (1667–1748) entered the prize competition of the Académie Royale des Sciences, which MacLaurin won with his *Démonstrations des loix du choc des corps*. Bernoulli's *Discours sur les loix de la communication du mouvement* was eventually accepted in 1726, and this may be what MacLaurin referred to. The treatise mentioned here was never published, as he explained in *A Treatise of Fluxions: In Two Books* (Edinburgh, 1742), 2 vols., 2:437–38n. See Letter 16 below.

7. From WILLIAM BRUCE[25]

Address: To Mr Francis Hutcheson Professor of Moral Philosophy in the University of Glasgow

MS: NLS, MS 9252, fols. 100–101

Dublin March 9th 1730/31[26]

My Dearest Cousen

You cannot imagine what uneasiness we suffered by your long Silence about the last parcel of your Goods, the Arrival of which we had no manner of Account of, till the letter End of last week when I had the favour of your short Epistle by the Hardiknute;[27] however the News you there tell us of the good State of my Cousen's Health has made abundant amends for all delays; I had prepared in my own Mind a severe Scold for you, but as it hapned to Prior in seeing his Mistress's Bosom,

> that Part of your Letter I with such pleasure surveyd that I forgot every
> word I designed to have said.[28]

the Orations you sent over[29] by Mrs Rainey's Servant were all delivered as you directed and the Gentlemen desired that their Acknowledgements

25. William Bruce (1702–1755), Dublin bookseller and later private tutor. He was the youngest son of Rev. James Bruce, Presbyterian minister at Killyleagh, County Down, whose wife was Hutcheson's mother's sister. He studied at Glasgow and in 1725 joined the bookselling firm of John Smith on the Blind Quay, Dublin, where he was involved in the publication of the first edition of Hutcheson's *Essay on the Nature and Conduct of the Passions and Affections* (1728). He was coauthor with Rev. John Abernethy of five papers on civil and religious liberty, published seriatim under the title *Reasons for the Repeal of the Sacramental Test* (Dublin, 1731) and republished in Abernethy, *Scarce and Valuable Tracts and Sermons* (London and Dublin, 1751), pp. 1–73. He later published two tracts critical of British economic policy in Ireland: *Some Facts and Observations Relative to the Fate of the Late Linen Bill* (Dublin, 1753) and a four-part *Remarks on a Pamphlet Entitled Considerations on a Late Bill for Paying the National Debt, &c.* (Dublin, 1754). He was buried in the same grave with Hutcheson in St. Mary's churchyard, Dublin, where a memorial stone survives.

26. Year given as 1730; see Editorial Principles above.

27. A packet boat.

28. Adapted from Matthew Prior (1664–1721), "A Lover's Anger" (1718), lines 14–16. The poem was set to music by Thomas Arne.

29. Copies of Hutcheson's inaugural lecture, *De naturali hominum socialitate oratio inauguralis* (Glasgow, 1730). See translation "On the Natural Sociability of Man,"

might be made to you in the most obliging terms; my Lord Cheif Baron[30] was so much pleased with the Present that he thought himself obliged to say something favourable about it immediatly on my delivering it to him, & so begun to praise the Letter & Printing of it which had almost made me burst out a Laughing it put me so strongly in Mind of the Panegyric you had written over on Glasgow's Butter & Veal, on your first going there: Mr Bowes promised to write you a long Epistle as soon as the Business of the Term was over, Mr Este also said he would write to you very soon; your Letter to Bishop Syng[31] was sent to him alongst with the Oration down to the Country, He is not expected in Town till the Session of Parliament: we are stitching up the parcel you last sent us as fast as we can and shall distribute about half a Score of them as you have ordered & have sett down Mr Abernathy[32] & Mr Craighead[33] amongst the Number that are to be Complemented.

---

in Francis Hutcheson, *Logic, Metaphysics, and the Natural Sociability of Mankind*, pp. 189–216.

30. Thomas Dalton (d. 1730), Chief Baron of the Irish Exchequer 1725–30, a protegé of Archbishop Hugh Boulter. See *Letters Written by His Excellency Hugh Boulter, DD, Primate of All Ireland*, 2 vols. (Oxford, 1769), 1:35, 106–107, 109, 197.

31. Edward Synge the Younger (c. 1690–1762), newly appointed bishop of Clonfert. Son of the archbishop of Tuam, he trained at Trinity College, Dublin, and quickly rose to prominence in the Church of Ireland. Hutcheson consulted him on his *Inquiry into the Original of Our Ideas of Beauty and Virtue* (1725), some of Synge's views having anticipated some of his own; and on his *System of Moral Philosophy*, which was posthumously dedicated to Synge by Hutcheson's son in 1755.

32. Rev. John Abernethy (1680–1740), Irish Presbyterian minister. Educated at Glasgow (MA c. 1696) and Edinburgh, he was minister at Antrim 1703–30, and thereafter at Wood Street, Dublin. In 1718 Abernethy, supported by both his congregation and his presbytery, resisted a call from the congregation of Usher's Quay, Dublin, which had the backing of the Synod of Ulster; but he lost support when a year later he delivered a sermon, "Religious Obedience Founded on Personal Persuasion" (printed in Abernethy, *Scarce and Valuable Tracts*, pp. 217–53), critical of the church's right to direct its ministers in matters of belief. Abernethy and those northern colleagues who refused to accept the authority of the Westminster *Confession of Faith*, known as "Nonsubscribers," were moved in 1725 into a separate Presbytery of Antrim, which was subsequently expelled from the Synod.

33. Robert Craghead (1684–1738), Irish presbyterian minister. Raised in northwest Ireland and trained at Glasgow, Edinburgh, and Leiden, he was ordained minister at Capel Street, Dublin, in 1709 as colleague to Rev. Francis Iredell. In the developing controversy, Craghead sided with the Nonsubscribers, Iredell with the Subscribers.

the Muzlen, Callico & Tea Chest, together with the Baskets long ago demanded, are all ready for the first opportunity to Newry which I am told will offer some time this Week the Muzlen came to £2:15 the Calico at 6s 6d a yeard 4 yeards & ½ to £1:9:3 & the Tea Chest to 12. I must beg that you would preserve the Account I formerly sent you if you have not already destroyed it for I have lost one of my Memorandum Papers & cannot well tell how Matters Stand. I got Alec Hamilton to speak to your Cousen James about Burges's Money, & the Answer was that the shereif had taken security for it by some rent charge which would pay up the whole in a Couple of years, & your friend desired that you might take no farther trouble, for that He would be as carefull of every thing that concerned your Interest as he would were the business his own.

there are no news in this place worth mentioning to you, for what would have been agreeable enough Chitt Chatt in Drumcondra Lane would be tedious Impertinence to you now: however it will be always agreeable to you to hear that your friends in this Country are well & that they always remember you & My Cousen[34] with the strongest affection; Captain Willson came to Town last Week I never in my Life saw him look better, he left the family in Tully all in good health, & seems to be conceiving good hopes of his unfortunate Son; he intends writing to you before he leaves Town. Cousen Hans in the last Letter I had from him compleans of your never having wrote to him since my Cousen went over, I know you have a very numerous Correspondence besides much other business which may serve as a very good Excuse for Silence as to some of us, but not as to him: all my Cousen's female Correspondents complain also heavily of her Silence, & particularly it costs Miss Campbell many a Tear, she wants to know whether she received a Couple of Letters which she wrote to her immediatly before she went off from Belfast, she has had thoughts of writing to her often since, but instead of setting down to write she sitts down to cry, upon which I have advised her to bottle up her Tears & send them properly labelled instead of a

---

34. Hutcheson's wife, Mary, daughter of Francis Wilson from Tully, County Longford. Throughout the correspondence the concept of "cousin" is used in a wider meaning than today.

Letter & desire they may be taken as the more natural Expressions of the thoughts of her Heart. I never spent so dull & languishing a Winter since I remember the spending of any but if you keep your word and I live to see it, I hope the Summer will make me forget it: I am much afraid my poor Brother Patrick is in a dangerous way, I wish you would ask Dr Johnston what his opinion is of him. Patrick consulted him Just before he came over & has been following his Praescriptions ever since please to remember me in the most respectfull & affectionat manner to my Cousen, to Mr Johnston & all other friends.

> I am
> > Dear Cousen
> > > your most obliged & most afectionate friend
> > > Will. Bruce

---

8. From PATRICK LANG[35]

Address lacking

MS: NLS, MS 9252, fols. 80r–81v

Greenoak[36] Sept 4 1732

Sir

I had probable Grounds to expect that My Letter would come Safe to Your Hand; however I shall be more cautious for the future. That which I blame there in the Management of that Sacred Institution is a fault which runs through the most part of their Sermons, chiefly such as they have at such Times VIZ that of showing the Humane Nature in a very bad Light. What others think of this I do not know, for My Self I am a Man, & can't endure to hear the Humane Nature run down at such a Rate without feeling a Selfish or Generous Indignation (which you will)

35. Patrick Lang (fl. 1730–31), son of Andrew Lang, merchant of Greenock, matriculated in the Logic class of John Loudon on November 14, 1730. He would have reached Hutcheson's class a year later.

36. Greenock, the port town to the west of Glasgow, on the Clyde estuary.

arise in My Mind. For that Escape I hope You will pardon me: Humanum est errare, Divinum vero ignoscere.[37] And You will be the more enclined to this if You consider I am at present at Greenoak where people are not Generally so bigotted as at Glasgow.

Since the Sacrament of the Lords Supper is a Duty, & in My Opinion, highly incumbent on every Christian, about which we should endeavour to have adequate Ideas & since You seem to doubt of Mine, I shall lay down what, at present, is My opinion of it, that if it be false, You may correct it, if Just You may approve of it; And, believe me, I would rather gain Your Approbation than have Millions of Worlds for My admire<r>s. And here I shall not confine My Self to either Orthodox or Heterodox Opinions (as they call them) concerning our Saviour, but endeavour to show it as it is a Duty which all Christians are bound to perform.

Christ came into the World a person if not the Son of God, Yet of a Nature Superior to Ours.

Mankind have reaped a Great many blessings from him, he having if not redeemed them from Death by the price of his blood at least set before them an Example of a Holy Life & laid down the precepts of a Divine Morality; to the truth of which he g<a>ve Testimony in Sealing it with his own blood.

Whatever rightly disposed Mind reflects upon such a form it must certainly raise Love & esteem for that being to a high Degree: And every One must be sensible how much Esteem for the Teacher engages us to practice his precepts.

Since a publick profession of this Love in Communion with others Naturally tends to raise & strengthen this Affection in Our Selves & others, And further since he requires it of us to show forth his Death till he come again I think it is every Mans Duty to partake of it.

This in My Opinion seems to agree with what the Scripture says about it. And from this it is easy to see what Disposition the Mind ought to be

---

37. A Latin proverb, found in variant forms, made popular in English through Alexander Pope's rendering in *An Essay on Criticism* (London, 1711), line 525: "To err is human; to forgive divine."

under at recieving & what is that Self Examination Necessary before we partake.

I must own that when ever I set my self to think on religious Subjects I do all I can to drive away Melancholy & Fear for Superstition & Begottry have alwayse appeared to me in such a Bad Light that I do all I can to free My Self of them They are Truths Greatest Enemys; the Greeks have observed this hence the Word in their Language that Signifys to be Mad comes from another Signifying a Daemon.

In my calm Meditations I could often see that however Young folks pique themselves often in laughing at what is popular in these Affairs Prudence & Manners restrain Wise Men from any such thing whatever their private Sentiments may be, tho I say I have been convinced of the Truth of this yet I feel that Desire of Distinction & Singularity (which you tell me is incident to Young folks of Studious Tempers) prevail even in My private Meditations tho I do all I can to stop it. And such things as seem to be contrary to common Opinion I examine strictly wither or not they proceed from such a principle. Yet I dont doubt but I am often Misled by it, for like other Desires it generally insinuates its own Justness.

LIVY[38] in his Relations is very Natural & Lively he does not amuse his readers with quaint Conciets, pointed turns of Witt or jingling Antitheses in which kind of writing the Words & the Wit of the Author Strike our Fancy but we never in the least are touched with the Matter. Our Minds are too much fixt on the Words to regard any thing else. In some of his Relations he seems to be inspired with poeticall fury & No Wonder it should be so Such Noble Generous Actions as he relates must certainly fill the Soul with Rapture & Amazement & even left it above it self. He makes use of No More Words than are necessary to Make himself fully Understood. In him are contained a Great Many particulars of the Roman Antiquitys. I dont in the least Doubt but Many of his Harangues are composed by himself. I can't persuade My Self that these discourses he relates in the Cases of Coriolanus & Melius & others in the Earlyer Ages

38. Titus Livius (59 BCE–CE 17), *Ab urbe condita* (History of Rome from Its Foundation).

of the Common Wealth could be handed down when the Credentials for their History (I believe) are very weak. He endeavour's to give his Reader a distinct prospect of the Roman Affairs by placing his Narrations where they shall give m<o>st light to the other parts of the History (as Cambray[39] thinks an Historian ought to do) However he does not leave the order of Time much as far as I read. There is one thing that would in my Opinion beautify a History very much which I dont remmember I met with in Livy & it is this After an Historian has given us any Series of Actions at proper Distances to give a Short View of the Whole. This would refresh the Readers Memory & Strike lively upon the Imagination. You know how delightfull it is to a Traveller when he has gone through a large Country from some Height to take a View of the Country all at Once, & in My humble Opinion it would be as pleasant in a History: Livy indeed at some Distances eases the Mind of his Reader by quiting the thread of his Story & bringing in some proper Digression. This, in My opinion, is a Beauty in Livy & His Book would not have been worse to have had more of them interspersed through it tho the Orations in a great Measure supply this want. You will pardon me that I did not read many of Gronov<ius>'s Notes[40] when I tell You that the Greatness of the Actions so intirely Swallowed up My Mind that I could not give over till once I Saw the End of the Story. The Consul never called the People together to Chose his Army & the Tribunes withstand him but I was Anxious for the Welfare of the City. I was afraid lest the Enemy should ruin them while they were jarring together I was Angry with both Partys both Patrician & Plebeian for being so obstinate Nay Many a Time I have been Marching My Self Armed Cap a pe to retard the Motions of the Enemy. These great Actions raise in Me a Love & Esteem of every thing that is Virtuous & an Abhorrence of the practices of those who Sacrifice the Good of their Country their Friends to gratify some Headstrong passion or obtain some private Good. History at the same Time that it is a Glass to futurity if it be well Write it naturally tends to raise an Hatred & Abherrence of Vice &

39. François de Salignac de la Mothe-Fénelon (1651–1715), archbishop of Cambrai.
40. Johann Friedrich Gronovius (1611–1671) published an annotated edition of Livy's history of Rome that appeared in several editions.

Strengthen Good Affections by representing great & good Vitious & Mean Actions in their true Colours.

I can't refrain laughing when I consider in what pompous Stile he relates those little bickerings that happened between Rome & her first Enemys. What large Armys could the<y> bring into the field? What signal Victorys could they gain? Yet he describes them with as much pomp & in as high a Stile as if the fate of the Whole World depended upon the Issue of the Battle.

Matchiavel[41] was certainly in the right in chosing the first Decade of Livy to comment on for all the Changes that can happen in a State are there related Monarchy Absolute & Limited, Aristocracy (not pure. I dont think there can be any such thing of any Continuance) which stood from the Expulsion of the Tyrant till the Tribunes of the People were chosen then the Commonwealth began & by Degrees with great Struggle the Commons got into all the places of power so that in this respect the Commonwealth was equal. There was still something wanting to make the Republick eternal. (Nihil ab omni parte beatum)[42] There were two Orders in the Commonwealth each of which reckoned their several Interests opposite. Besides this there was some Inequality in their Government the Senate sometimes debating & determining & the People in their turn using the same powers. this I think in part arose from the Distinction of Nobles, & Common people. These would have been but small Evils had a Just Agrarian been Settled at the beginning of the State for it was almost impossible to Settle it afterwards. In reading Livy I take a great Deal of pleasure in calling to Mind such Political Reflections as I have had from You, Harrington, Matchiavel, Sidney & Moil.[43]

You see how dangerous it is to give the least favour to an Impertinent fellow for whereas in Gratitude they should not trouble their Benefactor the kinder he is to them they trouble him the More.

I am Naturally Loquacious & Chiefly in things that relate to Learning & Our Conversation here is generally about Bussiness so that I must vent My

---

41. Niccolò Machiavelli (1469–1527), *The Discourses on the Ten First Books of Titus Livius* (1531).

42. Horace, *Odes* II.16.27: "Nothing <is> in every respect happy."

43. Algernon Sidney (1623–1683); Walter Moyle (1672–1721).

Self tho it be at the Expence of Gratitude & Good Manners And there is none that I know will be more apt to pardon the frailtys of Humane Nature than Your Self. Pardon this Boldness & be so kind as to think that it proceeds from a Confidence in your Goodness. Pardon it in

Your Most devoted Pupil
Patrick Lang

9. From WILLIAM BRUCE

Address: To Mr Francis Hutcheson Professor of Philosophy in the University of Glasgow

MS: NLS, MS 9252, fols. 78–79

Dublin December[44] 23d 1732

My Dear Cousen

It is well for yourself as well as others that your two principal Pleasures in Life are those of doing Good and of Obliging your friends for by this time youll have probably found that these are the Employments which it is expected your Life should be spent in, all that you have to insist on is that the Latter is never to be required when Inconsistant with the former, and indeed with this Limitation the Expectation is not unreasonable; It is upon this supposition that I now join young Mr Ross who writes to you by this Post & whose Letter will probably be delivered to you at the same time with this, in earnestly requesting your Interest in behalf of Mr Clifton's Son of Edenburgh who is now one of your Pupills, in Order to his being put upon Snells Bursury at the next Election;[45] the Young Fellow's merit I am utterly a Stranger to, but upon Supposition that his Pretensions in this respect are equal to those of the other Candidates it would give me very great pleasure if by your Influence he was made to Succeed,

---

44. *Written* "10ᵇʳ." Here, and in Letters 11, 18, and 25, William Bruce uses the numeral instead of the Latin word in the name of the month: Decem-ber.

45. William Clifton, son of William Clifton, Esq., Edinburgh, matriculated in Hutcheson's class in 1732, graduating MA in 1733. He transferred to Balliol College, Oxford, on May 8, 1733, and graduated BA from there in December.

because it is an affair which Mr Ross has exceedingly at heart, a young Gentleman, in my opinion worthy to be obliged and that, even for a better reason than what prevailed on our Saviour to serve the Centurion[46] for HE LOVETH THE CAUSE OF VIRTUE & LIBERTY & IS WILLING TO VOTE FOR THE REPEAL OF THE TEST.[47]

your friends here and in the Country are all well except poor Patrick who is still growing worse; but I shall not now trouble you with any News, Cousen Jack is just come to Town & I hope I shall in a few days be able to give you an Agreeable Account of that affair Colonel Hutcheson came to Town yesterday he gives you and family his most afectionate Service & bids me tell you that he had ordered Mr Young[48] in Belfast to remitt you £40. Eng which he left in his hands as he came up he was prevented from coming your way by a Severe Storm that overtook him on his Journey. all friends here most afectionately remember you, please to give my most respectfull service to Cousen Hutcheson Miss Willson Squire Everard &c.

I am

my Dear Cousen

with great Esteem

your most obliged & most sincere

friend & servant

Will. Bruce

---

46. Luke 7:1–10; Matthew 8:5–13.

47. See Letter 2.

48. Alexander Young, Belfast merchant, died intestate in 1754. His mother, Mary Hutcheson, was the sister of Rev. John Hutcheson, Francis Hutcheson's father (above, Letter 4). See Jean Agnew, *Belfast Merchant Families in the Seventeenth Century* (Dublin, 1996), p. 252. Later correspondence with Thomas Drennan (below, Letters 53, 56, and 57) shows that Young was close to bankruptcy in 1744–46.

10. From WILLIAM BRUCE

Address: To Mr Francis Hutcheson Professor of Philosophy in the University of Glasgow

MS: NLS, MS 9252, fols. 89–90; slight loss of wording due to seal

Dublin August 24th 1734

My Dearest Cousen

I had the pleasure of both your Letters since your return from the Whey, for which I am extreamly obliged to you, did all your benevolent actions so effectualy take place, you would certainly be the most benefi-cent Man on the face of the Earth. Some few days before I received your last Letter Mr Hamilton of Carlow went into the North, but I am heartily sorry that I did not know before, that Judgement was entered up and a Warrant given him to acknowledge Satisfaction for with great appeerence of Zeal he lamented the want of the Bond which I am now tempted to suspect was a little farcicall, it being hardly conceavable that he can be so far ignorant of these matters as not to know that this would sufficiently enable him to give as ample a release as any Man or any Law could require; I shall not fail to atack him on this Head as soon as I have an opportunity; the Man's dispositions I verily beleive are honest, but he is certainly neces-sitous to a most pityable degree & when this is the Case, a weak Judge-ment differs but very little in its Effects from a corrupt Heart. I think you are perfectly right in your Advice to Cousen Rhoda, I immediately ac-quainted her with it & she readily agreed to it, so I am to write to Cousen Trail to night and doubt not but he will readily take the Money in what-ever sums her Conveniency will require, She is at present in Town along with Mrs King but is talking of returning to Tully some time next week. I am heartily sorry that any Tittle Tattle of the kind you mention in rela-tion to Doctor Arebuckle[49] should ever have got abroad, these things never

---

49. James Arbuckle (d. 1742) was a poet and essayist who studied at Glasgow Uni-versity (MA 1720, followed by divinity studies), where he was politically active. He abandoned plans for the ministry and moved to Dublin in 1724 where he became a member of the circle around Robert, Viscount Molesworth. He founded and contrib-uted extensively to *The Dublin Weekly Journal* from 1725 until it folded in 1727. It was here that Hutcheson published his early essays on Mandeville and on laughter that are edited in the present volume, pp. 195–243. See *ODNB*; M. A. Stewart, "John Smith and the Molesworth Circle," *Eighteenth-Century Ireland*, 2 (1987): 89–102.

fail to meet with dispositions where they make a lasting impression let them be ever so groundless & with respect to the Doctor I am convinced in my Conscience they are absolutely false; It is true his Friends have been often rallieng him for coming so very seldom among them at nights since his Marriage but I always understood these to be only quarrels of a friendly sort, I could indeed have wished that his Indulgences to his friends in this Article had been a little more frequent as well for the sake of keeping their friendly afections in Life & Exercise as for my own Satisfaction, but we need only reflect a little on the unmanly & unthinking Manner in which the time of these interviews is most frequently consumed in order to find out a very sufficient Excuse for a Man who has such an Agreeable Companion & Entertainment at Home in treating them with neglect; this however is all in the Doctor's Conduct as far as my observation has hitherto reached that can with the least shadow of Justice be laid hold of, to Justifie the Charge, & how utterly insufficient it is for that purpose I leave every reasonable person to Judge; nothing would make me deceive you in this Matter, nor am I under any temptation to do it; if the Doctor's Conduct was offensive, my affection for him would naturaly lead me to take notice of it to you in order to your setting him right, but I afirm it to you I have never yet discovered any appearence in it that either looked like an Indifference towards his Friends or an unmanly Elation of Mind on Account of his Fortune, I am perswaded he is a worthy Man & bating some foibles in his temper which you are as well acquainted with as I, his Character is to me one of the most unexceptionable I know in the World.

I am glad to hear that you purpose to see London next Summer I think you would do well to order Matters so with respect to your Class that the Business of it might be over by the middle of Aprile for you ought if possible to take your Journey before the beginning of May; I cannot be sure that my Judgement is quite free from partiality as to what I have so often wished you to think of tho I have this Evidence in my favour that I have found myself thinking always in the same manner about it notwithstanding the State of my health has at some times cut off all prospect of having any share in the pleasure of it were it ever so quickly to have taken Effect; I have always taken it for granted that the requisite compliances could be made by you without doing Violence to your mind, and I cannot deny but that I was pleased to find it so tho I despair of ever being able to bring my own Mind into such a Latitude, but on this Supposition it has all along been as Evident to me as any thing of such a contingent nature could well be that a short while's Conformity must necessarly enlarge your Capacity of Usefullness vastly beyond your present Situation, or any other that you can rationaly lay your Account for without it: I perfectly agree with you that for all the purposes of a family & private conveniency you are Rich enough already but it is for this very reason that I want to have your Income enlarged, where Money afords such a facility of doing Good a Man of your Heart & dispositions can never have too large a Revenue; but my prospect of your Usefulness is far from being confined to that one Article; your Conversation would in all likelyhood come to lye principaly among the Men of high Stations & active Life, & by the few trials you have already made, you have abundant reason to expect that tho your Influence may not be equal to the supernatural operation of forming their Minds to a regular Course of Sobriety & Virtue yet it would notwithstanding be sufficient in a variety of Instances to animate them to Actions of Beneficence & Patrio-tism & often to restrain them from doing Hurt, a Situation which of all others a Man of Wisdom & Virtue should in the present State of the World desire to be placed in, but neither is your Influence with the Great all that I should expect, a Course of a few years it is by no means improbable would place yourself in the Number of the Great I know I shall be laughed at for this as altogether Chimerical & Visionary but the good old aphorism "that what has been, may be" will for ever stand in my own way from thinking it so, You cannot you say descend to the Modern Arts of growing Great, and I say God forbid you could, it would break my heart to see you become a B——p at such Expense, but modern Arts are only necessary to modern Minds Hoadly & Clark[50] neither used them nor wanted them; all that I would desire of you amounts to only a partial obedience of our Saviour's express command, not to conceal the Light that <is> within you,[51] & not to suffer any peculiarity of Taste to pre<vail> against that most important moral obligation of doing Good in proportion to the abilities you have re-ceived from the liberal hand and Providence of God.—but I have good expectations from next Summer's Jant.—there are little or no News in this

---

50. For Benjamin Hoadly and Samuel Clarke, see Letter 2, notes 6 and 8.
51. Luke 11:35.

Country worth mentioning, Dean Percival died tother day[52] but it is not yet known who will succeed him; all your friends & acquaintances in this place as far as I know are well except Mrs Finlay who has for a few days past been afflicted with a paralytic disorder that in some measure affects her Speech; the Colonel is perfectly recovered & He & I are to go in ten days to the North; I should be fond of hearing from you while I am there you may direct to the Care of Paddy Smith in Belfast. Some time ago I wrote to Mr Stalker[53] to pay in the Ballance of his Account to you which is £11:19:10 Irish what remains in your hand after paying John Millar's demand on Wear Dr Arbuckle desires he may have Credit for in some Account He has with you I also wrote lately to Cousen Trail in Edenburgh[54] setting him right in some things he had mistaken in the Account of a small parcel we had sent him; if you have an opportunity you may assure him we will use him as well as it is possible for any Bookseller in this Place to do; & you may assure Mr Stalker of the same, all we would desire is to know what price the Copies that we have no property in have been charged at by other Booksellers from his place; because that must be our Rule of charging them tho we have reason to beleive that we have been led in to charge some of them higher by the Assurances that they gave us that they were never charged lower than the prices they mention to us; we think it injustice to undersell any Man in his own Copy, but by the Number of good Copies that we have now a property in we certainly can aford to sell as cheap as any, getting all the Books of the Dublin Market in exchange for our Copies; we shall send you half a dozen Burnets by the first ship. please to remember me in the most afectionate & respectfull manner to my Cousen & the dear little Boy, it gave us all a great deal of pleasure to hear of his good State of Health, please also to give my afectionate service to Mrs Wallace Squire Everard & all other friends.

> I am Dearest Cousen yours in the fullness of my heart
> Will. Bruce

Mrs Arebuckle is still rowling about but they look for her falling asunder every day

52. Rev. William Perceval, 1671–1734, archdeacon of Cashel and dean of Emly.
53. Andrew Stalker, Glasgow bookseller.
54. John Trail or Traill, bookseller in Edinburgh.

11. From WILLIAM BRUCE

Address lacking

MS: NLS, MS 9252, fols. 91–92; poor legibility on the second leaf

Craigavade October[55] 21 1734

My Dear Cousen

I understand from Jack[56] since I came into the Country that there is a Letter of yours lying for me in Dublin & that he has open'd it, I hope it is not in answer to the last I wrote to you because if I remember right I there told you that I was intending a Visit to the North & expected to receive a Letter from you directed to Belfast & I should not be well pleased that an Answer to that Letter should fall into any hands but my own; I take it however for granted that no Inconveniency can follow from the Liberty Jack has taken because he tells me that the only important thing in it was in relation to my Brothers Boys[57] being sent over this Winter except an order for procuring some Casks of Tongues; as to this last I have sent directions to the Cooper whom I imployd before that in Case I do not get to Town before the best of the Season for providing these sort of things be over to purchase them for me & have them ready for sending over by the first opportunity & I have wrote to Jack to send to the Cooper as soon as he knows of a ship for Irwin.[58] we are all much obliged to you for your Concern about my Cousens,[59] but it was both my Brother's Opinion & mine that it would be best they should spend another year at home; they have all time enough before them for procuring Knowledge, & as yet I cannot think their Minds sufficiently opened & prepaired for making the best of a University Education; at the same time this is with respect to their Morals the most critical & dangerous Season of Life & therefore I would fain have some Evidence that their Minds

55. *Written* "8ᵇʳ."
56. Bruce's business partner, John Smith.
57. James and Samuel Bruce, sons of Rev. Michael Bruce, Nonsubscribing minister at Holywood, County Down. In the event, James matriculated under Hutcheson at Glasgow on November 14, 1735; Samuel a year later under John Loudon, graduating MA in 1740.
58. Irvine.
59. Apparently an error for "Nephews."

were sensible of the Power of the Principles of Virtue & Prudence before they were trusted so much to their own Government; if they shall hapily preserve their Innocence & escape the dreadful Contagion that is now so prevalent I shall be in no pain about their being pushed into the World but I honestly confess to you that their present danger fills me with a more painful Solicitude than any thing else has hitherto been able to give me since I came into the World: —the young Gentleman who does me the favour to be the Bearer of this I find is giving some of his friends in this Country a good deal of Solicitude of the same Sort tho mixed with a Concern & Policy that is in my opinion altogether forreign from it; It is their united Judgement however that his best Security both with respect to his Morals & his Fortune consists at present in his being again put under your Inspection; your consenting to this after all the Uneasiness you underwent last session is in their opinion as well as mine an Evidence of uncommon Friendship but the Circumstances of this young Gentleman as they have been represented to me, at present stand thus;[60] It is in his Father's Power to disinherit him of much the best part of his Estate & tho the old Gentleman is exceedingly fond of him yet, it is intirely on the perswasion that his Conduct is as unexceptionable abroad as it appears to him at home and it is the firm beleif of those of his friends whom I have conversed with & who seem to know best the Secrets of that family that an opposite representation especialy from you would do all that is wanting to prevail with the Father to sett him aside; this the Young Gentleman I am told is also convinced of & has therefore or perhaps on better motives put on the strongest resolutions of living a regular obliging & Studious Life I am very well aware that "Hott Constitutions are apt to leap over cold Decrees"[61] & therefore am not ready except where I see some strong Symptoms of the Mind's feeling the power of the principles of Virtue to lay any great stress on such Violent purposes, but what upon the whole I would choose to recommend to you is this that seeing the Penalty is already fixed & is either to be inflicted or not according to your

60. The reference appears to be to Arthur Upton (1715–1768), eldest son of John Upton, Esq., of Castle Upton, County Antrim, and the only Irish student to matriculate under Hutcheson in 1733. He was later an Irish MP and a Privy Councillor.

61. Adapted from Shakespeare, *The Merchant of Venice*, Act I, scene 2.

representation as you are well acquainted with the follies & weaknesses of the youthful Heart and are also aware that such a Punishment will in the Estimation of the World be thought unnatural & quite disproportionate to any of its ordinary Sallies, that you make one part of the Divine Character the Rule of your Conduct & be not Severe in marking his Iniquities, I mean so as to make them Articles of Complaint.

all friends in this family most afectionately & Gratefully remember you & join with me in most afectionate & respectful service to my Cousen & my dear little Franky & to Mrs Wallace. I am

> my dear Cousen
> under a lively sense of the strongest obligations
> your most afect Cousen
> & most faithful friend
> Will. Bruce

---

12. To WILLIAM WISHART [62]

Address: To the Revd Dr William Wishart at his house in Bridgewater Square London

MS: EUL, La. II. 115, fols. 1–2

Glasgow May 29th 1735

Dear Sir

I had a letter from you about 3 weeks ago, and don't pretend this as a full answer. I am much obliged to you for your Care about the Greek books you mention. they are all exceeding Cheap. as to Themistius since it is so late an Edition [63] it may be had when we please and the faculty commis-

62. Rev. William Wishart (c. 1692–1753), minister of the Scots Church, London. He had been minister of the Tron Church, Glasgow, from 1724 to 1730, and as dean of faculty in 1729 presided over the university meeting that elected Hutcheson to a chair of philosophy. In 1737 he was appointed principal of Edinburgh University (*ODNB*).

63. Themistius (c. 317–388), commentator on Aristotle and senator in Constantinople. Himself a pagan, his religious neutrality made him useful to Christian emperors.

sioned none of those I troubled you about, but I ventured to order them of my self, I will wait till it be commissioned. I would not ommit this note by Dr Haynes,[64] whose behaviour with us has been very good in the main, & very obliging. He really acquitted himself well upon Examination.

Sir Francis Wronghead[65] whom you did not apprehend in my last is my worship. I have been projecting a Journey to London with John Paisley these several Moneths.[66] I continue in the same humour yet, but am not positive about it: And cheifly on account of my wifes state of health. if this continues good till the 3d or 4th of July I shall then set off: if not I cannot leave her. all I fear about her is the Danger of Miscarriage as they call it, which has Several times brought her to the last extremity. I am too sensible of my good luck in that Article of life which attached me to her, not to be pretty solicitous about her safety. If She continues well I hope to have the pleasure of spending a few weeks with you, but I have some causes of fear.

I condole with you most heartily about your friend Dr Rundle's Danger.[67] If our last accounts in the Printed Papers were true, He must be past all accident of Mortality before this time. I am forced to write this in

---

The book in question would have been an edition of his paraphrases of Aristotle or his orations.

64. Newton Haynes, son of Hopton Haynes, the Unitarian lay writer who was assay-master at the mint and close to William Whiston and Isaac Newton. Newton Haynes graduated LL.D. at Glasgow in 1735.

65. A character in *The Provok'd Husband* (1728), a comedy by Sir John Vanbrugh, posthumously completed by Colley Cibber.

66. See above, letter 10. John Paisley was a Glasgow surgeon who in 1733 was authorized to offer anatomy classes in the university (GUA 26647, fol. 130). His brother Rev. Patrick Paisley (1695–1736) succeeded William Wright (above, Letter 2) as minister of Kilmarnock in 1724; he was one of the young ministers suspected of theological laxity when the teaching of John Simson, the professor of divinity, was under investigation around 1727 (Robert Wodrow, *Analecta*, 4:412: see below, Letter 32).

67. Thomas Rundle, DCL (1687/8–1743), liberal Church of England clergyman, at this time chaplain to the Lord Chancellor, Charles Talbot. He had been chaplain to Talbot's father, William Talbot, when the latter was bishop first of Salisbury, then of Durham, where high living ruined Rundle's health. The illness mentioned in this letter was not fatal. Two months later Rundle was appointed bishop of Derry in Ireland, and served there for eight years. See below, Letter 21.

great hurry, and must leave all news to our long-wished-for meeting, or to a more leisure hour if I am disappointed. I am Dear Sir

Yours most sincerly,

Franc: Hutcheson

13. From THOMAS NETTLETON[68]

Address: For Mr Hutchinson Professor in the University of Glasgow

MS: NLS, MS 9252, fols. 98–99; slight loss of wording due to seal

Halifax Sept 25 1735

Dear Sir

I have at last adventur'd to send You these Papers by the hands of a young man who comes to Glasgow for the advantage of your Instruction;[69] He has been some time with Mr Buck of Bolton in Lancashire,[70] who is your Freind & Admirer, & has sent the Young man to finish his Studies under your Inspection; I believe He has a very promising Genius & should take it as a particular Favour if You wou'd asist & befreind him so far as You find He deserves it.

It is not without some Confusion that I lay this small Treatise before You,[71] but You have indeed some sort of right to it, because it is in part

---

68. Thomas Nettleton, FRS (1683–1742) studied at Leiden (MD, 1706) and built up a medical practice at Halifax, Yorkshire, where he was a prominent Dissenting layman. He wrote on barometric pressure and smallpox inoculation, and published an anonymous satire, *A Layman's Sermon in Defence of Priestcraft* (1733), in addition to the work noted below. See H. McLachlan, "Thomas Nettleton, M.D.," *Transactions of the Unitarian Historical Society* 9, no. 1 (October 1947): 21–27.

69. The reference appears to be to Thomas Whitehead of Bolton, Lancashire. He matriculated under Hutcheson on November 14, 1735, and graduated MA in 1738.

70. Rev. John Buck, English Dissenting minister at Bank Street, Bolton, in succession to Thomas Dixon, who had transferred his Dissenting academy from Whitehaven to Bolton in 1723 and continued it there until his death in 1729. This is the first evidence that the work of the academy continued in some form after Dixon's death.

71. The reference is to Nettleton's *Treatise on Virtue and Happiness*, which would be published in London the following year. It was a greatly expanded version of *Some*

borrow'd from You, being built upon those Principles which have been advanced by my Lord Shaftsbury & your self. You were the first who pointed out to us those Powers of Affection, which tho plain to observation, have not been sufficiently attended to by many Writers; which is the reason why their Accounts of Humane Nature have been lame & imperfect. You will perceive that this little System of Morality is built entirely upon what We feel & experience within our selves, & the Design of it is to recommend moral Goodness from those Principles which are interwoven with our Frame & Constitution, without intermedling with forreign Motives drawn from Rewards & Punishments in a future State, which is the Provence of Divines, but as we are far from derogateing from those Motives, & as there cannot be too many Inducements to Virtue, some being led by one, & some by another & in this degenerate Age there being so many who make but a jest of a future State, We might hope to be pardon'd at least, for attempting to perswade Persons that Virtue is their true Interest here as well as hereafter. I have nothing to plead, but a good intention, in excuse for so poor a Performance, I am sensible it is too dry & general, especially the first part, not illustrated with a sufficient Number of particular Instances, nor enliven'd with any Turns of Witt, to make it agreable to the Generality of Readers. The Stile is also too perplex'd, abounding with too many Epithets & Synonymous Terms, but I have been of late so much hurry'd in Bussiness that I have no leisure, if I had ability to correct it for the better. As I have built upon your Foundation, so I do not differ from You in any thing, that I know of, or at least in nothing considerable, but if I do shall be very desirous of better Information, & shall most readily receive Conviction from your hands.

I have not mentioned either My Lord Shaftsbury or your Self because I know not whether it wou'd be proper but if the Book shou'd be read by any body so as to undergo another Edition, I shall not only be ready but desirous to make the most ample acknowledgements I am able

---

Thoughts Concerning Virtue and Happiness: In a Letter to a Clergyman (London, 1729). A second edition was published in 1742 and a third, "corrected and very much improved by the author," appeared posthumously in 1751, but Nettleton never made the promised acknowledgment of his debt to Hutcheson.

I wou'd not take up too much of your time in revising such a Trifle, but shall take it as a particular Favour if You will give me your Advice & lend me your Asistance where You shall judge it necessary

I know not well how it must <be re>turn'd with safety & without much loss of time after You have done with it, but do suppose that You may meet with some opportunity for it, or I will endeavour to inform You how it may be done in my next by the Post, for I must give You the trouble of a Post Letter, in a short time & in it shall send You the Conclusion of this Piece for You will perceive that it is not finished; I am call'd off & have no time to add more but to assure You that I am

Sir

Your most oblidged
humble Servant
Thos. Nettleton

---

14. To GEORGE BENSON[72]

Address lacking

MS: John Rylands University Library, Manchester, UCC B1/13

Glasgow March 17th 1735/36

Sir

I had the favour of yours of the 27th of December last; it gave me great pleasure to hear from an old acquaintance whom after 20 years Separation without any Correspondence I had almost forgot.[73] If I don't forget such old Storys, we had several merry meals together at Mrs Boyses with

72. George Benson (1699–1762), English Dissenting minister and prominent biblical scholar, at this time minister in Southwark and from 1740 at Crutched Friars, London (*ODNB*). The letter is dated according to the old "Legal calendar," but the reference to the publication of Benson's work makes clear that it would be 1736 in the "Historical calendar"; see Editorial Principles above.

73. Twenty years previously, Benson was still at school in Great Salkeld, Cumberland. The likely reference is to their paths crossing at Glasgow during the 1717–18 university session. Benson matriculated in the moral philosophy class, conducted that

a mirth & appetite which we must not expect should continue with us; and had for our Desert, Dr May & Dr Whitaker upon the table as Mountebank & Merry Andrew upon the Stage.[74] I am heartily glad to hear your time is so usefully employed. This is a place where we have few buyers of books, and far fewer Subscribers to books not published. t'is not possible to engage people to Subscribe who may probably buy what is once well received. I gave Mr Gordon a Copy of your proposals<.> he had an hearty zeal to serve you, but I believe neither of us had much Success. I Subscribe for two Copies. He will inform you of what he can do on the other side.[75] I am

Sir

Your most obedient

humble servant

Francis Hutcheson

the bearer Mr Gordons son will deliver 14 shillings the first payment for two Copies for me

---

year by Gershom Carmichael; Hutcheson was in the last year of his divinity studies and still serving as tutor to the new Earl of Kilmarnock.

74. This reference to the popular entertainment with the traditional figures of Mountebank and his sidekick Merry Andrew may be a reminder to Benson of their youthful interest in the Bangorian controversy around Benjamin Hoadly, bishop of Bangor; see anonymous (Daniel Defoe ?), *Merry Andrew's Epistle to His Old Master, Benjamin, a Mountebank at Bangor-Bridge, on the River Dee, near Wales* (London, 1719).

75. John Gordon, a Glasgow merchant, added his own note overleaf on the difficulty of securing sales. Benson's *History of the First Planting the Christian Religion: Taken from the Acts of the Apostles, and Their Epistles* was published in two volumes (London, 1735). In the subscribers' list, Hutcheson is identified as paying for two sets, Gordon for one.

15. To THOMAS DRENNAN[76]

Address: To the Revd Mr Thomas Drennan in Belfast

MS: GUL, MS Gen. 1018, no. 2

Glasgow Jan. 31 1737

Dear Thom

Yours of the 20th Instant surprized me much. Mr Arbucle sent over in December a letter to John Stark giving credit to Mr Williamson for £40. The boy brought it me, I went with him to John Stark, and having to pay Masters for the whole Session, a Gown Books a quarters Lodging he took the value of £20 Irish, viz £17-18-9. this he employed me to pay out for him and give him as he needed, and before me Drew a Bill for £20 Irish on Mr Arbucle which he gave to John Stark. The Boy received no more money from any Mortal but from me and has drawn for no more but the said £20 Irish. John Stark Died about 8 days after this payment, his Executors shewed me his Letter-book, and besides in consequence of Mr Arbucles Letter Mr Hartson should pay Mr Arbucle only for what Mr Williamson draws, and not any draughts of John Stark. there must be some gross blunder in this Matter, I fear on Mr Arbucles Side. Pray pay no money till he shews you Mr Williamson<s> Bills on him. But Mr Starks Executors tell me they must have a new letter of Credit before they will advance any more. I fancy you need not let Mr Hartson be at any trouble in this matter I will advance Mr Williamson what he shall further need and draw on Mr Hartson in favour of Brother Robin at as low Exchange as any one here. I happen to want to remit, which is very seldom the case with me.

76. Rev. Thomas Drennan (1696–1768), minister of the First Presbyterian Church, Belfast, from 1736. Born in Belfast, he studied under Gershom Carmichael at Glasgow (MA 1716) and attended the divinity class under John Simson. He was licensed for the ministry at Belfast in 1726. Then, if not before, he joined Hutcheson as tutor at his Dublin academy, winding up its affairs in 1731 after Hutcheson moved to Glasgow. Drennan joined the Nonsubscribing Presbytery of Antrim and was ordained minister at Holywood, County Down, succeeding William Bruce's brother, Rev. Michael Bruce, in 1731. He was the father of William Drennan (1754–1820), physician, poet, and political writer.

Pray let Mr Duchal[77] know that I am concerned that Mr Shane has not returned this session, that I lent him in May last 2 guineas, and have not heard any thing about him since. If his father inclines to pay it he may do it to you, and you can get it sent to me.

I am glad your present situation is agreeable to you, I must insist on your promise of a visit whenever you find Honest Mr Haliday in good health that he could take the whole burden for a moneth or six weeks. Robert Simson[78] with you & Charles Moor[79] would be wondrous happy till 3 in a morning: I would be with you from 5 to ten; I can write you litle news Our College is very well this year as to Numbers and Quality of scholars. but the younger classes are less numerous, as people here grow less set on a College-Education for lads designed for business.

My wife has troubled you with a litle bundle of thread which she sent by one Clerk a lad who deals in Linnen Cloath the Thread must be sent to Dr Arbucle by the first safe opportunity. My most hearty respects to Mr Haliday Dr Smith Alexander Young & all honest fellows in Belfast.

I must tell you a shamefull Story of our College. My Letter I wrote from Dublin stopped Clotworthy O Neals getting his Degree upon his first Application. He got some folks in this Country who are tools of the Court to recommend the Matter to our Principal,[80] he made a Compliment of 20 guineas to the College Library, and the Principal watched an opportunity when there was a thin meeting b<ut> his tools all present, and carryed to give him a Degree in <Arts an>d that too only an honorary one, and declared so in the Diploma, without any certifying for his

77. Rev. James Duchal (d. 1761), Irish Nonsubscribing Presbyterian minister at Antrim, 1730–40, and later at Wood Street, Dublin (*ODNB*).

78. Robert Simson (1687–1768), professor of mathematics at Glasgow University. He was the nephew of John Simson, professor of divinity, and an authority on ancient mathematics (*ODNB*). See Letter 46 and Hutcheson's published letter to William Smith, pp. 253–71.

79. Charles Moor was an Ulster Scot who matriculated at Glasgow University under John Loudon in the 1714–15 session. On the evidence of this correspondence he appears to have gone into business in Belfast.

80. The principal of Glasgow University at this date was Rev. Neil Campbell (1678–1761) (*ODNB*), a kinsman of the Duke of Argyll. He was appointed in 1728.

Learning or Manners.[81] My Dissent is entered in the books & 4 more Masters declined signing it.

I am Dear Thom

yours most affectionatly

Franc: Hutcheson

---

16. To COLIN MacLAURIN

Address: To Mr Colin MacLaurin Professour of Mathematicks in Edinburgh

MS: Aberdeen University Library, MS 206, fols. 17–18

Glasgow Ap. 21 [1737][82]

Dear Sir

last post I had a return from Jammy MacKay from Bangor near Donaghadee,[83] his Parish, "The Moon plainly passed over the Orb of the Sun but did not appear to us quite Central, the upper part of the sun appearing greater than the under at the greatest darkness. My watch was pretty truly set, & I observed the Eclipse was not visible till more than ½ an hour after the time fixed in our Almanacks.[84] The same was ob-

81. Clotworthy O'Neill, second son of John O'Neill of Thanes Castle, County Antrim, matriculated under John Loudon in the 1723–24 session but failed to complete the course. He was granted an MA in 1736 and later became high sheriff of County Antrim.

82. Damaged page. The year is traceable to a visible eclipse of the sun between Hutcheson's settlement in Glasgow (1730) and the conclusion of William Bruce's employment as a bookseller (late 1737). See note 84 below.

83. Rev. James MacKay (1709–1781) was licensed for the Irish Presbyterian ministry at Armagh in 1731 and ordained at Bangor, County Down, in 1732, subsequently holding pastorates at Clonmel (1740) and First Presbyterian Church (Nonsubscribing), Belfast (1761). He was to be Thomas Drennan's last colleague in Belfast and would publish a memorial sermon for him (*The Happiness of the Righteous in a Future State, Explained and Improved*) in 1768.

84. John Watson's *The Gentleman and Citizen's Almanack* (Dublin, 1737), p. 3, predicted "A Great and visible Eclipse of the Sun, on Friday Feb 18" from 1:08 p.m. to 3.53 p.m.

served by several people here, who observed with good pendulum-Clocks. Counsellour Blackwood told me he observed the Eclipse with a good reflecting Telescope in Dublin, & a watch set by the Sun that day or the day before, and that it was not sensible till half an hour after the time set in our Almanacks. As I had no Instruments I can say nothing more Exact." This with hearty respects to you is all he writes on that Head.

I have constant accounts of the Impatience of our Virtuosi in Dublin about your Fluxions Your Friends are angry at the Delay & Bishop Berklys are triumphing already.[85] If he should have some silly Answer ready before yours be well published, I think you deserve it for your excessive Complaisance to a Man bursting almost with Vanity long ago. Pray did you ever see his *Demonstration of Passive Obedience & Non-resistance & Hereditary Right*, Printed under Queen Anns Tory Ministry?[86] Pray send me a Dozen of Copies[87] for A friend of mine in Dublin a Bookseller one Bruce at whatever rate you dispose of them to others & as soon as you can. I find Sandy Andersons friends are defeated by Our Principals Interest.[88]

---

85. A fluxion is the rate of change of a quality, such as speed. Berkeley's *The Analyst; or, A Discourse Addressed to an Infidel Mathematician*, directed against Newton's theory of fluxions, was published in London and Dublin editions in 1734. MacLaurin had intended to reply in a short pamphlet, but it developed into a full-scale *Treatise of Fluxions*, finally published in Edinburgh in 1742. In addition to stimulating more immediate English responses, Berkeley's work occasioned at least two Dublin publications, J. Walton's *A Vindication of Sir Isaac Newton's Principles of Fluxions, against the Objections Contained in The Analyst* (1735) and John Hanna's *Some Remarks on Mr. Walton's Appendix, which He Wrote in Reply to the Author of The Minute Philosopher, concerning Motion and Velocity* (1736). Berkeley had responded to Walton in *A Defence of Free-Thinking in Mathematics* (1735).

86. As a young Fellow of Trinity College Dublin, Berkeley had published *Passive Obedience, or The Christian Doctrine of Not Resisting the Supreme Power, Proved and Vindicated upon the Principles of the Law of Nature* in Dublin, with second and third editions in London, in 1712. Hutcheson is inaccurate on the title and the subject matter of this pamphlet, which included no reference to the principle of hereditary right. He pursued the criticism in his *System of Moral Philosophy*, II.17.6–7.

87. The letter is endorsed "About sending The Fluxions to Dublin."

88. Rev. Alexander Anderson, 1698/9–1738, onetime librarian of Glasgow University, was ordained minister of Sorbie, Wigtownshire, in the Galloway region of Scotland in 1724.

A Good man may be happy with a poor stipend even in Galloway<.> that is my only consolation about him.

I am Dear Sir

Your Most obedient

humble Servant

Franc: Hutcheson

I heartily congratulate your perfect recovery. My humble respects to your Lady.

---

17. To THOMAS DRENNAN

Address: To the Reverend Mr Thomas Drennan, in Belfast

MS: GUL, MS Gen. 1018, no. 3

Glasgow September 21st 1737

Dear Thom

Yours of the 2d instant I got only last Night upon my return from a Country Jaunt The Painter you mentioned came to this town about a Moneth ago without recommendations and no body employed him upon which he went to Edinburgh. He was gone before I got yours otherways I should have introduced him to what business I could. I hope before it be very long to let you see in print what has employed my leisure hours, for several Summers past; but I am at a loss how to get a right printer to employ being a stranger in London. I don't incline to put my name to what I print or give any proofs of the Author to any wasps in this Country, tis a System[89] of Morality in English, larger than both my former books. you need not talk of this. I had a letter from Will Bruce of the 8th Instant along with yours, as I have not time to write him this day, nor do I know where he may be, pray tell him or write to him, that I was a fortnight in

---

89. "short" deleted before "System." Hutcheson is referring to his drafts for *A System of Moral Philosophy*, a work that he had abandoned by 1741 (see Letter 38 below), but which was published posthumously (London, 1755). See the editors' introduction to the new edition (Carmel: Liberty Fund, forthcoming).

the Country at 20 miles distance, that I instantly inquired at our Banker about a Bill he drew and found that it had returned from Edinburgh with a protest and was sent to Ireland before I returned or knew of it about ten Days ago. I shall write him soon more fully to the Care of Paddy Smith. You'l see I hope before this time twelve moneth, what hinderd my Letter to you this summer. you really don't need such things

I am quite at a loss about Jack Wallace, what he should do? I thought he had no hopes of living in Ireland some time ago, and this compleats his ruin in any shape the Charge of Manslaughter it self must ruin him. Brother Jack & Hans Wallace will take two of his boys. I will join with Alexander Young and other friends to club for transporting the rest to Pensylvania. his wifes friends may perhaps take a young child or two. Pray let Alexander Young know what I propose. I shall be impatient to hear more of this Story. My hearty respects to all friends with you. I am Dear Thom

yours most affectionatly

Franc: Hutcheson

---

18. From WILLIAM BRUCE

Address: To Mr Francis Hutcheson Professor of Philosophy in the University of Glasgow

MS: NLS, MS 9252, fols. 110–11; slight loss of wording due to seal

Dublin November[90] 3d 1737

My Dearest Cousen

I did not think of troubling you so soon after my last, but was surprised yesterday with a Message which Mr Henry[91] sent me by Mr Abernathy which I am extreamly Solicitous to have your advise upon tho I am not certain but I shall be obliged to come to a Resolution before your

---

90. *Written* "9ber."

91. The Dublin banker Hugh Henry Bruce did accept the offer to be travelling tutor to the son.

Answer can reach me; the Message was to desire that I would take upon me the Tuition of his Eldest son for which He would allow me a hundred a year; the Young Gentleman is already a good Latin & Greek Scholar, He is to continue in this Country to the beginning of next Winter & then it is the present design to send Him to Glasgow; you are a very good Judge how unfitt I am in many important respects for such an Employment however my friends here make light of all my objections & the partial representation that has been made of me to Mr Henry causes him to make light of them too, but I know I shall never be able to discharge a Duty of this Sort either to my own Aprobation or Answerable to other People's Expectations: at the same time I own it has always apeared to me a most desirable Employment to form the Manners & Principles of a Youth who by his fortune is likely to be in a condition of being extensively Useful in the World; and had I any rational expectation of being Succesful in such an Undertaking, a Sense of Duty would oblige me to preferr it to my present Business tho the profits arising from the Latter are more considerable than what the Other will in all likelyhood aford: I have no objection to my present Business but that I think I am doing little or no good by following it & that as my Life is extreamly precarious I am involved too much by it in the afairs of the World which I would not willingly leave as a troublesome task for any friend after my Death to unravell: Jack & I have had as yet no Conversation on the Method of setling our afairs in case I should embrace this proposal but I beleive we shall not have any disputes, I am sensible it was in a great measure owing to his friendship that I was at first brought into it, & I shall think it my Duty to go out of it on as advantagious Circumstances to him as He can in reason or in point of Gratitude expect: I am at present a good deal perplexed; I know not how to refuse Mr Henry any thing that He can think proper to ask of me & yet I have great suspicions that a real Regard for him & his Son should be my reason for not complying with his present Desire: be sure to write me your sentiments honestly & your free advise & pray let it be if possible by the return of the Post, for I am much urged to be speedy in my resolutions. I have not now time to write you on any other Head only I must not forget to return you my hearty thanks for discharging our Bill you may draw on us for the Value when it suits your Conveniency:

the Tongues are ready for the first opportunity. All friends here are pretty well Mrs Arebuckle was much out of < . . .> with the cold but is purely recovered her sister Johnston came to Town on Sunday's night, she looks thin but appears otherwise in good Spirits & Health. Sister Nelly by her last Letter was grown worse than when I left Her. please to give my most respectful & afect service to my Cousen & to all friends.

I am

my Dearest Cousen

your most afect Cousen

& most faithful obliged friend.

Will. Bruce

pray write me freely about my Nephews

19. From WILLIAM BRUCE

Address: To Mr Francis Hutcheson Professor of Philosophy in the University of Glasgow

MS: NLS, MS 9252, fols. 104–5; slight loss of wording due to seal

Dublin January 12th 1737/8[92]

My Dearest Cousen

    I had the pleasure of yours of the 19th of last Month & would have acknowledged it sooner but have been every day expecting the Arival of the manuscript from Irwin which I have been often uneasie about, since the time I first heard of your having sent it thither; I dare hardly ask you whether you have kept a Duplicate, but if you have not, and the Papers be still at Irwin, I heartily wish you to send for them, for all the Advantage that can possibly arise from the perusal of them on this side the Water is not worth purchasing at the hazard of their being lost. I am most sincerely obliged to you for the useful Hints in relation to my new Employment; I perfectly agree with you in your notion of what should engage my principal

92. Date given as 1737.

Attention, but for some time at least this Purpose is only to be served by a prudent use of Circumstances & the hapy timing of a short Reflection aparently Casual & incidental: the Young Mind is fond to be taught Knowledge, but it seems to Stand in need of such a Culture as will suffer it to appear to Itself as growing in Wisdom by the free & natural exercise of its own inward Powers; this Theory is obvious, but I fear it requires greater Strength & hapiness of Genius than I shall ever possess, to render it effectual in Practice; I am employd at present pretty much as you would have me, we read the English History, in the Morning & Horace in the afternoon. He is a good Greek Scholar. He has read Herodotus since I came to him & had read Polybius & Thucidides before; I shall never attempt teaching him Mathematicks but I incline to give him some little notion of Logicks, enough to save him the necessity of entring Mr Loudon's Class[93] in case we are to be so hapy as to go over to your University but this is a Matter not yet determined nor indeed talked of since I came into the Family; It will I imagine be time enough to enter on that Study in Spring or the beginning of Summer, I quite forget what kind of a performance Carmichaels Compend is[94] but if you like it I would be glad you wou'd send me two of them or mention any treatise you think better.

It would by no means be proper to make any farther mention to Mr Henry concerning my Sallary; He told me what I beleive I already mentioned to you that I might freely trust him in relation to all money Matters, I assured him I did, and from that time I have not heard one word further concerning that Matter; I have seen so many Instances of human Wisdom's defeating itself by an excessive Prudence in providing

93. John Loudon (d. 1750), appointed one of the four regents at the University of Glasgow in 1699, had taught the full three-year philosophy curriculum until the establishment of the fixed professoriate in 1727, when he assumed exclusive responsibility for the first year of philosophical instruction, teaching a conservative syllabus in logic, metaphysics, and the philosophy of the human mind.

94. Gershom Carmichael, *Breviuscula introductio ad logicam* (Glasgow, 1720; 2nd ed., Edinburgh, 1722); translated ("A Short Introduction to Logic") in Carmichael, *Natural Rights on the Threshold of the Scottish Enlightenment*, pp. 285–317. Carmichael (1672–1729), appointed a regent at Glasgow in 1694, had assumed exclusive responsibility for the penultimate year's instruction in natural theology and moral philosophy on the establishment of the fixed professoriate in 1727 (*ODNB*).

against Contingencies that I chuse rather to act on the first natural suggestions of Discreation at a time when my Mind is least disturbed by any disponding Mood.

the Account you give me of my Cousens has aforded me more Substantial delight than the greatest certainty with respect to a future distant support could possibly yeild; if they shall once hapily engage in earnest in the paths of Wisdom & Virtue I shall have the prospect of a constant source of the most rational & manly Enjoyment that my Heart wishes for in this World and I honestly assure you I dread their Moral Miscariages much more than Death either theirs or my own. among other Advantages towards the Rational Creation you seem to have been sent into the World for my greatest Benefactor, your assistance was one of my principal helps in first forming my Mind to the Love of Virtue, you afterwards were most instrumental in bringing me into business by which I have been enabled not only to provide for my own Support but to become in some smal measure useful to my friends & now you are employd in the Office that of all others lies nearest my Heart; however unpolite this manner of writing may be I think it my Duty to put you now and then on tasting that most delicious Dish in all Nature's Banquet, which always exhilirates at the same time that it nourisheth.

I am still of opinion that you paid the Eight pound &c which you got from Trail[95] because I do not well see how Trail should otherwise have Credit for it in our <Books> I shall some time or other turn over your old Letters & <then> possibly the matter will be cleared up. I am surprised Cousen Trail[96] of Edenburgh does not write to me. there are no News in this Country worth mentioning only all friends in Town are well, Mrs Arebuckle seems to be in a better State of Health than she has been for some years. I had tother night a Conference with Maccauler who is John Johnston's Lawyer, concerning that unhapy Lawsuit betwixt Jammy & him, we differed in some things but He has advised his Client to put an End to it by a Reference. I am vexed I can get nothing done about honest Mr Millars afair Charles Moor is so desponding about it that I can hardly

95. See Letter 25.
96. See Letter 10.

get him to think of it. Sister Nelly continues much one way but complains that her Limbs grow weaker every day; Cousen Robert is perfectly recovered of his Indisposition. poor Cousen Alec's Wife has been much out of Order with a Sore Breast it has been lansed but there is still a kernel in it which it is feared must be cut out. It would delight you to see the tenderness & afection which Alec expresses on this Occasion.

Mr Henry and all friends here often remember you with great afection pray remember me in the strongest terms of esteem & respect to my Cousen & pray let me hear now & then how she enjoys herself, give my afect Service to my sweet Franky Mrs Wallace my Cousens & all other friends.

I am

my Dearest Cousen in the fulness of my Heart

your most afectionate Cousen & most faithful obliged

friend

Will. Bruce

---

20. From WILLIAM BRUCE

Address: To Mr Francis Hutcheson Professor of Philosophy in the University of Glasgow

MS: NLS, MS 9252, fols. 106–7

February 9th 1737/8[97]

My Dearest Cousen

I have three favours of yours to acknowledge one I received the beginning of this week another last Post, and the third which you sent to the Doctor[98] I got only last night; I communicated that part of yours relating to my Cousen and He promised faithfully to write to you by this post or the following; I would gladly flatter myself that Her Indisposition is by this time quite removed seeing it appeared to yeild to the Medicines

97. Date given as 1737.
98. Dr. Arbuckle.

which Dr Johnston prescribed, but my Mind will not feel easie till I have much better assurances; I can very well imagine what you have been Suffering since Sickness came into your Family; it is something to have it in our power to try whether those principles that in theory appear sufficient to render the Mind superior to any of the Accidents of Life have in truth that fortifieng force, I own I am strongly inclined to beleive that the Theory is just, but It takes a good deal of time and a great deal of Care to put the Mind in a proper State for doing Justice to the Experiment; I do not however mean that the Mind should part with any of its Social feelings but only to be able when it is necessary to call in some of the nobler afections which by their presence will restore tranquillity to the Mind even under the Sense of these feelings.

If you have not time I beg you may make one of my Nephews write me at least once a Week till my Cousen be perfectly recovered. I was in the Country when your Papers[99] arrived, and as they had been so long on the way I thought it most decent to waite on the Bishop[100] with Your Letter as soon as I came to Town; upon reading it He expressed a strong desire to see them & assured me He would read them over with all the attention He was master of & would set down faithfully all such remarks as occurred to him worth mentioning that He would be careful that no one should know He had any such Papers in his Hands and that He would dispatch them as soon as was consistant with an attentive perusal. He was just going after having said so far to enter on some things He had said to you in relation to the Subject of Morals when you saw Him in Dundalk but was interrupted by some Visitors; I find He has got it strongly in his Head that He has found out a Demonstration a Priore for the Goodness of God; I expect to hear it from him the next time I waite on him; I think you will be extreamly to blame if you make one alteration or observation which you are not fully satisfied about, to please him or any Man else, and if He has the Weakness to expect any Complacence of this kind or to be displeased if his remarks are not thought just He will only shew that He did not deserve such an Instance of your Regard and that is all the

99. See Letter 19.
100. Thomas Rundle. See Letter 21.

Pain you should Suffer about it; but I take him to have a better Mind. I am much concerned for the absurd Conduct in the London Booksellers, I think you would do well to insist on their Cancelling this Edition and publishing the Corrected Copy & in case they refuse you will certainly be at Liberty to print it yourself & will be justified by every Body in doing it I am not for a diminitive Edition, but the Amendments will not fail of Selling another Edition of the same kind with the former.[101]

I have had some free Conversation with Mr Haughton since I received your last Letter, He got one from Mr Bowman on the same Subject the Post before, but Jack does not make any such Proposal as is hinted in yours, tho I make no doubt but He will readily comply with it; Mr Haughton is not come to any Resolution, and I realy beleive because He is not yet able to form any distinct Judgement about it, what He wants is to have the remainder of Mrs Bowman's Fortune Setled in such a Manner that it will remain intire for Her & her Childeren in Case of Mr Bowman's Death & so vested in Trustees that all expectation may be utterly cut off of being able on any Importunity or other Emergency to get it aplyed to any other Use; and if you can find out that this Intention of His can be answered in Employing it as now proposed and a distinct Scheme be sent over how this is to be done It is my opinion Mr Haughton will consent. I own to you it has this good while appeared to me that there was a great deal to be said for Mr Haughton's Conduct He mett with a remarkable disapointment in Jack Bowman's Fortune & when He found that a part of his Daughters own fortune was likewise lost, is it any Wonder He should do all in his Power to secure the remainder? It is not judging rightly in this matter to weigh the Merits of the Husband with those of the Wife; for this is a Measure that cannot be reduced to any fixed Standard & must vary greatly in Mr Haughton's hands from what it would be in yours or Mine; It is his Duty to take the most likely means in his power to Secure a Support & Satisfaction to his Daughter, it is plain the former must necessarily appear

101. Bruce is referring to the heavily revised fourth edition of Hutcheson's *Inquiry into the Original of Our Ideas of Beauty and Virtue* (London, 1738), which had a complicated publication history. Apparently Hutcheson did intervene in somewhat the manner Bruce advised. See the modern (revised) edition by Wolfgang Leidhold (2008), especially the Note on the Text, pp. xxvi–xxviii.

to Him in some Danger & it is not unnatural to conjecture that putting the remainder out of Mr Bowman's or his Daughters Power would be taking away one Subject of their Debates & therefore no unlikely means of promoting Harmony betwixt them. She appears to me to be sincerely willing to return to Scotland. there are no News only all friends in Town are well & friends in the country no worse; I except Cousen Alics Wife from what I said of friends in Town She is still much indisposed but there are good hopes of her recovery I have nothing new with respect to myself; I observe an expression in your Letter that does not sound well, you do not want you say to be informed what the Terms are that Mr Henry has fixed on with respect to my allowance; is there any thing in this matter do you imagine or in any Matter that concerns me that I would not as readily acquaint you with as think it over in my own Mind? I never had one words Conversation with him on this Subject but once & that I mentioned to you. remember me in the most respectful & afectionate manner to my Cousen to my sweet Frank & to all other friends.

> I am Dearest Cousen yours in the honesty & fulness of my Heart
> Will. Bruce

---

21. To THOMAS DRENNAN

Address: To the Revd Mr Thos. Drennan, in Belfast

MS: GUL, MS Gen. 1018, no. 4

Glasgow Feb. 27th 1738

Dear Thom

I had several letters from you by lads who came over this Season, but where there is not some particular Reason for writing I am forced to defer answering till near the End of the Session. These 10 weeks past I have been more than ordinarly hurried with Sickness of one or other of my family, but we are all perfectly well again. Next summer I hope to have some leisure during our vacation, perhaps to write you more fully. You recommended to me one James Stuart from Dublin College. I wish he had continued there I am cautious of hurting a lads Character, but I much fear he has had some bad Influence to lead some people you wish very well, into idleness and drinking. We almost constantly suffer by such as come from Dublin College. I never desire to see one of them. He is straitned for Money, has not paid his Lodging yet, & I am sure t'is not from any high payments made to Masters. I wish their friends would employ some Merchant in Town to pay honest fair Accounts for them and give them what they are allowed for pocket Money. There is such suspicion of his conduct here, tho' we have no full proof, that I believe it will be insisted upon by severals of the Professours that he bring proper certificates of his regular deportment in Dublin College attested to be Genuine by some Hand we know If you are concerned about him you can get me a Certificate from one or two of the Fellows of his good behaviour. Jack Smith meets them often and his Attesting the Genuiness of the Certificate will do. Without this I cannot agree to his getting a Degree. we have been hurt by such steps formerly. I would not have you divulge my bad impressions of him to any but such friends as could either influence him to better conduct & pay his debts here, or remove him in time. Pray write to Dublin in time to find what was the real cause of his leaving that College. The Bruces are doing very well, Sam as fine a boy as one could wish: The elder did as well till he got acquainted with Stuart, you see the spring of my keenness against Stuart; and yet I still hope well of Jammy Bruce as I find not viciousness but some Levity and imprudent expences for his circumstances, don't let his mother or friends with you know my fears, as there is nothing yet appearing for which I would give them any Pain You would readily hear that in November Last I sent some Papers at Will Bruces desire to be perused by Dr Rundle;[102] a *traik*, as they call it here, attends them. they came to Will only on the 8th of Feb. by contrary Winds, and tho' my design was to get Will's & Abernethys Opinion, he without looking into them gave them immediatly to the Bishop,[103] where perhaps they may lye a good time to litle purpose; and it may be resented unless Synge sees them too. But I am in no haste about them.

My hearty respects to Mr Haliday, I hope he is come to a better state of health. I wish you be not a Lazy Couple at the Preaching. one of our

102. See Letter 17.
103. See Letter 20.

Mess Johns[104] could preach you both off your feet without fashing his thumb.

Dear Thom

I am yours most affectionatly

Fran: Hutcheson

---

22. To THOMAS DRENNAN

Address: To the Revd Mr Thos Drennan, in Belfast

MS: GUL, MS Gen. 1018, no. 5

Glasgow Ap. 17th 1738

Dear Sir

I cannot ommit this opportunity of letting you know that we all are well, and often remembering you. This goes by two excellent Boys Mesrs Upton,[105] both sober good natured & studious, especially the younger, whose health obliges him to return sooner than I intended, after having tried Medicines & riding every good day for some time past. I can write you litle news to your taste, Robert Simson,[106] if he were not indolent beyond imagination, could in a fortnights application finish another book which would surprize the Connoisseurs. About November Last I sent a M.S. to Will Bruce cheifly for his & Mr Abernethys perusal.[107] He shewed it to the Bishop of Derry who it seems is much pleased with it and promises me a long Epistle soon. I heartily wish you had seen it, but it did not get to Dublin till February, and was in the Bishops Hands till the beginning of this Moneth. I believe Will is perusing it now. I am not expecting it back again speedily. during our College Session I get nothing done, but

104. Mess Johns: run-of-the-mill Scottish preachers.

105. Clotworthy and Francis, sons of John Upton, Esq., Castle Upton, County Antrim. They matriculated together in Hutcheson's class on November 14, 1737. Clotworthy graduated MA in 1741 and became clerk comptroller to the Princess of Wales. His brother became commander of HMS *Ferret* and was lost with his ship in a storm off Louisburgh.

106. See Letter 15.

107. See Letter 21.

if I get them back during our vacation with remarks of my friends I shall endeavour to put the last hand to them. If I can get leisure next Moneth I shall endeavour to send you such a letter as I once gave you an imperfect promise of if my hand be not gone out of use. We have at last got a Minister in Glasgow to my taste.[108] As I know your Laziness, I really wish you & he could interchange sermons, now & then. I am surprized to find some people of very good sense, laymen more than Clergy here, not a litle pleased with some of the notions of the forreign Mysticks. they have raised my curiosity of late to look into their books. I shall some time or other let you know the result of my reading this way. I am persuaded their warm imaginations would make them Moving preachers. I am going to read Ma-Dame Borignon[109] when I have leisure. You'l make Sam. Haliday laugh heartily by telling him this particular. My most hearty respects to him. I am Dear Thom

Yours most affectionaly

Franc: Hutcheson

John Kane whom you once recommended to me is really a sober sensible Modest lad. Stuart I know not how to manage. in consequence of your last I had a letter from Patty Stuart to advance & draw on him for what is necessary to send him home. but I find this will be much more money than his friends in Ireland imagine. Pat writes me of his once having thought of sending him a Bill of £5, but I mistake it much if he don't need 15, or 20.

---

108. Rev. William Craig (1709–1784) had entered the university as a mature student in 1730 and graduated MA in 1736. He was ordained minister of Cambusnethen in 1737 and transferred to Glasgow's Wynd Church in 1738. As a student he had made friends with David Fordyce (1711–1751), future regent at Marischal College, Aberdeen, when Fordyce visited Glasgow and attended some of Hutcheson's lectures in the 1734–35 session. See Letter 59. Two letters survive from Fordyce to Craig, dated August 24 and December 23, 1735. Fordyce voiced criticism of Hutcheson's moral philosophy but expressed his admiration at Craig's ability to defend his teacher's views (NLS, MS 584, no. 971; MS 2670, fol. 158).

109. Antoinette Bourignon (1616–1680), Flemish mystic whose teachings had been popular among the Episcopalians of northeast Scotland in the late seventeenth and early eighteenth centuries. The General Assembly of the Church of Scotland had passed resolutions against her views in 1701, 1709, and 1710, and formally designated Bourignonism as a heresy to be abjured by all ordinands in 1711.

23. From WILLIAM BRUCE

Address: To Mr Francis Hutcheson Professor of Philosophy in Glasgow

MS: NLS, MS 9252, fols. 125–6; slight loss of wording due to seal

May 15th 1738

My Dearest Cousen

I had the pleasure of yours of the 3d of this Month; I have deferred writing to you from Post to Post this fortnight past in hopes one day after another to have it to tell you that I had at length got the Papers from the Bishop; but unhapily they are still in his Hands; near three Weeks ago He told me He had only about three Hours Reading to go throw; in a day or two after Lady Limeric came to Town to meet her Lord in his return from England, & their Lodging with the Bishop was his last apology for the delay; but without fail I am to get them to morrow or Wednsday; I am invited to two hours Conversation at the same time, whether on the Subject of them or on any other I do not yet understand: He never fails speaking of them in the highest expressions of esteem & liking; in which I verrily beleive He is perfectly Sincere; but I do not take this to be a high Complement to your Papers for I suspect a little that He is too apt to *Admire*: I did not forward your Letter to Bishop Syng because I had not the Papers & I was not willing that He should know they had been put into others hands before his own; I do not expect much from him, but I incline to waite on him in case I get the Papers in a day or two, & to let him know that I shall be obliged to return them in eight or ten days & that if He would incline to peruse them in that time to let him have them; as soon as I get them to sitt down to; I will Suffer nothing to interrupt me, for I assure you these delays have heigthened my appetite which was keen enough when I got them to make it uneasie to me to part with them out of my Hands; but happen what will I shall take care to have them conveyd to you before the time you mention; they will receive no improvements on this Side as far as I can judge that would in any measure compensate that delay which detaining them longer, by means of your Winters Hurry would occasion.

I shall not attempt making any acknowledgements to you for the Care you took, & vexation you have Suffered on Account of my Nephews; my Sense of Obligation was long before these late Instances of Friendship grown much too great for Words, but there is one Species of Actions by which it is likely I shall be often expressing It and that is by making new demands on your Beneficence as often as Circumstances shall require it with as little reluctance as in asking favours of Heaven. I have according to my old Style honoured your Bills; the expense tho it is extravagant & in several respects inconvenient would give me little pain if I could have the least distant hope that that unhapy giddy Boy would ever come to Good.

It gave me great uneasiness to find you expressing yourself with so much distrust of Mr & Mrs Henry's regard towards you in one of your late Letters, had I thought there were any alianation between you, It would have made the thoughts of going into the Family extreamly painful to me; I can think of no friendships where you can be the object of dislike; I do not remember to have heard Mrs Henry expressing Herself in any manner concerning you since I knew the family, but Mr Henry has often talked of you with great Esteem & often toasts your Health. I have not heard any thing from Mr Henry himself concerning his Intentions about our going abroad but I understand from Mr Abernathy that He inclines we should continue another winter in this Country, his view is to send his Second Son at the same time with his eldest & He will not be fitt for any University before the following Winter. I write you this in some Hurry but shall probably write you again by Post sometime this week: we have been very hapy in honest Mr Boyd[110] but I unfortunatly lost several days by being in the Country.

Everard Hutcheson longs to hear from you. It was a Complement which Jack Wilson purposely made to his Mother in letting her have the farm for so much under value for one year, He was advised to it by his friends & seemed well inclined to it himself; It would not have been in his <power> to have Stocked it suddenly & tho Mrs Wilson has a ve<ry go>od Bargain I doubt if Jack would have made more of it for one year. please to give my most respectful & most afectionate Service to my dear Cousen in whose good State of Health we all most heartily rejoice remember me most afectionately to Franc & to all other friends particularly to Mrs Sally Wallace; I hope she continues to be agreeable to you.

110. Not identified.

Cousen Alec who is now with me gives You his most afectionate Service
his Wife is pretty well recovered.

I am

my Dearest Cousen

in the fulness of my Heart

your most afectionate Cousen

& most faithful obliged Friend

Will. Bruce

---

24. To THOMAS DRENNAN

Address and date lacking

MS: GUL, MS Gen. 1018, no. 1

[Glasgow, around October 1738][111]

Dear Thom

The inclosed you'r not obliged to me for. I was intreated by an old
friend who was to preach a Synod Sermon to Suggest him some materials,[112]
which I undertook and thinking of you, cast them into form with en-
largements, but really in great haste while I was in a Gentlemans house
in the Country and interrupted every half hour. theyr not in Method
have repetitions, and things proper to this Country only. My friend here
used a good deal of it in a better method & a diction more suited to this
Country, and made an admirable Sermon, but tho' it were printed few
would ever dream that he had seen the inclosed tho they read both. And

---

111. This letter was written at a time between Drennan's joining Samuel Haliday as
co-pastor of the First Presbyterian Church, Belfast, in 1736 and Haliday's death in
March 1739. For further narrowing of the date, see note 112 below.

112. Hutcheson lived within the bounds of the Synod of Glasgow and Ayr. His
friend since college days, Rev. Robert Patoun or Paton, minister of Renfrew, preached
the annual Synod Sermon in October 1738. It was later published, without the author's consent, under the title *The Main Duty of Bishops* (Edinburgh, 1739) and contains unmistakable Hutchesonian elements. The term "bishop" was used in the New
Testament sense as understood by Presbyterians, meaning any minister of the church.

you are only the third person who knows any thing of the Matter. If it proves of litle use to you, I have got it franked for you, otherways it would have cost you too dear My hearty respects to honest Haliday & all friends in Belfast. give Mr Mustenden[113] the <inclos>ed pray let me hear all your news

I am Dear Thom

---

25. From WILLIAM BRUCE

Address: To Mr Francis Hutcheson Professor of Philosophy in the University of Glasgow

MS: NLS, MS 9252, fols. 128–29; slight loss of wording due to seal

December[114] 16th 1738

My Dearest Cousen

It was a great Disapointment to me when the Seven Pacquets which arrived together from Scotland on Wednsday last brought me no Letter from you; but my Solicitude to hear from you ever since has been greatly encreased by a Pamphlet which has been transmitted to Jammy Arebuckle by Mr Boyd; I freely acknowledge to you that as soon as I saw it I was struck with an aprehension which I have not since been able to get quitt of, that notwithstanding its Impertinence, falshood & Villany, It will be able in a great measure to destroy both your Satisfaction & Usefulness in your present Situation; while these fears are prevailing so strongly with me, you will not wonder that I am greatly Anxious to know your own Sentiments and Resolutions about it; I do not mean by this to express any Suspicion, for I have not the least, that your Mind is not so far Superior to any Attempts of this sort as to continue, not greatly moved whatever should be the Consequences of them, but to a Mind whose principal affection is to be useful to the World, It cannot be a Matter of

---

113. The name appears as "Mussenden" in Hutcheson's letter of August 5, 1743 (Letter 46).
    114. *Written* "10ber."

Indifferance to meet with so untoward an Interruption in a Road which
was evidently conducting you to that excellent End; there are however
other Paths in which you may continue the same Pursuit, & in some of
them to much greater advantage; at least as you very well know this has
been my settld Sense of things these many years past; We have indeed
always thought differently with respect to Conformity and it was your
Superior Latitude with respect to compliances of this Sort that was the
foundation of all my Expostulations with you in behalf of the expediency
of Schemes where this was implied as previously necessary; I still continue to think that the Dissenting Interest is one of the best safeguards of
good Sense in Religion & of Liberty in civil Life, & that Standing up
avowedly in defence of it is a more effectual way of serving those Interests
it is meant to support, as well as of doing honour to the Cause itself, in
Men of Superior Character & Distinction than by going with ever so
good Intentions into the Establishment; I do not deny but that there may
be several Cases in which it would be otherways and if you continue to
think that your Circumstances form one of those Cases, I earnestly beg
of you to entertain the thoughts of returning into your own Country, &
to signifie to me or to some of your friends in what shape or manner such
return would be agreeable to you; I am still perswaded the Primate[115] the
Bishop of Derry or even your friend Syng would be fond of inviting you
back: But if an Aversion of Establishments has grown upon you of late, or
your temper & Constitution become less fitted for a bustling & active
Life and above all If you have the Spirit of Martyrdom stongly upon you
for the Sake of Serving a very good Cause & making a Number of Old
friends hapier than they could ever have wished for then to become Minister of our new Congregation in Stafford Street[116] seems by Providence to
be marked out as your proper Retreat: almost the whole of your Labour
will consist in about an hour & half's Service once a Week, you will be at
Liberty to teach the principles of Virtue with much more freedom than
you even could do in your Class & probably with much greater Success in
Influencing the Heart; you will have the highest honour & Esteem from

115. Hugh Boulter (1672–1742), archbishop of Armagh.
116. See Letter 5.

all your Paritioners & be regarded as a Father by them all; you will have an enlarged Sphaere of Mediatorial as well as personal Benefecence and you may be assured of a pretty nu<mer>ous attendance at 2 guineas a peice in Case you will take the trouble of giving lectures of Morality in your own House three hours in the Week, and a Salary of £150 per annum besides the £16 of King's bounty shall be secured as the poor indeed but Benevolent Reward for your Ministerial Services; our Meeting House is only a large Room, which takes away all objection with regard to your Voice; this may apear as talking too seriously on a Matter that deserves to be treated only as a Jest, but to a Mind that has delivered itself from false associations in its conceptions of Dignity & Honour, however fanciful it may be thought It can never appear Absurd; Our Society have had hopes of Mr Duchal,[117] but I think it most likely He will not accept; several folks have taken it into their heads to be shy of encouraging our Association & Mrs Henry has thought the Cause of Caple Street[118] a matter worthy her Zeal in opposition to us; but if ever there was a Society of Christians upon the true Bottom of a Voluntary Association for promoting the purposes of Religion, without usurpation & tyranny on the one hand, or fanciful notions & claims of Rights directly derived from the appointment of Christ on the other, we are that Society, and I flatter myself will flourish in spite of all the opposition of our Enemies & Cowardice & low Complacence of our friends; we are regularly suplied by the Presbytery, and if you will become our Priest & King our Father & our Judge we will keep it open for you as long as you please.

I take it for granted Jammy Johnston has acquainted you that Mr Neven & I have put an End to the Lawsuit betwixt his Uncle & him; if you have any Curiosity to see the particulars upon which we strook the ballance I will send them to you I purposed to have transcribed them in this Letter for they will come into a page of a quarter of a Sheet, but I have not left Room; Jammy is hapily delivered out of a tedious Lawshuit & near £800 richer than by the ArchDeacon's award. there are no

117. See Letter 15.
118. See note 33, p. 21.

<News> among our friends worth mentioning the Doctors family and all friends in < . . .> as far as I know are well please to remember me in the most a<fectionate & m>ost respectful Manner to my Cousen to my sweet Franc & to all friends. I am my de<arest> Cousen your most faithful & most obliged friend

Will. Bruce

the Circumstance in relation to Mrs Henry's Zeal is to yourself but I do not mean by this that you may not mention it likewise to my Cousen; but let it go no farther, you may be sure it surprises me being utterly unexpected but it does not move me.

how do my Nephews & Cousen Hamy Trail[119] behave?

---

26. To HENRY HOME[120]

Address lacking

MS: NRS, MS GD24/1/553, fols 157ʳ–158ᵛ

[Glasgow, April 1739]

Sir

I deferred Acknowleging the most obliging Present I received of your Friends Book upon human Nature,[121] by my Lord Kilmarnock,[122] till I

---

119. Hamilton Trail, son of James Trail of Marybrook, County Down. He matriculated under Hutcheson on November 14, 1737, and graduated MA in 1744.

120. Henry Home (1696–1782), later Lord Kames. A member of the Scots bar since 1724, he would become a judge in the Court of Session in 1752 and a Lord of Justiciary in 1763. Best known as a legal scholar in his early years, he turned to philosophical publication with his *Essays on on the Principles of Morality and Natural Religion*, partly in criticism of David Hume, in 1751. He had given strong encouragement to Hume in his early years, acting in some degree as patron and mentor. In 1745 he was active in the unsuccessful campaign to secure the Edinburgh moral philosophy chair for Hume.

121. Books 1 and 2 of David Hume's *Treatise of Human Nature*. See Letter 30.

122. See Letter 1.

could find Leisure to peruse it: And unluckily I met with more than Ordinary interruptions by unavoidable business. I perused the first volume, & a great part, indeed almost all the second. And was every where Surprized with a great acuteness of thought and reasoning in a mind wholly disengaged from the prejudices of the Learned as well as those of the Vulgar. I cannot pretend to assent to his tenets as yet, these Metaphysical subjects have not been much in my thoughts of late; tho' a great many of these sentiments and reasonings had employed me about 10 or 12 years ago. The teaching in a College, and a more important Work of inspecting into the Conduct of several young folks committed to me, leaves very litle Leisure for close attention to a long scheme of Philosophy not in my Province. This Book will furnish me Matter of a good deal of thought next vacation, now coming on in less than 6 weeks. I shall have the greatest pleasure in communicating to the Ingenious Author whatever occurs probable to me on these subjects. I have for many years been more and more running into the Old Academy, despairing of Certainty in the most important Subjects, but satisfied with a sort of Probable knowlege which to an honest Mind will be sufficient for the Conduct of Life.

I should be glad to know where the Author could be met with, if a lazy Umbratick, very averse to motion, ever makes a ramble in a vacation.

I am Sir

Your most obliged and

Most obedient humble servant

Francis Hutcheson

27. To THOMAS DRENNAN

Address: To the Revd Mr Tho's Drennan in Belfast

MS: GUL, MS Gen. 1018, no. 6

Glasgow March 5th 1738/9

Dear Thom

I had yours of the 26th of Feb. on friday and could not answer Sooner. I had resolved when I first read yours to have wrote you in the Negative, being in as much hurry at present as I have been this session, by many letters of business as well as by my ordinary work. I have got on my hands almost the whole Paternal Care of my old Pupil Lord Kilmarnocks three sons here.[123] But upon reading over your letter this Morning, with the deepest concern for that worthy friendly generous Man, I could not refuse you altogether what you desire, tho' I conclude it must be much either an unreasonable diffidence in your self, or an unjust value your friendship makes you put upon what comes from me that occasions such requests.[124] I shall be forced to work in starts with many interruptions, which never succeeds right with me I beseech you be as busy as you can in some scheme of your own, and don't take any sudden interrupted attempts of mine as fit for all the purposes you say are expected by friends on this occasion. I hint to you my plan that you may work upon it and be the readier to patch up a right thing out of the two "A consideration of what sort of Life is most worthy and best suited to a Being capable of such high Endowments and Improvements and actions, destined to an immortal Existence, and yet subjected for a certain space to a mortal Existence in this world. And then without drawing a Character leaving it to the Audience to recollect how much of this appeared in our friends life."

I hope Jack Smith has sent down to your town a *Serious adresse to the Kirk of Scotland*, lately published in London.[125] it has run like lightening here;

---

123. See Letter 1.

124. Drennan had plainly written to Hutcheson warning him of Samuel Haliday's imminent death and seeking his advice on the substance of a suitable funeral sermon. Haliday died on the day that Hutcheson penned this response.

125. *A Serious Address to the Church of Scotland, with Relation to the Growth of Deism and Immorality: Examining Some Parts of Their Discipline and Constitution* (London, 1739).

and is producing some Effect the author is unknown, tis wrote with anger and contempt of the Kirk and Confession, but it has a Set of Objections against the Confession which I imagine few will have the Brow to answer.

My most hearty respects to all friends. I am Dear Thom

yours most affectionately

Fran: Hutcheson

I really suffer with you heartily on the loss of your worthy friend: You will miss him exceedingly, and so will your Cause.

A worthy lad in this town one Robert Foulis,[126] out of a true publick spirit, undertook to reprint for the Populace an old excellent Book, *a Persuasive to mutual Love & Charity* wrote by *White*, Oliver Cromwells Chaplain, it is a divine old fashioned thing.[127] some are cast off in Better Paper sold at 9d in Marble Paper. the Course ones are sold at 5d in Blue Paper, and at 4d to Booksellers. I wish your Bookseller would commission a Parcel. of both so<on>. There has been some whimsical Buffoonry about my Heresy of which I will send you a copy.[128]

The *persuasive* is in the old Edition an half-Crown book

---

126. Robert Foulis (1707–1776) studied with Hutcheson from 1730, while his brother Andrew (1712–1775) matriculated in 1727. From being booksellers the brothers became printers, led by Robert, whom Glasgow University recognized as its printer (*ODNB*).

127. Jeremiah White, *A Perswasive to Moderation and Forbearance in Love among the Divided Forms of Christians*, was edited from the author's manuscript by the English Behmenist mystic Richard Roach (London, 1708). White (1629–1707) believed in universal salvation and campaigned on behalf of the English Dissenters (*ODNB*). The Glasgow edition (1739) was retitled *A Persuasive to Mutual Love and Charity among Christians Who Differ in Opinion. Drawn from the Motives of the Gospel, and Proper for Healing the Present Divisions among Us*. It was ascribed to "a Minister of the Gospel" and published without any indication of provenance.

128. This is most likely a reference to a pamphlet entitled *A Letter to the Valiant and Undaunted Champion of Our Broken Covenants, the Reverend Mr. Ebenezer Erskine, in Relation to the Present Heresies, Backslidings, Defections, and Lukewarmness of the Times and His Apostolical Testimonies against Them* (London, 1738). The author was identified as Euzelus Philalethes, author of the forceful attack on Hutcheson, *Shaftsbury's Ghost Conjur'd*, i.e., Hugh Heugh (printed below pp. 292–337), but it was clearly the work of people in the immediate circle around Hutcheson who defended his teaching in the form of a rough satire on Heugh's writing.

28. To UNIDENTIFIED CORRESPONDENT

Address lacking

MS: NLS, MS 10875, fol. 160r; fragment forming a wrapper among legal papers of the estate of Airth

Glasgow March 16th 1739

< . . .> for four Moneths in a decent tho' frugal Manner. My Lord Rosse writes me that you have orders from the Duke of Montrose[129] to apply some part of the Profits of the Lordship of Lithgow for their support, and that you intend at present fifty pounds sterling. This sum will abundantly defray all their Charges in Glasgow during the session of our College; and leave a litle Surplus, I hope, toward their subsistence in Summer. They will need it as soon as you can conveniently remit it. You have abundance of friends here to entrust with the proper Application of it. If you choose to entrust me as my Lord Kilmarnock did, I shall take all possible care that nothing be squandered.

I am, Sir,
Your most obedient
humble Servant
Fran: Hutcheson

129. See Letter 49.

29. To Mrs BRABANT[130]

Address lacking

MS: Staatsbibliothek zu Berlin, Preussischer Kulturbesitz, Handschriften-abteilung, Slg. Darmst. 2a 1755 (1): Hutcheson, Francis. Transcribed from photocopy.

Glasgow College May 3d 1739

Madam

At your Son Mr Brabants[131] desire I give you the trouble of this to as-sure You that his whole Deportment with us in this College for these two Sessions has been perfect<ly> Sober regular and Studious; and his proficie<ncy> in Learning has been very good; so that I c<an> most heartily recommend him as a worthy virtuous young Gentleman, to any who desire information about him.

I am, Madam,
your most obedient
humble Servant
Francis Hutcheson

130. Widow of Robert Brabant, formerly merchant at Miltown, Dorset.
131. Thomas Brabant (*c.* 1720–1804), an English student from Dorsetshire, ma-triculated at Glasgow University November 14, 1737, as a member of Hutcheson's class in Moral Philosophy. He was a classmate of the Upton brothers mentioned in Letter 22 above. After Glasgow, he studied at Philip Doddridge's academy at Northampton.

30. From DAVID HUME[132]

Address: To Mr Francis Hutcheson Professor of Philosophy at Glasgow

MS: National Library of Scotland, MS 23151, no. 55; slightly torn

Ninewells near Berwick. Sept[r] 17 1739.

Sir

I am much oblig'd to you for your Reflections on my Papers. I have perus'd them with Care, & find they will be of use to me. You have mistaken my Meaning in some Passages; which upon Examination I have found to proceed from some Ambiguity or Defect in my Expression.

What affected me most in your Remarks is your observing, that there wants a certain Warmth in the Cause of Virtue,[133] which, you think, all good Men wou'd relish, & cou'd not displease amidst abstract Enquirys. I must own, this has not happen'd by Chance, but is the Effect of a Reasoning either good or bad. There are different ways of examining the Mind as well as the Body. One may consider it either as an Anatomist or as a Painter; either to discover its most secret Springs & Principles or to describe the Grace & Beauty of its Actions. I imagine it impossible to conjoin these two Views.[134] Where you pull off the Skin, & display all the minute Parts, there appears something trivial,[135] even in the noblest Attitudes & most vigorous Actions: Nor can you ever render the Object graceful or engaging but by cloathing the Parts again with Skin & Flesh, & presenting only their bare Outside. An Anatomist, however, can give very good Advice to a Painter or Statuary: And in like manner, I am perswaded,

---

132. David Hume (1711–1776), Scottish philosopher, essayist, and historian. His *Treatise of Human Nature* appeared in three volumes (1739–40), most of his extant correspondence with Hutcheson occurring between the publication of the first two volumes (January 1739) and the completion of the third. Their correspondence appears to have ceased when Hutcheson sided with Hume's opponents in a contest for the moral philosophy chair at Edinburgh University in 1744–45.

133. A phrase used by an anonymous writer to *The London Journal*, October 11, 1729, commending the author of an essay on charity, or the virtue of beneficence, "which shews you have a Heart warm in the Cause of Virtue." The essayist, writing under the pseudonym "Socrates," was the prominent Whig writer James Pitt, who had taken over editorship of the journal on May 31, 1729.

134. "Views" added; "Purposes" deleted in the manuscript.

135. "if not hideous" deleted after "trivial" in the manuscript.

that a Metaphysician may be very helpful to a Moralist; tho' I cannot easily conceive these two Characters united in the same Work. Any warm Sentiment of Morals, I am afraid, wou'd have the Air of Declamation amidst abstract Reasonings, & wou'd be esteem'd contrary to good Taste. And tho' I am much more ambitious of being esteem'd a Friend to Virtue, than a Writer of Taste; yet I must always carry the latter in my Eye, otherwise I must despair of ever being servicable to Virtue. I hope these Reasons will satisfy you; tho at the same time, I intend to make a new Tryal, if it be possible to make the Moralist & Metaphysician agree a little better.

I cannot agree to your Sense of *Natural*. Tis founded on final Causes; which is a Consideration, that appears to me pretty uncertain & unphilosophical. For pray, what is the End of Man? Is he created for Happiness or for Virtue? For this Life or for the next? For himself or for his Maker? Your definition of *Natural* depends upon solving these Questions, which are endless, & quite wide of my Purpose. I have never call'd Justice unnatural, but only artificial. *Atque ipsa utilitas justi prope mater et aequi.*[136] Says one of the best Moralists of Antiquity. *Grotius* & *Puffendorf*, to be consistent, must assert the same.[137]

Whether natural Abilitys be Virtues is a Dispute of Words. I think I follow the common Use of Language. *Virtus* signify'd chiefly Courage among the *Romans*. I was just now reading this Character of Alexander the 6th in Guicciardin. In Alessandro Sesto fu solertia e sagacità singulare: consiglio eccellente, efficacia a persuadere maravigliosa, e a tutte le facende gravi, sollicitudine e destrezza incredibile. Ma erano queste virtù

136. "That very utility that is the mother, almost, of the just and equitable" (Horace, *Satires*, I.iii:98). Hume is using the phrase as if it is a self-standing sentence about the nature of utility. *Utilitas*, the conventional equivalent in Latin philosophical writers of Greek *ophelimon*, frequently has the sense of "benefit" or "interest."

137. Hugo Grotius (1583–1645) and Samuel Pufendorf (1632–1694) had quoted the same sentiment of Horace and in the same terms, but in criticism of him. See Grotius, "Preliminary Discourse," art. 17, *The Rights of War and Peace*, p. 93, n. 1; Pufendorf, *Of the Law of Nature and Nations*, 4th ed. (London, 1729), book 2, chap. 3, art. 10, p. 128.

avanzate di grande intervallo da vitii &c.[138] Were Benevolence the only Virtue no Characters cou'd be mixt, but wou'd depend entirely on their Degrees of Benevolence. Upon the whole, I desire to take my Catalogue of Virtues from *Cicero's Offices*, not from the *Whole Duty of Man*.[139] I had, indeed, the former Book in my Eye in all my Reasonings.

I have many other Reflections to communicate to you; but it wou'd be troublesome. I shall therefore conclude with telling you, that I intend to follow your Advice in altering most of those Passages you have remarkd as defective in Point of Prudence; tho' I must own, I think you a little too delicate. Except a Man be in Orders, or be immediatly concern'd in the Instruction of Youth, I do not think his Character depends upon his philosophical Speculations, as the World is now model'd; & a little Liberty seems requisite to bring into the public Notice a Book that is calculated for so few Readers. I hope you will allow me the Freedom of consulting you when I am in any Difficulty; & believe me to be

Dear Sir

Your most oblig'd humble Servant

David Hume

P.S. I cannot forbear recommending another thing to your Consideration. Actions are not virtuous nor vicious; but only so far as they are proofs of certain Qualitys or durable Principles in the Mind. This is a Point I shou'd have established more expressly than I have done. Now I desire you to consider, if there be any Quality,[140] that is virtuous, without having a Tendency either to the public Good or to the Good of the Person, who possesses it. If there be none without these Tendencys, we may conclude, that their Merit is derivd from Sympathy. I desire you wou'd

---

138. Francesco Guicciardini (1483–1545), *Storia d'Italia* (1537–40), book 1 (book 1, chap. 2 in modern editions): "Alexander was possessed of alertness and unusual perceptivity, had excellent judgment, was wonderfully persuasive, and unbelievably prompt and deft in grave situations. But these virtues were far and away surpassed by vices, etc."

139. [?Richard Allestree (1619–1681)], *The Practice of Christian Grace. Or the Whole Duty of Man* (London, 1658).

140. "Quality" added; "Instance" deleted in the manuscript.

only consider the *Tendencys* of Qualitys, not their actual Operation, which depends on Chance. *Brutus*[141] riveted the Chains of *Rome* faster by his Opposition; but the natural Tendency of his noble Dispositions, his <pub>lic Spirit & Magnanimity, was to establish her Liberty.

You are a great Admirer of *Cicero*, as well as I am. Please to review the 4th Book, *de finibus bonorum et malorum*; where you find him prove against the *Stoics*, that if there be no other Goods but Virtue, tis impossible there can be any Virtue; because the Mind wou'd then want all Motives to begin its Actions upon: And tis on the Goodness or Badness of the Motives that the Virtue of the Action depends. This proves, that to every virtuous Action there must be a Motive or impelling Passion distinct from the Virtue, & that Virtue can never be the sole Motive to any Action. You do not assent to this; tho' I think there is no proposition more certain or important. I must own my Proofs were not distinct enough, & must be alterd. You see with what Reluctance I part with you; tho' I believe it is time I shou'd ask your Pardon for so much trouble.

---

31. To THOMAS STEWARD[142]

Address: To the Revd Mr Thomas Steward Minister in St Edmondsbury

MS: Magee University College, Londonderry, MS 46, no. 73

Glasgow Feb 12th 1740

Sir

I received by a very worthy sober studious young Gentleman Mr Armstrong, your most obliging letter in October last; and would have sooner acknowleged the Receipt of it and my obligations to you for the most

---

141. Marcus Junius Brutus (85–42 BCE).

142. Rev. Thomas Steward (c. 1669–1753), Presbyterian minister at Bury St. Edmunds, Suffolk, England. He had previously been minister at Cook Street, Dublin, and remained in correspondence with leading members of the Nonsubscribing Presbyterian community in Dublin (*ODNB*).

agreeable present of your Sermons[143] had I not been dissappointed of a private hand I expected to have wrote by. Your Sermons must be acceptable to all who have a just Sense of Piety & virtue, to promote which they are so much adapted; The Perusal of them gave me an Additional pleasure as they revived a lively memory of my old worthy Friend, whom I ever sincerely esteemed.

I have the most tender Sympathy with you in the fortunes of Your Family, and particularly in the loss of your Son, if such a Death should be called a loss, the bitter sense of which can endure but for a short time, and be succeeded by eternal Joy, when we return, along with him, to our heavenly Father, the Source of all that's amiable & excellent. I have the more tender feeling with you in this matter that I have often experienced the like Accidents of Mortality, having been married now 15 years, & having only one Boy surviving of seven Children born to me by a very agreeable woman. I bless God for the one he has spared to me, and that he has no bad genius.[144] If he proves a wise and good Man, I am very well in this world.

Since my settlement in this College, I have had an agreeable, & I hope not an useless Life; pretty much hurried with Study & business: but such as is not unpleasant. I hope I am contributing to promote the more moderate & charitable Sentiments in religious Matters, in this Country; where yet there remains too much Warmth & Animosity about matters of no great consequence to reall Religion. We must make allowances for the power of Education in all places. And have Indulgence to the weaknesses of our Brethren. It will always give me pleasure to hear of your Welfare. Our poor old Professor of Theology died about 10 days ago.[145]

---

143. Thomas Steward, *Fifteen Sermons upon Several Practical Subjects* (London, 1734).

144. Francis Hutcheson the Younger (1721–1780) had entered Glasgow University in November 1739. He would graduate MA (1744), MD (1750), and settle as a physician in Dublin. He became a well-known songwriter under the pseudonym Francis Ireland (*ODNB*).

145. See Letter 32.

I am in much fear about getting a good Successor to him, and wholly uncertain upon whom our Choice shall fall.

I am Reverend & dear Sir
Your most obliged &
most obedient Servant
Fran: Hutcheson

---

32. From WILLIAM BRUCE

Address: To Mr Francis Hutcheson, Professor of Philosophy in the University of Glasgow

MS: NLS, MS 9252, fols. 153–4; slight loss of wording due to seal or torn paper

March 1st 1739/40

My Dearest Cousin

I had the favour of yours wherein you mention the Death of the old Professor;[146] I am sorry there is such an opposition of Politicks with regard to his Successor; from any Judgement I have at this distance been able to form of it, It appears not well Judged that you should make so Zealous a Stand against M'cClauran,[147] or indeed that you should lay out a great measure of Zeal about the Matter; I have no knowledge of Mr Craig,[148] but beleive him to be a Gentleman of great abilities & Learning & of generous Sentiments; this is the Character that several of my acquaintance have concurred with you in giving him, and in my Opinion the last Article of it utterly disqualifies him for your Divinity Chair; after the Treatment that Simpson mett with, I wonder you should ever wish to see an honest Man who is in the least hazard of quitting the beaten road, in that Situation; If He is to keep the beaten Road, Mr M'cClauran will

---

146. John Simson (1667–1740), professor of divinity at Glasgow 1708–40, suspended from teaching from 1728 (*ODNB*).

147. John MacLaurin (1693–1754), brother of Colin MacLaurin (see Letter 6) (*ODNB*).

148. William Craig. See Letter 22.

answer that purpose as well as any Man, & can do it with a good Conscience & without any imputation of dishonesty; your friend on the contrary must find himself in the most undesirable Circumstances imaginable; the Suspicion of heresy will persue him from the time he takes possession of his office, & while his prudence will find it a difficult task to Secure him on that Quarter, He will be regarded as making Shipwreck of his honesty by the rest of the world; and however common this practise may be grown, I know no knowledge or Sett of Principles in the World that will compensate the mischeif that the Young Mind must almost unavoidably suffer from perceiving a Man whom It has been taught to hold in high Esteem, practising deceit & dissimulation in circumstances of such apparent Solemnity as in common estimation naturaly inferr the strongest obligations to the Contrary; while you continue in that University, it seems to me of small importance I mean with respect to real usefulness what kind of Man sitts in Calvin's Chair, & It would not appear unlikely that Mr M'cClauran's Character may bring as many Students to the College as Mr Craig's.

I would be glad to contribute in any measure to the Success of so noble & beneficent an undertaking as the Hospital at Edenburgh, I got one of the Quarto Pamphlets relating to it from Mr Barkley in this Town & put it into Mr Henry's Hands, but I am not certain that It will have the Effect I intended;[149] He is either not to be directly Solicited in such Matters or I am an unacceptable Solicitor; this does not hinder my taking still one means or other to bring all such Matters as appear deserving under the consideration of his Mind but only leaves me generaly at a loss with respect to their Success or influence. I am concerned you should Suffer any uneasiness on Account of my Situation. It is true I have mett with such Circumstances since I entered upon it, as had I been before aware of them would have for ever hindered my engaging in it; some of them utterly unexpected, & others in direct opposition to what I had reason given me to expect; but it is not often that I suffer such disapointments to contaminate

---

149. Probably *A Letter from a Gentleman in Town to His Friend in the Country, relating to the Royal Infirmary of Edinburgh* (Edinburgh, 1739), a quarto pamphlet signed by "Philasthenes" and mentioning Mr. John Barclay, merchant in Dublin, as one of the recipients of donations there (p. 14).

the essential Enjoyments of my Life; I have been learning this considerable while past that it is principaly owing to an uncorrected imagination or an undisciplined Heart when our Hapiness is held by the precarious tenure of the temper & Conduct of other folks except in Cases wherein the Mind feels it noble & sutable to its dignity to suffer distress.

Mr Henry told me soon after my first Engagements with him that He would make provision for me in his Will, I know He has since made his Will and to t<e>ll <y>ou the truth of my Heart I do not care to know any thing farther about it; I am convinced that I am doing but very little good as I am now Circumstanced & would not be fond to be embarrassed by the feelings of generosity or Gratitude in any greater degree than I should be at present in Case an opportunity of becoming more servicable to the Interests of Virtue & Hapiness should happily turn up; there is nothing of this sort yet in sight nor probably ever will be, but the more independant I keep my Mind, at all adventures, I find my self the more at ease for the present & have a more rational Security for Satisfaction under future Contingencies; but with all my Equanimity I foresee it will give me a good deal of pain if I should be forced to reside next Winter in Holland instead of Glasgow, all my hopes of getting this absurd measure broken are founded in your coming so Early into this Country as to talk this matter over with Mr[150] Henry before we sett out on our Progress; you may think this a wild imagination considering the source of the opposition to Glasgow, but I still fancy that there is so much Ingenuous shame in Mr Henry's Mind as would restrain him from gratifieng so unworthy a humour were you upon the Spott: It will certainly do irreparable Injury to his eldest son; by continuing so long in a french family & from an almost unconquerable aversion to Society & the Entertainments of it He is unable to express himself with tolerable propriety in his own Language were it only for two or three short Sentences in common chatt; what then must become of him on spending two or three years in a Country where He will be under a necessity of using another Language for all the principal purposes of Conversation to the manifest encrease of all the disadvantages he now labors under with respect to his own.

150. Perhaps "Mrs."

there are no News; you will no doubt have heard that Cousen Rhoda has been extreamly ill but is now in a promising way of recovery all other friends as far as I know are pretty well; Old Mrs Weld died the beginning of this week by which a Jointur<e . . .> per year dropt, which since Hamilton's bankrupcy was the principal support <of her d>aughters. please to give my most afectionate & most respectfull service to my Cousin <& to my> young Cousens & to all other friends. I <am . . .> Dearest Cousen

Yours in the fullness of my Heart
Will. Bruce

---

33. From DAVID HUME

Address: To Mr Hutcheson Professor of Philosophy at Glasgow

MS: NLS, MS 23151, no. 56

Ninewells near Berwick. March. 4. 1740

Dear Sir

You will find, that the Good-Nature & friendly Disposition, which I have experienc'd in you, is like to occasion you more Trouble; & tis very happy, that the same Good-Nature, which occasions the Trouble, will incline you to excuse it.

Since I saw you, I have been very busy in correcting & finishing that Discourse concerning Morals,[151] which you perus'd; & I flatter myself, that the Alterations I have made have improv'd it very much both in point of Prudence & Philosophy. I shall set out for London in three Weeks or a Month with an Intention of publishing it. The Bookseller,[152] who printed the first two Volumes, is very willing to engage for this; & he tells me that the Sale of the first Volumes, tho' not very quick, yet it improves. I have no Acquaintance among these Folks, & very little Skill in

151. Book 3 of *A Treatise of Human Nature*. See Letters 26 and 30.

152. John Noon. Book 3 was published by Thomas Longman, and the two publishers subsequently collaborated in promoting the work as a whole. See Letter 34.

making Bargains. There are two Favours, therefore, I must ask of you, viz to tell me what Copy-Money I may reasonably expect for one Edition of a thousand of this Volume, which will make a four Shillings Book; And, if you know any honest Man in this Trade, to send me a Letter of Recommendation to him that I may have the Choice of more than one Man to bargain with. Tis with Reluctance I ask this last Favour; tho' I know your Authority will go a great Way to make the Matter easy for me. I am sensible, that the point is a little delicate. Perhaps you may not care to recommend even to a Bookseller a Book that may give Offence to religious People: Perhaps you may not think it calculated for public Sale. I assure you, therefore, that I shall not take in the least amiss, if you refuse me. I shall only say with regard to the first Article, that the Book is pretty much alter'd since you saw it; & tho' the Clergy be always Enemys to Innovations in Philosophy, yet I do not think they will find any great Matter of Offence in this Volume. On the contrary I shall be dissappointed, if Impartial Judges be not much pleas'd with the Soundness of my Morals. I have sent you the *Conclusion*, as I have alter'd it, that you may see I desire to keep on good Terms even with the strictest & most rigid. You need not return this Copy, unless you point out any Passage, which you think it proper for me to alter.

My Bookseller has sent to Mr Smith a Copy of my Book, which I hope he has receiv'd, as well as your Letter.[153] I have not yet heard what he has done with the Abstract. Perhaps you have. I have got it printed in London; but not in *the Works of the Learned*; there having been an Article with regard to my Book, somewhat abusive, printed in that Work, before I sent up the Abstract. I am

Dear Sir

Your most obedient & most humble Servant.

David Hume

---

153. William Smith, a Belfast-born bookseller in Amsterdam, edited the *Bibliotheque raisonnée des ouvrages des savans de l'Europe* that carried a review of books 1 and 2 of Hume's *Treatise* in the issue of April–June 1740. See M. A. Stewart and James Moore, "William Smith (1698–1741) and the Dissenters' Book Trade," *Bulletin of the Presbyterian Historical Society of Ireland* 22 (1993): 20–27.

34. From DAVID HUME

Address: To Mr Francis Hutcheson Professor of Philosophy at Glasgow

MS: NLS, MS 23151, no. 57; slight loss of wording due to seal

Edinburgh March. 16 1740

Dear Sir

I must trouble you to write that Letter you was so kind as to offer to Longman the Bookseller. I concluded somewhat of a hasty Bargain with my Bookseller from Indolence & an Aversion to Bargaining, as also because I was told that few or no Bookseller wou'd engage for one Edition with a new Author. I was also determin'd to keep my Name a Secret for some time tho I find I have fail'd in that Point. I sold one Edition of those two Volumes for fifty Guineas & also engag'd myself heedlessly in a Clause, which may prove troublesome, viz. that upon printing a second Edition I shall take all the Copys remaining upon hand at the Bookseller's Price at the time. Tis in order to have some Check upon my Bookseller, that I wou'd willingly engage with another, & I doubt not but your Recommendation wou'd be very servicable to me, even tho you be not personally acquainted with him.

I wait with some Impatience for a second Edition principally on Account of Alterations I intend to make in my Performance. This is an Advantage, that we Authors possess since the Invention of printing & renders the *Nonum prematur in annum*[154] not so necessary to us as to the Antients. Without it I shou'd have been guilty of a very great Temerity to publish at my Years so many Noveltys in so delicate a Part of Philosophy: And at any Rate I am afraid, that I must plead as my Excuse that very Circumstance of Youth, which may be urg'd against me. I assure you, that without running any of the heights of Scepticism, I am apt, in a cool hour, to suspect, in general, that most of my Reasonings will be more useful by furnishing Hints & exciting People's Curiosity than as containing any Principles that will augment the Stock of Knowledge that must pass to future Ages. I wish I cou'd discover more fully the particulars wherein I

---

154. "[put your parchment in the closet and] keep it back till the ninth year" (Horace, *The Art of Poetry*, 388, in *Satires, Epistles, the Art of Poetry . . .*).

have fail'd. I admire so much the Candour I have observd in Mr Locke, Yourself, & a very few more, that I woud be extremely ambitious of imitating it, by frankly confessing my Errors: If I do not imitate it, it must proceed neither from my being free from Errors, nor from want of Inclination; but from my real unaffected Ignorance. I shall consider more carefully all the Particulars you mention to me; tho' with regard to *abstract Ideas*, tis with Difficulty I can entertain a Doubt on that head, notwithstanding your Authority. Our Conversation together has furnish'd me a hint, with which I shall augment the 2d Edition. Tis this. The Word, *simple Idea*, is an abstract Term comprehending different[155] Individuals that are similar. Yet the point of their Similarity from the very Nature of such Ideas is not distinct nor separable from the rest. Is not this a Proof, among many others, that there may be a similarity without any possible Separation even in thought?

I must consult you in a Point of prudence. I have concluded a Reasoning with these two Sentences. *When you pronounce any Action or Character to be vicious, you mean nothing but that from the particular Constitution of your Nature you have a Feeling or Sentiment of Blame from the Contemplation of it. Vice & Virtue, therefore, may be compar'd to Sounds, Colours, Heat & Cold, which, according to modern Philosophy, are not Qualitys in Objects but Perceptions in the Mind: And this Discovery in Morals, like that other in Physicks, is to be regarded as a mighty Advancement of the speculative Sciences; tho' like that too, it has little or no Influence on Practice.*[156] Is not this laid a litt<le too stro>ng? I desire your Opinion of it, tho I cannot entirely promise to conform myself to it. I wish from my Heart, I coud avoid concluding, that since Morality, according to your Opinion as well as mine, is determin'd merely by Sentiment, it regards only human Nature & human Life. This has been often urg'd against you, & the Consequences are very momentous. If you make any Alterations on your Performances, I can assure you, there are many who desire you woud more fully consider this Point; if you think that the Truth lyes on the

---

155. "comprehending" and "different" added; "representing" deleted. Hume revised the wording further before inserting it to be read as a footnote to book 1 in the Appendix to his *Treatise* (3:306–7).

156. Hume, *A Treatise of Human Nature*, 3.1.1.26.

popular Side. Otherwise common Prudence, your Character, & Situation forbid you touch upon it. If Morality were determin'd by Reason, that is the same to all rational Beings: But nothing but Experience can assure us, that the Sentiments are the same. What Experience have we with regard to superior Beings? How can we ascribe to them any Sentiments at all? They have implanted those Sentiments in us for the Conduct of Life like our bodily Sensations, which they possess not themselves. I expect no Answer to these Difficultys in the Compass of a Letter. Tis enough if you have patience to read so long a Letter as this. I am Dear Sir

Your most obedient humble Servant
David Hume.

Please to direct to me as usual.

---

35. To whom it may concern

Address lacking

Copy: transcript by Thomas Hollis printed in Francis Blackburne, *Memoirs of Thomas Hollis, Esq.*, 2 vols., London, 1780, vol. 2, p. 778[157]

[Glasgow 22. May, 1740]

These are to certify any whom it may concern, that Mr. Richard Baron[158] hath resided in this university for three compleat annual sessions; *viz.* from October, 1737, to the date of these presents, attending regularly the lectures of philosophy, mathematics, and languages, and

---

157. In volume 2 of the *Memoirs of Thomas Hollis*, Francis Blackburne printed extensive extracts from Hollis's publications as well as other materials, including this letter. Either Hollis or, more likely, Blackburne provided the heading: "A Testimonial from the university of Glasgow to the late Rev. Richard Baron." Underneath the names "Hutchinson" and "Simson" is added: "The original, I think, was in the handwriting of Mr. Hutchinson, T.H."

158. Richard Baron (d. 1768), who apparently did not matriculate, was a contemporary in Glasgow of the devoted Hutcheson admirer Thomas Brand (later Brand Hollis). Both became associates of Thomas Hollis in the propagation of radical Whig republican ideas.

behaving as it became a man of virtue and probity, and particularly applying himself studiously to the law of nature, and shewing a good genius, and an high regard for what is virtuous and honorable.

In witness whereof we sign these presents, at Glasgow-College, this
twenty-second day of May, 1740.

Francis Hutchinson, P. P.

Robert Simson, Math. P.[159]

---

36. From WILLIAM BRUCE

Address: To Mr Francis Hutcheson Professor of Philosophy in the University
of Glasgow

MS: NLS, MS 9252, fols. 158–59; slight loss of wording due to seal

May 9th 1741

My Dearest Cousen

I had two Letters from you since my last for which I return you my
hearty thanks; Mr Houghton is much obliged to the Provost & you for
the trouble you have taken in relation to his daughter, He always had an
intire Confidence in the Integrity of the both & was much concerned
that any inadvertant Expression of his had given offence, I will undertake
to answer for him that He did not mean to offend; few men whom I have
mett with have more Simplicity of mind, or a juster Sense of any favour
done by another: He is perfectly satisfied with the whole transaction and
has too high an Idea of the importance of your friendship to his Daughter
to do or say any thing that He could suspect would have the least tendency to lessen it: I hope the bands of Love will every day grow stronger
where little else seems wanting to make the conjugal alliance comfortable
and alike so, to both: a disposition to find fault is poison to any Mind; it
is a cursed sagacity to be able to find out a reason for being dissatisfied,
where our whole attention ought to be employed in keeping ourselves in

---

159. Robert Simson, professor of mathematics. See Letter 15.

such a temper as will be easiest pleased; this is a necessary ingredient & ought to be regarded as an essential Article in all Contracts that imply Intimacy or a constant intercourse of Communion; It would prevent a great deal of folly & unhappiness if all Persons could be brought to account this among their primary moral obligations.

I communicated what you wrote in relation to Stalker to Jack Smith[160] it was very kind in you to take so much trouble in setling the account and Jack is very ready as indeed He ought to be, to acquiesce in what ever terms you would advise; at the same time Mr Stalker has not acted the part I would have expected from him, when the Pamphlets relating to the Bishop of Cloyne[161] were sent to us we were told that such of them as did not sell might be returned without any mention being made of a limited time, & if I do not strangely forget I very soon let Mr Stalker know that the Pamphlet would not answer at our Market, but it is a trifle not worth any farther words; Mr Gladsteins never paid the Bill as it is called but as I remember it was only a Letter to Mr Gladsteins desiring him to pay a specified ballance of Account in to us: the only circumstance I could wish to know farther in relation to this silly afair is whether the Rapins History[162] for which He claims an Abatement were got after or before November 1735.

I delivered your Letter to Mrs Miller, she is extreamly disconsolate & seemed concerned that you could not find room for her in your house but I appeared surprized at her ever having any expectations of it; and I cannot help thinking that you have judged it perfectly properly in declining her request at the same time that I have not any doubt but that she very well deserves yours & my Cousens Esteem: there is a delicacy in these things that unavoidably partakes of the nature of a constant Constraint and at this time of Life it were a thousand pities that either yours or my Cousen's Enjoyment should be embarrassed by any ceremonial observances but such as the Custom of the Country has rendered unavoidable

160. See note 25, p. 20, and note 53, p. 33.
161. George Berkeley; see Letters 5 and 16.
162. Paul de Rapin-Thoyras (1661–1725), *History of England*, 15 vols. (1726–31). There were subsequent editions, but it is unclear which is in question here.

too many in all conscience as every thinking Person knows to their constant regrett. I thank you for mentioning my Nephews it has been some concern to me that I have not heard from either of them these three Months past; I beg you may heartily advise Jammy to enter into the Ministry if you think him qualified for it: It is what I have much at heart & I doubt he has no business to entertain any thoughts of travelling with Mr Blackwood,[163] otherwise a delay of two or three years would not be disagreeable to me. I take it for granted Sam Bruce will want Money to bring him home please to let him have what you see necessary & I will pay it to your order in this town. there have few Alterations hapned among our friends in this Country since my last, I had almost lost my sister Patrick & her eldest Daughter in a fever & flux that has caried off many thousand through out this Country within these few Months past, but both of them I thank God are now recovered, you probably have heard of the Accident that befell Miss Campbel about three weeks ago of a fall in the little room off the Shop by which her Arm was broken just at the knob that goes into the Socket of the Shoulder; I never knew any Person recover better, She bore it extreamly well for she would hardly allow that <it> gave her any pain, and now the bandage is taken off < . . .> a few days I hope it will be in all respects as well as the other. Doctor Johnston is returned from France & purposes as I understand to settle in Drogheda it is a pretty thrang Neighbourhood of Gentlemen & the Phisician at present in that Country is not held in much Esteem. all our friends as far as I know are well & such as I have an opportunity of seeing seem generally to have an afectionate remembrance of their freinds in Glasgow uppermost with them. I am sorry to find that we are not likely to have honest Cornwal this Summer, I hope his Pupil's conduct pleases him, it is surmised here that a complaint or an insinuation of the Contrary in a Letter to Mr Walplate is the reason of the young Lad's being ordered to go into England but I imagine it is all a mistake.

163. This is presumably John Blackwood, 2nd Baronet of Ballyleidy (1721–1799), who matriculated at Glasgow in 1739 and graduated MA in 1741 with a remarkable *Dissertatio philosophica de imperii civilis origine et causis* (Glasgow, 1741). Later he became MP for Killyleagh.

I shall long to hear from you. I have no News to mention in regard to my self. pray remember me in the most afectionate Manner to my Cousen & young Cousens & all friends.

I am my Dearest Cousen yours in the fulness of my heart
Will. Bruce

37. To THOMAS DRENNAN

Address: To the Revd Thomas Drenan in Belfast

MS: GUL, MS Gen. 1018, no. 7

Glasgow June 1st 1741

Dear Thom

I had some time ago a letter from you on the back of Alexander Youngs about one Upton Scot, and last post had a double letter from a friend of his in Antrim. I deliverd the inclosed as he desired, and we shall take all due care in that Matter, and send him information where necessary. The lad should be over here some days before Michaelmass.[164] So much for that trifle which I shall not neglect.

I must next write you about an affair that gives me a great deal of trouble. Bob Haliday is not in a right way as to his conduct. I gave him several of the Strongest admonitions I could, I had many fair promises I confined him in his expences, he seemed to take all well and to promise diligence. All seemed to me tolerable till of late that I find he has run in Debt with Comerads, and for some trifles in shops, and is quite idling away his time. Nay what is worse, I fear is hurting others. The Boy has a good genius, but that is the poorest Satisfaction to me about any one I wish well to; he is conceity, thinks himself a wit, scorns advice from such folks as Gabriel Cornwal or Mr McMechan; and trifles away money & time for

164. Upton Scot, son of Francis Scot of Templepatrick, County Antrim, matriculated in the Greek class of Alexander Dunlop (1684–1747) (*ODNB*) on November 14, 1741. He graduated MD in 1753 and emigrated to Annapolis, Maryland, becoming first president of the Medical and Chirurgical Faculty of Maryland.

nothing. I know not how to write to Mr<s> Haliday; but as matters appear to me at present, theres litle hope of his succeeding in any learned Profession. And consequently he can have no business here. Cornwall & McMechan dread him about their pupils, and both set upon me to send him home as soon as possible I am distressed for Mrs Haliday, whom I used to incourage with the best accounts of things. I would not send him home suddenly, till she were some way prepared for it, and must beg it of you to begin the Matter, and prepare her to receive him. If any friends were for giving him a further trial as to study, they should send him without my Knowledge about £10, to pay off concealed Debts. Our Countrymen very generally have such an affectation of being Men and gentlemen immediately, & of despising every thing in Scotland, that they neglect a great deal of good wise instruction they might have here. I am truly mortified with a vanity and foppery prevailing among our Countrymen beyond what I see in others; and a softness & sauntering forsooth which makes them incapable of any hearty drudgery at books. we had 5, or 6, young gentlemen from Edinburgh, Men of Fortune & fine genius, at my Class & studying Law. Our Irishmen thought them poor book-worms; and indeed they dreaded contracting acquaintance with Blackwood & Haliday, in particular. I have mortified Haliday very heartily last night. His spirits will perhaps be up to day or tomorrow. If you get him to Belfast you must let him know you are sensible of his weakness & trifling. In the mean time I should wish to hear from you before I send him home, and that you would write me as soon as you can what you think most adviseable. You must not shew this to Mrs Haliday, but let her know that I write you that I cannot get him to be tolerably diligent, or Cautious in his Expences. Cornwal leaves the lodging to morrow on a Jaunt to England. but Haliday is at no loss, as he despised his advice all along. you must get Jammy Bruce on trials as soon as you can. Blackwood is too much Master for him. Indeed in his case Stultitiam patiuntur opes.[165] Pray write Bob Haliday as soon as you receive this, and don't fail to write to me upon Chatting with Mrs Haliday. Bob wants a Comission. I have

---

165. "Wealth gives rein to foolishness" (Horace, *Epistles*, I.xviii.29). Concerning Blackwood, see note 163, p. 86.

said a great deal against the Army, as the last < . . .> all good shifts, to men who have not interest in Shires or votes in Parliament. But I fear nothing else will suite his Turn of temper, unless he alters a good deal I shall be impatient to hear from you.

> I am Dear Thom
>> your most obedient servant
>>> & comerad
>>>> Fran: Hutcheson

young Blackwood is really good natured & lively and more capable of study than Haliday, but too gay & expensive

Math Morthland tells me that Cousen Alexander Young & you are talking of a visit to us this summer. I assure you it would give us great Joy, but t'is to good to be true. Pray if you do let us know by a letter some time before that we may not be out of the way on any Jaunt.

---

38. To THOMAS DRENNAN

Address: <To the Rev> Thoms Drenan <at his> house in Belfast

MS: GUL, MS Gen. 1018, no. 8

Glasgow June 15th 1741

Dear Thom

My last, which was a most necessary step, would give you and poor Mrs Haliday so much Pain that I am again impatient to write you. I find my discourse and some other Engines I have employed about Bob Haliday have had such Effects on him as begin to give me better Hopes, & some discreet folks, particularly McMechan who were most earnest for my sending him home, are now encourageing me to let him stay. I find he is heartily Mortified, and has continued so above this fortnight, retired & studious, and owning his faults. The Boy has a very good Genius & worth the takeing care of, provided I could fall on the way to do it to purpose. You can scarce imagine how desolate we are in Glasgow & how safe during the summer; Pray let Mrs Haliday know this. I dont profess reconciliation yet, to him; but I cannot conceal my agreeable hopes from her. Pray write to Bob now and then, and <in a> very grave strain, exhorting him to caution and spiriting him up to a generous Ambition. The wretched turn their Minds take is to the silly Manliness of Taverns, Jack Blackwood was a bad sight this way to lads of smaller Fortunes tho' otherways of a fine Temper. But this Expence always leads into disingenuous shifts, and to some other mischeifs. Satisfy poor Mrs Haliday. I hope all will go well. Pray let me hear from you now & then. I shall not leave Glasgow except about 3 weeks in July for this whole Vacation, but have more Avocations by too numerous an Acquaintance than you can imagine. In short Thom, I find old Age not in gray hairs & other trifles but in an incapacity of Mind for such close thinking or composition as I once had. And have pretty much dropped the thoughts of some great Designs I had once sketched out. In running over my Papers I am quite dissatisfied with Method Style Matter & some Reasonings, tho' I dont repent my Labour, as by it, and the thoughts suggested by Friends, a multitude of which I had from W Bruce & Syng & still more in number from some excellent hands here,[166] that I am fitter for my business, but as to composing in order I am quite bewildered, and am adding confusedly to a confused Book all valuable Remarks in a farrago to refresh my Memory in my class lectures on the several Subjects. You'll find the like, Pray lay up a good stock of Sermons. you would see a noble one by one of my Scotch Intimates who sees all I do, Mr Leechman.[167]

My hearty Love to all friends. I am
Dear Thom yours
Franc: Hutcheson

166. The remainder of this sentence was heavily revised. Hutcheson originally wrote ". . . that I am quite bewildered, and am adding them confusedly to a confused Book to refresh my Memory in my class lectures on the several Subjects."

167. Rev. William Leechman (1706–1785), minister of Beith, Ayrshire, since 1736. Edinburgh trained (MA, 1724), he had also attended Hutcheson's classes while serving as chaplain in the family of Mure of Caldwell, who took their winters in Glasgow (see Letter 49, note 207, p. 109). Leechman had just published *The Temper, Character, and Duty of a Minister of the Gospel: A Sermon Preached before the Synod of Glasgow and Air, at Glasgow, April 7th, 1741* (Glasgow, [1741]). Through Hutcheson's influence he would become professor of divinity at Glasgow in 1743, and in 1761 he became principal of the University (*ODNB*).

39. To THOMAS DRENNAN

Address lacking

MS: GUL, MS Gen. 1018, no. 9; damage to foot of the page with loss of at least one line.

Glasgow July 8th 1741

Dear Thom.

Tho I have often heard the Rumour of your Courtship without believing it, as I never thought your Talent lay in Fortune hunting; yet of late I have had such assurances that you're actually married, as I could not question it any longer. My wife and I congratulate you most heartily, and wish you all the Joys of that new Relation and wish the same to Mrs Drennan, who shows a more valuable Turn of Mind by her Conduct than most Young Ladies in such Circumstances.[168] We both long to See you both, and rejoice that we shall find another Family of Hearty friends in Belfast. If any interposal of Mine be necessary to promote or hasten an entire Satisfaction of all other friends with this Step you have taken, pray let me know, & it shall not be wanting. So much in seriosity.

And now Thom, that you have at last executed what you so often threatened with Charles Moore,[169] in your just Indignation at the foolish metamorphoses of your Comerads by Marriage; display to us the glorious Example; let us see how we should behave! rake away to Dublin every quarter; leave the wife behind you; or if you take her along, don't mind her; stay at the Walshes head till 2 in the Morning; saunter in Jacks Shop all day among Books; dine abroad; & then to the Walshes head again, to Charles great Consolation & Edification. I'm sure you cannot be so foolishly fond or so stupid as to quit all comerads, to despise the Inspiration of the Grape you recommend from the Pulpit, and sacrifice all Merry Conversation for one Woman.

168. Drennan's bride was Ann Lennox (1719–1806), daughter of a prominent Belfast merchant, Robert Lennox. She was a younger sister of Elizabeth, wife of Hutcheson's cousin Alexander Young (Jean Agnew, *Belfast Merchant Families*, p. 231). In a later letter (Letter 42), Hutcheson acknowledged that his congratulations were premature. William Bruce, DD, gives as the date of the wedding August 8, 1741.

169. See Letter 15.

> —Neque enim, fortissime, credo
> Jussa aliena pati, aut dominas dignabere Teucras.[170]

But to return to temptation a litle < . . .> the condition necessary for them, and not in that which the present Advancement of your Fortune entitles You to. You are sensible how much the Fortune you get is the sacred right of another & her descendents; and your Friends should be sensible of the same, and not presume upon Account of it to enlarge their Demands on You. A Clear neat Annual Sum for them is your only way, and then they can proportion their Expences to it. in this you should keep within your wifes judgement of what is reasonable, as She will probably from her generous conduct to you be abundantly Liberal in this point, and leave to her rather Opportunities of further handsom thing<s> in her conduct to them, than cause the least uneasiness in her Mind as if they were too burdensome. Dear Thom I just write as I would talk to you if we were walking in Hackmer or on the long Bridge, where I hope before I am many years Elder to have some pleasant Walks with you & Mrs Drennan. Pray write me soon.

As to Mrs Haliday pray tell <her>[171] immediatly that her son is in a better way by far than I expected. He has staid within and read close these 3 or 4 weeks, continues to own his faults is getting some wiser people to interceed for him, is out of the Way of all Temptations and will be for 3 moneths. He is safer here than in the wildest highland Isle, for that time I hope to get a new turn wrought in that time. I am Dear Thom

> yours entirely
> Franc: Hutcheson

---

170. "for you, gallant steed, will not deign, I think, to endure a stranger's orders and a Trojan lord" (Virgil, *Aeneid*, X:864–66).

171. "<her>" added; "him" deleted.

40. From WILLIAM BRUCE

Address: To Mr Francis Hutcheson Professor of Philosophy in the University of Glasgow

MS: NLS, MS 9252, fols. 160–61; in poor condition, transcription sometimes uncertain

Straffan August 29th 1741

My Dearest Cousen

by a Letter of yours to Charles Moor I find you finished your Summers Jant prosperously & got back in the time you had fixed for your Interview with Mrs Wilson; I could have wished for the sake of that amiable Youth her Son[172] she had made as much haste to fulfill her part of the apointment; his spending so much time in Dublin must be a disadvantage tho I am fully perswaded He has done it most Innocently; had I continued in Town I would have taken all the care in my Power that It should not have been altogether unusefully; I found my Company was not irksome to him and I was delighted with his; but unluckily this family have continued here in the Country the most of the time that He has been in Town; I took an opportunity the little while we were together to give him some general notion of Geography & the Uses of the Globes, & purposed to have read over with him Horace's Epistles; I fear you will find him greatly deficient with respect to the Languages, but that under your direction he will soon be enabled to remedy, without the sense of it proving in the mean time matter of discouragement to him;—his Capacity is good and his temper the sweetest & best disposed for receiving Instruction of any I have known. I should have been too happy had the object of my immediate Care[173] been blessed in a resemblance either of one or tother; I was going to say my Case is to be pitied; but Pity you would probably reply was never intended for alleviating Distress but where the Circumstances did not easily admitt of a Remedy; I will tell you the truth, I went so far in pursuance of your advice—an advice approved in a great measure by

172. Joseph, son of Francis Wilson, Tully, County Longford. He matriculated under Hutcheson at Glasgow on November 14, 1741.

173. Hugh Henry's son Joseph.

my own Judgement & recommended by the concurrence of my other friends, as to let the Young Lad know that I intended to leave him; He burst immediately into tears & cryed if I did so he would be utterly ruined. I have expostulated with him several times, but it always issues in a violent fitt of distress and a passionat conjuring intreaty that I would not, if I have any tenderness for him abandon him to misery & ruin; this I own distresses me, and yet on the other hand, small is my prospect of doing him any Valuable Service such is his temper, Abilities and Situation by continuing with him, which distresses me still more; this is the short & honest Account of my present State, perplexing enough but possibly a little time may happily extricate me; I almost repent having said so much because of the tenderness of your Sympathetic Sense; but do not my dearest Francis imagine that these external matters destroy my self Enjoyment; I meant well when I entered on my present business, I hoped to have contributed to the Interests of Virtue & Happiness by my Instructions & Influence; I am disapointed, but not, at least so I flatter myself, through want of honest Zeal; and while I can keep clear of remorse I shall endeavour to quiet my Mind under the want of Success, by reflecting more intently on that Superior Wisdom which superintends the purposes of moral Agents alike with all natural Events; Vast indeed is the difference betwixt the happiness of doing Good & that arising from the consciousness of wishing it, but withall it is no Small Matter to cultivate the Disposition & keep the afections Vigorous & ready for Action; who knows what is before us!

I am in some little perplexity about Jammy Bruce I have not yet seen him, for I have not made my annual Visit to the North; I take it for granted He is to part from Mr Blackwood; is not He too young to enter into the Ministry, would He profit much by another <wi>nter[174] in Glasgow? I was much displeased with so<me>[175] passages in the latin Oration, I have not yet expostulated with him about them, but I fear He has been too opinionative & impatient of your Advice; pray let me know the truth in this matter. I have hardly any News, no doubt you have

174. "winter" partly obliterated by seal.
175. "some" partly obliterated by seal.

heard of our friend Thom's happy Lot;[176] I hear He was married last week, I could heartily have wished that Our friend Alec Young had acted differently on this occasion his Zeal has been most intemperate & I know not for whose Sake or on what Account. I can give you but a general account of our friends in Town for we have been here in the Country these five weeks & honest Charles Moore along with us all the while; but they are all well; the Morning we were to have gone in to Town Mrs Jones took her labour, our friend Arebuckle was sent for & came out that Evening but she was safely delivered of a Boy before He arrived; I mention this circumstance of his being sent for that you may see how various we are. honest Hugh Kennedy is soon to be married to Miss Bell Curtiss, her friends speak well of her temper and she is generaly thought very pretty, the fortune is three thousand at present & great expectations at the Mother's death; I know not whether I desired you in a former letter to write to Cousen Jack in Waterford to < . . .>. I wrote to him but He did not answer my letter, Congrave who was the opposite Candidate is lately dead But one Barker who was his Partner as a Banker has declared in his Stead; they stand in the high Church Interest in opposition to Mr Christmas a Gentleman not active enough perhaps in serving his friends but on the whole a very worthy Man < . . .>

I heard before I left Town that our friend Jammy Arbuckle was about taking out a Commission of the Peace & it gave me concern for I dread the Consequences of it & could heartily wish he were diverted from it; but possibly it is already too late. pray how has my Cousen enjoyed herself this Summer & what is her State of Health; mention me likewise the Young Squires; and pray let me know in your next if you made any progress in revising your papers this Summer, I think you would do well to put the finishing hand to them as soon as possible, oh for a few hours Interview, but ah how distant is that prospect. continue to love me and be assured of the strongest afection to you & yours < . . .> your most faithful friend and Cousen

Will. Bruce

176. See Letters 39 and 42.

41. From WILLIAM BRUCE

Address: To Mr Francis Hutcheson Professor of Philosophy in the University of Glasgow

MS: NLS, MS 9252, fols. 162–63

Belfast October 23d 1741

My Dearest Cousen

had I not been for some time past on my Annual Visitation you should have heard from me sooner, at present I can write you but very indistinctly having hardly got through a severe fitt of my headach that for some years past seems to have as debilitating an Influence on the Powers of my Understanding as on the grosser Springs of Animal Life. I send back Sam Fleming[177] with Satisfaction in order to make another tryal of his Studies because of the favourable Account you gave of his Conduct while He was over before but I confess his progress in Literature does not appear encouraging, possibly this may have been partly owing to a Contempt that was prevalent even in my time of that branch of Science as well as the teacher of it that He attended, if this was the Case, the present Season will aford him no excuse, but if He does not bring over better Evidence of his application & of his Understanding his Business than what I have yet found, I shall heartily advise him to quitt thoughts of his Books; indeed if he does not improve in his Elocution, it will be necessary for him to do for were there no other Cause He tells me He would preferr the prosecution of his Studies to any other business which makes me fond of carrying the Experiment as far as Prudence and an impartial regard to his real Interest will well allow. the truth is my dearest friend, the circumstances of my young folks give me some anxious thoughts, I would fain help some of them forward into a Condition of being useful to the rest before I am no more, and possibly an apprehension now & then that this Event is not very far off may make me more impatient of the slowness of their advances towards it than Reason will justifie: I am in all respects extreamly pleased with Sam Bruce only I suspect he has confined his Studies to too narrow a Circle, he does not seem to have been sufficiently aware that his

177. Samuel Fleming from Shankill, County Armagh, matriculated in 1740, MA 1743, MD 1750.

business at a University ought at first to be his acquainting himself with the rudiments of all the branches of general Learning, but this inadvertency may yet be corrected; my hopes concerning him prove often a fine Cordial to my Spirits; were he much better qualified than He is I should think him several years too young to enter into the Ministry but It would give me great Satisfaction if in this Interval any Opportunity should offer of getting the tuition of a young Gentleman by means of which he might be enabled to continue in the most advantageous situation for prosecuting his own Studies; he was offered the care of two little Boys in a Gentleman's family with ten pounds a year but I advised against it as throwing him into a disadvantageous light on his first setting out. Jammy continues still with Mr Blackwood, but how long he is to do so is very uncertain He is averse to entring on tryals nor have I liberty to urge him, He is too young, too little acquainted with the World, not well enough acquainted with the logical Subjects, too confident of the irresistable force of truth, and too fond of it meerly for being true, withal He is a very amiable young fellow and afords me great hopes of his proving a Wise and Worthy Man:

I gave Sam fleming little more than would bear his expences over & serve him for a few weeks, when he finds that he must have recourse to you it will make him cautious of expence, I beg the favour of <you only>[178] to supply him as you see requisite and I < . . .>[179] fully answer your Bills. Cousen Trail came with me to this Country but has had a severe return of the pain in his dark Eye, his son Hamilton has resolved on a Country Life and I hope wisely. please to remember me most afectionately to my Cousen & young Cousens to Cousen Rhoda Mrs Wilson & her ameable Daughter & Son and to all friends; I have nothing to write to you concerning my own afairs only Mr Henry told me before I came for the Nrth that He purposed that Bob & I should go to London in Spring: wh<at> you wrote about expostulating with the Boy or the Boys expostulating with his father you would not have wrote if you had known either the Boy or his father.

I am my Dearest friend
yours in the fulness of my heart
Will. Bruce

178. "you only" obliterated by seal.
179. Obliterated by seal.

42. To THOMAS DRENNAN

Address: To the Revd Mr Thomas Drenan in Belfast

MS: GUL, MS Gen. 1018, no. 10

Glasgow Apr. 12th 1742

Dear Thom

You are such a lazy wretch that I should never write you more. Not one word of answer to my congratulatory Epistle you got six weeks before you were Married. Not one word of Godly Admonitions about spending an Evening with friends at the Welches head, and other Pious Sentiments about the vanity & folly of staying at home in the Evenings. But my present occasion of writing is that you may deliver the inclosed to Mrs Haliday your self, and give her what advice you can about her son. He has not yet got habits of Vice in the sense of the World. But I fear he is conceited, pert, and self willed. I have often told him my Mind very freely. He was in haste to be a Man, & thought Company in Taverns mighty Genteel; and could rally the folly of Bookish studious lads & saw too much of the vanity of the sciences. I write freely to you his faults that you may the better direct your conversation with him. I am at a loss how to explain his account to Mrs Haliday she allowed him £10, or £9-5 British for any secret accounts. But I gave him in the beginning of November £3-12 to pay Anatomy Lectures & some Books, & two guineas for the Surgeon whose shop he attended for the *Materia Medica*. But I found he applyed the Money to other purposes; as he had done two guineas I had given him the former year to pay for a Class, And I had this to charge in his accounts again. This discouraged me about him: Otherways I had entrusted him with his own Money this year. He has spent above £120 these 2 Sessions, and there is not twenty of this for Cloaths or Books. Theres another point you must manage as discreetly as you can. about this time two years I had given him four guineas to give as a compensation to a very worthy Lad; one Whitley, who had assisted him all the preceeding Winter. He had offered it as I hear, but at the same time made such intreaties & representations of his distress how to clear some litle Debts that Mr Whitley returned it to him, for that purpose: Whitley is a very worthy lad and indigent. t'is quite wrong he should want it. I cannot give

Mrs Haliday the pain of writing this to her now: but you must take a proper season for it. I have had a great deal of pain by Bob Haliday & to litle purpose I believe he is at present confounded; Good Company & advice may perhaps do him more good now than at another time. We all ow this to his worthy father; and all is not lost that's in danger. My wifes & my most hearty respects to Mrs Drennan we wish her an happy hour

I am Dear Thom
yours most heartily
Fran: Hutcheson

Alexander Young wrote me several moneths ago as if you were all reconciled again, which gave me great Pleasure. Send the two inclosed for Newry or Dublin by the first post franked or not franked. If Mrs Haliday challenges the above articles double charged, tell her it was no oversight. Whitley is yet unpaid, so tis not charged again. Mrs Haliday will probably shew my advice about him for the future.

---

43. To THOMAS DRENNAN

Address: To the Reverend Mr Thomas Drennan in Belfast

MS: GUL, MS Gen. 1018, no. 11

Glasgow May 31st 1742

Dear Thom

I venture to congratulate you upon Mrs Drennans happy delivery before I hear of it, I heartily wish it every way fortunately. I knew not the meaning of your earnest desire that I should go over this summer till I heard from W Bruce that there are still some points of consequence to be setled between you & Messrs Young & Bigger.[180] He only writes me in

---

180. James Biggar or Bigger, another Belfast merchant, married to a half-sister of Alexander Young's wife and of Drennan's wife (Jean Agnew, *Belfast Merchant Families*, p. 231).

general so I could only write in general to Alexander Young to get all matters cleared so that both you and he might be safe. for I find both are in some danger in case any thing goes wrong with Mr Biggar. You must Dear Thom bestirr your self on your Wifes & families Account. Thom Nevin can direct you much better than I could. and tho' trustees have the name in Law yet you must take the real work in hand. Pray let me know how all Matters are. The bearer Mr Hay takes over some copies of a new translation of Antoninus, the greater[181] half of which, & more, was my amusement last summer, for the sake of a singular worthy soul one Foulis. but I don't let my name appear in it, nor indeed have I told it to any here but the Man concerned. I hope you'll like it; the rest was done by a very ingenious Lad one Moore.[182] Pray try your critical faculty in finding what parts I did & what he did. I did not translate books in a Suite, but I one or two, & he one or two. I hope if you like it that it may sell pretty well with you about Belfast I am sure it is doing a publick good to diffuse the Sentiments & if you knew Foulis you would think he well deserved all incouragement. My hearty respects to Mrs Drennan. I am Dear Thom

yours
Franc: Hutcheson

give the inclosed useless Bill to Mrs Haliday. I forgot to send it her<.> the sum was included in my last draught on her

---

181. For "greater" Hutcheson originally wrote "first."

182. Concerning Hutcheson's and Moor's translation of *The Meditations of Marcus Aurelius*, see Letter 52, note 225, pp. 114–15.

44. From DAVID HUME

Address: To Mr Hutcheson Professor of Philosophy at Glasgow

MS: NLS, MS 28151, no. 58

Edinburgh Jany. 10 1743

Dear Sir

I receiv'd your very agreeable Present;[183] for which I esteem myself much oblig'd to you. I think it needless to express to you my Esteem of the Performance, because both the Solidity of your Judgement, & the general Approbation your Writings meet with, instruct you sufficiently what Opinion you ought to form of them. Tho your Good Nature might prompt you to encourage me by some Praises, the same Reason has not place with me, however Justice might require them of me. Will not this prove, that Justice & Good-nature are not the same? I am surpriz'd you shou'd have been so diffident about your Latin. I have not wrote any in that Language these many Years, & cannot pretend to judge of particular Words & Phrazes: But the Turn of the whole seems to me very pure, & even easy & elegant.

I have subjoin'd a few Reflections which occurd to me in reading over the Book. By these I pretend only to show you, how much I thought myself oblig'd to you for the Pains you took with me in a like Case, & how willing I am to be grateful. P. 9. L. ult: et quae seq:[184] These Instincts you mention seem not always to be violent & impetuous, more than Self-love or Benevolence. There is a calm Ambition, a calm Anger or Hatred, which tho' calm, may likewise be very strong, & have the absolute Command over the Mind. The more absolute they are, we find them to be commonly the calmer. As these Instincts may be calm, without being weak, so Self-love may likewise become impetuous & disturb'd, especially where any great Pain or Pleasure approaches. P. 21. L. 11.[185] In opposition to this, I shall cite a fine Writer, not for the sake of his Authority,

183. Hutcheson's *Philosophiae moralis institutio compendiaria* (Glasgow, 1742). An enlarged and corrected edition appeared in 1745, and a translation by another hand, under the title *A Short Introduction to Moral Philosophy*, in 1747.

184. This is book 1, chap. 1, sec. vi, also in the 2nd edition.

185. Book 1, chap. 1, sec. xi.

but for the Fact, which you may have observ'd. Les hommes comptent presque pour rien toutes les vertus de coeur, & idolatrent les talens du corps & de l'esprit: celui qui dit froidement de soi, & sans croire blesser la modestie, qu'il est bon, qu'il est constant, fidele, sincere, equitable, reconoissant, n'ose dire qu'il est vif, qu'il a les dents belles ou la peau douce; cela est trop fort. Le Bruyere.[186] I fancy however this Author stretches the Matter too far. It seems arrogant to pretend to Genius or Magnanimity, which are the most shining Qualities a man can possess. It seems foppish & frivolous to pretend to bodily Accomplishments. The Qualities of the heart, lye in a medium & are neither so shining as the one, nor so little valu'd as the other. I suppose the Reason why Good nature is not more valu'd is its Commonness, which has a vast Effect on all our Sentiments. Cruelty & Hardness of Heart is the most detested of all Vices. I always thought you limited too much your Ideas of Virtue; & I find, I have this Opinion in common with several that have a very high Esteem for your Philosophy. P. 30 L. antepen: et quae seq.[187] You seem here to embrace Dr Butler's Opinion in his Sermons on human Nature;[188] that our moral Sense has an Authority distinct from its Force and Durableness, & that because we always think it *ought* to prevail. But this is nothing but an Instinct or Principle, which approves of itself upon reflection; and that is common to all of them. I am not sure that I have not mistaken your Sense, since you do not prosecute this Thought. P. 52. L. 1. I fancy you employ the Epithet *aerumnosam* more from Custom than your settled Opinion.[189] P. 129 et quae seq.[190] You some times, in my Opinion, ascribe the Original of Property & Justice to public Benevolence, & sometimes

186. Jean de la Bruyère (1645–1696), *Les caractères, ou Les moeurs de siècle* (1688), "Men reckon the Virtues of the Heart worth nothing, but idolize the Endowments of Mind and Body. He who says coldly of himself, and without thought of offending against Modesty, that he is good, constant, faithful, sincere, just and grateful; dares not say he is gay and sprightly, has fine Teeth and a soft Skin; that would be too vain" (*The Characters, or Manners of the Present Age*, in *The Works*, 2:233).

187. Book 1, chap. 1, sec. xvi. In the 2nd edition this is sec. xviii.

188. Joseph Butler (1692–1752), *Fifteen Sermons Preached at the Rolls Chapel*.

189. Book 1, chap. 2, sec. x. In the 2nd edition Hutcheson deleted "aerumnosam," "wretched."

190. Book 2, chap. 6.

to private Benevolence towards the Possessors of the Goods, neither of which seem to me satisfactory. You know my Opinion on this head. It mortifies me much to see a Person, who possesses more Candour & Penetration than any almost I know, condemn Reasonings, of which I imagine I see so strongly the Evidence. I was going to blot out this after having wrote it, but hope you will consider it only as a Piece of Folly, as indeed it is. P. 244 L. 7.[191] You are so much afraid to derive any thing of Virtue from Artifice or human Conventions, that you have neglected what seems to me the most satisfactory Reason, viz lest near Relations, having so many Opportunities in their Youth, might debauch each other, if the least Encouragement or Hope was given to these Desires, or if they were not early represt by an artificial Horror, inspird against them<.> P. 263, L. 14.[192] As the Phraze is true Latin, & very common, it seem'd not to need an Apology, as when Necessity obliges one to employ modern Words. P. 266. L. 18 et quae seq:[193] You imply a Condemnation of Locke's Opinion, which being the receiv'd one, I cou'd have wisht the Condemnation had been more express.

These are the most material things that occurd to me upon a Perusal of your Ethics. I must own I am pleas'd to see such Philosophy and such instructive Morals to have once set their Foot in the Schools. I hope they will next get into the World, & then into the Churches. Nil desperandum Teucro duce et auspice Teucro.[194]

191. Book 3, chap. 1, sec. vi.

192. Book 3, chap. 4, sec. iv. Hutcheson had used a conventional phrase ("toto coelo") to underline the total contrast between civil society and despotism, adding "ut aiunt," "as they say" (as the saying goes).

193. Book 3, chap. 5, sec. ii (1).

194. "You are to despair of nothing with Teucer as your leader and your guardian" (Horace, *Odes*, I.vii:27). In Greek mythology, Teucer was a heroic archer, banished from his native Salamis in Greece, who founded the greater Salamis in Cyprus. Horace envisages him exhorting his followers.

45. To WALTER SCOT OF HARDEN[195]

Address: To Walter Scot of Hardon Esqre

MS: NRS, MS GD157/2241

Glasgow May 12th 1743

Sir

It gives me great pleasure upon your sons[196] returning to you, that I can give you so good an Account of his whole behaviour with us, which was sober prudent and studious. As he had been much a stranger to Philosophy when he came to us, it was no Wonder that some things were pretty difficult to him at first; but by Mr Lindsays assistance he has done very well, and seemed to relish his Studies very heartily. I am much pleased to hear that you intend he should spend another winter with us. I am persuaded it will be much for his advantage, and it will give great pleaure to all of us whom he attends. he has time enough to spend some years at home before he goes for his improvement to any Universities abroad.

I am Sir
Your most obedient
humble Servant
Francis Hutcheson

195. Walter Scott (1682–1746), hereditary laird of Harden, Roberton.
196. Walter Scott of Harden (1724–1793) later married into the family of the earls of Marchmont. There is no record of his having been a matriculated student, but Alexander Carlyle included his name among the "Young Men of Fashion attending the College" in his day: "There never was but one Concert During the two Winters I was at Glasgow, and that was Given by Walter Scott Esqr of Harden who was himself an Eminent performer on the Violin; and his band of assistants Consisted, of two Dancing School Fidlers, and the Town Waits" (*Anecdotes and Characters of the Times*, pp. 43, 39). His descendants inherited the title Baron Polwarth.

46. To THOMAS DRENNAN

Address: To the Revd Mr Thomas Drenan in Belfast

MS: GUL, MS Gen. 1018, no. 12

Glasgow Aug 5th. 1743

Dear Thom

I have had 2 letters of late from Mr Mussenden,[197] one about 5 weeks ago with an Invitation to Mr Leechman to succeed Dr Kilpatrick.[198] Leechman was then just upon his marriage I concluded the Matter quite impracticable & returned an Answer to that purpose, & upon conversing Leechman found I was not then mistaken. He was lately very ill treated by our Judges, in a discretionary augmentation he applied for, which they could have given with full consent of parties. His Wife not so averse to removal as formerly. Indeed the difficulty is with him Self. You never knew a better sweeter man, of excellent literature, &, except his Air, and a litle roughness of voice, the best preacher imaginable. You could not get a greater blessing among you of that kind. As I have heard nothing from other Hands, I want fuller information. Are the people generally hearty for Leechman upon the Character they hear? Is there no other worthy Man on the field? Unless these points be cleard he will take no Steps. I remember one Millar an assistant. Pray is he to be continued, and no way afronted or neglected in this design? Leechman is well as he is and

197. Daniel Mussenden (d. 1763), a wealthy Belfast merchant active from early in the century, with commercial interests throughout the north of Ireland and trading links to Britain, northern Europe, the Baltic, the West Indies, and the Americas. He was a prominent lay elder of the Second Presbyterian Church, Belfast. On his reputation for probity in business, see Toby Barnard, *A New Anatomy of Ireland: The Irish Protestants, 1649–1770*, pp. 260–61.

198. Rev. James Kirkpatrick (d. 1743), Presbyterian minister in Belfast since 1706. The congregation exceeded the capacity of the existing church, and from 1708 Kirkpatrick led the new Second Congregation, making his name as a leading advocate of the Presbyterian cause by the publication of *An Historical Essay upon the Loyalty of Presbyterians in Great-Britain and Ireland from the Reformation to this Present Year 1713*. In the 1720s, with Rev. John Abernethy, he had been one of the leaders of a campaign to oppose enforced ministerial subscription to the Westminster *Confession of Faith*. In 1725 those congregations whose ministers refused to subscribe were moved into a reconstituted Presbytery of Antrim, which was excluded from the General Synod of Ulster in 1726. Concerning Leechman, see Letter 38.

happy, tho' preaching to a pack of horse-copers & smuglers of the rudest sort; He would do nothing hard or disagreeable to any worthy man: And has no desire of Change. But if the field be clear, it were *peccare in publica commoda*,[199] not to force him out of that obscure hole where he is so much lost. Pray dont fail to write me fully next post. He was the man I wished in the first place to be our Professor of Theology. I believe I had not occasion formerly of congratulating you upon the Birth of your Daughter. I wish you would write me more fully the state of all your affairs as to Mrs Drennans fortune. I hear very contrary accounts. and some insinuating as if Alexander Young with his composition with Campbel Hamilton, & being Tenant for Life was much embarrassed in his affairs. I have no news but that we expect immediatly from Robert Simson a piece of amazing Geometry, reinventing 2 Books of Appollonius, & he has a third almost ready.[200] He is the best Geometer in the World, reinventing Old Books, of which Pappus[201] preserves only a general Account of the Subjects. My wifes & my most hearty respects to Mrs Drennan & you, and to all friends. I am Dear Sir

your most obedient humble Servant
Francis Hutcheson

199. "To offend against the public good" (adapted from Horace, *Epistles*, II.i:3).

200. Concerning Robert Simson, see Letter 15 and Hutcheson's published letter to William Smith. He published *Apollonii Pergaei locorum planorum*, libri II, restituti a Roberto Simson, with the Foulis brothers in Glasgow (1749).

201. Pappus of Alexandria (c. AD 290–350).

47. To JOHN HENDERSON[202] or THOMAS DRENNAN

Address: To the Revd Mr John Henderson or Mr Thomas Drennan in Belfast

MS: GUL, MS Gen. 1018, no. 13

Glasgow September 20th 1743.

Revd & Dear Sir

I had the favour of yours by Mr Blow, but could not return an Answer by him, being much employed in promoting the affair you wrote about. I had also very urgent Letters from Messrs Mairs & Duchal[203] to the same Purpose. T'is very difficult to persuade a Modest worthy Man who is tolerably setled, to Adventure upon a New scene of Affairs among strangers. I shall use my utmost endeavours to prevail upon him, as I have been doing for some time past. I am sorry I cannot give you great hopes of success; but I dont yet so despair as to quit solicitation, as he is exceedingly moved with the affection & generosity of that people. My most humble & hearty respects to your Brethren of your presbytery whom I shall always remember with the greatest Esteem & affection. I am

Revd Sir

your most obedient

humble servt

Francis Hutcheson

My wife joins in most hearty respects to you & all friends with you.

202. Rev. John Henderson (c. 1684–1753), Irish Presbyterian minister at Duneane (initially joined with Grange), County Antrim, from 1713. He had completed studies at the Killyleagh Academy by 1704, was entered on trials by the Antrim Presbytery before June 1706, and received his preaching licence before June 1707. He joined the Belfast Society and was one of the ministers who in 1725 were formed into the Nonsubscribing Presbytery of Antrim.

203. See Letter 5, note 19, p. 13, and Letter 15, note 77, p. 43 respectively.

48. To THOMAS DRENNAN

Address lacking

MS: GUL, MS Gen. 1018, no. 14; letter damaged and faded

Glasgow Oct 29 1743

Dear Thom

I am sorry to tell you \<that> my utmost importunities had no effect \<upon Mr> Leechman. His wifes friends seemed to be \< . . .> with such Views as \< . . .> never come into; that is, to make Belfast \< . . .> Step, till they tryed for some years what m\< . . .> could make to remove him thence to Eden\<burgh>. In that View Mr Leechman abhorred to go to such a kind generous people; and his wifes friends as \<we>ll as his own urged much that he should not go with a view to Setle for Life in Belfast. For my own part I would prefer Belfast to either Edinburgh or Glasgow, unless one had many sons disposed to be Scholars. I am heartily sorry you're all disappointed. I Send you by the Bearer Dr Thomson two Copies of a trifle which I don't own as it was first most imperfectly & foolishly printed without my knowlege, from some loose hastily wrote papers, and now tho much enlarged & altered, yet I had not leisure either to examine the whole thoroughly or to correct the latin.[204] I am sure it will match De Vries and I therefore teach the 3d part of it *de Deo*.[205] I see \< . . .> my Compend of Morals a good many d\< . . .> oversights.[206] But I am so diverted with vari\<ety of b>usiness that I must do every thi\<ng> by such \< . . .> and \<h>ave something Desultory in the c\<ondition> of my Mind; besides something of Old \<Age cre>eping on. I congratulate Mrs Drennan & \<you on> your Son. I wish I had him once at my Class.

---

204. Hutcheson's *Metaphysicae synopsis: ontologiam et pneumatologiam complectens* (*A Synopsis of Metaphysics, Comprehending Ontology and Pneumatology*) was first published by Robert Foulis in an unauthorized edition (Glasgow, 1742). Hutcheson revised it for a second edition a year later with the main title changed to *Synopsis metaphysicae*, but it appeared with an imprint date of 1744. For a modern translation, see Francis Hutcheson, *Logic, Metaphysics, and the Natural Sociability of Mankind*.

205. Gerard de Vries (1648–1705), *De natura Dei et humanae mentis*.

206. Hutcheson's *Philosophiae moralis institutio compendiaria* had been published in 1742, with a revised edition in 1745. Hutcheson explained his revisions in the Preface to the latter.

But as we say here, *theres a lang time to the Sadling of a foal*. Remember he is mortal: I know you doat upon him, as I have done in like cases. My Frank still gives me both great hopes & fears. of a very unstaid temper, not capable of long application; but of a quick genius. Our most hearty respects to Mrs Drennan and all friends Pray send by first safe Hand the copy directed to Bishop Syng. I had a very fond letter from him, but a very melancholy one, last summer, he is wanting such elementary books for his son.

I am Dear Thom
yours most heartily
Franc: Hutcheson

pray dispatch the Book to the Bishop

Dr Thomson is a man well versed in the languages and was much commended by our Doctor upon <h>is Ex<ami>nation, as to his knowlege in Medicine, of which I am no judge. I am surprized he should < . . .>

---

49. To WILLIAM MURE[207]

Address: To William Mure Esquire Member of Parliament for the Shire of Renfrew London

MS: NLS, MS 11004, fols. 57–58

Glasgow November 23d. 1743

Dear Sir

Our Professor[208] died this morning. beside the Letters from Messrs Rosse to George,[209] (who I believe is fixed our friend already) Could you

---

207. William Mure (1718–1776), of Caldwell, Ayrshire, Scotland; studied law at Edinburgh and Leiden, Member of Parliament for Renfrewshire 1741–61; later Baron of the Scottish Exchequer. Tutored in early life by William Leechman, Mure later used his political influence to promote the careers and interests both of Leechman and of his associates. He was also a close friend and staunch ally of David Hume.

208. Michael Potter (1670–1743), professor of divinity.

209. George Bogle of Daldowie, rector of the university.

not obtain a letter from the Duke our Chancellor to Charles Morthland?[210] You may represent Leechman as acceptable to the best of this Society of his friends, viz: Messrs Dunlop Simson Hamilton Rosse[211] & my self, nay Morthland pretends to be for him too, Only Loudon & Anderson,[212] our Standard & Champion of Orthodoxy oppose him. That his Graces Letter to Morthland would not only fix him, but perhaps Loudon & Forbes.[213] You may represent what is abundantly known that he is universally approved for Literature & Eloquence, & that Anderson his cheif opposer made himself ridiculous to all men of sense by dangling after Whitefield & McCullogh. I want this should be known to Andrew Mitchel & Tweedale.[214] That we are not without hopes of carrying him by some of the other side, which might be thought a disagreeable Obligation, and would far rather have him attached by this favour to his Grace. He can scarce scruple to write a letter to his old friend Murthland to be communicated to Loudon & others, representing his good impressions of Mr Leechman and zeal to Oblige some friends of Mr Leechmans who Applied in his behalf for his graces recommendation, that so he might be carried by his graces friends. If you get Ch. Rosse or other members to join you in this request so much the better. I am perhaps too sanguine: But even Mr Dick[215] is declaring for him, but you know his instability. I am yours

you know my Hand

You might show this letter, if my name could do any thing or tell the Contents, only my name must not be mentioned in his Graces Letters to his friends here.

---

210. William Graham, 2nd Duke of Montrose (1712–1790), chancellor of the university since 1742; Charles Morthland, professor of Oriental languages, 1709–44.

211. For Dunlop, see Letter 37; Robert Simson, Letter 15; Robert Hamilton (1714–1756), professor of anatomy and botany; for Rosse, see Letter 1.

212. For Loudon, see Letter 19; William Anderson (c. 1690–1752), professor of ecclesiastical history.

213. William Forbes (c. 1669–1745), professor of law.

214. Andrew Mitchell (later Sir Andrew; 1708–1771), private secretary to John Hay, 4th Marquis of Tweeddale (1695–1762) (*ODNB*).

215. Robert Dick, the elder (c. 1690–1751), professor of natural philosophy.

50. To THOMAS DRENNAN

Address: To the Revd Thomas Drennan at his house in Belfast

MS: GUL, MS Gen. 1018, no. 15; undated

[Glasgow, end November 1743]

Dear Thom

Having this opportunity I must trouble you with a small affair. Upon Conversation with Mr Brown who came lately from Ireland along with Mr Alexander Haliday about the circumstances of some Ministers very worthy Men in your Presbytery; It occurred to me that a litle liberality could not be better exercised than among them. I am concerned that in my prosperous circumstances I did not think of it sooner. If you have any litle contributions made toward such as are more distressed than the rest, you may mark me as a subscriber for £5 per annum. And take the above ten pounds as my payment for the two years past. Alexander Young will advance it immediatly, as I wrote him lately that I would probably draw such a Bill without telling him the purposes.

I think it altogether proper you should not mention my name to your Brethren, but conceal it. I am already called new light here. I don't value it for my self, but I see it hurts some Ministers here who are most intimate with me. I have been these ten days in great hurry and perplexity, as I have for that time foreseen the Death of our Professor, who died last Wedensday: And some of my Collegues join me in labouring for Mr Leechman to succeed. We are not yet certain of the Event but have good hopes. If he succeeds it will put a new face upon Theology in Scotland. I am extremely concerned for your Divisions in Belfast. I find they talk of Jack Maxwel of Armagh, or young Kennedy. the talents of this latter I know not; but believe he has a very honest heart. Jack Maxwell is an ingenious lively fellow, for any thing I could discern. That Presbytery will miss him much. pray write me now sometimes. I am sorry the Event in your family made some hints in my last so seasonable. But your Son is now as well as if he had lived 60 years a Plato or a Caesar. or if he is not life is scarce worth spending under such a Providence. we should all long ὕδωρ καὶ γαιὰ γινεσθαι.[216] My hearty respects to Mrs Drennan I am Dear Thom

yours

Franc: Hutcheson

my hearty Compliments to Mrs Haliday. tell her her son is doing very well. pray did Dr Thomson deliver the 2 copies of a Trifle I sent for you & Bp Synge.[217]

---

51. To THOMAS DRENNAN

Address: To the Revd Thomas Drenan at his house in Belfast

MS: GUL, MS Gen. 1018, no. 16

Glasgow Feb. 20th 1743/4

Dear Thom

I am not a litle surprized that I have not heard from you these 4 moneths past, tho' there were some of My Letters which any other person would have thought required an Answer. I could tell you a good deal of News upon the unexpected Election of a Professor of Divinity, and the furious indignation of our zealots, but you deserve no news from any body. We have our own concern about the setlement of Belfast, but are to expect no Accounts from you of any thing. Pray tell Mrs Haliday her son is doing very well, that she should hear from me often did I not trust to Mr Browns informing her: And I never was more hurried than since our late Professors Death. Our hearty respects to Mrs Drenan, & sympathy with you on the loss of your Boy.

216. *Hudor kai gaia ginesthai*, "to become water and earth," a phrase adapted from Homer, *Iliad*, VII.99.

217. See above, Letter 48.

Dicimus autem hos quoque felices qui ferre incommoda vitae
Nec jactare jugum vita dedicere magistra.[218]

> I am Lazy Thom
> yours very heartily
> Franc: Hutcheson

Pray was the Bill paid I sent you some weeks ago, or some moneths < . . .>

---

52. To LORD MINTO[219]

Address: To the Right Honourable the Lord Minto Edinburgh

MS: NLS, MS 11004, fols. 57–58

Luss upon Lough lomond July 4th 1744

Your Lordships kind letter did not come to hand till last night as I have resided here for these 4 weeks past, and could not return an answer so soon as you might otherways have expected. I am very Sensible of my Obligations to your Lordship, and how far this friendly design toward me is owing to your influence. I don't doubt but an active young man might make that Situation in Edinburgh more profitable than my present one in Glasgow, and might be more extensively usefull in it. But as there is no Scarcity of very good hands who would be dayly improving, and I look upon my Self as upon the verge of Old Age & soon to decline, And am at present agreably situated, I can not entertain any thoughts of a Change of that kind.[220] Indeed my onely views, in My Castlebuilding, are returning to Ireland some few years hence, if once my son were in any way of

218. Nearly accurately quoted from Juvenal, *Satires*, XIII.20–22: "Yet we consider happy, too, people who've learned from life's teachings to put up with the unpleasant things in life and not to resist the yoke."

219. Sir Gilbert Elliot, Bt., Lord Minto (1693–1766), Dutch-trained advocate, was appointed a judge in the Court of Session, the Scottish supreme civil court, in 1726. By the time of this letter he was a member of the Court of Justiciary, the supreme criminal court, rising to the position of Lord Justice Clerk in 1763.

220. See Letter 55 below.

Subsistence, to spend the dregs of life among a numerous Set of old Comerads & Kinsmen. one year more makes me 50, & some litle Rheumatick disorders & gout make me much more. *Parvum parva decent; non me jam regia Roma*[221] you remember the merry story that follows, with an excellent Moral. As I am sensible both of your kind intentions to me & of your zeal for promoting Virtue & literature, I cannot omit naming to you Thom Craigy Professor of Hebrew in St Andrews,[222] Robt Trail who was lately in Lord Kilkerrens family.[223] Robt Pollock minister of Duddiston,[224] James Moore, now with Mr Hamilton of Baldoon[225] William Rowat

221. "Small things befit a lowly man; imperial Rome is not now for me" (adapted from Horace, *Epistles*, I.vii.44). There follows a cautionary tale of a small-time merchant tempted by a wealthy patron into taking on a farm beyond his station and capacity.

222. Thomas Craigie (d. 1751); studied at Glasgow, professor of Hebrew at St. Mary's College, St. Andrews, 1741–46. He succeeded Hutcheson as professor of moral philosophy at Glasgow in 1746 but was dogged by poor health. For further information on his relationship with Hutcheson, see James Moore and Michael Silverthorne, "Hutcheson's LL.D."

223. Robert Traill (1720–1775); studied at Edinburgh, minister of Kettins 1746 and Banff 1753, appointed professor of Oriental languages at Glasgow in 1761 but immediately transferred to the chair of divinity vacated by William Leechman (*ODNB*). Sir James Fergusson, Bt., Lord Kilkerran (1688–1759), of Kilkerran, Ayrshire, was a judge in the Court of Session, Edinburgh (*ODNB*). His eldest son, John (1727–1750), after attending two classes at Edinburgh University, was sent to Philip Doddridge's academy at Northampton in December 1743. He planned on a military career but died young of consumption. See Geoffrey Nuttall, *Calendar of the Correspondence of Philip Doddridge DD (1702–1751)*; also Colin MacLaurin to Lord Morton, n.d.: NRS, GD150/3486/3.

224. Robert Pollock (1709–1759); MA Edinburgh 1725, minister of Duddingston 1744, professor of divinity at Marischal College, Aberdeen 1745, combined with the principalship 1757.

225. James Moor (1712–1779); MA Glasgow 1732 and one of Hutcheson's early students there, university librarian 1742, professor of Greek 1746–74 (*ODNB*). Hutcheson and Moor had already collaborated on the translation of *The Meditations of the Emperor Marcus Aurelius Antoninus* (1742); see the modern edition by James Moore and Michael Silverthorne. "Mr. Hamilton of Baldoon" would have been a son of Basil Hamilton (d. 1742), hereditary laird of Baldoon, near Wigtown, Dumfriesshire. He was related to the earls of Selkirk, a title to which the eldest son, Dunbar Hamilton, a former student of Hutcheson's, succeeded in 1744. The new earl, according to William Leechman, was privileged to have received a copy of the unfinished manuscript of *A System of Moral Philosophy* from Hutcheson himself. See uncatalogued fragment of a letter, Leechman to [William Bruce of Dublin], datable

lately returned from his travels with Sir John Maxwells son,[226] Mr Cleghorn who was lately employed this way,[227] or George Muirhead.[228] I have more acquaintance with all the rest than Cleghorn, and yet I judged him a very acute man from Some few days conversation. I just name these persons to your Lordship because Sometimes very worthy men are overlooked who had they occurred to peoples thoughts might have pleased them well upon enquiry. Craigy & Moore are the two in my Acquaintance for whose Success I could best venture to promise: of the rest I have very good impressions according to my acquaintance of them.

> I am my Lord
> Your Lordships most obliged
> & most obedient humble servt
> Francis Hutcheson

You'll be pleased not to mention to any my presuming thus to name persons to you for that office.

---

on internal evidence c. June 1749, Bruce Papers, PRONI; see transcription in the Appendix to *A System of Moral Philosophy*, ed. Haakonssen and Maurer.

226. William Rouet (d. 1785); matriculated at Glasgow 1730, professor of Oriental languages there 1751–52, and of ecclesiastical history 1752–62.

227. William Cleghorn (1719–1754); MA Edinburgh 1739, succeeded to the appointment that is under discussion here in 1745. See M. A. Stewart, *The Kirk and the Infidel*; Douglas Nobbs, "The Political Ideas of William Cleghorn, Hume's Academic Rival"; Simon W. Grote, *The Emergence of Modern Aesthetic Theory: Religion and Morality in Enlightenment Germany and Scotland*, chap. 5. MacLaurin, after recommending Robert Traill as a possible tutor for the Earl of Morton's son, wrote: "I cannot think of any better at present, unless it be one Mr Cleghorn Dr Pringle's substitute who I fear would insist on higher terms & tho' a great Moral philosopher is not so good at Natural philosophy as Mr Traill" (MacLaurin, *Démonstrations des loix du choc des corps*).

228. George Muirhead (1715–1773); entered Glasgow University 1728, MA Edinburgh 1742; minister of Monigaff 1746, and Dysart 1748; professor of Oriental languages at Glasgow 1753, and of humanity (Latin) 1754 (*ODNB*).

53. To THOMAS DRENNAN

Address: To the Reverend Mr Thomas Drennan at his house in Belfast

MS: GUL, MS Gen. 1018, no. 18

Glasgow October 18th 1744

Dear Thom

I had yours by Mr Banks, but some unlucky businesses hindered me from returning you an Answer And as I find one of your former letters to me miscarried I did not choose to write by post. I had heard from several hands, what I believe you have hinted in the letter which I never received, that Alexander Young is in most embarrassed circumstances. This to me is Matter of very great surprize. Grant he payd £1700 to Campbel Hamilton: yet first & last he had got near that sum with his wife beside the freehold. And I don't find he has payd off his fathers Legacies to his younger Children. I doubt there have been great losses in trade which he has concealed. I am much at a loss how you & Mrs Drennan can be well secured. No other way occurrs to me but his consenting to a sequestration of 2/3ds of his Rents till you are payd off, & confining himself to £100 per annum. When Will Bruce comes to the North and makes an enquiry into the affair perhaps something better may occur. Cousen Alexander never told me particularly his affairs, only spoke as if his Rents with those of his wife were above £300 per annum. Nor do I know the sum of his Debts to you or others. But I hope such a sequestration might in 10 or 12 years make all clear. I should be very glad to hear all particulars from you. My writing to him can be of no consequence but to make him conclude that I had my information from you. I hope to see you at Belfast God willing next June, and get a clear view of your affairs. I take such precaution as to my own affairs that I cannot lose any thing considerable in his hands: And I found him such an obliging friend to me that I would not grudge a litle loss to relieve him, tho his straits have I doubt led him into very unjustifiable measures toward others. My wife & franky, who is perfectly well again join in hearty respects to Mrs Drennan & you.

I am Dear Sir

your most obedient humble servant

Fran: Hutcheson

54. To THOMAS DRENNAN

Address: To the Revd Thomas Drennan at his House in Belfast

MS: GUL, MS Gen. 1018, no. 17; undated

[Glasgow, late 1744]

Dear Sir

You have the above Bill for the purposes I mentioned last year. But your letters are so general that I am not yet sure that you received it except by Alexander Youngs Account. I sent a litle Book to you by Dr Thomson for Bishop Synge along with a letter I know not whether you got it or not.—but *go thy ways* Thom, I shall never make a good correspondent of you. I am heartily concerned at the trouble you meet with in your affairs. And am amazed what can be the cause of Alexander Youngs Straits. I long to spend a summer with you & friends in Ireland, what has detained me is Mrs Wilsons family, who don't incline to leave Glasgow till they leave it for Good & all: My wife cannot leave them. Mrs Wilson is a discreet friend, her daughter a very agreable Girl, & her son Joseph is one of my Idols. I never knew a better genius a sweeter temper or more prudence in such years: his body does not belie his Mind. I truly doubt of their going over next summer, but I am intending to be over, tho' I should go alone. We have at last got a Right Professor of Theology, the only thorough right one in Scotland. The numbers of young Divines are not half what they used to be, all over Scotland, and yet we have already more than I ever remember here. The numbers of scholars in the Classes is also smaller, but we have far more than our Share of them & those of a better sort who attend many private Classes. You'll see how we flourish in printing. Old Dunlop the greatest Hero I have known, under two most formidable growing distempers keeps his heart, and teaches with great Reputation & spirit. but I dread we shall soon lose him we have elected his son in place of poor Rabbi Dagesh who died last summer.[229] our most hearty respects to Mrs Drenan Franky continues perfectly well since our highland expedition, & will grow tall in all appearance.

229. Alexander Dunlop the Younger (c. 1717–1750) was appointed to his chair of Oriental languages on October 22, 1744, so the letter postdates that date.

I heartily condoled with you on your loss. I am Dear Thom yours most affectionatly

Franc: Hutcheson

send the two inclosed for Newry by first post.

---

55. To GAVIN HAMILTON[230]

Address: To Baily Gavin Hamilton & the Councill of the City of Edinburgh

Copy: Edinburgh City Archives, Council Records, vol. 65, p. 158 (minutes of April 10, 1745)

Glasgow, April 8th 1745

Sir,

I received Your Letter of the 4th Instant, along with an Extract of the Councills act Electing me professor of morall Philosophy in the university of Edinburgh. I must in the first place return my most humble acknowledgments of Gratitude To the Honourable the Magistrats and Councill of Edinburgh for their kind Intentions, & favourable opinion they are pleas'd to Entertain of Me; And assure them that it is with Sincere regret that I find it Impossible for me to Answer their Expectations; But as I had heard of their design some time agoe, And thus had full Leisure to Consider it I could not keep the Councill any time in suspence, by any expectation of my Acceptance of a Charge which in my present Stage of Life I cannot undertake. I must therefore request it of you to Communicate this Letter to the Councill, to let them know that I cannot undertake the said office; which accordingly I do hereby Decline that they may not be retarded in proceeding to a new Election.

I heartily wish the City good Success in their next Choice, and In all their affairs: And that their university may flourish in all parts of Literature.

I am, Sir,

Your most Obliged and most obedient humble Servant
Francis Hutcheson

---

230. Gavin Hamilton (1704–1767), Edinburgh bookseller and papermaker (*ODNB*).

56. To THOMAS DRENNAN

Address: To the Revd Mr Thomas Drennan at his house in Belfast

MS: GUL, MS Gen. 1018, no. 19

Newry July 19th 1745

Dear Thom

I heartily wish I had seen you after your return. Cousin Bruce & I after turning over your affairs in every shape, could think of Nothing better than what follows, considering the necessity of keeping all Creditors quiet that the Subject may not be consumed by forms of Law.

1. That Charles Johnston have entire possession of the whole Lands of Listuther & Ballydyan & keep down all Interest by paying the several Creditors, and particularly receive all Rents due last May, to this Alexander Young entirely consents. 2. that you receive your self for the future your Rents of the Quarter of Cotton due last May, and chuse any of the Tenants you please till a formal Division be made. 3. That Alexander Young & his wife levy a fine upon the unsetled quarter, and make the same over to Mrs Johnston which stops one preferable Claim for £430. < . . .> that he get any more money he can upon the said quarter to pay off any persons who may be so urgent as to take executions & disturb all our measures. 4. that Alexander Young either put your self or some person you trust in Actual possession of his Share of the Saltworks, & have his name entered as partner in the books of the Company, under this trust that all the annual Profits be applied to discharge the Arrear of Interest due to you: but in case you are paid up three years hence all your Debt, by a sale of his lands, that Alexander Young be reinstated in his Share of the Saltworks. to this he also consented heartily.

Upon the best state we could make there will be due to you of Interest £362, allowing to Alexander Young all the Articles he could mention, such as £70 for Diet & lodging to Mrs Drennan & £18 for your share of Charges of a lawsuit in defence of Cotton: And then you are paid up £160 of your Principal by the Money received for his share of the houses sold. or if you charge this as Interest then there remains all your Principal & £200 of Interest. In plain terms, while Interests are paid by Charles Johnston matters grow no worse & there < . . .> hopes of Justice to Creditors when Lenox comes to Age. But if the Creditors push at present there will be lost in Law 2 or £300 of the Subject besides a new set of involved vexatious suits. You may shew this to Mr Maxwell & Mr young as what seemed to me like result of our Conversations. The making over to you the unsetled Quarter of Cotton would I fear provoke other Creditors with prior judgements & confound all. If Mr Young goes on Candidly in the above scheme I hope you will be safe. If he does not I cannot dissuade you from doing the utmost for your safety, < . . . wi>ll get abundant compensation for his Estate in Listuther &c: if he gets the unsetled Quarter of the Cotton & his own half of it disencumbered of such Leases as his father has a power to make. In the mean time you must see the absolute necessity for the strictest frugality as to your own expences, considering the Dangers attending your Fortune My Most hearty respects to Mrs Drennan & Cn Bruce: who will confirm < . . .>. I am Dr Thom

yours most affectionatly
Francis Hutcheson

< . . . Ar>magh < . . .> to me at Brother Roberts in Newry

Mr Young desires, (what can do you no hurt) that the trustee whose name is in the Books of the salt company should give no declaration of trust, least the share should be attacked by other Creditors. In this case I am persuaded he may trust your self.

---

57. To THOMAS DRENNAN

Address: To the Revd Mr Thomas Drennan at his house in Belfast

MS: GUL, MS Gen. 1018, no. 20

Glasgow March 25. 1746

Dear Thom

I receivd a letter this day from Cousin Alexander Young telling me that his Sister Rhodas attorney had served him with Notice to pay up her portion next moneth, and desiring my interposition for a delay. If Men of Law assure her that her Claim against his lands is good as it must be preferable to all others, I think she should content herself while the Interest is tolerably paid her, & I am sure you agree in this. If her claim upon the lands is not sure I truly know not what to advise, tho' I cannot suspect it otherways, unless by a Plea that her Brother holds them under Campbel Hamilton & not by his fathers Will: This I believe would not do; but no body likes Lawsuits. Nay In that Case he would be Tenant in fee simple and all his lands lyable to every even the latest Bonds, so that I think she may rest satisfied upon receiving her Interest. By one creditors pushing thus all the rest are set upon him, and must destroy a great part of their own subject by the Expences of Executions Any lawyer or Attorney by seeing the Deed declaring the uses of the Fine Levyed by Campbel Hamilton can tell whether it excludes the Legacies or Debts: If the uses or trusts (I know not how they call them) be to Alexander Young his heirs and assigns the lands are lyable to every Legacy & Bond. Mr Maxwell will explain these things better than I can. I hope to see you all next vacation. We have had a dull winter, more so after the departure of the vagabonds than before, as my wife & I have both been tender. but I hope we are recruiting: & so is Jo Wilson who seems recovered, I may say from Death occasioned by an ulcer in his Lungs. The Duke is advancing from Aberdeen to Attack the Rebels, who are to dispute his passage of a very deep River with bad Fords the Spey.[231] If we get more news tomorrow you shall have a postscript Pray let Mr McCartney know that his of the 17th came to hand only this night. to morrow it shall go to Greenock in case the french ship is not arrived, that notice may be sent to our ships of Force on this coast. Our most hearty respects to Mrs Drennan \Cn Rhoda/ Dr Smith & all friends. Pray write me of all your affairs.

I am Dear Thom
yours most sincerly
Franc: Hutcheson

I conclude this notice is only to quicken the payment of Interest. no doubt she should have her Interest constantly paid. I hope Charles Johnston will be empowered to pay it as he gets the rents. Theres no news of Consequence to day. Only the ship Mr McCartney wrote about came in to Clyde, as she said, for tobaccos, where she will get double what she wants.

---

231. The Duke of Cumberland led the British government's army via Banff, Elgin, and Nairn to confront the Jacobite insurrectionist army at Culloden on April 16, 1746, crossing the River Spey on April 12.

58. To THOMAS DRENNAN

Address: To the Revd Mr Thomas Drennan at his house in Belfast

MS: GUL, MS Gen. 1018, no. 21

Glasgow Apr. 16th 1746

Dear Thom

The occasion of this is to certify for the Bearer William Donaldson that he has behaved with great diligence & sobriety during his residence with us, and as far as I could judge by Examinations seemed to have a pretty good apprehension of what I taught. You'll be pleased to let his friends know this good Account I give you; as I cannot find time for all the letters they desire.

Our publick news of the 15th from Edinburgh was that the Duke had passed the Spey, that 2000 Rebels on the Banks fled precipitatly upon his pointing his cannon at them. They may reassemble, & as they are very cunning may yet have some Artifice to surprize. but I cannot but hope that they are dispersing & their cheifs making their Escape. You have heard no doubt of our taking from them the Hazard sloop they had taken at Montrose. She returned from France with 150 men, & Arms & Amunition & had landed them. But Lord Rea very boldly attacked them with a smaller number & took them all prisoners, with £13000 Sterling.[232] The same Man of War took another of their ships with Arms & amunition, which had siezed 12 small merchant Men in Orkneys for their use. The Duke has endeared himself to some of his very Enemies by his good sense & humanity void of all State or pride.

I had this day a letter from a Presbytery of Pensilvania of a very good turn, regreting their want of proper Ministers & Books: expecting some assistance here. it was of a very old date in October last. I shall speak to some Wise men here, but would as soon speak to the Roman conclave as to our Presbytery. The Pensilvanians regret the want of true literature:

---

232. George Mackay of Skibo (c. 1715–1782), younger son of George Mackay, 3rd Lord Reay and a captain in the government army, did his deed at Tongue on March 26, 1746. Angus Mackay, *The Book of Mackay*.

That Whitefield[233] has promoted a contempt of it among his followers, &
bewailing some wretched contentions among themselves. The only help
to be expected from you is sending some wise men if possible. I shall send
them My best advice about Books & Philosophy, & hope to be employed
to buy them Books, cheaper here than they are to be got any where. I long
for a full letter about all your chat & news. I am in a great deal of private
distresses about Jo Wilson & his sister, the later in the utmost danger &
the other scarce recovered from Death, My wife too very tender. I am
intending to take them over if I am[234] alive this summer: but by a set of
most intricate business upon which the soul of this College depends, &
all may be ruined by the want of one Vote, I cannot leave this till after the
26th of June & we go to Dublin first.[235] Our hearty respects to Mrs Drennan & all friends.

I am Dear Thom yours
Franc: Hutcheson

233. George Whitefield (1714–1779), the Methodist preacher, had considerable
and controversial impact during tours of the Colonies in 1739–41 and 1744–48
(*ODNB*).

234. The manuscript has "can."

235. Hutcheson is referring to the election of James Moor as profesor of Greek.
Moor was elected on June 27. See Letter 52 above.

59. To DAVID FORDYCE[236]

Address lacking

Copy: undated excerpt in David Fordyce to George Benson, August 20, 1746: John Rylands University Library, Manchester, UCC B1/13[237]

[spring 1746][238]

I am sensible of Mr B——n's Merit. But some of us who dable in Divinity spare not to declare him unsound; one of our Body, when he was accidentally mentioned in Faculty spoke of him with Abhorrence, as an avowed Socinian.[239] As the Matter of a degree is not worth great Contention, others of us who esteem his Learning would not raise any Flame by moving for a Compliment which many think is a sort of espousing his Principles. Indeed I think, Academic Honours import no such Thing: but this would be matter of high Debate. If your Society are less awake upon such Points, his Learning no doubt deserves that Honour.

236. David Fordyce (1711–1751), MA Marischal College, Aberdeen, 1728; regent at Marischal College from 1742 (*ODNB*). He had visited Glasgow University and attended some of Hutcheson's lectures in 1734–35. See Letter 22 above. He was the author of *Dialogues concerning Education* and of "The Elements of Moral Philosophy," first published anonymously in volume 2 of Dodsley's *Preceptor* (London, 1748), and posthumously republished under the author's name as a book in its own right. Fordyce had been the moving force in securing Benson's DD degree from Marischal College in 1744 and had tried to use Hutcheson's good offices to negotiate a similar honor for him from Glasgow University. Hutcheson's reply, extracted here, is prefaced with the words: "I had wrote Mr Hutcheson of Glasgow about a Diploma from their Society, to which he sent this Answer."

237. For Benson, see Letter 14 above. News of Hutcheson's death on August 8 had apparently not yet reached Fordyce at his home at Eggie, near Aberdeen, at the time of this letter to Benson.

238. Hutcheson's original response is likely to have been dispatched to Fordyce while Hutcheson was still in Glasgow and before he went to Ireland, which we know from Letter 58 was not going to be until at least June 26. Some time after that he went over to Dublin, and died there on August 8.

239. Benson's theology was Arian rather than Socinian. See R. K. Webb in *ODNB*.

Documents Relating to Hutcheson's
Appointment at the University of Glasgow

1. *Faculty Minutes, December 19, 1729*[1]

This being the day appointed for the Election of a person to supply the Vacancy made by Mr Carmichaels death, The principal produced a letter from the Rector[2] dated Edinburgh the 16th instant signifying he was sorry it was not possible he could be present at the Election upon this day and wishing a happy choice for the good of the University:

Then after several of the members had discoursed about a fit person the Question was put Who shall be elected to succeed to the Vacant profession of philosophy, according to the terms of the minut of the 12th instant;[3] And the Clerk having call'd the roll, It was carried by the majority[4] That Mr Francis Hutchinson of Dublin should be Elected to succeed to the said Vacancy, And therefor the Faculty in consideration of the known merit learning and great reputation of the said Mr Hutchinson, and of his other good qualities Did and hereby Do Elect him in the forsaid terms to succeed to the vacant profession of philosophy in this University, And the Faculty appoint a letter to be written by the principal to the Rector to acquaint him with the Election, and another to Mr Hutchinson to inform him of his being Elected and to desire him to come over as soon as possible.

1. Faculty Minutes, 1727–1730: GUA 26635, pp. 146–47.

2. The rector of the University, 1729–31, was Francis Dunlop, laird of Dunlop. A largely absent functionary, he attended only for Hutcheson's inauguration on November 3, 1730 (GUA 26647, p. 21).

3. The decision was taken on December 12 not to make a comparative trial of several candidates, but to elect one prior to trial "to be admitted after Examination & Approbation of him by the faculty" (GUA 26635, p. 143).

4. The vote was seven to five in favor of Hutcheson. See Charles Morthland to Mungo Grahame of Gorthy, October 22, 1729 (NRS, GD220/5/1106/7).

2. *Faculty Minutes, January 22, 1730*[5]

The Principal read a letter he had received from Mr Francis Hutcheson in Dublin, in answer to the letter he had wrote to him Signifying his Election to the Vacancy made by Mr Carmichaels death, wherein Mr Hutcheson after thanking the faculty for the honour they have done him, hopes in a very little time to declare his Acceptance of their kind invitation, but sayes it is not possible he can come over this winter; Upon which the principal proposed to the faculty to consider how the Vacant Class might be effectuallie taught during the remainder of this Session, and after some discourse thereupon the faculty delayed the determination of this affair till Next meeting.[6]

3. *Faculty Minutes, February 20, 1730*[7]

The principal read a letter from Mr Hutcheson dated at Dublin the third of February seventeen hundred & thirty signifying his Acceptance of the facultys invitation and Election of him to succeed to the Vacancy made by Mr Carmichael's death, and desiring he may be alloued to delay his coming over till September Next; The faculty desired the principal might write to him that if he found it inconvenient to come over sooner he might delay coming till the forsaid time.

The faculty Appoints the following Subjects to be given to Mr Hutcheson in order to his making discourses upon them to be delivered in presence of faculty Viz.

In Logick, De Scientia, fide et Opinione inter se collatis.

In Ethicks, An sit una tantum morum lex fundamentalis, Vel si sint plures, quaenam sint?

5. GUA 26635, p. 151.

6. It was subsequently agreed that the professor of ecclesiastical history, William Anderson, should have temporary supervision of the class, with additional stipend, but he would "not be obliged to have any publick praelections during the said time" (GUA 26635, p. 153).

7. GUA 26635, pp. 158–59.

In Physicks, De gravitatione Corporum versus se mutuo.[8]

But the faculty do not think it Necessary to send him these subjects till towards the rising of the College.[9]

4. *Faculty Minutes, November 3, 1730*[10]

This day the Principal reported that Mr Francis Hutcheson formerly Elected Professor of Philosophy had subscribed the Confession of Faith in presence of the presbytery of Glasgow upon the twenty Ninth of last month[11] According to the Act of Parliament thereanent, And this being the time appointed for his admission, the Rector administered to him the Oath de fideli According to the usual form, which he subscribed in the New Register Book.

5. *Minutes of the University Meeting, November 3, 1730*[12]

Coll. Gl. tertio die Novembris An. D. M.DCCXXX.

Quo die in Numerum Magistrorum Academiae Glasguensis cooptatus est Franciscus Hutcheson, qui admissionis suae Sacramentum secundum formulam ab Academiae Moderatoribus praescriptam praestitit ut sequitur

Ego Franciscus Hutcheson cooptatus in numerum Magistrorum Academiae, promitto Sancteque Iuro, me favente Dei gratia, muneris mihi demandati partes, Studiose fideliterque obiturum, et in hujus Academiae rebus ac rationibus gerendis ac procurandis, et commodis ac ornamentis augendis Nihil reliqui ad Summam fidem et diligentiam facturum, Nec ante Sexennium, nisi

---

8. "On knowledge, faith, and opinion, compared with one another." "Whether there is only one fundamental law of nature, or, if there are more, what they are?" "On the mutual gravitation of bodies towards one another."

9. The discourses were delivered on October 20, 1730, "with all of which the faculty unanimously declared they were perfectly well satisfied as convincing proofs of his knowledge in the several parts of philosophy and faculty in teaching the same." They set the date for Hutcheson's inauguration as November 3, and authorized him in the meantime to "begin his teaching of the moral-philosophy Classe" (GUA 26647, p. 21), the existing professors of philosophy having at a specially convened meeting on October 10 waived any claim to that class.

10. GUA 26647, p. 22.

11. The Presbytery minutes for this date are lost.

12. Minutes of the University Meeting, 1730–1749: GUA 26639, p. 5.

impetrata Venia, ab iis quorum interest, Stationem hanc deserturum et omnino non nisi consultis, et ante tres menses praemonitis Academiae Modera-toribus, finito etiam Anni curriculo discessurum.

Franciscus Hutcheson
Rob: Simson Cl: Fac.[13]

13. "At the College of Glasgow, November 3rd, 1730. On this day Francis Hutcheson was appointed by the Masters of the University of Glasgow to be one of their number, and took the oath of admission according to the form prescribed by the governors of the University as follows: 'I, Francis Hutcheson, having been appointed by the Masters of the University of Glasgow to be one of their number, do promise and solemnly swear that, with God's gracious help, I will zealously and faithfully perform the duties of the office entrusted to me, and that I will not fail in any way to show the greatest fidelity and diligence in the affairs of this University, both in fulfill-ing its principles and in advancing its interests and enhancing its lustre. Nor within a period of six years will I relinquish this appointment without first seeking the indul-gence of those whose business it is, and in no circumstances will I leave before con-sulting with the governors of the University, giving three months notice, and completing the courses for the year.' (Signed) Francis Hutcheson; Rob: Simson, Clerk of the Faculty."

Hutcheson's Will

MS (uncertified copy): PRONI, D/971/34/D/1[1]

In the Name of God Amen I Francis Hutcheson one of the Professors[2] in the University of Glasgow North Britain make this my last Will and Testament Committing my soul to the Mercy of God through Jesus Christ and my body to be Interred at the Discretion of my Executors I thus dispose of my Estate Real and Personal First I give and bequeath to my Wife One annuity of twenty pounds Sterling out of the Lands of Ballyhachmer[3] in the Parish of Holywood & County of Down to be paid her at the usual Terms in equal portions Yearly dureing her life as also all the Residue of my Personal Estate after payment of my Debts and Legacies   Item   I give and devise to my Brother Robert Hutcheson in Newry all my Estate and Interest in the Lands of Drumnacross Garrinch & Knock<s>keagh in the Parish of Clonbrony and County of Longford in Ireland under this trust that he Yearly pay to my Wife in two equal portions all the Rents Issues and Profits of the said Lands during her natural life and after her decease under the further trusts hereinafter mentioned And I will and

---

1. This is a folded parchment lacking original signatures and with no physical seal, and was not verified for accuracy. It is endorsed on the back with the date of the original, and there is also a reference to the sum paid for probate (£2 10s. 8d.). These endorsements are dated December 20, 1746, and initialed "A.H.," which may therefore be the date the copy was made or received. Inside the folded document is a signed, authenticated copy of the probate certificate, recording that the original will was proved in Dublin on August 21, 1746, thirteen days after Hutcheson's death, before "Philip Tisdall Esquire Doctor of Laws, Judge or Commissary of His Majesty's Court of Prerogative for Causes Ecclesiastical."

2. Wrongly written "Possessors": the judge's certificate has the correct designation "Professor."

3. Modern Ballyhackamore.

appoint that the above annuities and Legacy be in full Lieu & full Barr of all Jointure Dower or thirds[4] she can any way Claim   Item   I give and devise to my only son Francis Hutcheson that Moyety of the Lands of Drummaleg in the Barony of Castlereagh & County of Down in Ireland which is now in my possession under the Limitations hereinafter mentioned   Item   I give and devise to my said Son Francis my Lands of Ballyhachmer aforesaid (subject to the aforesaid Annuity) with their appurtenances to hold the same during his natural life and as tenant for life only, not impeachable for Waste and after his decease to the first Son of my said Son Francis lawfully to be begotten and to the heirs Male of the body of such first Son And for want of such Issue of his first Son to the Second third fourth fifth and every other Son of my said Son Francis lawfully to be begotten severally and successively and their Issue Male lawfully begotten respectively according as they shall be in Seniority of Age and Priority of Birth And in default of such Issue I devise the same to my said Brother Robert Hutcheson his heirs and Assigns for ever I also empower my said Son Francis to set Leases for thirty one Years or three lives of the said Lands of Ballyhachmer at the best Rent can be had and to settle a Jointure upon the same to any Wife he shall marry not Exceeding Forty pounds Sterling yearly and to charge and encumber the said Lands of Ballyhachmer for the portion or portions of Daughters or Younger Sons with such Sums not exceeding in whole Seven hundred pounds Sterling And as touching the Estate above devised to my Brother Robert in the Lands of Drumnacross Garrinch and Knockskeagh I do hereby declare that it is under the following Trusts that if my son Francis shall at any time within four Years after he attains to the Age of twenty one Years By such Deeds as the Council learned in the Law of my Brother Robert appoint or devise make such a Settlement of that Moyety of Drummalig above devised to him as shall make him my said Son Francis tenant for life only with Remainders over to there first Second third fourth and every other Son of my said Son Francis and their heirs Male severally and successively as in the above entail of the Lands of Ballyhachmer and in default of such Issue to my Brother Robert and his heirs reserving to him my Son Francis like powers of set-

4. The third part of a deceased husband's estate claimable by his widow.

tling Leases at the best Rents that can be had and settling an Annuity of
twenty pounds Sterling Yearly and charging the said Lands with four hundred pounds for the daughters or Younger Sons of the said Francis my son
And if my son Francis shall in like manner concurr at the desire of my
Brother Hans Hutcheson in any Legal Deeds to make a like Settlement of
the other Moyety of Drummalig now <in> possession of my Brother Hans
Subject to all the purposes of my Brother Hans his Marriage Settlement
(so that my son Francis shall be tenant for life only but reserving to him
the same powers of settling Leases of the said last mentioned Moyety & of
Charging the same with the same annual Sum for a Jointure to any Wife
my said Son shall Marry and charging the said last moyety with the same
Sum for portions to Daughters or Younger Children of my said son Francis
as are appointed to be [illegible] the other Moyety (provided the said Moyety <now possessed>[5] by my Brother Hans be discharged of any Burdens
in Consequence of his my Brother Hans's Marriage Settlement) my said
brother Robert shall in that Case make over and Convey the said Lands of
Drumnacross Garrinch & Knockskeagh to my said Son Francis and his
Issue lawfully to be begotten and for default to my Brother Hans during
his natural life and to his Issue lawfully begotten and in default of such
Issue to my Right heirs But if my son Francis refuses to concurr in such
Deeds so to settle the Lands of Dramaleg as aforesaid that then my Brother
Robert shall retain the said Lands of Drumnacross Garrinch & Knock-
skeagh to himself and his heirs and Assigns for ever   Item   I give
and bequeath to my Couzin William Bruce of Dublin One hundred
pounds Sterling to be disposed of among his Friends at his Discretion   Item   I appoint my Executors to employ One hundred pounds
Sterling as they think fit in Educating any of the Grand Children of my
Aunt Wallace   Item   I appoint my Executors to raise one half of
what my Couzin Alexander Young[6] owes me on account and divide the
same at their discretion among the Grand Children of my Aunt Young and
release to the said Alexander Young the Remainder   Item   I appoint

    5. Reading uncertain.
    6. Hutcheson's letters to Drennan in his last years had been much taken up with
his cousin's imminent bankruptcy.

my Executors to pay an Annuity of five pounds Sterling to my Couzin Sarah Wallace during her life   Item   I bequeath to my Four Brothers and my Sister Rhoda twelve pounds each   Item   I bequeath to the University of Glasgow twenty pounds Sterling to be added to the late Primate Bolters foundation[7] and ten pounds to the Towns Hospital in Glasgow Lastly I nominate and appoint my Wife Mary Hutcheson and my two Brothers Hans and Robert Hutcheson the Executors of this my last Will and Testament written with my own hand the Words (at the best Rent can be had) being Interlined in the fifteenth Line, and the Word (Sterling) in the Sixteenth and I declare that all the Sums mentioned are intended in Sterling Money / Signed and Sealed at Glasgow this thirtieth Day of June in the Year of our Lord One thousand Seven hundred & Forty Six Signed Sealed published & Declared before these Witnesses James Moore Library Keeper and Robert and Andrew Foulis Booksellers in the University of Glasgow FRANCIS HUTCHESON (Seal) JA: MOOR Witness ROBERT FOULIS Witness ANDREW FOULIS Witness

7. Hugh Boulter (1672–1742), archbishop of Armagh, had established a trust in 1733, the interest from which was to support poor students from Ireland and England who were attending Glasgow University.

*Public Correspondence
and Occasional Writings*

Letters to *The London Journal,*
1724–25

1.

SATURDAY, *November* 14. 1724.

To the Author of the London Journal.[1]

SIR,

I Send you the inclos'd Paper, containing some Reflections on our common Systems of *Morality,*[2] that if you like the Specimen you may communicate it to the *Publick*; and at the same Time let your *Readers* know, that they may shortly expect *An Essay upon the Foundations of Morality, according to the Principles of the Ancients,*[3] in a Book, entitl'd, *An Enquiry into the Original of our Ideas of* Beauty *and* Virtue. I am

SIR, Your, &c,

PHILANTHROPOS.

1. The "Author" of *The London Journal* (1722–25) was Benjamin Hoadly (1676–1761), who employed the pseudonym "Britannicus." See *The Works of Benjamin Hoadly,* vol. 3, where letters signed Britannicus, September 15, 1722, to January 9, 1724–25 are attributed to Hoadly. See also Francis Hutcheson, *Two Texts on Human Nature,* p. 159.

2. In his reference to "our common Systems of Morality," Hutcheson had principally in mind the works of Samuel Pufendorf, *De Jure Naturae et Gentium* (1672) and *De Officio Hominis et Civis* (1673). On the use of Pufendorf's works in universities and academies in the early eighteenth century, see Timothy J. Hochstrasser, *Natural Law Theories in the Early Enlightenment*; James Moore, "Natural Rights in the Scottish Enlightenment"; and Knud Haakonssen, "Natural Jurisprudence and the Identity of the Scottish Enlightenment."

3. It is instructive that Hutcheson should have described his forthcoming *Inquiry into the Original of Our Ideas of Beauty and Virtue; in Two Treatises* as "An Essay on the Foundations of Morality." This was indeed the theme of the second treatise of the *Inquiry,* as the argument of that work made clear: (1725), pp. 101, 125, 153, 179, etc.; (2008), pp. 85, 101, 118, 136, etc.

Nec furtum feci, nec fugi, si mihi dicat
Servus: Habes pretium; loris non ureris, aio.
Non hominem occidi : non pasces in cruce corvos.
Sum bonus et frugi: Renuit, negat atque Sabellus,
Cautus enim metuit foveam lupus, accipiterque
Suspectos laqueos, & opertum Milvius hamum.
Oderunt peccare boni Virtutis amore;
Tu nihil admittes in te Formidine poenae:
Sit spes fallendi, miscebis sacra profanis.
—Hor. Lib, I. Epist. 16.[4]

A Very small Acquaintance in the World may probably let us see, that we are not always to expect the greatest *Honour* or *Virtue* from those who have been most conversant in our *Modern Schemes* of *Morals.* Nay, on the contrary, we may often find many, who have, with great Attention and Penetration, employ'd themselves in these Studies, as capable of a *cruel,* or an *ungrateful* Action, as any other Persons: We shall often see them as backward to any thing that is *generous, kind, compassionate;* as *careless* of the Interest of their *Country*; as *sparing* of any Expence, and as *averse* to undergo any Danger for its Defence, as those who have never made the *Law of Nature* their Study: Nay, we shall often find them plentifully stor'd with nice Distinctions, to evade their Duty when it grows troublesome, and with subtle Defences of some *base* Practices, in which many an *undisciplin'd Mind* wou'd scorn to have been concern'd.

Nor shall we observe any singular Advantages arising from their Studies, in the Conduct of themselves, or in the State of their *Minds.* We may often find them *sour* and *morose* in their Deportment, either in their Fam-

---

4. "If a slave were to say to me, 'I never stole or ran away': my reply would be, 'you have your reward; you are not flogged.' 'I never killed anyone': 'You'll hang on no cross to feed crows.' 'I am good and honest': Our Sabine friend shakes his head and says, 'No, no!' For the wolf is wary and dreads the pit, the hawk the suspected snare, the pike the covered hook. The good hate vice because they love virtue; you will commit no crime because you dread punishment. Suppose there's a hope of escaping detection; you will make no difference between sacred and profane" (Horace, *Epistles,* I.xvi.46–54, in *Satires, Epistles and Ars Poetica*). The first four lines of this epistle had been quoted to the same effect by Shaftesbury, in "Sensus Communis," part 3, sec. 4, in *Characteristics*, p. 59.

ilies, or among their Acquaintances; they shall be *easily put out of Humour* by every trifling Accident; soon *dejected* with common Calamities, and *insolent* upon any prosperous Change of Fortune. Are all the Efforts of humane Wisdom, in an Age which we think wonderfully improv'd, so entirely in- |effectual in that Affair, which is of the greatest Importance to the Happiness of Mankind? Shall we lay it all upon a *Natural Corruption* in us, growing stronger, the more Opposition it meets with? Or may we not rather suspect, that there must be some *Mistakes* in the leading Principles of the Science; some *wrong Steps* taken in our Instruction, which make it so ineffectual for the End it professes to pursue?

All Virtue is allow'd to consist *in Affections of Love toward the Deity, and our Fellow Creatures, and in Actions suitable to these Affections.*[5] Hence we may conclude, 1st, "That whatever *Scheme of Principles* shall be most effectual to excite *these Affections,* the same must be the *truest Foundation of all Virtue.* And, 2dly, Whatever *Rules of Conduct* shall lead us into a Course of Actions acceptable to the *Deity,* and most beneficial to *Mankind,* they must be the *true Precepts of Morality.*" We shall enquire into these two Heads more distinctly.

Our *Affections* toward rational Agents seem generally incapable of being engaged by any Considerations of *Interest. Interest* may engage us to external good *Offices,* or to Dissimulation of *Love,* but the only thing which can really excite either *Love,* or any other *Affection,* toward rational Agents, must be an Apprehension of such *Moral Qualifications,* or *Abilities,* as are, by the *Frame* of our *Nature,* apt to move such *Affections* in us. How ridiculous would it be to attempt, by all the Rewards or Threatenings in the World, to make one *love* a Person, whom he apprehended to be *Cruel, Selfish, Morose* or *Ungrateful*; or to make us *hate* a Person, whom we imagine *Kind, Friendly* and *Good natured*? Some Qualities of Mind necessarily raise *Love* in every considering Spectator, and their Contraries

---

5. The notion that all virtue consists "in Affections of Love towards the Deity, and our Fellow Creatures" is found in the Gospels: Matthew 22:37–39 and Luke 10:27–28. It was also characteristic of the moral philosophy of the Stoics as Hutcheson understood them: see "Maxims of the Stoics," collected by Thomas Gataker and appended to *The Meditations of the Emperor Marcus Aurelius Antoninus,* trans. Francis Hutcheson and James Moor (1742), pp. 296–303; (2008), 155–59.

Hatred; and where these Qualities don't appear, we in vain attempt to purchase either *Love* or *Hatred*, or expect to threaten Men into either of them. And this is the Reason of what a very ingenious *Writer*[6] justly observes, *viz.* That Men's Practices are very little influenced by their *Principles*. The Principles he means, are those which move Men to *Virtue* from Considerations of *Interest*.

Now let us observe how our *Moralists* inculcate these great Foundations of all *Virtue*, the *Love of God*, and of our *Neighbour*. One of the great Authors of Morality [Puffendorf] reasons thus, as one wou'd be led to imagine, from the chief Argument he pursues: "All our worldly Happiness depends upon Society, which cannot be preserved without sociable Dispositions in Men toward each other, and a strict Observation of any Rules adapted to promote the Good of Society. Nothing is looked upon as more effectual for this End, than the Belief of a *Deity*, the *Witness* and *Judge* of human Actions; and therefore, as we expect to promote our civil *Interest*, we shou'd believe in a *Deity*, and worship him with *Love* and *Reverence*."[7] As to the Belief of a *Deity*, that *Author* does indeed suggest other Arguments for it than this, *that it is necessary to support Society, therefore it is true.* And by suggesting other Grounds and Motives to love him, in different Places of his Works, he seem'd sensible of the Deficiency of his grand Argument; for, it is certain, that <2>Views of worldly *Interest* are as unfit to beget *Love* and *Reverence* in our Hearts, as to form Opinions or Belief in our Understandings however, they may procure Obsequiousness in our outward Deportment, and Dissimulation of our Opinions.

6. Thomas Mautner suggested, in Hutcheson, *On Human Nature*, p. 43, that the "very ingenious writer" was Pierre Bayle. In *Pensées diverses sur la comète* (1680), sec. CLXXVI (*Miscellaneous Reflections Occasion'd by the Comet*, p. 361, Bayle remarked that man is "that kind of Creature, who, with all his boasted Reason, never acts by the Principles of his Belief." It may seem controversial that Hutcheson would describe as "very ingenious" a skeptic whose ideas on other subjects he would dismiss in his later writings. But Hutcheson did not hesitate to describe as ingenious other writers with whom he disagreed: e.g., Archibald Campbell and Bernard Mandeville, in his inaugural lecture: "Mirum in modum ingeniosi adversarii," *De Naturali Hominum Socialitate* (1730), p. 19. And he may have known, through his friendship with Robert Molesworth, of Shaftesbury's great esteem for Bayle as a philosopher and as a friend.

7. Pufendorf, *The Whole Duty of Man*, book 1, chap. 3, secs. 9–12, pp. 56–60.

The greater Part of *Moralists* are indeed asham'd of this Scheme; but how do they mend it? "They first give us rational Arguments for the Existence and Power of the *Deity*, and his Government of the Universe: He is represented as fond of Glory, jealous of Honour, sudden in Resentment of Affronts, and resolute in punishing every Transgression of his Laws: His *natural Laws* are whatever Conclusions he has made us capable of drawing from the Constitution of *Nature,* concerning the Tendency of our Actions to the *Publick Good.*"[8]

The better sort of our latter *Moralists* always attempt to prove "his good Intentions toward the Happiness of Mankind; and hence infer, that if we co-operate with his Intentions, we may expect his Favour; and if we counter-act them, we must feel the severest Effects of his Displeasure." Now it must be own'd, that Writers on this *last Scheme* do really suggest one good Motive to *Religion* and *Virtue,* by representing, the *Deity* as *Good,* but upon this they dwell no longer than is necessary to finish a Metaphysical Argument; they hurry over their Premises, being impatient till they arrive at this Conclusion, *That the Deity will interest his Power for the Good of Mankind,* that thus they may get into their Favourite *Topicks* of *Bribes* and *Terrors,* to compel Men to love *God* and *one another,* in order to obtain the Pleasures of *Heaven*, and avoid *Eternal Damnation.*[9] But what kind of *Love* can be excited by such *Motives?* In humane Affairs we shou'd certainly suspect whatever was procur'd merely by such Means, to be little better than *Hypocrisy.*

With how much more Ease and Pleasure wou'd an ingenuous Mind be led, by the very *Frame of its Nature,* to love the *Deity,* were he represented "as the Universal Father of *All*, with a boundless Goodness consulting the Interests of *All* in the most regular and impartial Manner; and that of

8. Hutcheson may have had in mind the Supplements appended to Pufendorf's *De Officio Hominis et Civis,* by Gershom Carmichael (Edinburgh, 2nd ed., 1724). See *Natural Rights on the Threshold of the Scottish Enlightenment,* chaps. 2 and 5, pp. 21–29 and 46–53.

9. Richard Cumberland, like Carmichael, would have qualified in Hutcheson's mind as one of "the better sort of our latter Moralists." See *A Treatise of the Law of Nature,* chap. 5, pp. 495ff.

each *Individual*, as far as 'tis consistent with the Good of the *Whole*. Did we set before Men's View, as far as we can, the wise Order of *Nature*, so artfully adapted to make Men happy: Did we let them see what Variety of Pleasures *God* has made us capable of enjoying by our *Senses*, by our *Understandings*, by our *generous Instincts* toward *Friendships, Societies, Families*: Did they apprehend the Necessity of subjecting human *Nature* to the *Friendly Admonitions* of sensible *Pain* and *Compassion*, to excite us to preserve our selves, and those who are dear to us; nay, to preserve the most indifferent Persons in the World: Cou'd we enlarge Men's Views beyond themselves, and make 'em consider the whole *Families* of *Heaven* and *Earth*, which are supported by the indulgent Care of this *Universal Parent*; we shou'd find little need of other sort of Arguments to engage an unprejudiced Mind to love a *Being* of such extensive *Goodness*."

To be concluded in our next.

2.

SATURDAY, *November* 21. 1724.

The Conclusion of the former Paper.

As to our *Fellow-Creatures,* it is much more difficult to give a tolerably engaging Representation of them. Every Body is furnish'd with a thousand Observations about their Wickedness and Corruption; so that to offer any thing in their behalf, may make a Man pass for one utterly unacquainted with the World. And yet without giving better Representations of them, than our Systems of *Morality* do, we may bid farewell to all Esteem of, or Complacence in, Mankind: For tho' a strong *Humanity* of Temper may entertain Compassion and good Wishes toward such an abandon'd *Crew*, yet these Wishes must be very joyless, despondent, and weak, if Men are really as bad as they are represented. Many of our *Moralists*, after Mr. *Hobbs*, are generally very eloquent on this Head. "They tell us, that Men are to each other what *Wolves are to Sheep*; that they are all *injurious, proud, selfish, treacherous, covetous, lustful,* revengeful:[10] Nay, the avoiding the Mischiefs to be fear'd from each other, is the very Ground of their Combinations into *Society*, and the sole Motive in this Life of any external good Offices which they are to perform." We scarce ever hear any thing from them of the *bright Side* of *Humane Nature.* They never talk of any kind *Instincts to associate*; of *natural Affections*, of *Compassion*, of *Love of Company*, a *Sense of Gratitude*, a *Determination* to honour and love the Authors of any good Offices toward any Part of Mankind, as well as of those toward our selves; and of a *natural Delight* Men take in being esteem'd and honour'd by others for good Actions: which yet all may be observ'd to prevail exceedingly in *humane Life.*

Cou'd we lay aside the Prepossessions of our Systems a little, and some of their* *Axioms,* (better suited to an omniscient *Being,* than to poor Mortals,) we shou'd find, "That every Action is *amiable* and *virtuous*, as far as it evidences a Study of the Good of others, and a real Delight in their Happiness: That innocent *Self-Love,* and the Actions flowing from it, are *indifferent:* And that nothing is *Detestably wicked*, but either a direct Study and Intention of the Misery of others, without any further View; or else such an entire Extinction of the *kind Affections*, as makes us wholly indifferent and careless how pernicious our selfish Pursuits may be to others." In this Light it wou'd appear indeed, that there are many Weaknesses in *Humane Nature*: We shou'd find *Self-Love* apt to grow too strong by bad Habits, and overcoming the *kind Affections* in their more remote Attachments; we shou'd find too much Rashness in receiving bad Notions, concerning Those whose Interests are opposite to our own, as if they were Men so opposite to the *Publick Good*, that it were a good Deed

10. Hobbes, *Leviathan,* chapter 13. Hutcheson would offer a similar paraphrase of Hobbes's description of the natural condition of mankind in his inaugural lecture *On the Natural Sociability of Mankind* (1730). See *Logic, Metaphysics and the Natural Sociability of Mankind*, pp. 198–99.

* *Bonum ex integra Causa: Malum ex quolibet Defectu.* ["The good derives from a cause that is entire or complete, evil from any deficiency whatsoever."] This maxim appears frequently in the writings of St. Thomas Aquinas, e.g., *Summa Theologiae*, 2.1. Question 18, article 4, and is consistent with the ethics of scholastic moralists who held that the good can be discovered only in perfect happiness or beatitude. See below, note 15.

to |suppress them. But for this goodly Effect we are often indebted to *Education*, and to many a grave Lesson which *Nature* wou'd never have taught us. We shou'd find Men sudden and keen in forming their *Parties* and *Cabals*, and so fond of them, that they overlook the Inhumanity towards others which may appear in the Means used to promote the Interests of the espoused *Faction*.[11] And yet notwithstanding all this, we shall find one of the greatest Springs of their Actions to be *Love* toward others. We shall find strong *natural Affections, Friendships, National Love, Gratitude*; scarce any Footsteps of *disinterested Malice*, or study of Mischief, where there is no Opposition of *Interests*, a strong *Delight* in being honour'd by others for kind Actions; a tender *Compassion* towards any grievous Distress; a *Determination* to love and admire every thing which is good-natur'd and kind in others, and to be highly delighted in reflecting on such Actions of their own: And on the other hand, a like *Determination* to abhor every thing cruel or unkind in others, and to sink into Shame upon having done such Actions themselves. We shall see a Creature, to whom mutual *Love* and *Society* with its Fellows is its chief Delight, and as necessary as the Air it breathes; and the *universal Hatred* of its Fellows, or the want of all *kind Affections* toward others in it self, is a State worse than Death. In short, we shall see in *Humane Nature* very few Objects of *absolute Hatred*, many Objects of high *Esteem* and *Love*, and most of all of a Mixture of *Love* and *Pity*. Their Intention, even when their Actions are justly blameable, is scarcely ever *malicious*, unless upon some sudden transitory Passion, which is frequently innocent, but most commonly honourable or kind, however imperfectly they judge of the Means to execute it.

As to the Method these *Moralists* take to make us love our Neighbours, I doubt much if ever the *Hopes* or *Terrors* of Laws wou'd have produc'd those *noble Dispositions*, of which we have had many Instances in *Patriots*, Friends and Acquaintances. With what an ungainly Aire wou'd a good Office appear from one, who profess'd, that he did not do it out of Love

11. Hutcheson elaborated on the theme that parties, cabals, and factions are generally productive of conflict and malice in the second edition of the *Inquiry* (1726), sec. 4, art. 4 IV (2008), pp. 142–43.

to us, but for his own Interest in Civil Life, or to avoid Damnation! How fruitful should we find *Humane Nature* in Distinctions, and Subterfuges, to avoid any laborious, expensive, or perilous Services to their Country? Were *Interest* the only Spring of such Actions, a selfish Temper, before it wou'd act, wou'd state an Account with *Virtue* to compare her *Debt* and *Credit*, and be determin'd to Action or Omission, according as the Balance favour'd her or not. A superstitious Temper might be terrify'd by *Religion*, to submit to the hard Terms of a generous or publick spirited Action, to avoid *Damnation*, and procure *Heaven* to itself; but upon Motives of *Interest*, we shou'd never find a Man who cou'd entertain such a Thought as *Dulce & Decorum est pro Patria mori*.[12]

Were Men once posses'd with just Notions of *Humane Nature;* had they lively Sentiments of the *natural Affections* and *kind Passions,* which it is not only capable of, but actually influenc'd by, in the greatest Part of its Actions; did Men reflect, that almost every Mortal has his own dear Relations, Friends, Acquaintances; did we consider all the good-natur'd kind Solicitudes which they have for each other; did we see the vast Importance of *Laws, Constitu<2>tions, Rights* and *Privileges;* and how necessary they are to preserve such vast Multitudes as form any *State* in a tolerable Degree of Happiness, and in any Capacity to execute their kind Intentions mutually with any Security: Did Men understand the Distress, the Dejection of Spirit, the Diffidence in all kind Attempts, and the Uncertainty of every Possession under a *Tyrant;* these Thoughts wou'd rouse Men into another kind of *Love* to their *Country*, and *Resolution* in its *Defence*, than the mere Considerations of *Terror* either in this World or in the next.

Again, in the more private Offices of *Virtue*, it is generally *Compassion* to visible Distress, assisted by *Gratitude* to *God and our Redeemer*, which moves the *Religious* to Charity; and the *Bulk* of Mankind are most powerfully moved by some apparent virtuous Dispositions in the miserable Object along with the Distress. The poor Creatures we meet in the Streets, seem to know the Avenues to the humane Breast better than our *Philosophers*: They never tell us we shall be *damned* if we don't relieve them. The

---

12. "Sweet and proper it is to die for one's country" (Horace, *The Odes*, 3.2.13); cited also by Shaftesbury, "Sensus Communis," part 2, sec. 3, in *Characteristics*, p. 48.

old Cant, *God will reward you*, is of no great Force: *A Wife and many small Children*, when we know they speak Truth, has much more Influence. A visible Distress, a Shame to be troublesome, an ingenuous Modesty, with an Aversion to discover their Straits, if we imagine them sincere, do seldom fail of Success. We see then that *Gratitude, Compassion*, and the Appearance of *virtuous Dispositions*, do move us most effectually: And how little many of our *Moralists* employ of their Labours, in giving us such Representations or *Motives*, every one sees who is not a Stranger to their Writings.

What is here said does no way imply, that the Considerations of *Rewards* and *Punishments* are useless: They are the only, or best Means of recovering a Temper wholly vitiated, and of altering a corrupted *Taste* of Life, of re-straining the *selfish Passions* when too strong, and of turning them to the Side of *Virtue*; and of rousing us to Attention and Consideration, that we may not be led into wrong Measures of Good from partial Views, or too strong Attachments to Parties. But still there must be much more to form a *truly great and good Man*.

The second Subject, was to consider the *Rules of Conduct* laid down by *Moralists* as to particular *Duties* of Life. As for our *Duty* to the *Deity*, we are recommended to other Instructors:[13] The *Moralists* treat this Subject very superficially.

As to our *Duties* to our selves, they give us many Directions to restrain our *Passions*. "We are told that they hurry us into Violations of *Laws*, and expose us to their *Penalties*; that many of these *Passions* are immediately uneasy and tormenting, even in their own *Nature*."[14] These are no doubt just Conclusions from *Reason* and Experience. But then a *Passion* is not always flexible by Reasons of *Interest*. A Man in deep *Sorrow* will not be immediately easy, upon your demonstrating that his *Sorrow* can be of no Advantage to him, but is certainly pernicious. *Anger, Jealousy, Fear*, and

13. In Pufendorf's *The Whole Duty of Man*, book 1, chap. 4, p. 60n Barbeyrac di-rects the reader to Jean LeClerc's *Pneumatologia*, sec. 3, and to the fourth discourse of *Selecta Jura Naturae et Gentium de Pietate Philosophica* by Gulielmus Budaeus, enti-tled *de Pietate Philosophica*.

14. See *The Whole Duty of Man*, book 1, chap. 5, sec. 8, pp. 77–78 for Pufendorf's list of the passions that must be controlled by the mind.

most other *Passions*, are not suppressed by proving that we are the worse for them. The only way to remove them, is to give *just Ideas* of their Objects. Shew to a *sorrowful, dejected Mind*, that its State may still be happy: Let it see that its Loss is repairable, or that it has still an Opportunity of valuable Enjoyments in Life: If it mourns the Loss of a *Friend*, let it see that *Death* is no great Evil; and let other *Friendships* and *kind Affections* be raised, and this will more easily remove the *Sorrow*. Let the *wrathful Man* see that the resented Actions have been only the Effects of *Inadvertency* or *Weakness*, or, at worst, of strong *Self-Love*; and not of *deliberate Malice*, or a *Design to affront*; and he will find few Occasions for his *Passion*, when he's convinc'd that he has not to do with *Devils*, who delight in Mischief, but with *good-natured, tho' weak and fallible Men*. Let the *Coward* see, that the prolonging Life which must soon end, is but a sorry Purchase, when made by the Loss of *Liberty, Friendship, Honour* and *Esteem*. The *Covetous* and *Ambitious* must surely feel the Uneasiness of their *Passions*, and yet they still continue *Slaves* to them, till once you convince them, that the Enjoyments of the *highest Stations* and Fortunes, are very little above those which may be obtain'd in very moderate Circumstances. Unless *just Representations* be given of the Objects of our *Passions*, all external Arguments will be but Rowing *against the Stream*; an endless Labour, while the *Passions* themselves do not take a more reasonable Turn, upon juster Apprehensions of the Affairs about which they are employed.

The *School-men* in their *Morals,* by their Debates about the *Summum Bonum*, wou'd make one expect just Representations of all the Objects which solicit our *Affections*; but they flew so high, immediately to the *Beatifick Vision and Fruition*, and so lightly passed over, with some trite com |mon-place Remarks, all ordinary human Affairs, that one must be well advanced in a *visionary Temper* to be profited by *Them*.[15] They seldom mention the Delights of *Humanity, Good-nature, Kindness, Mutual Love, Friendships, Societies of virtuous Persons*. They scarce ever spend a

15. For the scholastic distinction between beatific vision and fruition, see Eustachius, *Ethica, sive summa moralis disciplinae*, pp. 20–27, and Carmichael, *Natural Rights*, pp. xii, 11n.8, and 23n.7. Hutcheson continued to employ the distinction between formal and objective beatitude in *Philosophiae moralis*, pp. 65–66, and *A Short Introduction to Moral Philosophy* (1747), pp. 59–60; (2007), pp. 66–67.

Word upon the earthly Subjects of *laborious Diligence in some honest Employment*; which yet we see to be the *ordinary Step*; by which we mount into a *Capacity of doing Offices*: And hence it is, that we find more virtuous Actions in the Life of one *diligent good-natur'd Trader*, than in a whole *Sect* of such speculative *Pretenders to Wisdom*.

The later *Moralists*, observing the Trifling of the *School-men*, have very much left out of their *Systems*, all Enquiries into Happiness, and speak only of the external Advantages of *Peace and Wealth* in the Societies where we live. But this is, no doubt, a great Omission, since amidst *Peace and Wealth*, there may be *Sullenness, Discontent, Fretfulness*, and *all the Miseries of Poverty*.

As to our *Duty toward others*, our later *Moralists* hurry over all other Things till they come to the Doctrine of *Rights*, and *Proper Injuries*; and like the *Civilians*, whose only Business it is to teach how far *refractory or knavish Men* shou'd be compell'd by Force, *they* spend all their Reasonings upon *Perfect* or *External Rights*.[16] We never hear a *generous Sentiment* from them any further. "Some *borrow'd Goods*, for instance, perish by an *Accident*, which wou'd not have befallen them with the *Proprietor*. This *Accident* is no way chargeable upon any *Negligence in the Borrower*. Who shall bear the Loss? *A generous Lender* wou'd think with himself, Am I far wealthier than the *Borrower*? I can more easily bear the Loss. The *Borrower*, in like case of superior Wealth, wou'd reason the same way. If their Wealth was equal, each wou'd bear his Share; or an *honest Neighbour*, if the Loan was *gratuitous*, would scorn to let any Man repent of his having done him a Kindness." But *Thoughts of this* kind never come into the Heads of many of these *Moralists*. *Mankind are*, with them, *all resty Villains*: Our only Inquiry is, which Side will it be most convenient to compel? This Question is indeed very necessary too, because there are bad Men who need *Compulsion to their* Duty. But may not better Sentiments prevail with a great many? All Men are not *incorrigible Villains*. There are

---

16. In the *Inquiry* Hutcheson argued that although only perfect and external rights can be enforced, there is more virtue in the recognition of the imperfect right of another to one's benevolence even though such a right cannot be enforced: (1725), sec. 7, arts. 4 and 7 (arts. 6 and 9 in 2nd ed.); (2008), pp. 183–86 and 189–91.

still a great many who can be mov'd with Sentiments of *Honour* and *Humanity*.

Shou'd we run over other Matters of *Right*, we shall find them treated in the same manner. Seldom ever a *generous, or manly Sentiment*. We only see how far in many Cases the *Civil Peace* requires that we shou'd force Men to Action: And we see, at the same time, how far we may play the Villain *with Impunity*, when we can evade their *great Foundation of Virtue*, viz. *the Force of a Penalty*. In short, according to the *Motto* prefix'd to this *Essay*, "*The avoiding the Prison or the Gallows, appears a sufficient Reward for the Virtue which many of our Systems seem to inspire.*"

PHILANTHROPOS.

3.

Saturday, *March* 27, 1725

To *BRITANNICUS*.[17]

SIR,

I think that No *Attempt* to recommend *Virtue* to the World, and especially to the *Highest* Part of it, upon whose Example and Influence so

17. This was the seventh letter from Philopatris to Britannicus published in *The London Journal* in January, February, and March 1725. Philopatris was an Englishman newly arrived in Ireland. It is highly probable that Philopatris was Hugh Boulter (1672–1742), bishop of Bristol. He left England for Ireland with his secretary, Ambrose Philips, in November 1724 to take up an appointment as archbishop of Armagh and primate of all Ireland. Boulter had collaborated with Richard West (1691–1726), who was appointed lord chancellor of Ireland in 1725, and Gilbert Burnet (1690–1726) in writing essays for *The Free-thinker,* edited by Ambrose Philips in 1719–20. The themes addressed by Boulter in his essays for *The Free-thinker* are similar to concerns expressed by Philopatris: contempt for Popery; friendship with Presbyterians, who differ "from us only in some Outward Forms and modes"; and an appreciation of philosophy and religion as they were understood by "the finest Gentlemen among the Ancients." William Leechman remarked that while Hutcheson lived in Ireland, he enjoyed "a large share in the esteem of the late Primate Bolter" and that he "lived in great intimacy with Richard West" (Preface to Francis Hutcheson, *A System of Moral Philosophy*, p. ix).

much of the Virtue of the *Lower Rank* of Men depends, when this *Attempt* is prosecuted in an agreeable engaging Manner, should pass without the Regard and Notice due to it. This makes Me beg leave to mention to You, and (if You please) to the World, a *New Treatise*, intituled, *An* Inquiry *into the* Original *of our* Ideas *of* Beauty *and* Virtue. The great View of the Book is best express'd in the *Author's* own Words, *Pref.* p. vi. where He tells us—"His principal Design is to shew, That *Human Nature* was not left quite indifferent in the Affair of *Virtue*, to form to itself Observations concerning the *Advantage* or *Disadvantage* of Actions, and accordingly to regulate its Conduct." After having observ'd from the unavoidable Circumstances of Human Nature, that "Few of Mankind could have form'd those long Deductions of *Reason*[18] which may shew some Actions to be in the whole *Advantageous* to the *Agent*, and their contrary *Pernicious*"; He adds, "The AUTHOR of *Nature* has much better furnished us for a *virtuous Conduct,* than our *Moralists* seem to imagine, by almost as quick and powerful Instructions, as We have for the Preservation of our Bodies.—*He* has made *Virtue* a *Lovely Form*, to excite our Pursuit of it; and has given us *strong Affections* to be the Springs of each virtuous Action." The *Writer* would willingly raise in Mankind "a *Relish* for a *Beauty* in *Characters,* in *Manners,*" as well as in other Things. And this He concludes with a *Reflection*, which I own was what moved Me to look into the Book, and to give You the present Trouble. "I doubt, (*says He,*) We have made *Philosophy,* as well as *Religion,* by our foolish Management of it, so austere and ungainly a Form, that a Gentleman cannot easily bring Himself to like it; and Those who are Strangers to it, can scarcely bear our Description of it: So much is it changed from what was once the Delight of the *Finest Gentlemen* among the *Antients*; and their *Recreation*, after the Hurry of

---

18. Hutcheson's diffidence about the capacity of mankind to engage in "long Deductions of Reason" in the ordinary course of moral and social life (*Inquiry*, 1725, pp. vi–vii, 115, 143; 2008, pp. 9, 94, 112) was shared by Boulter: "It will not be to my purpose to enter into abstracted Notions, or metaphysical Definitions . . . all Knowledge more immediately useful to Society, may with a little Pains be brought down to *Common Sense. . . .*" *The Free-Thinker*, vol. 1, no. 14, p. 60 (London, 1722). The attribution of no. 14 to Boulter is provided in no. 55 of the 1740 edition (the 3rd edition) of *The Free-Thinker*.

Publick Affairs!"[19] One would hope, such a *Reproof* as This, may not fall to the Ground without Use; not only as it is levell'd at some *Writers* of *Morals*, but as it ends with a *Satire* upon the *Indolence* and *Unconcern* about a *Matter* of the greatest Importance, too visible in that Part of the World, who have so much *Leisure* that their *Time* is a Burthen to them; and who yet waste so much of it in the Pursuit of the most Unmanly Relishes, that hardly a Moment is left for the supreme Relish of *Human Nature* in its most exalted State. If I could excite their Curiosity, to enter into such *Subjects*; whether They found entire Satis|faction in the *Scheme* of this *Author*, or not; yet They would find a noble Entertainment for an Inquisitive Mind, mixed with a very agreeable and uncommon Delicacy of Thought; which must at length lead them to what will be the *Ornament* as well as Happiness of their Lives.

I shall only point out *One* Part of the *Book*, which may give an *Idea* of the *Whole*; and that is, the *Second Section* of the *Second Treatise*, p. 125.[20] *Concerning the* Immediate Motive *to* virtuous Actions. Here the *Author's* main and favourite Notions may appear from the following Propositions. "1. Every Action, which we apprehend as either *morally good* or *evil*, is always supposed to flow from *some Affection* toward *rational Agents*; and whatever we call *Virtue* or *Vice*, is either some such *Affection*, or some *Action* consequent upon it. Or it may perhaps be enough to make an Action, or Omission, appear *vitious*, if it argues the Want of such Affection toward rational Agents, as we expect in Characters counted *morally good*. 2. None of these Affections which we call *Virtuous,* do spring from *Self-love,* or Desire of *private Interest;* since all *Virtue,* is either some such *Affections,* or *Actions* consequent upon them; from whence it necessarily follows, That *Virtue* is not pursu'd from the *Interest* or *Self-love* of the *Pursuer,* or any Motives of his own Advantage." For the Proof of this, He instances in the Two Affections, which are of most Importance in *Morals*, Love and

---

19. *Inquiry* (1725), p. vii; (2008), pp. 9–10. Boulter also admired the "warm Expressions, and rapturous Sentences, scattered through the Writings of the Ancient Philosophers in Praise of Truth" and thought that from those writings he "could furnish out a Paper might justly put Numbers of Christians to the Blush" (*The Free-Thinker*, vol. 1, no. 10, pp. 68–69).

20. *Inquiry* (1725), p. 125; (2008), p. 101.

HATRED. As to the *Love,* call'd the *Love* of *Complacence,* or *Esteem*; This, He says, appears at first View *disinterested,* and so its *contrary;* i.e. *entirely excited by some Moral Qualities,* Good *or* Evil, *apprehended to be in the* Objects, *&c.* "As to the *Love* of *Benevolence,* [He goes on in a Manner worth transcribing, p. 129.] the very Name excludes *Self Interest.* We never call that Man *Benevolent,* who is in fact useful to others, but at the same time only intends his *own Interest,* without any desire, of or delight in, the *Good* of *others.* If there be any *Benevolence* at all, it must be *disinterested*; for the most useful Action imaginable, loses all Appearance of *Benevolence,* as soon as we discern that it only flowed from *Self-love* or *Interest.* Thus, never were any human Actions more *advantageous,* than the Inventions of *Fire,* and *Iron*; but if these were casual, or if the *Inventor* only intended his *own Interest* in them, there is nothing which can be call'd *Benevolent* in them. Wherever then *Benevolence* is suppos'd, there it is imagin'd *disinterested,* and design'd for the *Good* of others. But it must be here observ'd, That as all Men have *Self-love,* as well as *Benevolence,* these two Principles may jointly excite a Man to the same Action; and then they are to be consider'd as two Forces impelling the same Body to Motion; sometimes they conspire, sometimes are indifferent to each other, and sometimes are in some degree opposite. Thus, if a Man have such strong *Benevolence,* as would have produc'd an Action without any Views of *Self-Interest*: that such a Man has also in View *private Advantage,* along with *publick Good,* as the Effect of his Action, does no way diminish the *Benevolence* of the Action. When he would not have produc'd so much *publick Good,* had it not been for Pro<2>spects of *Self-Interest*; then the Effect of *Self-Love* is to be deducted, and his *Benevolence* is proportion'd to the remainder of *Good,* which pure *Benevolence* would have produc'd. When a Man's *Benevolence* is hurtful to himself, then *Self-Love* is opposite to *Benevolence,* and the *Benevolence* is proportion'd to the Sum of the *Good* produc'd, and the Resistance of *Self-Love* surmounted by it. In most Cases it is impossible for Men to know how far their Fellows are influenc'd by the one or other of these Principles; but yet the general Truth is sufficiently certain, That this is the Way in which the *Benevolence* of Actions is to be computed. If any enquire, Whence arises this *Love* of *Esteem,* or *Benevolence,* to good Men, or to Mankind in general; if not from some nice

Views of *Self-Interest*? Or, how we can be mov'd to desire the Happiness of *others,* without any View to our *own*? It may be answer'd, That the *same Cause* which determines us to pursue Happiness for our selves, determines us both to *Esteem* and *Benevolence* on their proper Occasions; even the very *Frame* of our *Nature,* or a *generous Instinct,* which shall be afterwards explain'd." [21]

YOU see the *Author* does not exclude the Pursuit of *our own* Happiness; but is labouring to found *Virtue* upon something more *divine,* and exalted, than *Self-love.* He then proceeds to "other *Affections,* as *Fear,* or *Reverence,* arising from an Apprehension of *Goodness, Power* and *Justice*"— and then goes on to answer the principal Objections against his Notion. After which He concludes the Argument with an ingenious Thought about the *Foundation* of what we call *National Love,* or the *Love* of our *Native Country.* "Whatever Place, (*says He,* p. 147.) [22] we have lived in for any considerable Time, there we have most distinctly remarked the *various Affections* of *human Nature*; we have known many *lovely Characters*; we remember the *Associations, Friendships, Familys, natural Affections,* and other *human Sentiments.* Our *moral Sense* determines us to approve these *lovely Dispositions* where we have most distinctly observ'd them: And our *Benevolence* concerns us in the Interests of the Persons possess'd of them. When we come to observe the like as distinctly in *another* Country, we begin to acquire a *national Love* towards it also; nor has our *own* Country any other Preference in our Idea, unless it be by an *Association* of the pleasant Ideas of our Youth, with the *Buildings, Fields,* and *Woods,* where we received them. This may let us see how *Tyranny,* and *Faction,* a *Neglect* of Justice, a *Corruption* of Manners, and *anything* which occasions the Misery of the Subjects, destroys this *national Love,* and the *dear Idea* of a COUNTRY."

I shall only add, that what He here calls our *Moral Sense,* He has before explained in the *former Part* of his Work: And shall conclude with expressing my Hope, that This *Treatise,* and *Another* in particular, [23] which

21. *Inquiry* (1725), p. 129–31; (2008), pp. 103–4.
22. *Inquiry* (1725), pp. 147–48; (2008), p. 115.
23. William Wollaston, *The Religion of Nature Delineated.*

has lately appeared with so great and just an Applause, may revive and excite in Men of Fortune and Leisure the Study of the Philosophy of *Virtue,* and the Nature of *True Religion.* This would soon throw a Lustre upon their whole Conduct. It would give *Decency* to every Part of their own *Behaviour,* and Happiness to their Country, and to all the World around them. I am,

SIR, *Your,* &c.

PHILOPATRIS.

4.

Saturday, *April* 10 1725

To *Britannicus.*[24]

SIR,

It was with great Pleasure that I read the *Letter* you lately published from *Philopatris,* relating to the *Inquiry into the Original of our Ideas of Beauty and Virtue;* both because in it he recommends to the World a very *ingenious* Treatise; and because he professes, his Design and Hopes were *to excite the Curiosity* of Men of *Leisure* and *Inquisitiveness,* to *enter into such Subjects; to study the Philosophy of Virtue, and the Nature of true Religion.*[25] And I am the more pleased with his *Design;* because I am much afraid, that, without some *Study* and *Cultivation,* the bare *moral Sense* of *Virtue,*

---

24. The three letters of Philaretus (lover of virtue or excellence), published in five installments between April and December 1725, were written by Gilbert Burnet (1690–1726). Burnet was one of the most able and prolific defenders of Benjamin Hoadly in the Bangorian controversy; like Hugh Boulter and Richard West, he contributed essays to *The Free-Thinker;* his sister, Elizabeth, was married to Richard West (*ODNB*).

25. Burnet's religious beliefs were very close to Hutcheson's. He thought that "the truly Religious Man is the most Rational, the most Generous, the best-natured Creature living." He was also, like Hutcheson, a staunch defender of the right of private judgment in matters of religion. He differed from Hutcheson, however, in his insistence on the primacy of reason in the determination of virtue and "true Religion": "I know no Rule to judge of Religion by in the general, but Reason" (*The Free-Thinker* vol. I, no. 22, pp. 158–59).

which the Author of the *Inquiry* very justly observes to be implanted in Men, would continue lurking in their Breasts, without ever exerting it self in any *constant* and *regular* Course of useful and agreeable Products. Without this, it may indeed ferment, and annoy them, *within*: But it will never spring up sufficiently to have any *lasting* and *uniform* Influence on their Actions *without*. It may make them *sensible* when they are in the *wrong*: But it will scarce have Force enough to prevail upon them to keep themselves always in the *right*; unless they will afford some Time, and some Pains, to consider coolly of it; and suffer themselves to feel the Weight of the *Arguments* and *Reasons* for it.

And, as nothing seems to me more likely to stir up the Attention of Mankind to this *Study,* than hearing the different Opinions of Men on such Subjects, when they are delivered in a truly Philosophical Manner; and appear to proceed from a *real* Desire of *Truth,* without any Mixture of *Contention* and *Cavil*; I have taken the Liberty to send you my Thoughts on this Subject; leaving it wholly to your Judgment, whether they deserve to be conveyed into the World, or not.

I could not but be sensibly touch'd with the noble Design of the Author of the *Inquiry,* to deduce the *Excellency* and *Obligation* of *moral Actions* from one plain and simple Principle in Nature, which he calls a *Moral Sense.* And, allowing his *Principle,* his *Conclusions* are most justly and accurately drawn. But when I considered his *Principle* itself more closely, I could not find in it that *Certainty,* which *Principles* require. I saw indeed, there was some such thing in humane Nature. But I was at a Loss to know how it came there; and whence it arose. I could not be sure, it was not a *deceitful* and *wrong Sense.* The *Pleasure* arising from the Perceptions it afforded, did not seem sufficient to convince me that it was *right.* For I knew that *Pleasure* was very apt in many Things to mislead us, and was always ready to tinge the Objects it was concerned in with false and glaring Colours. And I could not see any good Reason to trust it more in one Case, than in another. |It appeared to me too uncertain a Bottom to venture out upon, in the stormy and tempestuous Sea of Passions and Interests and Affections.

I wanted therefore some further *Test,* some more certain Rule, whereby I could judge whether my *Sense,* my *moral Sense* as the Author calls it, my *Taste* of Things, was *right,* and agreeable to the *Truth* of Things, or not.

And till I obtained this Satisfaction, I could not rest contented with the bare *Pleasure* and *Delight* it gave me. Nay, indeed, without this, I could not indulge my self in this *Pleasure,* without a secret Uneasiness arising from my Suspicions of its not being *right*; and from a kind of constant Jealousy I entertain of every *Pleasure,* till I am once satisfied it is a *reasonable* one.

The Perception of *Pleasure* therefore, which is the Description this Author has given of his *Moral Sense,* P. 106, seems to me not to be a certain enough Rule to follow.[26] There must be, I should think, something *antecedent* to justify it, and to render it a *real Good.* It must be a *Reasonable Pleasure,* before it be a *right* one, or *fit* to be encouraged, or listened to.

If it be so, then it is the *Reason* of the thing, and not the *Pleasure* that accompanies it, which ought to conduct us: And the first Question must always be; "Is the Action *Reasonable*? Is it *Fit,* that I should allow my self to accept of the *Pleasure* it promises me?"

The Constitution of all the Rational Agents that we know of is *such* indeed, that *Pleasure* is inseparably annexed to the Pursuit of what is *Reasonable.* And *Pleasure* ought never to be considered as something independent on *Reason;* no more than *Reason* ought to be reckon'd unproductive of *Pleasure.* But still the Ideas of *Reason* and *Right* are quite different from those of *Pleasure,* and must always in Reasoning be considered distinctly: *Reason* as the Ground of Inward *Pleasure,* and that *Pleasure* as the Encouragement to follow *Reason.*

Reason and *Pleasure* may both of them be properly enough stiled *Internal Senses*; and, with relation to *Moral Actions, Moral Senses.* But still they must be conceived as different *Senses*: *Reason,* as the *Sense* of the *Agreement* or *Disagreement* of our *Simple Ideas,* or of the *Combinations* of them, resulting from their Comparison: *Pleasure,* as the *Sense* of Joy which any *Ideas* afford us.

Now this *Internal* or *Moral* Sense, which we call *Reason,* is the *Rule* by which we judge, and the only *Rule* we can judge by, of *Truth* and *False-*

---

26. In the *Inquiry* (1725, p. 106; 2008, p. 88) Hutcheson had described the "immediate Goodness" we perceive in certain actions as a perception of pleasure "by a *superior Sense*, which I call a *Moral one*."

hood; and, in *moral Actions,* of *moral Good* or *Evil,* of what is *Right* or *Wrong, Fit* or *Unfit.* And the other *Internal* or *Moral Sense* of *Pleasure* or *Pain,* whereby we conceive *Joy* in discerning *Truth,* or *Pain* in feeling ourselves embarrassed with *Falsehood*; or, in *moral Actions,* by reflecting upon in ourselves, or observing in others, *Moral Good* or *Moral Evil*; is not it self the *Rule* by which we judge, or can judge, of *Truth* or *Falsehood,* of *Moral Good* or *Evil*; but only the Consequence of finding that we judge *right,* and according to *Reason.* And this latter *Sense* indeed constitutes our *Idea* of *Beauty;* by which Word, I think, we mean no more than *what pleases us.* <2>

But *Things* do not seem to us to be *True* or *Right,* because they are *beautiful,* or *please us*; but seem *beautiful,* or *please us,* because they seem to us to be *True* or *Right.* And always, in our Apprehensions of Things, (I mean, those *Apprehensions* of things, about which we are now concern'd,) the *Reason* of the thing, or the *Sense* of it's being *True* or *Right,* is antecedent to our *Sense* of *Beauty* in it, or of the *Pleasure* it affords us.

Thus, in a *Theorem,* or *Problem,* in *Geometry,* we perceive *Beauty.* But we first discern *Truth*; or we should never find out any *Beauty* in it. And so, in *Moral Science,* we first conclude, that a certain Action is *Right*: And then it appears to us likewise *Beautiful.* But, while we are in any Suspense about it, and doubt whether it is in it self *Right* or *Wrong*; or if we know it to be *Wrong*; we can never feel any *Beauty* in it. I do not say, there is always a Distance of Time between these two *Sentiments,* viz. of *Truth* or *Right,* and *Beauty.* If there is, the *Perceptions* of our Mind are often in this Case too nimble for us to measure it. But I speak only of the *Order* in which we should consider *them,* and the *Dependence* they have on one another. And in this Sense, I say, *Beauty,* in the Nature of Things, follows, or depends upon, our previous Apprehension of *Truth,* or of *Right.*

It may be said indeed, by way of *Objection* to what I have advanced, That "the *Sense* of *Beauty* or *Pleasure* moves faster than the *Sense* of *Truth* or *Right*: That, in particular, the *former* is immediate upon many *Moral Actions* proposed to us; but the *latter* does not operate but after a *long Deduction of Reasoning,* which many are incapable of, who yet discern *Beauty,* and feel *Pleasure* in such Actions." But the *Answer* is pretty easy: It is true, we often find *Beauty* and *Pleasure* in *Propositions* and *Actions,* where there is no *Truth* or *Right*. But then it must be, where we *imagine* we find *Truth* or *Right* in them. In this we may deceive our selves: But still that *Deception* is the Ground of our *Sense* of *Beauty* or *Pleasure* in such a case, tho' it may be a *False* Ground. And if we know, or imagine, that there is an absence of *Truth* or *Right,* we shall never feel any such *Sense* of *Beauty* or *Pleasure* there. Sometimes, we perceive *Truth* or *Right,* by a kind of natural Penetration and Sagacity of the Mind, before we have staid to weigh distinctly every one of the Steps which lead to it. And then, taking the Conclusion for granted, we esteem it *Beautiful* or *Pleasant.*

This may happen to some in the abstruser Sciences, who have Heads perfectly well turned for them. Whenever a *Proposition* is named to them, if it be not of too complex a Nature, they shall immediately discern whether it is *True* or *False,* even before they go thro' every Step of the *Demonstration.* And, upon this Confidence in their own Penetration and Sagacity, they shall perceive *Beauty* or *Pleasure* in the *Proposition.* And, when they enquire further, if they find they judged *right,* it confirms them in that *Beauty* or *Pleasure* which they conceived from a more partial and slight View, and increases it. If they find they judged *wrong,* the *Beauty* immediately vanishes away, and a Sentiment of the contrary succeeds. Few, indeed, are capable of such quick *Perceptions* in those kind of Sciences, where the Conclusions are forced to pass thro' many Steps. But almost all Mankind are capable of them in *Moral Science,* where the Conclusion and the Premises lie within a narrower Compass.

To instance in *Benevolence.* Every Man, of any Degree of Understanding, who has observed himself, and others, immediately with one Glance of Thought, perceives it *Reasonable* and *Fit,* "That the *Advantage of the Whole* should be regarded more than a *Private Advantage,* or the *Advantage* of a *Part* only of that *Whole.*" And, taking this quick Conclusion for granted, even before he has examined every Step that conduces to it, he sees *Beauty* in every *Moral Action* by which the *Advantage of the Whole* is designed: Not because it is *Advantageous* or *Useful* to *Himself,* or even to the *Whole;* but because he sees, or thinks he sees, it to be *Fit* and *Reasonable* that the *Advantage of the Whole* should take place. And the *Beauty* he apprehends in the *Action* seems to consist in this, "That it agrees, or seems to agree, with what is in itself *Fit* and *Reasonable*." And the more he considers the Proposition, *viz.* "That it is *Fit* and *Reasonable* that the *Advantage of the Whole* should be preferred," and, by proving it, feels the *Truth* of it more strongly in his Mind; the more he will be confirmed in esteeming *Benevolence* to be Beautiful, as a Disposition conducing to *That* which is *Fit* and *Reasonable* in |itself; and the same as to *Actions* proceeding from that *Disposition*. But, if it were possible a Mind could be so framed, as to feel the *contrary* to be *Truth* and *Right*; no doubt, all the *Beauty* of *Benevolence*, or *Benevolent Actions*, would immediately vanish out of that Mind. And, I am afraid that Men may, by long endeavouring to deceive themselves into this false Opinion, bring themselves at last to believe it, or at least to imagine they do; and by that means destroy in themselves all *Sense* of *Beauty* in *Benevolence*, as well as work out by Degrees the *Disposition* itself which Nature has fixed so deeply in their Breasts. But I hope there are few such Monsters in Humane Nature; or, at least, that ever arrive at the highest Pitch of this Depravity.

I do not mean by what I have advanced to diminish the Force of the strong *Motives* to *Virtue,* arising from the *Beauty* or *Pleasure* which our *Natural Affections* make us perceive and feel in *morally Good* Actions. I know they are the most successful Solicitors to every thing that is *Right* and *Reasonable,* if duly attended to, and not mistaken, or misused. And we should be comfortless and forlorn Creatures, if we had no *Affections* and inward Warmth of Sentiments to spur us on to what Dry *Reason* approves of. But I would not have Men depend upon their *Affections* as *Rules* sufficient to conduct them, tho' they are the proper Means to animate them to, and support them in, such a Conduct as *Reason* directs. I would have them search still higher for the Foundation and Ground of those very *Motives*. And I am persuaded they will find that *Reason* is as necessary to account for them, and to justify their Effect; as it is needful to guide and direct them afterwards.

And I have no small *Pleasure* in observing, that all the accurate Deductions and Reasonings of the *Author* of the *Inquiry* may easily be adapted to the Principle here laid down; *viz. Reason*, or our *Internal Sense* of *Truth* and *Falshood, Moral Good* and *Evil, Right* and *Wrong*, accompanied, and fortified, by another succeeding *Internal Sense* of *Beauty* and *Pleasure,* feeling those things which are *Reasonable* and *True* to be at the same time *Delightful*: and, on the Reverse, of *Deformity* and *Pain,* terrifying us from following after *Falshood,* or giving our selves up to any thing that is *Unreasonable.*

But I find too many Thoughts on this Subject crowding into my Mind, to dispose them within the Compass of a *Letter.* And therefore, if it be acceptable, I shall take some further Opportunity of addressing myself to you: And, in the mean while, am

SIR,

Your, &c

PHILARETUS.

5.

SATURDAY, *June* 12, 1725

To *Britannicus.*

SIR,

I Send you the following Thoughts upon the Subject of PHILARETUS's Letter of *April* 10, and shall study to imitate his gentlemanly and *truly philosophical* Manner of Writing on so useful a Subject.

There are certain *Words* frequently used in our Discourses of *Morality,* which, I fancy, when well examined, will lead us into the same Sentiments with those of the Author of the late *Inquiry into Beauty and Virtue.* The Words I mean are these, when we say that Actions are *Reasonable, Fit, Right, Just, Conformable to Truth. Reason* denotes either our Power of finding out *Truth,* or a Collection of Propositions already known to be *True. Truths* are either *Speculative,* as "*When we discover, by comparing our Ideas, the Relations of Quantities, or of any other Objects among themselves*"; or *Practical,* as "*When we discover what Objects are naturally apt to give any Person the highest Gratifications, or what Means are most effectual to obtain such Objects.*" *Speculative Truth* or *Reason* is not properly a *Rule* of Conduct, however *Rules may be* founded upon it. Let us enquire then into *Practical Reason,* both with relation to the *End* which we propose, and the *Means.*

To a Being which acts only for its *own Happiness,* That *End* is *Reasonable,* which contains a greater Happiness than any other which it could pursue; and when such a Being satisfies itself with a smaller Good for itself, while a greater is in its Power, it pursues an *Unreasonable End.* A Being of this Temper, as to the *Means,* would call those *Reasonable,* which were effectual to obtain their *End* with the smallest Pain or Toil to the Agent; with such a Being, the Cruelty of the *Means,* or their bad Influence on a *Community,* would never make them pass for *Unreasonable,* provided they had no bad Influence on his own Happiness.

But if there are any Beings, which by the very Frame of their Nature desire the Good of a *Community,* or which are determin'd by *kind Affections* to study the Good of others, and have withal a *Moral Sense,* which causes them necessarily to approve such Conduct in themselves or others, and count it amiable; and to dislike the contrary Conduct as hateful: To such Beings, That *End* is *Reasonable,* which contains the greatest Aggregate of *Publick Happiness,* which an Agent can procure; and the pursuing of the Good of a small *Party,* or *Faction,* with neglect of more *universal* Good, to *such Natures* would seem *Unreasonable.* If these Beings have also *Self-Love,* as well as Natural *Benevolence* and a *Moral Sense,* and at the same Time find that their own highest Happiness does necessarily arise from *Kind Affections and Benevolent Actions,* That *End* which would appear *Reasonable,* would be *Universal Happiness,* the very Pursuit of which, is supposed to be the greatest Happiness to the several Agents themselves; for thus both Desires are at once gratified, as far as they are capable of doing it by their own Actions. By such Beings as these, the *Means of Publick Good* will be counted *Unreasonable,* when they occasion Evil to the Agent, greater than the Good obtained by them to the Publick; or when other *Means* equally in our Power might have obtained the same, or an equal Publick Good with less Detriment, either to the Agent himself, or to other Persons: And, in like Manner, the *Means of Private Good* will be reputed *Unreasonable* by such Beings, when they contain a prepollent *Publick Evil,* or a *Greater Evil* towards others, than is contained in Means equally effectual for obtaining the same, or equal Private Good. Under this Class of Beings, the Author of the *Inquiry* seems to rank our own Species, Mankind.

If any one should ask concerning *Publick* and *Private* Good, Which of the two is most *Reasonable*? The Answer would be various, according to the Dispositions of the Persons who are pas|sing Judgment upon these *Ends*. A Being entirely *Selfish*, and without a *Moral Sense*, will judge that its own Pursuit of its greatest private Pleasure is most *Reasonable*. And as to the Actions of others, it can see, whether the Actions be naturally apt to attain the *Ends* proposed by the *Agents*, or whether their Ends interfere with its own *Ends*, or not; but it would never judge of them under any other Species than that of Advantage, or Disadvantage, and only be affected with them as we are now with a fruitful Shower, or a destructive Tempest. Such a Being might have the abstract *Idea of Publick Good*; but would never perceive any Thing amiable in the Pursuit of it. The only Debate, which such a *Mind* could entertain concerning *Ends*, would be only this, Whether this *Object* or another, would conduce most to its own greatest Advantage or Pleasure.

But if the same Question be proposed to *Beings* who have a *moral Sense* of Excellence in publick Affections, and a Desire of publick Good implanted in their Nature; such Beings will answer, that it is *Reasonable* that smaller *Private* Good should yield to greater *Publick Good*, and they will disapprove of a contrary Conduct: But without this *Sense* and *Affections*, I cannot guess at any *Reason* which should make a Being approve of Publick Spirit in another, farther than it might be the Means of Private Good to it self.

If one should still farther enquire, is there not something *absolutely Reasonable* to any possible *Mind* in *Benevolence*, or a Study of Publick Good? Is it not *absolutely Reasonable*, that a Being who does no Evil to others, should not be put to Pain by others? It is very probable every *Man* would say, that these Things are Reasonable. But then, all Mankind have this *Moral Sense* and *Publick Affections*. But if there were any *Natures disjoined from us*, who knew all the *Truths* which can be known, but had no *Moral Sense*, nor any Thing of a superior Kind equivalent to it; such *Natures* might know the Constitution of our Affairs, and what *Publick* and

Private Good did mean; they would grant, that equal Intenseness of Pleasure enjoyed by Twenty, was a greater Sum of Happiness than if it were enjoyed only by One; but to them it would be *indifferent,* whether One or more enjoyed Happiness, if they had no benevolent Affections. Such *Natures* might see from the Constitution of our Affairs, that a *social* Conduct would be the most probable Way for each single Person of Mankind to secure his own Happiness, in the Neighbourhood of a Set of Beings like themselves, with social Affections, and a Sense of Honour and Virtue; but these *disjoined Natures,* without a *Moral Sense,* would see nothing *Reasonable* in the good Affections of one Man towards another, abstractly from Considerations of the Advantage of the Virtue to the virtuous Agent: And if this *disjoined Nature* observed such a Conjuncture, wherein a Man who had stupified his *Moral Sense,* so as to be above Remorse, could with Privacy, Force, or cunning Management, furnish himself with the highest Pleasures he then could relish, at the Expense of Misery to Multitudes; if this *disjoined Nature* had no Notion of a good Deity, and of a State of future Rewards or Punishments, it would see perhaps that the Conduct of this Man was not apt to promote the Publick Good, nor the *Reasonable* Means for that End: But it would also acknowledge that this was *Reasonable* Conduct in the Agent, in order to obtain private Happiness to it self. If there be any other Meaning of this Word *Reasonable,* when apply'd to Actions, I should be glad to hear it well explained; and to know for what *Reason,* besides a *Moral Sense* and *Publick Affections,* any Man approves the Study of Publick Good in others, or pursues it himself, antecedently to Motives of his own private Interest.

What has been said of *Reasonable* and *Unreasonable,* may be also apply'd to that *Fitness* and *Unfitness of Things,* which some speak of in |their Moral Writings.[27] It is certain, that abstracting from the Observation or Relish

---

27. Samuel Clarke, in *A Discourse concerning the Unchangeable Obligations of Natural Religion, and the Truth and Certainty of the Christian Revelation,* pp. 60–61, reasoned that just as there are "certain necessary and eternal differences of things"; so there are "certain consequent fitnesses and unfitnesses of the application of different things or different relations one to another . . . founded unchangeably in the nature and reason of things, and unavoidably arising from the differences of the things themselves."

and Approbation of any other *Mind,* some Objects are *apt* or *fit* to give greater Pleasures to the Person who enjoys them, than others: It is certain also, that some Means are more effectual to obtain an End than others. In this Sense, there is a natural *Fitness* and *Unfitness* both in Ends and Means. Thus one Tenour of Conduct is naturally more *fit* among Men to promote Publick Good, than another; and to *Men,* who have a *Moral Sense* and *Publick Affections,* a *Benevolent* Conduct is more *fit* to promote the Happiness of the Agent than the Contrary; more fit to engage the Favour of a good Deity, than a malicious Conduct: And any *Mind* whatsoever, who knew our State, and believed a good Deity, might perceive this *Fitness* in Benevolence to promote both Publick Happiness and that of the Agent, both in this Life and the next. But a *Mind* without a *Moral Sense,* altho' it saw this natural *Fitness* of Benevolence to obtain these Ends, would never *approve* of Benevolence, unless this *observing Mind* had kind Affections toward Mankind, (so that the Happiness of Men were an End agreeable to this *Mind;*) or a *Moral Sense* did determine it to *admire* and *approve* a Publick Spirit wherever it observed it. Without a *Moral Sense,* a Mind would *approve* nothing but what was *Fit* for its own Ends, altho' it might also observe what was *Fit* to promote the Ends of others. That *absolute antecedent Fitness in the Nature of the Things themselves,* of which some talk, must either mean this *Sensation of Excellence* which we necessarily receive by our *Moral Sense,* or it is to me perfectly unintelligible, since it is supposed *antecedent to any Views of Private Interest, or any Sanctions of Laws*; and for *Publick Interests,* it must be a *Moral Sense,* or a *Benevolent Instinct,* which can make any Man regard them.[28]

As to the Words *Just, Right,* and their Opposites *Unjust* and *Wrong,* antecedently to any Opinion of *Laws,* or *Views of Interest,* the same may be said of them which was said of the former Words, *Reasonable, Fit,* and *Unfit;* they seem to have no other Meaning, but *agreeable* or *disagreeable* to a *Moral Sense.*

[*To be concluded in our next.*]

---

28. Hutcheson's arguments against Clarke's theory of the natural fitnesses and unfitnesses of things in morals are developed more fully in *Illustrations upon the Moral Sense,* sec. 2.

6.

SATURDAY, *June* 19, 1725.

The Conclusion *of the former Letter.*

As to another Character of Actions, *viz. Agreeable to Truth,*[29] We know that by Custom, *Words* or *Sounds* are made Signs of *Ideas,* and *Combinations* of *Words* Signs of *Judgments.* We know that Men generally by *Words* express their *Sentiments,* and profess to speak, as far as they know, according to what is Matter of Fact; so that their Profession is to speak *Truth.* In like Manner we judge of Actions: We know what is the usual Conduct of Men upon certain Occasions, from the Dispositions which we generally imagine to be in Mankind, if they have the same Opinions of Objects which we have, and which Men generally profess to have. And hence we conclude, from a Man's acting otherwise, that he has either other *Opinions* of Objects, or other *Affections* than those which we have our selves, and expect to find in other Men.

Thus a Man who kills another, who had done him no harm, by his Action *declares,* or *gives us Occasion* to conclude, either that he does not take that Object which he treats in this Manner to be a Man; or if he knows what Object he acts upon (as we generally imagine he does on such Occasions) he *declares,* or *gives us Ground* to conclude, that he has not those *Affections,* or that *Moral Sense* of Actions, which we generally expect in Mankind. So that this *Disagreeableness to Truth* in such an Action, at last must end in a *Moral Sense,* unless the Person be *mad,* and really have false Appearances of Objects.

As to these Phrases, *treating Things as they are,* or *according to what they are, or are not,* they arise from our *Moral Sense.* This Sense suggests to us what Treatment of Objects is amiable, and what is odious. Virtue, or a *Regard to Publick Good,* in Conformity to this *Sense,* is so universally professed by Mankind, and acknowledged to be the only Conduct which they can approve, that we say, Men do not act *suitably to the Nature of Things* who do not pursue Publick Good: But it is our *Moral Sense* of

29. William Wollaston, in *The Religion of Nature Delineated,* argued that moral judgments of good and evil are nothing but judgments concerning truth and falsehood. Hutcheson's arguments against this theory are developed below, and in section 3 of *Illustrations upon the Moral Sense.*

Excellence in a Publick Spirit, which suggests to us this Idea of *Suitableness* of Conduct to Natures; which *Suitableness* we involve in the Particles *as, according,* and such like. Had we our selves been *wholly selfish,* and lived in a System of Beings *wholly selfish,* without a *Moral Sense,* in which System we should have had no Ground to have expected any Regard to the Good of each other, in our Fellows; their doing Evil to each other, or procuring *private Pleasure* by the *Pains of Multitudes,* when they had *Force* to do it successfully, would have been *treating Things as they would have been upon this Supposition;* nor should we have perceived any *Opposition to Truth* in such Actions.

It were to be wished that Writers would guard against, as far as they can, involving very complex Ideas under some short *Words* and *Particles,* which almost escape Observation in Sentences; such as, *ought, should, as, according;* nay sometimes in our *English* Gerunds, *is to be done, is to be preferr'd,* and such like. Some Writers treat the Pronoun *his,* as if it were the Sign of a simple Idea; and yet involve under it the complex Ideas of *Property,* and of a Right to *natural Liberty.* As the School-men made *Space* and *Time* to vanish into Nothings, by hiding them in the Adverbs *when* and *where,* or by including them in the Compound Words *Coexistent, Corresponding, &c.*[30]

As to *Philaretus's* Letter, he has not happen'd to observe the Author of the *Inquiry's* Definition of the *Moral Sense,* p. 124;[31] and seems by this means to have misapprehended him in some Things.

As to his Questions, *"Whence this Sense arose?"* The Author of the *Inquiry* takes it to be implanted by the Author of Nature. *Philaretus* wants *to be sure that this Sense is not Deceitful or Wrong.* If by a *wrong* or *deceitful* Sense, he means a *Sense* which shall make *That* pleasant for the present,

---

30. Hutcheson described at greater length how "the schoolmen seem to be talking in empty phrases, without advancing knowledge," when they "avoid employing the nouns *time* and extended *space* by making use of the adverbs *where, anywhere,* and *when,"* in *A Synopsis of Metaphysics,* part 1, chap. 3, sec. 4, in *Logic, Metaphysics and the Natural Sociability of Mankind,* pp. 85–86.

31. In the *Inquiry* (1725, p. 124; 2008, p. 100) Hutcheson defined the moral sense as "a Determination of our Minds to receive amiable or disagreeable Ideas of Actions, when they shall occur to our Observation, antecedently to any Opinions of Advantage or Loss to redound to ourselves from them."

which shall have pernicious Consequences; the Author of the *Inquiry* has attempted to prove, that the Pleasures of the *Moral Sense* are the most *lasting* and so-|lid in human Life. And, as he does not profess to give a *complete Treatise* of *Morality,* he recommends to us *Cumberland* and *Puffendorf,* who shew that *Benevolence* and a *social* Conduct is the most probable way to secure to each Individual, Happiness in this Life, and the Favour of the Deity in any future State to be expected; that so all Obstacles to our *Moral Sense,* and our *kind Affections,* from false Views of *Interest,* may be removed. *See* p. 251 *of the Inquiry.*[32]

Philaretus wants to know if this *Moral Sense* of something amiable in Benevolence be *Right* and *Reasonable,* or *fit* and *justifiable.* If by these Words he means, whether the Actions which this Sense at any time makes him *approve,* shall be *always approved* as *Morally Good* by him? The Author tells him, that this *Moral Sense* and our *Benevolent Affections* do make us pursue Publick Good as the End, find our greatest Pleasure in such Pursuits, and approve of all Benevolent Actions in others; but then the Author also in many Places recommends the most serious Application of our *Reason,* to enquire into the *natural Tendencies* of our Actions, as the *Means* to attain this End, that we may not be led by every *slight Appearance* of *particular Good,* to do Actions which may have *prepollent evil Consequences.* And this Inadvertence he makes one great Source of *Immoral Actions,* which both we ourselves and all others will condemn, when we observe the prepollent evil Consequences which the Agent might have foreseen. *See* Art. 8, 9, 10, of the third Section, and p. 150, and the whole fourth Section. If he means, "Will this *Sense* lead me to my own greatest

---

32. Hutcheson distinguished two different senses of obligation in the *Inquiry,* sec. 7 (1725, pp. 249–51; 2008, pp. 177–78): one is a sense of obligation which follows from the definition of moral sense (see the previous note): *"a Determination, without regard to our own Interest, to approve Actions, and to perform them"*; the other is *"a Motive from Self-Interest, sufficient to determine all those who duly consider it, and pursue their own Advantage wisely, to a certain Course of Actions."* The latter sense of obligation may arise from considering, *"as Cumberland and Pufendorf have prov'd"* that *"a constant Course of benevolent and social Actions . . . [is] the most probable means of promoting the natural Good of every Individual."* As he makes clear in the penultimate sentence of the following paragraph, the second sense of obligation was not the principal subject of the *Inquiry.*

Happiness, to a constant Self-Approbation, and engage the Favour of the Deity, if my Actions be conformable to this Sense, according to the best Knowledge of the natural Tendencies of my Actions?" The Author partly proves this, and partly refers to other Writers for what was not to his present Design, p. 251. Our *Moral Sense* and Affections determine our End, but *Reason* must find out the *Means*.

Philaretus thinks, that this Sense is not a proper *Rule*. The Author recommends to Moralists, to examine also into the State of Humane Affairs, to know what Course of Action will be most effectual to promote Publick Good, the End which our *kind Affections* and *Moral Sense* incline us to pursue, p. 253. And if a further Rule be necessary, it must come from *Revelation*.

Philaretus fears, that "*this Bottom is too uncertain to set out upon, amidst the Storms of our Passions and Self Interests.*" The Author suggests, that we have Benevolent Passions as well as Selfish; and recommends it to Moralists to explain, as he partly does himself, how all our *Selfish Affections* would conspire, if we understood our own *true Interest,* to persuade us to the same Actions which Benevolence excites us to, and our Moral Sense determines us to approve. And the Author of the *Inquiry* frequently suggests, that in the present State of Humane Nature, many other additional Motives to the Study of Publick Good are very necessary, besides our *Moral Sense* and *kind Affections.* These Motives or *Reasons* for pursuing *Publick Good,* and *preferring* it to Private, which he hints at, are such as some way or other may prove, that the *Pursuit* of *Publick Good* does most effectually promote the *truest Interest* of the Agent, either as the Pursuit of *Publick Good* is acceptable to the Deity, and will be rewarded by him; or as this *Pursuit* gives the Agent pleasant Reflections upon his own Conduct; or, as it engages the Love, Esteem, and mutual good Offices of Mankind; and is withal generally consistent with the *highest* and *truest* Enjoyment of other *Pleasures,* nay, is the very Spirit and Life of the most of our Pleasures: Whereas a *contrary Temper* has all the *contrary pernicious Effects.* We have a Perception of *moral Good and Evil,* of something *amiable or hateful* in Actions, antecedently to any of these *Reasons;* and yet the Author of the *Inquiry* knows no other *Reasons* for *virtuous Actions;* and hence he concludes, that our first Ideas arise from a *Sense.* All Action is designed for some *End;* if the *End* be *reasonable,* and the Action, with all its Consequences, *naturally |apt* to attain it, the Action is *Reasonable:* The *End* must be either the Good of the Agent, or of the *Publick,* or both consistently with each other. *Philaretus* owns, that Actions are *reasonable, fit, right,* &c. without regard to the Interest of the Agent: They are *reasonable* then with regard to *Publick Interests.* Now for what Reason *should* the Publick Interest be regarded? What means that *should?* Is it, that *this Regard to the Publick is the Interest of the Agent?* or *that it will be rewarded by the Deity?*——No: It is *fit* antecedently——*Fit!* for what End? for Publick Good or Private Good? Publick Good, to be sure: Because, *that the Advantage of the Whole should take place, is fit.* Again, *fit!* for what End?——Not for Private, but Publick Good.——Why should I in my Actions regard Publick Good?——For what Reason?——Why, it is *fit* for Publick Good that I should do so. In this Circle we must run, until we acknowledge the first Original of our moral Ideas to be from a *Sense;* [33] or, which is to the same purpose, till we acknowledge that they arise from a *Determination by the Author of Nature, which necessitates our Minds to approve of Publick Affections,* and of *consulting the Good of others:* And then we have room enough for our *Reason* to direct us in that Tenour of Action, which shall produce the greatest and most extensive Good in our Power, and to confirm our Publick Spirit by Motives of *Self-Interest,* and to prove it to be *reasonable* in that Sense. I mistake *Philaretus* very much, from his Letter, if his Zeal for the *Reasonableness* of Virtue does not flow from a lively *Moral Sense* and very *Noble Affections:*

And am his, and your
most obedient obliged, Servant,
PHILANTHROPUS.

33. That all deliberation about the ends of actions must terminate in a sense was a notion that Hutcheson, following Henry More, also attributed to Aristotle. See *A Synopsis of Metaphysics,* in *Logic and Metaphysics, and the Natural Sociability of Mankind,* p. 128, n. 7. See also below, pp. 363–64 for Hutcheson's very favorable judgment of More's moral philosophy in his Preface to *Divine Dialogues.*

7.

To *BRITANNICUS.*

SIR,

When I read *Philanthropus's* Letter in the *Journals* of the 12th and the 19th of *June,* I was mighty glad to meet with a Person of his Ingenuity and Candour, so willing and so able to examine my Sentiments of Things. And as I conceive no small Hopes, by his Means, to be either convinced that I am yet in the wrong, or to be more fully satisfied that I am in the right, by hearing all that he has to say against my Opinion; I shall beg the favour of you, if you judge it proper, to convey these Speculations to Him, by publishing them to the World.

I entirely agree with him as to the Method he proposes in arguing on these Subjects, *viz* to *examine* into the Meaning of the *Words used in our Discourses of Morality.* And therefore, I will immediately define what I mean by the Words which *Philanthropus* mentions, viz. *Reasonable, Fit, Right, Just, Conformable to Truth;* that we may see whether they stand for the same Ideas with *him,* that they do with *me;* and that if they do not, we may agree what *Ideas* they shall stand for.

By *Reason,* I understand, strictly speaking, that Method of Thinking, whereby the Mind discovers such *Truths* as are not *Self Evident,* by the Intervention of *Self-evident Truths;* and such Truths as are *less evident,* by such as are already supposed to be *more* so. The Perception of *Evident Truths,* is *Knowledge;* which is therefore acquired and improved by Reasoning, *i.e.* by connecting remote or less evident *Truths* with *self-evident* or *more evident* ones.[34] All *Propositions* which we perceive as *True,* whether immediately, or by the Means of other intermediate Perceptions, we call *Truths.* They are all, strictly speaking, *Speculative;* i.e. they are seen and perceived by the Mind. But when such *Truths* are Relative to the *Actions* of rational Agents, they are in common Usage stil'd *Practical Truths.* And

34. See also Samuel Clarke's *Discourse Concerning the Unchangeable Obligations of Natural Religion,* p. 50: "These things are so notoriously plain and self-evident, that nothing but the extremest stupidity of Mind, corruption of Manners, or perverseness of Spirit, can possibly make any Man entertain the least doubt concerning them."

they are always the *Conclusions* made from Those, which, by way of Distinction are called *Speculative Truths*. *Speculative Truths* are not themselves Rules of Action, but only the Practical Truths (or Conclusions) drawn from them. The Instance which Philanthropus gives of *Practical Truth*, according to these Definitions, seems rather to belong to *Speculative Truth*. For the *discovering what Objects are naturally apt to give any Person the highest Gratifications, or what Means are most effectual to obtain such Objects*, is discovering the same *Species* of *Truth* with the *Relations of Quantities, or of any other Objects among themselves*, both *speculative Truths*, or *Theorems*. But the inferring from thence in what Manner *Persons* are *obliged* to act towards such Objects, or what Means they are *obliged* to employ, in order to obtain them, would be the discovering *Practical Truths* properly so call'd. *Reasonable*, signifies the Result of employing *Reason*. *Thinking* according to this Result, is called *Thinking Reasonably*: And *Acting* according to it, *Acting Reasonably*. Sometimes indeed the Word *Reason* is used to signify the *Faculty of Reasoning*, or of employing *Reason*. But this is in a less proper and strict Sense. When again the Word *Reason* is used *to denote a Collection of Propositions already known to be true*, it is likewise improperly and figuratively used, and means no more than *Reasonable*, or the Result of *Reasoning*.

Now I think it will plainly follow from this Definition of the Word *Reasonable*, if it be a right one, that the *Reasonableness* of the *Ends* of *Moral Agents* does not depend on their Conformity to the *Natural Affections* of the Agent, nor to a *Moral Sense* representing such *Ends* as *amiable* to him; but singly on their Conformity to *Reason*. *Reason* would always represent the *End* in the same Manner to the *Rational Agent*, whatever his *Affections*, or *Inward Sense* of *Amiableness*, were. And, supposing a Being framed so as to have only *selfish Affections*, and yet to be endued with a Faculty of *Reasoning*; such a Being, if he employs that Faculty, must |see it to be highly *unreasonable* that *his* private Interest or Pleasure should take Place to the Destruction of the Interest or Pleasure of all other Beings like *himself;* tho' for want of *kind Affections*, he would be void of any Disposition[35]

---

35. A note at the end of Philaretus's subsequent letter instructs that "Collateral" should be inserted before "Disposition."

to act in that Manner, which to his Understanding must necessarily appear *Reasonable*. Nay, such a Being would perceive his *Natural Affections* to be very *unreasonable Affections*. I do not believe indeed he could possibly have a *Sense* of *Amiableness* in a Conduct agreeable to such *Affections*; because it seems absurd that any thing should appear *Amiable* to a rational Creature which so evidently contradicted *Reason*. But if he could be supposed to have such a *Sense,* it would be a *Sense* as *unreasonable* as his *Affections* were. And neither of them, nor both together, could possibly render a Conduct pursuant to them *Reasonable*.

That which perhaps may be apt to mislead us in this Point is, That we find in Fact it is always *Reasonable* to act according to *Natural Affection,* and the *Moral Sense*. And thence we may too hastily conclude, that such a Conduct is *Reasonable,* for this Reason, because our *Natural Affections* and *Moral Sense* move us to it. But, if we examine more closely, I believe we shall find the Reverse to be the Truth, *viz.* That we deem our *Affections* and our *Moral Sense* to be *Reasonable Affections,* and a *Reasonable Sense,* from their prompting us to the same Conduct which *Reason* approves and directs. And thus *Reason* is the Measure of the *Goodness* or *Badness* of our *Affections,* and *Moral Sense,* and consequently of the Actions flowing from them, and not *vice versâ*.

Philanthropus acknowledges that *every Man would say that Benevolence, or a Study of Publick Good, is absolutely Reasonable to any possible Mind.* But he thinks they would say so, only because all Mankind have a *Moral Sense* and *Publick Affections*. And he thinks they would not say so, if they had not; but would be *indifferent.*

I agree with him, that they would be *Indifferent* as to any *Affection* they would feel towards others, disposing them to do or to wish them any Good. But they would not, they could not, be *Indifferent* as to perceiving it *Reasonable* that the *Publick Good* should be preferred to *Private Good*; and consequently, that it was in itself *Reasonable* that every *Rational Agent* should study the *Publick Good*. They would not only see the *Speculative Truth,* That *an equal Intenseness of Pleasure enjoyed by Twenty was a greater Sum of Happiness, than if it were enjoyed only by One.* But they would likewise see this *Practical Truth* to be the Consequence of it, "That it was therefore *Reasonable* that the *Happiness* of the *Twenty* should be considered preferably by all *Rational Agents* to the *Happiness* of the *One,* where all things else were supposed equal, and there were no peculiar Circumstances to justify a Distinction."[36]

And it is from this Perception of the *Reasonableness* of regarding the *Happiness* of *Many* more than the *Happiness* of a *Few,* that we discern and admire the *Wisdom* of our Maker, in implanting *Social* and *Publick Affections* in his Creatures, to be subservient to this *wise* and *reasonable* End. Whereas, if we had not this previous Apprehension of *Reasonableness,* antecedent to, and independent on, any *Affections,* or *Sense* of them, we could not judge it to be more *wise* or *reasonable* to have bestowed such *social Affections* on Men, than to have given them only *selfish Affections,* prompting them to take care of themselves alone, without any respect to the *Cruelty of the Means, or the bad Influence on a Community.* In short, without such a previous Apprehension of what is *Reasonable* in itself, all conceivable Constitutions of Creatures would have been equally *wise;* which is evidently absurd.

Reasonable therefore, when said of *Actions,* or of the *Ends* of *Rational Agents,* denotes the Agreeableness of those *Actions,* and those *Ends,* not to the *Natural Affections* of such *Agents,* nor to a *Moral Sense* rendering the Compliance with those *Affections* amiable; but to *Reason* |only. And those *Affections,* as well as that *Moral Sense,* are themselves denominated *Reasonable,* when they move us to such *Actions,* or *Ends,* as *Reason* prescribes to us, and directs us to; and must be stiled *Unreasonable,* if they diverted us from *them,* or disposed us to the contrary.

The next Word, *FIT,* is a relative Word, expressing the relation of Means to an End. And therefore an *absolute antecedent Fitness in the Nature of Things,* meaning thereby *Antecedent* to any *End,* either existing, or in Supposition, is absolute Nonsense. But when Moralists speak of *Antecedent Fitness,* they mean only *Antecedent* to the actual Constitution of Things, and *Fit* upon Supposition of certain Circumstances existing, which perhaps may never really exist. As for instance; if never any Creatures had been produced, it would nevertheless have been always *Antecedently true,* that, if they should ever be so and so constituted, it would be *Fit* that they

36. See below, pp. 180–81, for Hutcheson's response to Burnet's argument.

should act towards one another in such and such a manner. For, upon Supposition that the perfectly wise and good Author of Nature should produce any Rational Agents, it was always *Antecedently Fit* that they should use the best *Means* to *Happiness,* since their Happiness must be the chief *End* for which the wise and good Author would bring them into Being. And, further, supposing they should be framed with *Natural Affections* leading to this *End,* it was likewise *Antecedently Fit* that they should exercise those *Affections,* and follow *their* Motions; not barely because they are supposed to have such *Affections,* (for that Consideration alone discovers no *End,* and consequently no *Fitness*), but because they are supposed to have such *Affections* leading to such an *End.* It is not *Fit* that they should perform such Offices, barely because they have such *Affections.* But, because it was *Antecedently Fit,* that they should perform such Offices, it was likewise *Fit* that they should be endued with such *Affections.* And, for the same Reason, it was *Fit* that they should exert those *Affections* when they have them.

This Explanation of the Word *Fit* may easily clear up that seeming Circle which *Philanthropus* observes in arguing upon this Proposition, "It is *Fit* that the Advantage of the Whole should take place." *Fit,* says he, *for what End?—Not for Private, but Publick Good.* Now indeed to argue that it is *Fit* for *Publick Good,* that *Publick Good* should take place, is arguing in a Circle, and proving nothing. But, if we consider that, when we say, "It is *Fit* that *Publick Good* should be regarded," the *End* to which the *Fitness* there relates is not *Publick Good* considered barely in itself; but the wise and good *End* of the Creator, to render all his Creatures as happy as their Constitution will admit of: Then it will be no Circle, to argue that the Regard of *Publick Good* is a *Fit* Means for obtaining this wise and good *End* of the Creator. If the Question be, *Why should I in my Actions regard Publick Good?*—The proper and first Answer is, "Because it is the *Fit* Means of obtaining the *Publick Good,* that every constituent Member of that *Publick* should regard it." But if it be further demanded—*Why ought the Publick Good to be sought after?*—Then the right Answer is—"Because it is *Fit* for the accomplishing the wise *End* of our Creator, to make all his Creatures Happy, that it shou'd be so." And if it be further urged—"Why is that *End* to be regarded?" The Answer is—"Because it is a *wise* and *reasonable End.*"

Indeed the *Fitness* of *Means* to an *End* lays no Obligation, but as the *End* is *Reasonable*. And therefore when Moralists say that any Thing is *Antecedently Fit,* they always suppose the *End* to be *Reasonable. Means* may be very *apt* to promote a *very unreasonable End.* But, in a Moral Sense of the Word, such *Means* would never be said to be *Fit,* and far less to constitute such an *Antecedent Fitness* as Moralists speak of in their Writings. I will trouble you with what remains, next Week; and am,

Yours, &c

PHILARETUS.

8.

SATURDAY. *August* 7, 1725

To *BRITANNICUS.*

SIR,

The next to be considered is the Word RIGHT, which denotes nothing more in effect than *Reasonable;* only taking it for granted that *Reason* represents to us the Nature of Things truly as it is.

The Word JUST denotes only *Right* applied specially to what we owe to other Persons. And therefore, what has been said of the Word *Reasonable,* may be applied to these Words *Right* and *Just.*

The Expression AGREEABLE TO TRUTH, when used with respect to Actions, is to the same Effect with *Agreeable to Reason.* For, tho' *Truth,* meaning thereby such Propositions as express the Nature of Things as it is, is the real Foundation of all *Moral Good* or *Evil*; yet, as this *Truth* must be apprehended by the *Agent,* before it can be a *Rule* for his Actions, so *Truth* considered as a Rule to act by, *i.e. Moral Truth,* is the same with *Reason,* or what *Reason* dictates. And *Acting Agreeably to Truth,* can mean no more than Acting agreeably to our *Knowledge* of it, *i.e.* to *Reason*; for

Reason leads us to that *Knowledge*. *Reason* informs us how Things are, as far as it goes. And if we treat Things not as our *Reason* tells us they *are,* but as our *Reason* tells us they *are not,* we act contrary to our *Apprehension* of *Truth,* or to *Moral Truth*; and, acting therein perversely, become *morally Evil* Agents: Whereas, if we act the Reverse, we are denominated *morally Good* Agents. Acting contrary to our *Natural Affections* does not immediately render us *morally evil* Agents, nor acting agreeably to them *morally good* Agents; because our *Affections* do not of themselves immediately inform us how things *are,* or *are not*. But, mediately, the acting agreeably or disagreeably to *them,* may denominate us *morally Good* or *morally Evil,* as those *Affections* are Indications of the Will and Design of our Creator; and as the acting in Opposition to his Will, is acting as if he had not been our Benefactor, and as if we owed him no Return of Gratitude and Obedience. And, further, the thwarting our *Natural Affections* may constitute us *morally Evil* Agents, as being in effect the denying that we have such *Affections,* by acting as if we had them not. And, in this Case, the *moral Evil* will consist in acting contrary to this *Truth,* That we have such *Affections*. But still all this supposes these *Affections* to be *Good, Right, Reasonable Affections*. For, if they are not so, then the thwarting them will not render us *evil,* but *good Agents*. For in that case, *Reason* would be a much surer Indication of the Will and Design of our Creator, than the *Affections* can be: And the acting as if we had not *Natural* EVIL *Affections* would render us *morally good* Agents.

But, as such a Supposition of *Natural* EVIL *Affections* can only be put for Argument's Sake, and can never really exist; it being impossible that a wise and good Being should give his Creatures a *Natural Bias* to *Evil*; the Conclusions from *Reason,* and from *Natural Affection* duly examined, will always be the same: For the *Natural Affections,* and the *Moral Sense* attending them, are so ordered by the Author of Nature, that they coincide with the Dictates of *Reason*. And therefore, whatever follows from the Consideration of *their* Movements, will likewise follow from a due Attention to the Discoveries of *Truth* which our *Reason* will open to us. The only Difference is, that the *One* is a sufficient Principle to argue from; the *Other* is not. For, when, in the Regress of the Analysis, as I may call it, we arrive at *Natural Affections,* or a *moral Sense* accompanying them, and take them for our ultimate Principle; we do not feel sufficient Satisfaction to make any demonstrative Conclusion from them: Whereas, when we go back to *Reason* in our Investigation, *i.e.* when we resolve the Propositions into *self-evident* or *evident Truths,* then we find no further Doubt in our Mind, but meet with a *Principle* which |we cannot but acquiesce in. In one Case, we still leave our *Principle* to be proved. In the other, we reach a Principle, which is self-evident, or certainly demonstrable. When we have observed certain *Natural Affections* in our selves, the Question still remains, whether these Natural Affections are *Good* or *Evil, Right* or *Wrong, i.e.* agreeable to *Reason,* or disagreeable to *it,* which requires further Proof to determine it: But when we rest our Foot upon such *Truths* as are evident or demonstrated, we leave nothing unproved; but arrive at as much Certainty as we are capable of, and can go no farther.

Thus I have examined all the *Terms* which *Philanthropus* proposes. And, as I understand them, they would lead me to look upon *Reason* as That which alone discovers and delivers to us the *proper* Rule and Measure of *Action*; as That which lays the *proper,* and indeed, strictly speaking, the *only Obligation* upon us to act in a certain manner; since we are always self-condemned, whenever we contradict its Conclusions and Directions. And, as for all those *natural Affections,* whether *Social* or *Selfish,* which the Author of our Nature has interwoven in our Frame, all the consequent *Relishes* and *Tastes* which he has endued us with; they are indeed additional Motives to Right Acting, as they render our Duty pleasant and comfortable to us, and the contrary displeasing and comfortless; they render us the more inexcusable in departing from the *Rules* of *Reason,* since they were given us to promote the Observance of them: But they can never fix upon us any *proper* and *strict Obligation,* farther than as they are made Objects of *Reason,* and furnish us with Topicks to *reason* from, and are found to agree with *Reason.*

And, I believe, if we consider the Matter closely, we shall find that we cannot so much as form an Idea of *Obligation,* without introducing *Reason* as its Foundation. Supposing we have *Natural Affections* disposing us to certain *Actions,* how are we *obliged* to comply with such *Dispositions?*—Why—because it is *Reasonable* to do so. Have we a *Moral Sense,* or *Relish,* for such *Actions* and *Dispositions?* How are we *obliged* to gratify that *Relish*? Why—it is *Reasonable* to gratify it. How are we at all *obliged* to consult our own *Interest* or *Pleasure*? Are we not at Liberty to give up that *Interest* or *Pleasure*?—No—it is *Unreasonable* to do it—we are self-condemned if we do it in such and such Cases. And therefore, we are *obliged* in such Cases *not* to do it. In short, all sort of *Obligation* to any thing, implies some *Reason* to give it Force, without which it is a mere Phantom of the Imagination.

Philanthropus thinks, I have not *happened to observe the Author of the Inquiry's Definition of the Moral Sense,* p. 124, *and that I have by this means misapprehended him in something.* If I have, I shall be extremely glad to be set right. But I think I have all along understood him to mean by his *Moral Sense,* as he defines it, *A Determination of our Minds to receive* Amiable *or* Disagreeable *Ideas of Actions, when they occur to our Observation, antecedently to any Opinions of Advantage or Loss to redound to ourselves from them.* That there is such a *Sense* implanted in us by the Author of our Nature, I make no Question. I believe every one may feel it in himself, And when I asked, *whence this Sense arose?* I did not mean to express any Doubt about its Existence; but only to signify the Necessity of enquiring into the Original of it, in order to determine whether it was a *Right Sense,* or not; by which I meant, whether it prompted us to *Right Actions,* or to judge *Rightly* of *Actions,* or not; and whether the *Actions,* or *Agents,* in which it delighted, or to which it was averse, were really *Morally Good* or *Morally Evil* in themselves: The *Test* of which Inquiry, I took to be *Reason*; and that this *Sense* was *Good* or *Bad, Right* or *Wrong,* as it *agreed* or *disagreed* with *Reason*; and not *Reason,* as it *agreed* or *disagreed* with this *Sense.* |As to Philanthropus's Admonition against squeezing too much Meaning into some *short Words and Particles,* by which means the crowded Sense often passes almost unobserved in the Sentence, I think it very just; and have endeavoured to avoid that Fault in Writing this, as much as I could.

I am persuaded that *Philanthropus* is no more an Enemy to the *Reasonableness* of *Virtue,* than I am to the *Amiableness* of *it.* But the Question at present is, "From what Principle *Moral Obligation* is to be deduced; and what it is that immediately denominates *Actions,* and *Agents, Morally Good,* or *Morally Evil.*" In which Inquiry I shall always be glad of, as I shall be ever ready to receive, further Information from so ingenious a Writer as *Philanthropus*.

I am, *SIR.*

His and Your obliged humble Servant,

PHILARETUS.

In Philaretus's Letter, *last Week*, Col. 2, line 5, *instead of* Void of any Disposition to act, *read* void of any Collateral Disposition to act.

9.

SATURDAY, *October* 9, 1725.

To *Britannicus*

SIR,

After hearty Thanks to PHILARETUS for engaging me in a further Enquiry into the Foundation of *Virtue,* please to communicate to him these Thoughts on his Letters of *July* and *August 7.*

Our Debate is drawn into narrower Bounds, by his reducing ultimately all other *Moral Attributes* of Actions to *Reasonableness* or *Conformity to Truth.* I allow his Definitions; nor do I apprehend he would have disallowed my Instance of *Practical Truth,* had he defined the Word *Obligation.*

The *Reasonableness* of an Action, or its *Conformity to Truth,* or *the Power of finding out Truth,* I fancy needs further Explication. *True Propositions* may be made concerning all Objects, Good or Evil; there must be a *Conformity* between every true Proposition and its Object: If then all Conformity between an Object and a *Truth,* be *Goodness,* all Objects must be good. If there be any particular Kind of Conformity which constitutes *Moral Goodness,* I wish it were explained, and distinguished from that *Conformity* between every *Object* of our Knowledge and the *Truths* which we know.

In every *Truth* some *Attribute* is affirmed or denied of its *Subject.* In *Truths* about Actions some *Attribute* is affirmed or denied of Actions.

Whatever *Attribute* is affirmed of any Action, the contrary *Attribute* may be as *truly* affirmed of the contrary Action or Omission: Both these Propositions shall be true, and their Objects, *viz.* the *Actions,* shall be conformable to them. If then this *Conformity* be *Moral Goodness,* the most contrary Actions shall both be Good, being both conformable to their several *Truths:* This *Conformity* then cannot denominate the One Good more than the Other. It must be some other *Attribute,* which can be ascribed to one, and not to the other, which must make the Distinction, and not *the agreeing with a Truth;* for any one may make as many Truths about Villany as about Heroism, by ascribing to it the contrary *Attributes.*

But not to pass over this Debate with a *Logical* or *Metaphysical* Argument.[37] When we ask the *Reason* of an Action, we sometimes mean *the Truth which excites the Agent to it, by shewing that it is apt to gratify some Inclination of his Mind.* Thus, Why does a sensual Man pursue Wealth? The *Reason,* in this Meaning of the Word, is this *Truth,* viz. Wealth is useful to purchase Pleasures. At other Times, by the *Reason* of Actions we mean, *the Truth which shews a Quality in the Action of any Person, engaging the Approbation either of the Agent or the Spectator; or which shews it to be Morally Good.* Thus why do I observe the Contracts I have made? The Reason is this, "Mutual Observation of Contracts is necessary to preserve Society." The former *Reasons,* after GROTIUS, I call *exciting Reasons,* the latter *justifying Reasons.*[38]

Now *Philaretus* seems to me to maintain, "That there is some *Exciting Reason* to *Virtue,* antecedent to all *kind Affections,* or *Instinct* toward the Good of Others: And that in like Manner there are some *justifying*

37. In *A Compend of Logic* and in *A Synopsis of Metaphysics* Hutcheson made a point of distinguishing between logical truth ("the agreement of the signs with the thing signified" or "the agreement of a proposition with the things themselves") and moral or ethical truth ("the agreement of the signs with the sense of the mind" or "the agreement of a proposition with the sentiment of the mind"): see *Logic, Metaphysics, and the Natural Sociability of Mankind,* pp. 24 and 80.

38. Hugo Grotius distinguished between the reasons rulers give to justify war and the motives that prompt them to go to war: "Thus in the War of *Alexander* against *Darius,* to take Vengeance of the *Persians,* for the Injuries they had formerly done the *Greeks,* was the justifying Reason, whilst the Motive was a strong Desire of Glory, Empire, and Riches, in Conjunction with Confident Hopes of Success": *The Rights of War and Peace,* p. 1097, and see ibid. p. 389.

Reasons, or Truths, antecedent to any *Moral Sense,* causing Approbation."
The Author of the *Inquiry,* I apprehend, must maintain, "that *Desires,*
Affections, Instincts, must be previous to all *Exciting Reasons;* and a *Moral*
Sense antecedent to all *Justifying Reasons.*"

The *Exciting Reasons* are such as shew an Action to be fit to attain its
End: But nothing can be an *End* previous to all Desires, Affections, or
Instincts, determining us to pursue it: *They* must then be previous to all
Exciting Reasons or *Truths,* unless we say that there may be *Exciting Rea-*
sons to Actions, where no *End* is intended; or that *Ends* are intended pre-
viously to all *Desire* or *Affection.*

But are there not *Exciting Reasons* even antecedent to any *End,* moving
us to propose one |*End* rather than another? To this ARISTOTLE long ago
answered, That there are *Ultimate Ends,* not desired with a view to any
thing further; and *Subordinate Ends,* desired with a view to something
further.[39] There are *Exciting Reasons,* or *Truths,* about subordinate Ends,
shewing their Tendency toward the *Ultimate End;* but as to the *Ultimate*
Ends, there is no Truth or Reason exciting us to pursue them. Were there
Exciting Reasons for all Ends, there could be no *Ultimate End;* but we
should desire One thing for the Sake of Another in an infinite Series.

Thus, ask a Being who has *selfish Affections,* why he pursues Wealth?
He will assign this Truth as his Exciting Reason, "that Wealth furnishes
Pleasures or Happiness." Ask again, why he desires his own Happiness or
Pleasure? I cannot divine what Proposition he would assign as the *Reason*
moving him to it. This is indeed a true Proposition, "There is a Quality
in his Nature moving him to pursue Happiness"; but it is this *Quality* or
Instinct in his Nature which moves him, and not this Proposition. Just so
this is a Truth, "that a Certain Medicine cures an Ague"; but it is not a
Proposition which cures the Ague, nor is it any Reflection or Knowledge
of our own Nature which excites us to pursue Happiness.

If this Being have also *publick Affections;* what are the *Exciting Reasons*
for observing Faith, or hazarding his Life in War? He will assign this
Truth as a Reason, "such Conduct tends to the Good of Mankind." Go a

---

39. Aristotle, *Nicomachean Ethics,* I.1.3–4. See also *Illustrations upon the Moral*
Sense (1728), p. 217; (2002), p. 139.

Step further, Why does he pursue the Good of Mankind? If his *Affections* be really disinterested, without any selfish View, he has no *Exciting Reason*; the Publick Good is an ultimate End to this Series of Desires.

When *Philaretus*, to evade a Circle, brings in the End of the *Deity*, as a Reason of pursuing publick Good; if he means an *exciting Reason*, let him express the Truth exciting Men to pursue the End proposed by the *Deity*.[40] Is it this, "No Creature can be Happy who Counteracts it"? This is a Reason of Self-Love exciting all who consider it. But again, what Reason excites Men to pursue their own Happiness? Here we must end in an Instinct. Is this the Truth, "The *Deity* is my Benefactor"? I ask again the Reason exciting to love or obey Benefactors? Here again we must land in an Instinct. Is this the *Truth*, "The End of the *Deity* is a Reasonable End"? I ask again, What is the *Truth*, a Conformity to which makes the Desire of Publick Good reasonable in the *Deity?* What Truth either excites or justifies the *Deity* in this Desire? As soon as I hear a pertinent Proposition of this Kind, I shall recant all I have said. If the *Exciting Reason* of Men's complying with the *Deity* be this Truth, "Men are *obliged* to comply, or it is their Duty"; Then we are excited because we are obliged, or bound in Duty; and not because it is Reasonable so to do, or because it is conformable to a Truth. For this also is a Truth, "Disobedience is contrary to Obligation"; yet no body imagines that Conformity to this Truth, either makes Disobedience *Morally* Good, or excites to Pursue it. But whoever will define the Words, *Oblige, Owe, Duty,* will find himself at as great a Loss for ultimate *exciting Reasons,* previous to *Affections,* as ever.

In like Manner, where he says, "that to a Being void of *Publick Affections,* the pursuing the Happiness of Twenty, rather than his own, is *Reasonable*"; I want to know the Truth exciting such a Nature to Pursue it. Sure it is not this, that "the Sum of Twenty Felicities is a greater Quantity than any One of them." For unless by a *Publick Affection* the Happiness of others be made desirable to him, the Prospect of a great Sum in the Possession of others will never excite him; more than the Knowledge of this

---

40. In *Illustrations upon the Moral Sense* (1728), pp. 220–22; (2002), pp. 141–42 the argument of this and the following paragraph are paraphrased under the heading: "The common Reasons examined."

Truth, "That One Hundred equal Stones are a greater Bulk than One," will excite a Man, who has no Desire of Heaps, to cast them together.

If *Philaretus* intended in these two last Cases | *Justifying Reasons,* then it leads to the next Part of our Debate, about *Justifying Reasons:* The true Way of deciding it, is not a frequent Assertion, "that we approve Actions antecedently to a *Sense*"; but producing the very *Truths* for Conformity to which we approve Actions ultimately. Here the former Argument might be repeated, "that we may form *true Propositions* concerning all sorts of Actions Good or Evil: Each sort of Action is conformable to the Truths formed concerning it; this *Conformity* then cannot distinguish *Good Actions* from *Evil.* But to pass this Argument.

Philaretus owns, that "*Truths* which only shew an Action to be fit to attain its *End,* do not justify it." The *Justifying Truths* must be about the Ends themselves. Now what are the *Justifying Truths* about Ultimate Ends? What is the Truth, for Conformity to which we approve the Desire of Publick Good as an End, or call it a *Reasonable End*? Is it this, "Publick Good is a reasonable End"? This amounts to a very trifling Argument, *viz.* It is reasonable because it is reasonable. Is it this one; "This Desire excites to Actions which really do promote Publick Happiness"? Then, for Conformity to what *Truth* do Men approve the promoting of Publick Happiness? Is it this *Truth,* "Publick Happiness includes that of the Agent"? This is only an exciting Reason to Self-Love. Is this the *Justifying Truth,* "Publick Happiness is the End of the *Deity*"? The Question returns, What *Truth* justifies Concurrence with the Divine Ends? Is it this, "The *Deity* is our Benefactor"? Then what *Truth* justifies Concurrence with *Benefactors*? Here we must end in a *Sense.* Or shall we assign this Reason, "Concurrence with the Divine Ends is morally good, because those Ends are *Reasonable Ends*"? Then what is the *Reason* or *Truth,* for Conformity to which we call the Divine Ends *Reasonable*? They are not good or conformable to Reason, because he wills them to be so. Here I own, I must ultimately resolve all *Approbation* into a *Moral Sense,* as I was forced to resolve all *Exciting Reasons* into *Instincts.*

Philaretus often insinuates two Objections; 1st. "There must be some *antecedent Standard,* by which we judge the *Affections* or *Moral Senses* themselves to be *right* or *wrong*." As to *Affections,* we judge of them ultimately by the *Moral Sense,* according as they are kind or malicious. But as to the *Moral Sense* itself, it can no more be called morally *Good* or *Evil,* than we call the Sense of Tasting, *sweet* or *bitter.* Each Person judges the *Sense* of others by his own: But no Man can immediately judge of his own *Moral Sense,* or Sense of Tasting, whether they be right or wrong. Reason may shew Men, that their *Moral Sense,* as it is now constituted, tends to make the Species *Happy*; and that a *contrary Sense* would have been pernicious; and therefore we may, by a Metonymie, call it *happy,* as we call our Taste *Healthy,* when it leads us to delight in Objects tending to our Health.

The other Objection is this, "that if there is no *Moral Standard* antecedent to a *Sense,* then all *Constitutions of Senses* had been alike *Good and Reasonable* in the *Deity.*" To this it may be answered, that we can conceive no *exciting Reasons* of the Divine Actions, antecedent to something in the *Divine Nature,* of a nobler Kind, corresponding to our Kindness and sweetest Affections; by which the *Deity* desires universal Happiness as an *End.* The Divine Wisdom did, no doubt, suggest the implanting of such a Sense in Men, to be the fittest Means of obtaining this End. The Justifying Reasons of the Divine Actions, when *we* judge of them, must end in our *Moral Sense,* which makes us approve such a kind beneficent Constitution of our Nature. Had we wanted a *Moral Sense,* yet the *Deity* might have judged of his own Actions as he does now; but we should have had no Moral Ideas, either concerning the *Deity,* or our selves. Our Reason might have suggested indeed, that if the *Deity* did study our Happiness as an End, the omitting to give us ◇ such a Sense, if we could have had an Idea of it, was omitting the proper Means for obtaining his End. But *Moral Good* or *Evil* would have been to us unknown.

> *I am his and your*
> *very humble Servant,*
> PHILANTHROPUS.

10.

SATURDAY, *November* 27, 1725

To BRITANNICUS.

SIR,

If you are not already tired with this Debate your self, I would by your Means presume once more on *Philanthropus's* Patience; and beg you to convey these Thoughts to him, in Answer to his last Letter of *Oct. 9.*

He observes rightly, that the Argument is *drawn into narrower Bounds*; and seems willing to put the Issue of the Whole upon this single Question, "Whether, or no, there are *Reasons* previous to all *Desires, Affections, Instincts,* or any *Moral Sense* arising from them?"

The Question then is, "Whether *Truth,* apprehended by our *Reason,* is the Principle from which we must argue to prove any thing to be *morally Good* or *Evil;* or whether our *Desires, Affections, Instincts,* and a *moral Sense* attending them, distinct from the Faculty of *Reason,* compose that Principle?"

Philanthropus thinks, *Truth* cannot be the Principle; because "we may form *True Propositions* concerning all Sorts of Actions, *Good* and *Evil;* and each Sort of Action is conformable to the *Truths* formed concerning it: And therefore this Conformity cannot distinguish *Good* Actions from *Evil.*—But, upon this Principle, all Objects must be *Good.*—And the most contrary Actions shall be both *Good.*" This is the Substance of his *Logical* or *Metaphysical Argument.*

But he, by a great Mistake here, puts the Conformity, or *agreeing with a Truth, i.e.* any one single Truth; for the *Conformity with Truth,* as *Truth* signifies the true State and Connexion and Relation of Things, taken all together.[41] For, when it is said that *Moral Goodness* consists in the Acting

41. In this paragraph Burnet adopted a position similar to Clarke's, and different from Wollaston, who held that many particular actions have moral significance and these actions signify propositions that may be true or false. Hence Leslie Stephen's characterization of Wollaston's moral philosophy: "Thirty years profound meditation had convinced Wollaston that the reason why a man should abstain from breaking his wife's head was, that it was a way of denying that she was his wife" (*English Thought in the Eighteenth Century,* 1:130). Hutcheson elaborated on his response to Wollaston in *Illustrations upon the Moral Sense,* section 3. See also letters to *The London*

in *Conformity to Truth*; the Meaning is not, that it consists in Conformity to any one single and detached *True Proposition,* but to the whole Chain and *Compages* of *Truth*; in acting agreeably to the State and Connexion and mutual Relation of Things.

For instance, tho' it is a *True Proposition,* "That such an Action gives me Pleasure"; yet it may not be a *morally good* Action, because it may contradict and interfere with other *Truths;* as, "That, tho' it pleases *me,* it hurts *another*"; and, "That the Nature of that other requires Pleasure as well as mine"; or, "That, tho' it gratifies me for the present, it may probably be followed by Pain afterwards"' and the like: And because it may be contradictory to the Nature and Constitution of Things, which is the Chain and Series of *Truth.*

But, not to dwell longer on this *Logical or Metaphysical* Objection, (which is entirely founded upon his mistaking the sole Idea which is annexed to the Word *Truth* in this *Question,*) I shall proceed to examine his *Moral* Objections.

Philanthropus divides *Reasons* for Actions, after GROTIUS, into two Sorts; *Exciting Reasons,* and *Justifying Reasons.* And I am willing to follow him in this Partition: Tho', in Truth, the *Exciting Reason* to an Action, and the *Justifying Reason* for it, ought always to be the same in Substance, and should only differ in the Form of putting them. The *Exciting Reason* should amount to this, in order to be a valid Reason; "This Action is Right, therefore I will do it"; and the *Justifying Reason,* "It was *Right,* therefore I did *right* in doing it."

But the Dispute is, what Method we are to take to prove that *This* Action *is,* or *was, Right.*

Now this I would prove from its Conformity to the Nature and Constitution of Things, about which I form in my Mind certain *True Propositions*; and thence call it *Truth.* And in this Disquisition I would take into Consideration my own Nature; the Nature of Things without me; and my Relation to *them,* and *theirs* to me. And under this Head all natural

---

Journal (1728) for a defense of Wollaston by Aletheiophilos (lover of truth) and the response from Philocalus (lover of warmth) that presented further criticisms of Wollaston's theory in the manner of Hutcheson.

Desires, Affections, Passions, Appetites, Instincts, Relishes and *Senses,* both in myself and others, come to be examined, as Indications of the Condition and End of Nature. And when, from all these Considerations, I find certain *True Propositions* resulting, concerning the |Nature of Things; then *Moral Goodness,* I say, consists in acting agreeably to those *True Propositions,* and *Moral Badness* in acting disagreeably to them.

But *Philanthropus* thinks this Point may be proved singly from the *Ends* which our *Desires and Affections* propose to us; and from a *Moral Sense,* or Taste, approving of what is agreeable to *them*: Wherein I think he wants ground to rest upon. He esteems *That* to be the whole Proof, which seems to me but a Branch of the Reasoning; and the Quarry whence we are to fetch some of the Materials which help us in examining those Propositions which are the Foundations of our Rules for acting.

He proceeds to sustain his own, and overturn the contrary Opinion, by this Principle, "That there can be no *exciting Reason* to an *Ultimate End*"? In which I agree with him and ARISTOTLE:* But the very Point in Question is, "What is, or ought to be, the *Ultimate End* of Actions." And the greatest part of *Moral Goodness* consists in choosing a right *Ultimate End.* He who proposes his *Pleasure* as his *Ultimate End,* can scarce be a very good Man: Whereas he who makes *Truth* his *Ultimate End,* can scarce be a bad Man. He acts like a rational Creature, and does not desire or wish that *Truth* may lie on *this* side or *that* side of the Question; but studiously and sincerely pursues it whithersoever it leads him.

The Question is not, what is seen in Experience to lead Men to act. I confess, their *Passions* and *Affections* generally do lead them. And it is their Happiness, and the Wisdom of their Creator, that they have such *Affections* and *Passions* as naturally tend, till they corrupt them, to produce in many Instances the same Effects, which *Reason* both dictates before, and approves afterwards. But still 'tis *Reason* alone which informs us beforehand that such Actions *would be* Right, as well as afterwards that such Actions *were* Right. And of this indeed I think there can be no doubt to any one who has ever felt *Reason* working in his Breast.

---

* *Nichomach. Ethic.* Lib. I, C.1. [1093b]

Philanthropus observes, that *to avoid a Circle I bring in the End of the Deity.* But I must remind him that this was only under the Definition of the Word FIT; which being a *Relative* Word, respecting some End or other, must have a *Correlative* answering it: Whereas the Words *True, Reasonable, Right,* are *Absolute* and not *Relative Terms,* and therefore need no *Correlate.* Now I said, if we form this Proposition, "It is *Fit* that *Publick Good* should be regarded," it must be *Fit* for the attaining some *End.* And this *Fitness* is a *Moral Fitness,* and *Right* in it self, if the *End* be a *wise and reasonable End.* I mentioned the *Deity,* not as meaning that this *End* was *wise,* because it was the *End* of the *Deity*; but because all *Ends* must subsist in some *Intelligent Agent*; and the *Deity* is an *Intelligent Agent,* who is perfectly wise, and always proposes *wise Ends* to himself.

Philanthropus proceeds to ask, "What is the Truth *exciting* Men to pursue the End proposed by the Deity?" And he offers me my Choice of several *Truths,* which tho' they are all very weighty Truths, yet are not those I should choose to build upon in this Argument. The single *Truth* I would pitch upon is, "Because the *End is a reasonable End*" And the *Truth,* which makes this *End,* (*viz.* Publick Good or Happiness) a *Reasonable End* is, "*That it is best, that all should be happy.*" This is the "*Truth,* a Conformity to which makes the Desire of Publick Good reasonable in the Deity" and, I add, in all rational Creatures, who would imitate the Wisdom and Goodness of the *Deity.*

If any one asks, Why it is *Best*? I would answer him, as I would do, if he asked me Why Four is more than Two? It is self-evident. I should be sorry indeed to argue, as PHILANTHROPUS afterwards puts it, "That *Publick Good* is a reasonable End, because it is a reasonable End." I should think it sufficient to prove it to be *Best,* and should not be afraid of affirming it to be *reasonable* to pursue what is *Best.* The only Point is to prove what is *Best.* And this |can only be done, by considering and examining by *Reason,* not feeling by *Instinct* or *Sense,* how the Matter of Fact stands, and what is actually *Best* in it self. Just as when I am examining, whether I ought to assent to a Proposition; I would not say, It is True, because it is True: but would consider the Evidence of it; and if I perceived it to be True, would assent to it.

The self-evident *Truth* then, "That it is in it self *Best* that All should be Happy," is immediately perceivable by all rational Natures. But the Question of Fact, wherein that *Best* consists, makes the Difference of *more* or *less Moral Goodness* in *Intelligent Agents,* according to the greater or narrower Extent of their Knowledge; considered together with their Disposition to act, and, in Fact, acting agreeably to their Knowledge; and also using the Means to acquire and improve that Knowledge. In this the All-knowing Author of Nature, being infallible and unchangeable, *He* is most perfectly *Good* in a *Moral Sense.* Inferior Beings are, *more* or *less,* capable of being so, proportionably to their Capacity of Knowledge: And are, in Fact, *morally Good* or *Evil,* as they act according to, or contrary to, that Knowledge which they are possess'd of, or may acquire.

But that which I fancy misleads *Philanthropus* in this Point is, that by *Exciting,* he means, exciting as the *Passions* and *Affections* do, by giving us Uneasiness when we do not follow their Movements; (which is indeed a Guard to our Virtue, but not the Ground of it:) Whereas by *Reason's exciting,* I mean only its proposing an Action to us as most *eligible* and *right*; which, tho' it may be attended with Pleasure or Uneasiness from an additional *Moral Sense,* yet is distinct from it, and not dependent upon it. And on the same ground he often confounds a Thing's being *desirable* to us, with its being esteemed *reasonable* by us: Whereas Men often *desire* what they think, and are conscious, is very *unreasonable*; and know That to be very *reasonable,* which they by no Means *desire.* For which I appeal to the common Experience of Mankind.

What I have said about *exciting Reasons,* may be easily applied to all that *Philanthropus* demands, concerning *justifying Reasons*; and therefore I need not consume the Time in doing it; nor mistrust the Judgment of my Readers so far. But I may possibly say more on this Head, if ever I come to examine *Philanthropus's* Answers to the *two Objections,* which he says I often insinuate.

I shall conclude at present, with giving my Meaning of the Word *Obligation,* since *Philanthropus* desires it more than once; tho' I thought I had in Effect done it in my last.

Obligation is a Word of a Latin Original, signifying *the Action of Binding*; which therefore, in a *Moral Sense,* (for the Question here is not about corporal Force) must import the *Binding* an Intelligent Agent by some Law; which can be no other than that of *Reason.* For all other Ties are reducible to this; and this is Primary, and reducible to no other Principle.

I find I can thwart my *Desires* and *Affections,* and yet approve what I do in contradiction to them. I can approve of Actions by a *Moral Sense*; and yet, upon Examination by Reason, rectify that *Sense,* as I can my *external Senses*; and condemn what *it* approved. But my *Reason* I can never contradict, but it flies in my Face; I stand self-condemned, and bring my self in guilty, tho' all the Earth should acquit me. And I never heartily comply with its Dictates, but I acquit my self, tho' all the World should condemn me. And I do not find, that *Desire,* or *Affection,* or *Passion,* or any kind of *Sensation,* has any Influence in the Case; except it be, to increase or diminish Pleasure and Self-complacency, as we comply with, or reject the Dictates of *Reason,* and are thereby a kind of natural Rewards and Punishments; or perhaps, to extenuate our Guilt, and excuse us in some Degree, on the Strength and Violence of the Temptation. I am.

> *SIR, Yours,* &c.
> PHILARETUS.

11.

Saturday, *December* 25, 1725

> The day itself will justify the giving the *Reader this Paper* upon so serious and important a Subject as the Nature and Foundation of VIRTUE; the Restoration of which to its native Force, and original Authority over the intelligent World, was the Great Delight of Christianity itself.

To BRITANNICUS

SIR,

I Would fain, methinks, clear the Account I have, in several former Letters, given of the *Basis* and *Groundwork* of True Virtue, from all seeming and plausible Difficulties: And therefore, I now beg Leave to conclude, by examining the Answers which *Philanthropus* gives to the *Two Objections,* he says, *I often insinuate.*

The *First* Objection is, "That there must be a Standard to judge of the *Affections* and *Moral Senses* themselves, whether they are *Right* or *Wrong*."[42]

To this *Philanthropus* returns for Answer, That "we judge of the *Affections* by the *Moral Sense*. But, as to the *Moral Sense* it self, it can no more be called *morally Good* or *Evil,* than we call the Sense of *Tasting,* Sweet or Bitter.—No Man can immediately judge of his own Moral Sense, or Sense of Tasting, whether they be *Right* or *Wrong*."

Now, the Question is not, whether the *moral Sense* can be called *morally Good* or *Evil,* which I admit it cannot, properly and strictly speaking; because *moral Good* and *Evil* belong to *Agents,* and their *Actions,* not to *Affections* or *Inclinations*. For the Person chooses; and his Action arises from his own Choice: And therefore *He* is accountable. But his *Affection,* or *Inclination,* or *Sense,* is implanted in him, and not in his own Power: And therefore he is not accountable either for having it, or for wanting it; and consequently it has nothing *moral* in it; since *Morality* implies the being accountable and answerable; and cannot take Place where Force is used, or Power is wanting. A Man is no more a *morally good* Man for being made *affectionate,* than for being made hungry when his Stomach is craving. But, as Hunger prompts us to eat when the Machine requires Repair, where perhaps *Reason* might forget or neglect it, were it left to itself; so *natural Affection,* and the *Sentiments* belonging to it, urge us to render good Offices to others, which our Reason, tho' it approves them, and even proposes them to our Thoughts as the best Things we can do, yet might be too slack and remiss in stirring us to perform them, without such indefatigable Solicitors continually prompting us. But still the doing such good Offices is a *morally good* Action; not because *Affection,* or *Sentiment,* inclines us so, (for then Cruelty, in Case a cruel *Affection,* or *Sentiment,* was natural to us, would be *morally good* too;) but because our Mind perceives it to be *Best* to do so; perceiving immediately, and intuitively, this Truth; "That it is best that the Species should be happy"; and

42. Hutcheson continued the argument with Burnet on this subject in *Illustrations upon the Moral Sense,* (1728), pp. 234–38, 239–42; (2002), pp. 149–51, 151–54.

deducing this further Truth by Reason, "That Benevolence is the properest and fittest Means to procure the Happiness of the Species."

But the true Question is, "Whether the *moral Sense* may be called *Right* or *Wrong,* or not": For we grant it cannot be properly called *morally Good* or *Evil.* And this it certainly may, as well as any other Sense. It is not parallel to the calling the Sense of Tasting, *sweet* or *bitter;* as PHILANTHROPUS has wrongly put it, and in doing so directly begs the Question. For *sweet* and *bitter* are on all Hands allowed to be Denominations of particular distinct Sensations: Whereas we deny that *moral Good* and *Evil* are at all Denominations of *Sensations,* but of *Dispositions* and *Actions* of Agents. But it is exactly parallel to the calling the Sense of Tasting *Right* or *Wrong.*

Now this we certainly may do, and in fact very frequently do, in *this* and all other *Senses,* internal as well as external. We judge any |*Sense* to be wrong, or vitiated, when it represents Things otherwise than we know it would do, if we were in a right State of Body. And, even in our best State, our *Senses* often deceive us; and are, or may be, rectified by our *Reason.* A Truth so well known to all natural Philosophers, that I need not spend Time in proving it. In the same manner the *Moral Sense* must be esteemed wrong, or vitiated, where it contradicts our Reason, in which the Health and Vigour of the Mind consists. If all Men were naturally selfish, and ill-natured to others; and by any *internal Sense* found Delight in reflecting on Actions conformable to such a malign *Affection*; still all Men endued with *Reason,* and employing their *Reason* in examining such Things, must perceive it to be a *wrong Sense* that relished such Actions; a Sense which represented Things very differently from what they really were. And it would be as ill Reasoning to conclude, from such a vitiated *internal Sense,* the *Moral Goodness* or *Badness* of an Action, as it would be to conclude the true *Taste* or *Colour* of a Body, (that is, what Sensation of *Tasting* or *Seeing* it would give us in a right Habit of Body) from the *Taste* or *Colour* which a Fever or a Jaundice makes it put upon us. But, as in the *External Senses* our *Reason* must be the Test to inform us whether they are perfect in their kind, or defective and vitiated; so it is likewise in the *Internal Senses.* And without this Standard of *Reason* to recur to, all *Senses* would be equally *Right,* merely because they were *Senses*; which we know is contrary to fact.

But I think *Philanthropus* here gives the Point up in effect himself. For he admits *that Reason may shew Men, that their moral Sense, as it is now constituted, tends to make the Species happy; and that a contrary Sense would have been pernicious.* Why—if this be allowed, we have the greatest *Truth* we wanted, and the most complex, and difficult to be demonstrated. And one *Truth* more, and that a self-evident *One,* will afford us a solid Bottom, on which the whole Structure of Morality may safely rest. And that is, "That it is better that the Species should be Happy, than that it should not." This is such an unmoveable *Truth,* that it will bear all the Weight we can lay upon it. And, consequently, whatever Actions, or Dispositions of the Mind, are the proper Means to this *End,* (*viz.* to obtain the Happiness of the Species,) are in themselves evidently *morally Good,* being agreeable to this self-evident Truth, "That it is *best* that the Species should be Happy." And, if we find in our selves *Affections,* or Sentiments, leading to this End, we judge them to be *Right Affections,* tho' I would not choose to stile them *morally Good.* And so, *vice versâ.*

But, if it be farther asked, "Why it is *best* that the Species should be happy?" I own no Reason can be assigned for it; no more than a Reason can be assigned, "why the Whole is equal to all its Parts," or "a Part is less than the Whole"; or "Things equal to the same Third, are equal to one another." No Reason can be ever given for a self-evident Axiom: For all Reasoning is only an Appeal to some self-evident Principle or other. And if I could find a Man of so different a Make of Understanding from mine, that what was self-evident to me was not so to him, I should have no Medium by which I could argue with him any longer on that Head; but we must part, and own that we cannot understand each other: Only in that case we should not be angry at one another, for what neither of us could help.

Again, if it be farther demanded, "For whom is it *best,* that the Species should be happy?" I answer; For themselves, and for every one who has any Thing to do with them, and who is capable of perceiving, "That *Happiness* is *better* than *Misery*; and of seeing this Consequence, That therefore, He does for the *better* who promotes *Happiness* any where, than He who promotes *Misery.*" And this, I should |think, every Intelligent Being must perceive, if he applies his Mind to it at all.

The other *Objection Philanthropus* takes notice that *I insinuate* is: "That if there is no *moral Standard* antecedent to a *Sense,* then all Constitution of Senses had been alike good and reasonable in the Deity": I meant, *for the Deity to appoint and cause.*

To this he answers; "That we can conceive no *exciting Reasons* of the Divine Actions, antecedent to something in the *Divine Nature,* of a nobler kind, corresponding to our Kindness and sweetest Affections; by which the *Deity* desires universal Happiness as an *End*—The *justifying Reasons* of the Divine Actions must end in our *moral Sense,* which makes us approve such a kind beneficent Constitution of our Nature."

But I would here ask *Philanthropus,* by what kind of Reasoning it is, that we attribute *Benignity* to the *Deity?* Is it only because we find *benign Affections* in our selves? If so; then, on the same Ground, we may attribute Pain and Uneasiness to *Him,* because we sometimes feel them; or any other *imperfect Sentiment,* which is familiar to *us.* But the Truth is, we conclude, that the *Deity* cannot but be *benign;* because, by some *previous Standard* in our own Minds, we judge *Benignity* to be a Perfection; something in itself Right and Excellent; and therefore cannot be wanting where there is infinite Perfection. And this brings us back to the Inquiry; "How, and by what Standard, we are to judge of our *Affections* and *Senses?*" Which was fully considered under the *former Objection,* and needs not be repeated here. So that we go much higher in our Enquiry than the bare Consideration of *Affection,* or a *moral Sense* in our selves. I own, indeed, we cannot but conceive something in the *Deity,* in some measure analogous to our kindest *Affections*; as that he takes infinite Pleasure in communicating Good to his Creatures. But this Consideration by it self would only lead us to conclude him infinitely *Happy,* and not *Good* in a moral Sense. We esteem him essentially *Good,* because he knows all *Truth,* and always acts according to it. He infallibly knows what is *Best*; and will always do what is *Best* upon the whole, all things considered. For Instance, his infinite Knowledge represents to him *Happiness,* as something that is *better* than *Misery.* And thence we firmly conclude, that he will always propose the *Happiness,* and not the *Misery,* of his Creatures, as his *End* in creating them. And, if he creates them with a Capacity for *Happiness,* he will not make it impossible for them to be *Happy*: Tho' perhaps it may be in the Nature of Things impossible to make them capable of the *Happiness* of Intelligent and Free Agents, without leaving it in their own Power to make themselves *Miserable* if they will; which will therefore still be *best,* to put in their own Election, tho' the Consequence may be evil to them thro' their own perverse Choice.

And I think here *Philanthropus* again gives up the Cause; when he admits that *our Reason might have suggested, that, if the Deity did study our Happiness as an End, the omitting to give us such a Sense, if we could have had an Idea of it, was omitting the proper Means for obtaining his End.*

Then surely there can be no doubt, that the *Deity* intended us to be *Happy* when he created us: Nor can we suppose that he intends us to be *Happy,* and yet with-holds from us the necessary Means of *Happiness.* For the not doing the one would be acting contrary to what He knows to be *best*: And the other would be acting contrary to his own Design. Neither of which can find Place in an Intelligent, Free, and Perfect Being.

So that upon the whole, I think, these *Objections* have not been answered by *Philanthropus.* And indeed, they seem to me *such* as cannot be removed, and must entirely overturn his Notions of *moral Good* and *Evil.* <>

But I cannot part with PHILANTHROPUS, till I assure him once more, that I think the Treatise of the *Original of Virtue,* which gave occasion to this Debate, as well as the other concerning *Beauty* and *Order,* exceedingly ingenious, and well argued from the Principles laid down. And if the Author had laid his Principles deeper, he would have made his Discourse as useful and solid, as it is delightful and entertaining. And I should not esteem my Labour lost, if by what I have said I could provoke him to undertake the Proof of the Rectitude and Excellence, as well as of the Existence, of his *Moral Sense.* I am fully persuaded he would be much more capable of deducing that Series of Truths, which is necessary to the compassing such a Design, than,

Your, &c.

PHILARETUS

Letters to *The Dublin Weekly Journal,*
1725–26

1.

No. 10. *Saturday, June* 5, 1725.[1]

Rapias in jus malis ridentem alienis.—Hor.[2]

To Hibernicus.

There is scarce any thing that concerns *human Nature,* which does not deserve to be inquired into: I send you some Thoughts upon a very

---

1. The letters to *The Dublin Weekly Journal* are reproduced here from the revised edition in book form: *A Collection of Letters and Essays on Several Subjects, Lately Publish'd in* The Dublin Journal, 2 vols. (London, 1729). In the first publication this letter was addressed "To the Author of the *Dublin Weekly* Journal," and it opened with this preamble: "Sir, The following Essay, being the Performance of a very learned and ingenious Gentleman, I presume it will be an acceptable Present to the Publick, and am, Sir, Your very humble Servant, Hibernicus." Behind the nominal editor of the journal, Hibernicus, was James Arbuckle (d. 1742), a native of Belfast and a former student at the University of Glasgow. It was Arbuckle who identified Hutcheson publicly as author of the two series of letters to the journal, writing: ". . . it becomes me to divest my self of a great deal of Reputation I have got by the Papers of some other Gentlemen who have more frequently lent me their Assistance. The Learned and Ingenious Author of the *Inquiry into the Original of Our Ideas of Beauty and Virtue,* will therefore, I hope excuse me if to do this Piece of Justice on my self, I am obliged to name him for the three Papers upon Laughter, which are written in so curious and new a strain of thinking; and also for the Forty-fifth, Forty-sixth, and Forty-seventh Papers, containing so many judicious and valuable Remarks on that pernicious Book the *Fable of the Bees*" (*The Dublin Weekly Journal*, No. 104, March 25, 1727). By the time the letters were republished in book form, Arbuckle was no longer associated with *The Dublin Weekly Journal*, and the title page of the book suggests that the letters had in fact been published in the rival *Dublin Journal*. This falsehood is repeated in the headings to the letters of June 12 and 19, 1725, just as the 1729 text does not reproduce the original journal's banner at the top of each letter: "The Dublin Weekly Journal." In the following notes the *Dublin Weekly Journal* is referred to as *DWJ*.

2. Horace, *Satires*, II.3.22: "brought forcibly to justice, he will transform himself and laugh maliciously."

common Subject, *Laughter*; which you may publish, if you think they can be of any use, to help us to understand what so often happens in our own Minds, and to know the Use for which it is design'd in the Constitution of our Nature.

Aristotle, in his *Art of Poetry*, has very justly explained the Nature of one *Species* of *Laughter*, *viz.* the *Ridiculing of Persons*, the Occasion or Object of which he tells us, is ἁμάρτημά τι καὶ αἶσχος ἀνώδυνον καὶ οὐ φθαρτικόν; *Some Mistake, or some Turpitude, without grievous Pain, and not very pernicious or destructive*. But this he never intended as a general Account of all sorts of Laughter.[3] <78>

But Mr. *Hobbes*, who very much owes his Character of a *Philosopher* to his assuming positive solemn Airs, which he uses most when he is going to assert some palpable Absurdity, or some ill-natur'd Nonsense, assures us,[4] that "*Laughter* is nothing else but *sudden Glory*, arising from some sudden Conception of some Eminency in our selves, by comparison with the Infirmity of others, or with our own formerly: For Men laugh at the Follies of themselves past, when they come suddenly to remembrance, except they bring with them any present Dishonour."[5]

This Notion the Authors of the *Spectators* No 47, have adopted from Mr. *Hobbes*. That bold Author having carry'd on his Inquiries, in a singular manner, without regard to Authorities; and having fallen into a way of speaking,[6] which was much more intelligible than that of the *Schoolmen*, soon became agreeable to many free Wits of his Age. His grand View was to deduce all human Actions from *Self-Love*: by some bad Fortune he has over-look'd every thing which is *generous* or *kind* in Mankind; and represents Men in that Light in which a thorough Knave or Coward beholds them, suspecting all Friendship, Love, or social Affection, of Hypocrisy, or selfish Design or Fear.

The learned World has often been told that *Puffendorf* had strongly imbib'd *Hobbes's* first Principles, altho he draws much better <79> Con-

---

3. Aristotle, *Poetics*, V.2.1449a. This paragraph was added in 1729.
4. In the *DWJ* the paragraph opens thus: "Mr. *Hobbes* has been at Pains to enquire into this Matter; he tells us, . . ."
5. Hobbes, *The Elements of Law*, part I: *Human Nature*, chap. 9, art. 13, p. 54.
6. *DWJ*: "speaking and thinking."

sequences from them; and this last Author, as he is certainly much preferable[7] to the generality of the *School-men,* in distinct intelligible Reasoning,
has been made the grand Instructor in Morals to all who have of late
given themselves to that Study: Hence it is that the old Notions of *natural Affections,* and kind *Instincts,* the *Sensus communis,* the *Decorum,* and
Honestum, are almost banish'd out of our Books of Morals; we must
never hear of them in any of our Lectures for fear of *innate Ideas:* All
must be *Interest,* and some selfish View; Laughter it self must be a Joy
from the same Spring.[8]

If Mr. *Hobbes's* Notion be just, then first, There can be no *Laughter* on
any Occasion where we make no *Comparison* of our selves to others, or of
our present State to a worse State, or where we do not observe some *Superiority* of our selves above some other Thing: And again, it must follow,
that every sudden Appearance of *Superiority* over another, must excite
Laughter, when we attend to it. If both these Conclusions be false, the
Notion from whence they are drawn must be so too.

I*st.* Then, that *Laughter* often arises without any imagined Superiority
of ourselves, may appear from one great Fund of Pleasantry, the *Parody,*
and *Burlesque Allusion*; which move *Laughter* in those who may have the
highest Veneration for the Writing alluded to, and also admire the Wit of
<80> the Person who makes the Allusion. Thus many a profound Ad-
mirer of the Machinery in *Homer* and *Virgil,* has laugh'd heartily at the
Interposition of *Pallas* in *Hudibras,* to save the bold *Talgol* from the
Knight's Pistol, presented to the Outside of his Skull:

> *But* Pallas *came in Shape of Rust,*
> *And 'twixt the Spring and Hammer thrust*
> *Her* Gorgon Shield, *which made the Cock*
> *Stand stiff, as 'twere transform'd to Stock.*[9]

7. *DWJ:* "vastly preferable." Joseph Addison thought that Hobbes's discourse on
Human Nature "in my humble opinion is much the best of all his works": *The Spectator,* vol. 1, no. 47 (London, 1718), p. 178. On the use of Pufendorf's works in universities and academies in the early eighteenth century, see above, p. 135, note 2.

8. *DWJ:* "from some selfish Interest."

9. Samuel Butler, *Hudibras,* part 2, canto 2, lines 29–32, p. 128.

And few who read this, imagine themselves superior either to *Homer* or *Butler*; we indeed generally imagine ourselves superior in Sense to the valorous Knight, but not in this Point, of firing rusty Pistols. And pray, Would any Mortal have laughed, had the Poet told, in a simple unadorned manner, that his Knight attempted to shoot *Talgol,* but his Pistol was so rusty that it would not give fire? and yet this would have given us the same ground of sudden Glory from our Superiority over the doughty[10] Knight.

Again, to what do we compare our selves, or imagine ourselves superior, when we *laugh* at this fantastical Imitation of the *Poetical Imagery,* and Similitudes of the Morning?

> *The Sun, long since, had in the Lap*
> *Of* Thetis *taken out his Nap;*
> *And, like a Lobster boil'd, the Morn,*
> *From black to red began to turn.*[11]

<81> Many an Orthodox *Scotch Presbyterian* (which Sect few accuse of disregard for the holy Scriptures) has been put to it to preserve his Gravity, upon hearing the Application of *Scripture* made by his Countryman Dr. *Pitcairn,* as he observ'd a Crowd in the Streets about a Mason, who had fallen along with his Scaffold, and was over-whelmed with the Ruins of the Chimney which he had been building, and which fell immediately after the Fall of the poor Mason; *Blessed are the Dead which die in the Lord, for they rest from their Labours, and their Works follow them.*[12] And yet few imagine themselves superior either to the Apostle or the Doctor. Their Superiority to the poor Mason, I'm sure, could never have raised such Laughter, for this occur'd to them before the Doctor's Consolation; in this Case no Opinion of Superiority could have occasioned the *Laughter,* unless we say, that People imagined themselves superior to the Doctor in Religion: but an imagined Superiority to a *Doctor* in *Religion,* is not a

---

10. *DWJ*: "valorous."

11. *Hudibras*, part 1, canto 2, lines 781–84, p. 51.

12. Archibald Pitcairne (1652–1713), eminent Scottish physician. Like Samuel Butler, he wrote satires on Presbyterianism; *The Assembly, a Comedy, by a Scots Gentleman* (1722) was the most famous of these. The citation is Revelation 14:13.

matter so rare as to raise *sudden Joy;* and, with People who value Religion, the Impiety of another is no matter of *Laughter.*

It is said, "* That when Men of Wit make us laugh, it is by representing some Oddness or Infirmity in themselves, or others." Thus Allusions made on trifling Occasions, to the most solemn *figured Speeches* <82> of great Writers, contain such an obvious Impropriety, that we imagine ourselves incapable of such Mistakes as the Alluder seemingly falls into; so that in this Case too, there is an imagin'd Superiority. But in answer to this, we may observe, that we often laugh at such Allusions, when we are conscious that the Person who raises the *Laugh,* knows abundantly the justest Propriety of speaking, and knows, at present, the *Oddness* and *Impropriety* of his own Allusion as well as any in Company; nay, laughs at it himself: We often admire his Wit in such Allusions, and study to imitate him in it, as far as we can. Now, what sudden Sense of Glory, or Joy in our Superiority, can arise from observing a Quality in another, which we study to imitate,[13] I cannot imagine. I doubt, if Men compared themselves with the Alluder, whom they study to imitate, they would rather often grow grave or sorrowful.

Nay, farther, this is so far from Truth, that imagined Superiority moves our *Laughter,* that one would imagine from some Instances the very contrary: For if *Laughter* arose from our imagined *Superiority,* then, the more that any Object appear'd *inferior* to us, the greater would be the Jest; and the nearer any one came to an Equality with us, or Resemblance of our Actions, the less we should be moved with *Laughter.* But we see, on the contrary, that some Ingenuity in *Dogs* and *Monkeys,* which comes near to <83> some of our own Arts, very often makes us merry; whereas their duller Actions, in which they are much below us, are no matter of Jest at all. Whence the Author in the *Spectator* drew his Observation, *That the Actions of Beasts which move our Laughter, bear a Resemblance to a human*

---

* See the Spectator. [In *The Spectator*, vol. 1, no. 47 (London, 1718), p. 180, Addison wrote: "I am afraid I shall appear too Abstracted in my speculations if I shew that when a Man of Wit makes us laugh, it is by betraying some Oddness or Infirmity in his own Character, or in the Representation which he makes of others."]

13. "to imitate" added in 1729.

Blunder,[14] I confess I cannot guess; I fear the very contrary is true, that their imitation of our grave wise Actions would be fittest to raise Mirth in the Observer.

The second Part of the Argument, that *Opinion of Superiority* suddenly incited in us does not move *Laughter,* seems the most obvious thing imaginable: If we observe an Object in pain while we are at ease, we are in greater danger of Weeping than *Laughing:* And yet here is occasion for *Hobbes's* sudden Joy. It must be a very merry State in which a fine Gentleman is, when well dressed, in his Coach, he passes our Streets, where he will see so many ragged Beggars, and Porters and Chairmen sweating at their Labour, on every side of him. It is a great pity that we had not an Infirmary or Lazar-house to retire to in cloudy Weather, to get an Afternoon of *Laughter* at these inferior Objects: Strange, that none of our *Hobbists* banish all *Canary Birds* and *Squirrels,* and *Lap-Dogs,* and *Puggs,* and *Cats* out of their Houses, and substitute in their Places Asses, and Owls, and Snails, and Oysters to be merry upon. From these they might have higher Joys of Superiority, than from those with whom <84> we now please ourselves. *Pride,* or an high Opinion of ourselves, must be entirely inconsistent with Gravity; Emptiness must always make Men solemn in their Behaviour; and conscious Virtue and great Abilities must always be upon the Sneer. An Orthodox Believer who is very sure that he is in the true way to Salvation; must always be merry upon Hereticks, to whom he is so much superior in his own Opinion; and no other Passion but Mirth should arise upon hearing of their Heterodoxy. In general, all Men of true Sense, and Reflection, and Integrity, of great Capacity for Business, and Penetration into the Tempers and Interests of Men, must be the merriest little Grigs imaginable; *Democritus* must be the sole Leader of all the Philosophers; and perpetual *Laughter* must succeed into the Place of the Long Beard,

> *To be the Grace*
> *Both of our Wisdom and our Face.*[15]

14. This citation is a paraphrase of the remainder of the sentence quoted above from *The Spectator,* no. 47: "and that when we laugh at a Brute or even at an inanimate thing, it is at some Action or Incident that bears a remote Analogy to any Blunder or Absurdity in reasonable Creatures" (p. 180).

15. *Hudibras,* part 1, canto 1, ll. 239–40.

It is pretty strange, that the Authors whom we mentioned above, have never distinguish'd between the words *Laughter* and *Ridicule:* this last is but one particular Species of the former, when we are *laughing* at the Follies of others; and in this Species there may be some pretence to alledge that some imagined Superiority may occasion it; but then there are innumerable Instances of *Laughter,* where no Person is ridiculed; nor does he who *laughs* compare himself to any thing what<85>soever. Thus how often do we *laugh* at some out-of-the-way Description of natural Objects, to which we never compare our State at all. I fancy few have ever read the *City Shower* without a strong Disposition to *Laughter*; and instead of imagining any Superiority, are very sensible of a Turn of Wit in the Author which they despair of imitating: Thus what relation to our Affairs has that Simile in *Hudibras,*

> *Instead of Trumpet and of Drum,*
> *Which makes the Warriour's Stomach come,*
> *And whets Mens Valour sharp, like Beer*
> *By Thunder turn'd to Vinegar*[16]

The *Laughter* is not here raised against either Valour or martial Musick, but merely by the wild resemblance of a mean Event.[17]

And then farther, even in Ridicule itself there must be something else than bare Opinion to raise it, as may appear from this, that if any one would relate in the simplest manner these very Weaknesses of others, their extravagant Passions, their absurd Opinions, upon which the Man of Wit would rally, should we hear the best Vouchers of all the Facts alledged, we shall not be disposed to *Laughter* by bare Narration; or should one do a real *important Injury* to another, by taking advantage of his Weakness, or by some pernicious Fraud let us see another's Simplicity, this is no matter of *Laughter:* and yet these important Cheats do really discover our *Superi*<86>*ority* over the Person cheated, more than the trifling Impostures of our *Humourists.* The Opinion of our Superiority may raise a sedate Joy in our Minds, very different from *Laughter*; but such a Thought seldom arises in our Minds in the hurry of a cheerful Conversation among

16. Jonathan Swift, "A Description of a City Shower," in *Poetical Works,* pp. 91–93; first published in *The Tatler,* no. 238, p. 1710.

17. This sentence was added in 1729.

Friends, where there is often a high mutual Esteem. But we go to our Closets often to spin out some fine Conjectures about the Principles of our Actions, which no Mortal is conscious of in himself during the Action;[18] thus the same *Authors* above-mentioned tell us, that the Desire which we have to see tragical Representations is, because of the secret Pleasure we find in thinking ourselves secure from such Evils; we know from what Sect this Notion was derived.

> *Quibus ipse malis liber es, quia cernere suave.* Lucr.[19]

This Pleasure must indeed be a secret one, so very secret, that many a kind compassionate Heart was never conscious of it, but felt itself in a continual state of Horror and Sorrow; our desiring such Sights flows from a kind *Instinct* of Nature, a secret Bond between us and our Fellow-Creatures.

> *Naturae imperio gemimus cum funus adultæ*
> *Virginis occurrit, vel terra clauditur Infans.*
> *. . . Quis enim bonus . . .*
> *Ulla aliena sibi credat mala.*[20]   —Juven.

18. *DWJ*: "himself amidst the very Action."

19. Lucretius, *De Rerum Naturae*, book 2, line 4, pp. 84–85: "to perceive what ills you are free from yourself is pleasant."

20. Juvenal, *Satires*, XV, lines 138–42: "Nature's command that we sigh when we meet the funeral of a marriageable virgin or when a baby is burried in the ground, too young for the pyre's flame. . . . who is good. . . . [who] considers the distress of others irrelevant to themselves [?]" This and the following letter to *The Dublin Weekly Journal* were not signed; only in the third letter did the author identify himself as Philomeides.

2.

No 11. *Saturday, June 12, 1725.*

To the AUTHOR of the *Dublin Journal.*[21]

> *Humano capiti cervicem, pictor equinam*
> *Jungere si velit, & varias inducere plumas*
> *Undique collatis membris, ut turpiter atrum*
> *Desinat in piscem mulier formosa superne,*
> *Spectatum admissi, Risum teneatis amici?*
> —HOR.[22]

SIR,

In my former Letter, I attempted to shew that Mr. *Hobbes's* Account of *Laughter* was not just. I shall now endeavour to discover some other Ground of that *Sensation, Action, Passion,* or *Affection,* I know not which of them a Philosopher would call it.

The ingenious Mr. *Addison,* in his Treatise of *The Pleasures of the Imagination,* has justly observ'd many sublimer Sensations than those commonly mention'd among Philosophers:[23] He observes particularly, that we receive Sensations of Pleasure from those Objects which are *great,*[24] *new,* or *beautiful*; and on the contrary, that Objects which are more *narrow* and *confined,* or *deformed,* and *irre<88>gular,* give us disagreeable Ideas. It is unquestionable, that we have a great number of *Perceptions,* which one can scarcely reduce to any of the five Senses, as they are commonly explained; such as either the Ideas of *Grandeur, Dignity, Decency, Beauty, Harmony*; or on the other hand, of *Meanness, Baseness, Indecency, Deformity*; and that

---

21. *DWJ*: "the *Dublin Weekly Journal.*"

22. "If a painter chose to join a human head to the neck of a horse, and to spread feathers of many a hue over limbs picked up now here now there, so that what at the top is a lovely woman ends below in a black and ugly fish, could you, my friends, if favored with a private view, refrain from laughing?" (Horace, "The Art of Poetry," lines 1–5, in *Satires, Epistles and Ars Poetica,* p. 451). Also quoted by Addison, in *The Spectator,* vol. 1, no. 63, p. 243 (London, 1718).

23. Addison's essays on the pleasures of the imagination appear in *The Spectator,* nos. 412–21.

24. *DWJ*: "just."

we apply these Ideas not only to material Objects, but to *Characters, Abilities, Actions.*[25]

It may be farther observed, that by some strange *Associations* of Ideas made in our Infancy, we have frequently some of *these Ideas* recurring along with a great many Objects, with which they have no other Connection than what Custom and Education, or frequent Allusions[26] give them, or at most, some very distant Resemblance. The very *Affections* of our Minds are ascribed to inanimate Objects; and some Animals, perfect enough in their own kind, are made constant *Emblems* of some Vices or Meanness; whereas other Kinds are made *Emblems* of the contrary Qualities. For Instances of these *Associations,* partly from Nature, partly from Custom,[27] we may take the following ones; *Sanctity* in our *Churches, Magnificence* in publick Buildings, *Affection* between the Oak and Ivy, the Elm and Vine; *Hospitality* in a *Shade,* a pleasant Sensation of *Grandeur* in the Sky, the Sea, and Mountains, distinct from a bare Apprehension or Image of their Extension; *Solemnity* and *Horror* in shady Woods. An Ass is <89> the common Emblem of *Stupidity* and *Sloth,* a Swine of *selfish Luxury*; an Eagle of a *great Genius*; a Lion of *Intrepidity*; an Ant or Bee of *low Industry,* and *prudent Oeconomy.* Some inanimate Objects have in like manner some accessary Ideas of *Meanness,* either for some natural Reason, or oftner by mere Chance and Custom.[28]

Now, the same ingenious Author observes, in the *Spectator* Vol. I. No 62. that what we call a *great Genius,* such as becomes a heroick Poet, gives us Pleasure by filling the Mind with *great* Conceptions; and therefore they bring most of their Similitudes and Metaphors from Objects of

25. See *An Essay concerning the Nature and Conduct of the Passions and Affections,* (1728), p. 5; (2002), p. 17, where Hutcheson distinguished between the perceptions of the external senses and "the Pleasant Perceptions arising from *regular, harmonious, uniform* Objects; as also from *Grandeur* and *Novelty.* These we may call, after Mr. Addison, the Pleasures of the *Imagination*; or we may call the Power of receiving them an *Internal Sense.* Whoever dislikes this Name may substitute another."

26. "or frequent Allusions" added in 1729.

27. "partly from Nature, partly from Custom" added in 1729.

28. See *Inquiry,* sec. 4, art. 4 (1725), p. 38; (2008), p. 44: "A fruitful Fancy would find in a Grove, or a Wood, an Emblem for every Character in a Commonwealth, and every turn of Temper, or Station in Life"; and sec. 6, art. 11 (1725), p. 76; (2004), pp. 67–68 for an explanation of the "Diversity of Fancys" by the association of ideas.

Dignity and Grandeur, where the Resemblance is generally very obvious.[29] This is not usually called *Wit,* but something nobler. What we call grave *Wit,* consists in bringing such resembling Ideas together, as one could scarce have imagined had so exact a Relation to each other; or when the Resemblance is carry'd on thro' many more Particulars than we could have at first expected: And this therefore gives the Pleasure of *Surprize.* In this *serious Wit,* tho we are not solicitous about the *Grandeur* of the Images, we must still beware of bringing in Ideas of *Baseness* or *Deformity,* unless we are studying to represent an Object as base and deformed. Now this sort of *Wit* is seldom apt to move *Laughter,* more than *heroick* Poetry. <90>

That then which seems generally the Cause of *Laughter,* is "The bringing together of Images which have *contrary* additional Ideas, as well as some Resemblance in the principal Idea: This *Contrast* between Ideas of *Grandeur, Dignity, Sanctity, Perfection,* and Ideas of *Meanness, Baseness, Profanity,* seems to be the very Spirit of *Burlesque;* and the greatest Part of our Raillery and Jest are founded upon it."

We also find ourselves moved to *Laughter* by an overstraining of *Wit,* by bringing Resemblances from Subjects of a quite different kind from the Subject to which they are compared. "When we see, instead of the Easiness, and natural Resemblance which constitutes true *Wit,* a *forced straining* of a Likeness, our *Laughter* is apt to arise; as also, when the only Resemblance is not in the Idea, but in the Sound of the Words." And this is the Matter of *Laughter* in the *Pun.*

Let us see if this Thought may not be confirmed in many Instances. If any Writing has obtained a high Character for *Grandeur, Sanctity, Inspiration,* or *sublimity* of Thoughts, and *boldness* of Images; the Application of any known Sentence of such Writings to low, vulgar, or base Subjects, never fails to divert the Audience, and set them a *laughing.* This Fund of *Laughter* the Antients had by Allusions to *Homer:* Of this the Lives of some of the Philosophers in *Dio*<91>*genes Laertius* supply abundance

---

29. In *The Spectator,* vol. I, no. 62, p. 241 (London, 1718), Addison remarked "that natural Way of writing, that beautiful Simplicity, which we so much admire in the Composition of the Ancients; and which no Body deviates from, but those who want Strength of Genius to make a Thought shine in its natural Beauties."

of Instances. Our late *Burlesque* Writers derive a great part of their Pleasantry from their introducing, on the most trifling Occasions, *Allusions* to some of the bold Schemes, or Figures, or Sentences of the great Poets, upon the most solemn Subjects. *Hudibras* and *Don Quixote* will supply one with Instances of this in almost every Page. It were to be wished that the Boldness of our Age had never carry'd their ludicrous Allusions to yet more venerable Writings. We know that Allusions to the Phrases of *holy Writ* have obtained to some Gentlemen a Character of *Wit,* and often furnish'd *Laughter* to their Hearers, when their Imaginations have been too barren to give any other Entertainment. But I appeal to the Religious themselves, if these Allusions are not apt to move *Laughter,* unless a more strong Affection of the Mind, a *religious Horror* at the Profanity of such Allusions, prevents their allowing themselves the Liberty of *laughing* at them. Now in this Affair I fancy any one will acknowledge that an Opinion of Superiority is not at all the Occasion of the *Laughter.*

Again, any little Accident to which we have joined the Idea of *Meanness,* befalling a Person of great Gravity, Ability, Dignity, is a matter of *Laughter,* for the very same reason; thus the strange Contortions of the Body in a Fall, the dirtying of a decent Dress, the natural Functions which we study to con<92>ceal from sight, are matter of *Laughter,* when they occur to Observation in Persons of whom we have high Ideas: nay, the very human Form has the Ideas of *Dignity* so generally joined with it, that even in ordinary Persons such mean Accidents are matter of Jest; but still the Jest is increased by the *Dignity, Gravity,* or *Modesty* of the Person; which shews that it is this *Contrast,* or *Opposition* of Ideas of *Dignity* and *Meanness,* which is the Occasion of *Laughter.*

We generally imagine in Mankind some degree of *Wisdom* above other Animals, and have high Ideas of them on this account. If then along with our Notion of *Wisdom* in our Fellows, there occurs any Instance of *gross Inadvertence,* or *great Mistake;* this is a great cause of *Laughter.* Our Countrymen are very subject to little Trips of this kind, and furnish often some Diversion to their Neighbours, not only by Mistakes in their Speech, but in Actions. Yet even this kind of *Laughter* cannot well be said to arise from our Sense of *Superiority.* *This* alone may give a sedate Joy, but not be a matter of *Laughter*; since we shall find the same kind of *Laughter* arising in us, where this Opinion of *Superiority* does not attend it: For if the most ingenious Person in the World, whom the whole Company esteems, should thro' inadvertent hearing, or any other mistake, answer quite from the Purpose, the whole Audience may *laugh* heartily, without the least <93> abatement of their *good Opinion.* Thus we know some very ingenious Men have not in the least suffer'd in their Characters by an extemporary *Pun,* which raises the *Laugh* very readily; whereas a premeditated *Pun,* which diminishes our Opinion of a *Writer,* will seldom raise any *Laughter.*

Again, the more violent Passions, as *Fear, Anger, Sorrow, Compassion,* are generally look'd upon as something great and solemn; the beholding of these Passions in another, strikes a Man with Gravity: Now if these Passions are artfully, or accidentally raised upon a small, or a fictitious Occasion, they move the *Laughter* of those who imagine the Occasions to be small and contemptible, or who are conscious of the Fraud: this is the occasion of the *Laugh* in *Biting,* as they call such Deceptions.

According to this Scheme, there must necessarily arise a great Diversity in Men's Sentiments of the *Ridiculous* in Actions or Characters, according as their Ideas of *Dignity* and *Wisdom* are various. A truly wise Man who places the Dignity of human Nature in good Affections and suitable Actions, may be apt to *laugh* at those who employ their most solemn and strong Affections about what, to the wise Man, appears perhaps very useless or mean. The same *Solemnity* of Behaviour and *Keenness* of Passion, about a Place or Ceremony, which ordinary People only employ about the absolute Necessaries <94> of Life, may make them *laugh* at their Betters. When a Gentleman of Pleasure, who thinks that good Fellowship and Gallantry are the only valuable Enjoyments of Life, observes Men with great *Solemnity* and *Earnestness,* heaping up Money, without using it, or incumbering themselves with Purchases and Mortgages, which the gay Gentleman with his paternal Revenues, thinks very silly Affairs, he may make himself very merry upon them: And the frugal Man, in his turn, makes the same Jest of the Man of Pleasure. The successful Gamester, whom no Disaster forces to lay aside the *trifling Ideas* of an Amusement in his Play, may *laugh* to see the serious Looks and Passions of the gravest Business, arising in the *Loser,* amidst the Ideas of a Recreation. There is indeed in these last Cases an Opinion of *Superiority* in the *Laughter;* but this is not the proper occasion of his *Laughter;*

otherwise I see not how we should ever meet with a composed Countenance any where: Men have their different Relishes of Life, most People prefer their own Taste to that of others; but this moves no Laughter, unless in representing the Pursuits of others, they do join together some whimsical Image of *opposite* Ideas.

In the more polite Nations there are certain Modes of Dress, Behaviour, Ceremony, generally received by all the better sort, as they are commonly called: To these Modes, *Ideas of Decency, Grandeur,* and *Dignity* <95> are generally joined; hence Men are fond of imitating the Mode: And if <in>[30] any polite Assembly, a contrary Dress, Behaviour, or Ceremony appear, to which we have joined in our Country the contrary Ideas of *Meanness, Rusticity, Sullenness,* a Laugh does ordinarily arise, or a disposition to it, in those who have not the thorough good Breeding, or Reflection, to restrain themselves, or break thro' these customary Associations.

And hence we may see, that what is counted ridiculous in one Age or Nation, may not be so in another. We are apt to *laugh* at *Homer,* when he compares *Ajax* unwillingly retreating, to an *Ass driven out of a Cornfield*; or when he compares him to a *Boar*:[31] Or *Ulysses* tossing all Night without Sleep thro' Anxiety, to a *Pudding frying on the Coals*.[32] Those three Similies, have got low mean Ideas joined to them with us, which it is very probable they had not in *Greece* in *Homer's* days; nay, as to one of them, the *Boar,* it is well known, that in some Countries of *Europe,* where they have *wild Boars* for Hunting, even in our Times, they have not these low sordid Ideas joined to that Animal, which we have in these Kingdoms, who never see them but in their dirty Sties, or on Dunghills. This may teach us how impertinent a great many Jests are, which are made upon the Style of some other antient Writings, in Ages when Manners were very different from ours, tho perhaps fully as rational, and every way as human and just.[33] <96>

---

30. "in" seems to have been inadvertently deleted in 1729.
31. *The Iliad of Homer,* book XI, p. 249.
32. Homer, *The Odyssey,* book XX, p. 304.
33. In the *DWJ* the letter ends with the promise: "(This to be continued)."

3.

No 12. *Saturday, June* 19, 1725.

To the AUTHOR of the *Dublin Journal.*[34]

> *Ridiculum acri*
> *Fortius & melius magnas plerumque secat res.*

SIR,

To treat this Subject of *Laughter gravely,* may subject the Author to a Censure, like to that which *Longinus* makes upon a prior Treatise of the *Sublime,* because wrote in a manner very unsuitable to the Subject.[35] But yet it may be worth our pains to consider the Effects of *Laughter,* and the Ends for which it was implanted in our Nature, that thence we may know the proper Use of it: which may be done in the following Observations.[36]

First, WE may observe, that *Laughter,* like many other Dispositions of our Mind, is necessarily pleasant to us, when it begins in the natural manner, from some *Perception* in the Mind of something ludicrous, and does not take its rise unnaturally from *external Motions* in the Body. Every one is consc<97>ious that a State of *Laughter* is an easy and agreeable State, that the Recurring or Suggestion of ludicrous Images tends to dispel *Fretfulness, Anxiety,* or *Sorrow,* and to reduce the Mind to an *easy, happy State*; as on the other hand, an easy and happy State is that in which we are most lively and acute in perceiving the *Ludicrous* in Objects: Any thing that gives us Pleasure, puts us also in a fitness for *Laughter,* when something ridiculous occurs; and ridiculous Objects occurring to a sour'd Temper, will be apt to recover it to Easiness. The implanting then a *Sense* of the *Ridiculous,* in our Nature, was giving us an *Avenue* to Pleasure, and an easy *Remedy* for Discontent and Sorrow.[37]

---

34. *DWJ*: "the *Dublin Weekly Journal.*" The quotation is from Horace, *Satires,* Book I, Satire X, lines 14–15: "Ridicule often decides serious matters more effectively and in a better manner than severity."

35. Longinus, *On the Sublime,* p. 123.

36. "which may . . . Observations" added in 1729.

37. Hutcheson also described a sense of humor as one of the reflexive senses in *A Synopsis of Metaphysics,* part 2, chap. 1, sec. 5: "we may discern yet another reflexive sense: a sense of things that are *ridiculous* or apt to cause laughter, that is, when a

Again, *Laughter,* like other Affections, is very contagious; our whole Frame is so sociable, that one merry Countenance may diffuse Cheerfulness to many; nor are they all Fools who are apt to *laugh* before they know the Jest, however curiosity in wise Men may restrain it, that their Attention may be kept awake.

We are disposed by *Laughter* to a *good Opinion* of the Person who raises it, if neither our selves nor our Friends are made the *Butt. Laughter* is none of the smallest Bonds of common Friendships, tho it be of less consequence in great Heroick Friendships.

If an Object, Action or Event be truly *great* in every respect, it will have no natural Relation or Resemblance to any thing <98> *mean* or *base;* and consequently, no mean Idea can be joined to it with any natural Resemblance. If we make some forced remote Jests upon such Subjects, they can never be pleasing to a Man of Sense and Reflection, but raise Contempt of the Ridiculer, as void of just Sense of those things which are truly great. As to any great and truly sublime Sentiments, we may perhaps find that, by a playing upon Words, they may be applied to a trifling or mean Action, or Object; but this Application will not diminish our *high Idea* of the great Sentiment. He must be of a poor trifling Temper who would lose his relish of the Grandeur and Beauty of that noble Sentence of *Holy Writ,* mentioned in a former Paper, from the *Doctor's* Application of it.[38] *Virgil Travesty* may often come into an ingenious Man's Head, when he reads the Original, and make him uneasy with impertinent Interruptions; but will never diminish his Admiration of *Virgil.*[39] Who dislikes that Line in *Homer,* by which *Diogenes* the *Cynick* answered a Neighbour at an Execution, who was inquiring into the Cause of the Criminal's Condemnation? (which had been the Counterfeiting of the antient Purple)[40]

---

thing arouses contrary sensations at one and the same time" (*Logic, Metaphysics, and the Natural Sociability of Mankind,* p. 120).

38. See the reference to Archibald Pitcairn in the first *DWJ* letter, p. 198, n. 12.

39. Charles Cotton, *Scarronides, or Virgil Travesty, on the First and Fourth Books of the Aeneid.* Cotton was also a translator of Hobbes: see Noel Malcolm, "Charles Cotton, Translator of Hobbes's De Cive," pp. 259–87.

40. Diogenes Laertius, *Lives of Eminent Philosophers,* VI, 57, p. 59: "Fast gripped by purple death and forceful fate."

ἔλλαβε πορφύρεος θάνατος καὶ Μοῖρα κραταιή.

Let any of our Wits try their Mettle in ridiculing the Opinion of a *good and wise Mind* governing the whole Universe; let them try <99> to ridicule *Integrity* and *Honesty, Gratitude, Generosity*, or the *Love of one's Country*, accompanied with *Wisdom*. All their Art will never diminish the Admiration which we must have for such Dispositions, wherever we observe them pure and unmixed with any low views, or any Folly in the Exercise of them.

When in any Object there is a *Mixture* of what is truly *great* along with something *weak* or *mean*, Ridicule may, with a weak Mind which cannot separate the *great* from the *mean*, bring the whole into Disesteem, or make the whole appear weak or contemptible: But with a Person of just Discernment and Reflection it will have no other Effect, but to separate what is great from what is not so.

When any Object either good or evil is aggravated and increased by the Violence of our Passions, or an *Enthusiastick Admiration*, or *Fear*, the Application of Ridicule is the readiest way to bring down our high Imaginations to a Conformity to the real Moment or Importance of the Affair. Ridicule gives our Minds as it were a bend to the contrary side; so that upon Reflection they may be more capable of settling in a just Conformity to Nature.

Laughter is received in a different manner by the *Person ridiculed*, according as he who uses the Ridicule evidences good Nature, Friendship, and Esteem of the Person whom he laughs at; or the contrary. <100>

The enormous *Crime* or grievous *Calamity* of another, is not of it self a Subject which can be naturally turned into Ridicule: The former raises Horror in us, and Hatred; and the latter Pity. When *Laughter* arises on such occasions, it is not excited by the *Guilt* or the *Misery*. To observe the Contortions of the Human Body in the Air, upon the blowing up of an Enemy's Ship, may raise *Laughter* in those who do not reflect on the *Agony* and *Distress* of the Sufferers; but the reflecting on this Distress could never move *Laughter* of it self. So some fantastick Circumstances accompanying a Crime may raise *Laughter*; but a piece of cruel *Barbarity*, or treacherous *Villany*, of it self must raise very contrary Passions. A Jest is not ordinary in an *Impeachment* of a Criminal, of an Invective Oration: It rather diminishes than increases the *Abhorrence* in the Audience, and may justly raise Contempt of the Orator for an unnatural Affectation of Wit. Jesting is still more unnatural in Discourses design'd to move *Compassion* toward the distressed. A forced unnatural Ridicule on either of these occasions, must be apt to raise in the guilty or the miserable Hatred against the *Laughter*; since it must be supposed to flow from Hatred in him toward the Object of his Ridicule, or from want of all Compassion. The guilty will take *Laughter* to be a Triumph over him as contemptible; the miserable will interpret it as hardness of <101> Heart, and Insensibility of the Calamities of another. This is the natural Effect of joining to either of these Objects, mean ludicrous Ideas.

If smaller *Faults,* such as are not inconsistent with a Character in the main amiable, be set in a ridiculous Light, the guilty are apt to be made sensible of their Folly, more than by a bare grave Admonition. In many of our faults, occasion'd by too great Violence of some Passion, we get such *Enthusiastick* Apprehensions of some Objects, as lead us to justify our Conduct: The joining of opposite Ideas or Images, allays this *Enthusiasm*; and, if this be done with good Nature, it may be the least offensive, and most effectual Reproof.

Ridicule upon the smallest faults, when it does not appear to flow from kindness, is apt to be extremely provoking; since the applying of mean Ideas to our Conduct, discovers *Contempt* of us in the Ridiculer, and that he designs to make us contemptible to others.

Ridicule applied to those Qualities or Circumstances in one of our Companions, which neither he nor the Ridiculer thinks *dishonourable,* is agreeable to every one; the *Butt* himself is as well pleas'd as any in Company.

Ridicule upon any small *Misfortune* or Injury, which we have received with sorrow or keen resentment, when it is applied by a third Person, with appearance of good <102> Nature, is exceeding useful to abate our *Concern* or *Resentment,* and to reconcile us to the Person who injured us, if he does not persist in his Injury.

From this Consideration of the *Effects* of *Laughter,* it may be easy to see for what *Cause,* or *End,* a *Sense* of the ridiculous was implanted in Human Nature, and how it ought to be managed.

It is plainly of considerable *Moment* in Human Society. It is often a great occasion of *Pleasure*, and enlivens our Conversation exceedingly, when it is conducted by good Nature. It spreads a pleasantry of Temper over Multitudes at once; and one merry easy Mind may by this means diffuse a like Disposition over all who are in Company. There is nothing of which we are more communicative than of a good *Jest:* And many a Man who is incapable of obliging us otherwise, can oblige us by his Mirth, and really insinuate himself into our kind Affections, and good Wishes.

But this is not all the Use of *Laughter*. It is well known, that our Passions of every kind lead us into wild *Enthusiastick Apprehensions* of their several Objects. When any Object seems great in comparison of our selves, our Minds are apt to run into a perfect *Veneration*: When an Object appears *formidable*, a weak Mind will run into a *Panick*, an unreasonable, impotent Horror. Now in both these Cases, by our *Sense of* <103> *the ridiculous*, we are made capable of Relief from any pleasant, ingenious Well-wisher, by more effectual Means, than the most solemn, sedate reasoning. Nothing is so properly applied to the *false Grandeur*, either of Good or Evil, as Ridicule: Nothing will sooner prevent our excessive Admiration of *mix'd Grandeur*, or hinder our being led by that, which is, perhaps, really *great* in such an Object, to imitate also and approve what is really *mean*.

I question not but the Jest of *Elijah* upon the false Deity, whom his Countrymen had set up, has been very effectual to rectify their Notions of the Divine Nature; as we find that like Jests have been very seasonable in other Nations. *Baal*, no doubt, had been represented as a great Personage of unconquerable Power: But how ridiculous does the Image appear, when the *Prophet* sets before them, at once, the poor Ideas which must arise from such a limitation of Nature as could be represented by their *Statues*, and the high Ideas of *Omniscience*, and *Omnipotence*, with which the People declared themselves possessed by their *Invocation*. *Cry aloud, either he is talking, or pursuing, or he is on a Journey, or he is asleep.*[41]

This Engine of Ridicule, no doubt, may be abused, and have a bad Effect upon a weak Mind; but with Men of any Reflection, there is little

41. 1 Kings 18:27.

fear that it will ever be very pernicious. An Attempt of Ridicule <104> before such Men, upon a Subject every way great, is sure to return upon the Author of it. One might dare the boldest Wit in Company with Men of Sense, to make a Jest upon a completely great *Action,* or *Character.* Let him try the Story of *Scipio* and his *Fair Captive,* upon the taking of *Cartagena;*[42] or the old Story of *Pylades* and *Orestes;*[43] I fancy he would sooner appear in a Fool's Coat himself, than he could put either of these Characters in such a Dress. The only danger is in Objects of a *mixed Nature* before People of little Judgment, who by Jests upon the weak side, are sometimes led into Neglect, or Contempt, of that which is truly valuable in any Character, Institution, or Office. And this may shew us the Impertinence, and pernicious Tendency of general undistinguished Jests upon any *Character,* or *Office,* which has been too much over-rated. But, that Ridicule may be *abused,* does not prove it useless, or unnecessary, more than a like possibility of *Abuse* would prove all our Senses, and Passions, impertinent, or hurtful. Ridicule, like other *edged Tools,* may do good in a wise Man's hands, tho Fools may cut their Fingers with it, or be injurious to an unwary By-stander.

The Rules to avoid Abuse of this kind of Ridicule, are, First, *Either never to attempt Ridicule upon what is every way great, whether it be any great Being, Character, or Sentiments:* Or, if our Wit must some<105>times run into Allusions, on low occasions, to the Expressions of great Sentiments, *Let it not be in weak Company, who have not a just discernment of true Grandeur.* And, *Secondly,* Concerning Objects of a *mixed Nature,* partly great, and partly mean, *Let us never turn the meanness into Ridicule, without acknowledging what is truly great, and paying a just Vineration to it.* In this sort of jesting we ought to be cautious of our Company.

42. See Livy, *Ab Urbe Condita* (*From the Founding of the City*), book L, pp. 190–94, where Livy relates the story of Scipio's clemency in returning a beautiful woman taken captive in the conquest of New Carthage (Cartagena) to the man to whom she was betrothed. Scipio also provided a generous dowry for the couple. The groom subsequently became, at Scipio's request, an ally of Rome.

43. The "old Story" of the friendship of Orestes and his cousin, Pylades, was a narrative of their collaboration in the murder of Clytemnestra (Orestes' mother) and her husband, in revenge for the murder of Agamemnon, the father of Orestes. The story was retold and reworked by Homer, Aeschylus, Sophocles, and Euripides.

Discit enim citius, meminitque libentius illud,
Quod quis deridet, quam quod probat & veneratur.
                                                    —Hor.[44]

Another valuable Purpose of *Ridicule* is with relation to smaller *Vices,* which are often more effectually corrected by *Ridicule,* than by grave Admonition. Men have been laughed out of Faults which a Sermon could not reform; nay, there are many little *Indecencies* which are improper to be mentioned in such solemn Discourses. Now *Ridicule* with *Contempt* or *Ill-Nature,* is indeed always irritating and offensive; but we may, by testifying a just Esteem for the *good Qualities* of the Person ridiculed, and our *Concern* for his Interests, let him see that our *Ridicule* of his Weakness flows from Love to him, and then we may hope for a good Effect. This then is another necessary Rule, *That along with our ridicule of smaller faults we should always join Evidences of good Nature, and Esteem.* <106>

As to *Jests* upon *Imperfections,* which one cannot amend, I cannot see of what use they can be: Men of Sense cannot relish such Jests; foolish trifling Minds may by them be led to despise the truest *Merit,* which is not exempted from the casual Misfortunes of our Mortal State. If these Imperfections occur along with a vitious Character, against which People should be alarmed and cautioned, it is below a wise Man to raise Aversions to bad Men from their necessary Infirmities, when they have a juster handle from their vitious Dispositions.

I shall conclude this Essay with the words of Father *Malebranche,* upon the last Subject of *Laughter, the smaller Misfortunes of others.* That *Author* amidst all his *Visions* shews sometimes as fine Sense as any of his Neighbours. *Book* IV. *Ch.* XIII.[45]

There is nothing more admirably contrived than those natural *Correspondences* observable between the *Inclinations* of Men's Minds and the Motions of their Bodies.—All this secret *Chain-Work* is a Miracle, which can never sufficiently be admired or understood. Upon Sense of

44. Horace, Epistle 2.1: lines 261–63: "for men more quickly learn and more gladly recall what they deride than what they approve and esteem" (Horace, *Satires, Epistles and Ars Poetica,* pp. 418–19).
45. Nicholas Malebranche, *Treatise concerning the Search after Truth,* p. 166.

some surprizing *Evil,* which appears too strong for one to overcome with his own strength, he raises, suppose, a *loud Cry*: This *Cry* forced out by the Disposition of our *Machine,* pierces the Ears of those who are near, and makes them understand it, let them be of what Nation or Quality soever: <107> For it is the Cry of all *Nations,* and all *Conditions,* as indeed it ought to be. It raises a Commotion in their Brain, and makes them run to give *Succour* without so much as knowing it. It soon obliges their *Will* to *desire,* and their *Understanding* to *contrive,* provided that it was just and according to the Rules of Society. For an indiscreet *Outcry* made upon no occasion, or out of an idle Fear, produces, in the Assistants, *Indignation* or *Laughter* instead of *Pity.*—That indiscreet *Cry* naturally produces *Aversion,* and desire of revenging the Affront offered to *Nature,* if he that made it without cause, did it willfully: But it ought only to produce the Passion of Derision, mingled with some Compassion, without Aversion or desire of Revenge, if it were a *Fright,* that is a *false Appearance* of a pressing Exigency, which caused the *Clamour.* For *Scoff* or *Ridicule* is necessary to re-assure and correct the Man as *fearful;* and *Compassion* to succour him as *weak.* 'Tis impossible to conceive any thing better ordered.

> *I am, Sir,*
> *Your very humble Servant,*
> PHILOMEIDES.

4.

No 45. *Saturday, February 4, 1725/6*

To HIBERNICUS.

Nunquam aliud natura aliud—apiential dicit.—Juv.[46]

SIR,

A great part of your Readers must have heard of a Book entitled, *Private Vices publick Benefits.* I do not intend any Answer to that Book; but rather hereafter to shew it to be unanswerable, notwithstanding the zealous Attempts of some of the Clergy.[47] Yet it is to be hoped that that Author's Performance will not supersede the Labours of others on the same Subject, without design of answering what he has wrote.

It is not the Interest of every Writer to free his Words from Ambiguity. *Private Vices publick Benefits,* may signify any one of these five distinct Propositions: viz. *Private Vices are themselves publick Benefits:* Or, *Private Vices naturally tend, as the direct and necessary*[48] *Means, to produce publick Happiness:* Or, *Private Vices by dextrous Management of Governors may be made to tend to publick Happiness:* Or, <371> *Private Vices natively and necessarily flow from publick Happiness:* Or lastly, *Private Vices will probably flow from publick Prosperity thro' the present Corruption of Men.* Were it proper to crowd your Margin with Citations, you should have several Passages of that Book for each of these five Sentences, as if it were the Meaning of the Title. Far be it therefore from a candid Writer to charge upon him any one of these Opinions more than another; for if we treat

46. "Never does nature say one thing and wisdom another" (Juvenal, Satire XIV, p. 321, in *Juvenal and Persius,* pp. 286–87).

47. See Hutcheson's third letter on *The Fable of the Bees,* pp. 233–43 below. Among the clergymen who attempted to answer Mandeville, the most notable were William Law (1686–1761), *Remarks upon a Late Book, Entituled* The Fable of the Bees; or Private Vices, Public Benefits. *In a Letter to the Author. To which is added, a Postscript, containing an Observation or Two upon Mr. Bayle* (1724); and Richard Fiddes (1671–1725), *A General Treatise of Morality, Form'd upon the Principles of Natural Reason Only. With a Preface in Answer to Two Essays Lately Published in* The Fable of the Bees (1724). Cf. F. B. Kaye, in his 1924 edition of *The Fable of the Bees,* 2:401–7.

48. "and necessary" added in 1729.

him fairly, and compare the several Parts of his Work together, we shall find no ground for such a Charge.

What his *own private Happiness* is, any one may know by reflecting upon the several sorts of pleasant *Perceptions* he is capable of. We imagine our Fellows capable of the same, and can in like manner conceive *publick Happiness.* They are happy who have what they desire, and are free from what occasions Pain. He is in a *sure State* of Happiness, who has a sure Prospect that in all parts of his Existence he shall have all things which he desires, or at least those which he most earnestly desires, without any considerable pains. He is *miserable* who is under grievous Pain, or who wants what he most violently desires.

There is one old Distinction of our Desires, according as some of them are *preceded* naturally by a Sense of Pain, previously to any *Opinion* of Good to be found in the Object; <372> which is desired chiefly in order to remove the Pain; whereas other Desires arise only upon a *previous Opinion* of Good in the Object, either to ourselves, or to those we love. These Desires, tho' they do not *presuppose* any sense of Pain *previous* to the Opinion, yet may be attended with Pain, when the Object imagined to be good is uncertain. The former sort of Desires are called *Appetites*; the latter *Affections,* or *Passions.*[49] The Pains of the Appetites when they are not gratified are unavoidable. But the Pains of many disappointed *Passions* might have been prevented, by correcting the *false Opinions,* or by breaking foolish *Associations of Ideas,* by which we imagine the most momentous Good or Evil to be in these Objects or Events, which really are of little or no consequence in themselves.[50]

No Reason or Instruction will prevent *sensible Pain,* or stop a *craving Appetite.* Men must first be free from violent bodily Pain, and have what will remove Hunger and Thirst, before they can be made happy. Thus

49. The "old Distinction" between the appetites and the affections or passions is traced to "the scholastics" in Hutcheson, *A Synopsis of Metaphysics,* part 2, sec. 6 in *Logic, Metaphysics, and the Natural Sociability of Mankind,* p. 136. The distinction is elaborated more fully in *An Essay on the Nature and Conduct of the Passions and Affections,* sec. 4 (1728), pp. 89–92; (2002), pp. 67–68.

50. See *An Essay,* (1728), pp. 93–98; (2002), pp. 69–72 on the dangers of "foolish" and "confused" associations of ideas.

much is absolutely necessary. If there be but small Pleasure attending the Enjoyment of the bare *Necessaries* of Life, yet there is violent Pain in their absence Whatever farther Pleasures Men enjoy, we may count so much *positive Happiness above Necessity.*

The World is so well provided for the support of Mankind, that scarce any Person in good health need be straitened in bare <373> *Necessaries.* But since Men are capable of a great diversity of Pleasures, they must be supposed to have a great variety of *Desires,* even beyond the Necessaries of Life. The commonest Gratifications of the Appetites do not satisfy them fully: They desire those Objects, which give some more *grateful Sensations,* as well as allay their Pain; they have Perceptions of *Beauty* in external Objects, and desire something more in Dress, Houses, Furniture, than mere *Warmth* or necessary *Use.* There is no Mortal without some *Love towards others,* and desire of the Happiness of some other Persons as well as his own. Men naturally perceive something *amiable* in observing the *Characters, Affections* and *Tempers* of others, and are struck with a *Harmony in Manners,* some Species of *Morality,* as well as with a *Harmony of Notes.* They are fond of the *Approbation* of each other, and desirous of whatever either directly procures Approbation and Esteem, or, by a confused Association of Ideas, is made an Evidence of any valuable Ability or kind Disposition. Wealth and Power are in like manner desired, as soon as we observe their Usefulness to procure any kind of Pleasures.

Since then our *Desires* are so various, and all Desire of an Object, while it is uncertain, is accompanied with some *Uneasiness*; to make a Society happy, it must be necessary, either to gratify all Desires, or to suppress, or at least to regulate them. The <374> universal Gratification is plainly impossible, and the universal suppressing or rooting them out as vain an attempt. What then remains, in order to publick Happiness after the necessary supply of all *Appetites,* must be to study, as much as possible, to *regulate* our Desires of every kind, by forming just *Opinions* of the real Value of their several Objects, so as to have the strength of our Desires proportioned to the real Value of them, and their real Moment to our Happiness. Now all Men of Reflection, from the Age of *Socrates* to that of *Addison,* have sufficiently proved that the truest, most constant, and lively *Pleasure,* the happiest enjoyment of Life consists in *kind Affections* to our

Fellow-creatures, *Gratitude* and *Love* to the Deity, *Submission* to his Will, and *Trust* in his Providence, with a Course of suitable Actions. This is the true Good in our power, which we can never too strongly desire. The Pleasures of this kind are so great and durable, and so much above the power of Fortune, so much strengthened by the probable Hope of every other valuable Pleasure of Life, especially the *Esteem* and *Love* of our Fellows, or at least of the better part of them, that other Pleasures seem almost to vanish when separated from them; and even the greatest Pains seem supportable if they do not exclude them. By this means we may be sure, if not of all the Pleasures we can desire, yet of those which we most desire, and which <375> may make our Existence agreeable to ourselves in the absence of others.

This thorough Correction of our Opinions will not indeed extinguish our *Appetites,* or prevent all Pain; but it will keep our Appetites *unmixed with foreign Ideas,* so as to be satisfied with the plainest nourishing Food, without being disturbed by Imaginations of *Worth, Dignity,* and *Merit,* in a manner of Living which is not in our power. We may in like manner break the foolish Conjunction of *Moral Ideas* with the finer sort of *Habitation, Dress, Equipage, Furniture,* so as not to be dejected upon the unavoidable want of such things; we may learn to look upon them as they really are, without imagining them necessary to a happy and honourable Life, however they may be some *additional Advantage* to it.

Then we may observe, that tho this correcting our Opinions and Imaginations will make the *Absence* of the Pleasures above Necessity very tolerable to us, and cut off many vain Anxieties, yet no Person is thereby rendered insensible of any *real Pleasure* which these Objects do give. Tho we shall not look upon them as the *Chief Good* in Life, or preferable to the Publick Interest, to our Virtue, or our Honour; yet, when they can be enjoyed consistently with superior Pleasures, our Sense of them may be as *acute* as that of others. An affectionate Temper never stupified the *Palate;* Love of <376> a Country, a Family, or Friends, never spoiled a Taste for *Architecture, Painting,* or *Sculpture;* the Knowledge of the true *Measures and Harmony of Life,* never vitiated an *Ear,* or Genius for the *Harmony of Musick or Poetry.* This certainly is the only way in our power of preserving the full Relish for all the Pleasures of Life, and yet securing our selves against its Pains.

But if the fullest present Enjoyment cannot make the human Mind easy and fully satisfied; if we be disturbed by the Uncertainty either of external *Objects,* or of our own *Existence* in this World; if any are subjected to such acute Pains, that nothing can make them amends for them in this Life; if no Man can be sure but this may be his Condition in the future part of his Existence in this Life; if the present *seeming Disorders* and *Calamities,* sometimes befalling the best of Men, and the *insolent Prosperity* of the worst, disturb an honest compassionate Heart: The Hope of a *Future State* is the only universal Support to all Conditions of good Men, which can make them fully satisfied with their Existence at all adventures; especially if the Means of obtaining this future Happiness are no way opposite to their greatest present Happiness.[51]

'Tis too improbable, I own, that all Men will ever thus correct their vain Opinions and Imaginations: But whoever do so in any measure, are so much the happier: <377> And if all did so, all would be as near Happiness as our present State will allow. No Trade, no Manufacture, or ingenious Art would be sunk by it, which produces any *new Pleasures* to the Senses, Imagination, or Understanding, without bringing along with it *prepollent Evil.*

It is obvious to all, that in a Nation of any tolerable Extent of Ground, three fourths employed in *Agriculture* will furnish Food to the whole. Were this Land divided to all, except a few Artificers to prepare Instruments of Husbandry, the whole Nation must want all the Pleasure arising from other Arts, such as fine convenient *Habitations,* beautiful *Dress, Furniture,* and handy *Utensils.* There would be no Knowledge of *Arts;* no agreeable *Amusements* or *Diversions;* and they must all be idle one half of their Time, since much of the Husbandman's Time is now spent in providing Materials for more curious Arts. Would it be advisable to any

---

51. On "the hopes of a future state universal," see *A Synopsis of Metaphysics*, part 2, chap. 4, in *Logic, Metaphysics, and the Natural Sociability of Mankind*, pp. 148–49; and *A System of Moral Philosophy*, book 1, chap. 9, sec. 14, pp. 199–202.

impartial Mind, who regarded the good of the whole, to keep them in this State, and to prohibit all Arts but Husbandry, with what was absolutely necessary to it, confining them to their Huts, and Caves, and Beasts Skins, to secure them from Cold; allowing them no farther Compensation for the Conveniences they might procure by Industry, than the pleasure of *Idleness* for half their Lives? What other Answer do we need to this Question, than what every one will give for himself?[52] <378>

What Man, who had only the *absolute Necessaries* of Meat and Drink, and a Cave or a Beast's Skin to cover him, would not, when he had leisure, labour for farther *Conveniences,* or more *grateful Food*? Would not every Mortal do so, except some few *pretended Gentlemen* inured to Sloth from their Infancy, of weak Bodies and weaker Minds, who imagine the lower Imployments below their Dignity? Does not the universal choice of Mankind, in preferring to bear *Labour* for the *Conveniences* and *Elegancies* of Life, shew that their Pleasures are greater than those of *Sloth,* and that *Industry,* notwithstanding its Toils, does really increase the Happiness of Mankind? Hence it is that in every Nation great Numbers support themselves by Mechanick Arts not absolutely necessary; since the Husbandman is always ready to purchase their *Manufactures* by the Fruits of his *Labours,* without any Constraint; which they would not do if the Pleasures or Happiness of *Idleness* were greater. This may shew us how little Justice there is in imagining an *Arcadia,* or *unactive Golden Age,* would ever suit with the present state of the World, or produce more Happiness to Men than a vigorous improvement of Arts.[53]

---

52. Mandeville had remarked that in a society where men are engaged in nothing but agriculture they will have "no Arts or Sciences, or be quiet longer than their Neighbours will let them; they must be poor, ignorant, and almost wholly destitute of what we call the Comforts of Life": *The Fable of the Bees*, Remark Q, (1924), 1:183; (1724), p. 199.

53. In "The Moral" that follows "The Grumbling Hive," Mandeville had written: "they, that would revive / A Golden Age, must be as free, / For Acorns, as for Honesty": *The Fable of the Bees*, (1924), 1:37; (1724), p. 24. And in "A Search into the Nature of Society," he wrote: "In such a Golden Age, no Reason or Probability can be alledged why Mankind ever should have rais'd themselves into such large Societies as there have been in the world, as long as we can give any tolerable account of it": *Fable of the Bees*, (1924), 1:346; (1724), p. 346.

The comparative Wealth of any Country is plainly proportioned to the *Quantity of the whole Produce of Husbandry, and other Mechanick Arts* which it can export. Upon the Wealth of any Country, when other cir<379>cumstances are equal, does its *Strength* depend, or its *Power* in comparison with others. Now if any alledge that the improvement of Arts by foreign Trade, is at least pernicious to the Publick Good, by its occasioning many Calamities to Families, and Deaths in Shipwrecks; that therefore the whole would have been happier without it; let us only consider, that in computing the good or evil Consequences of any Actions, we are not only to consider the bare *Quantities* of Good or Evil, but the Probabilities on both sides. Now had a Country once as many Inhabitants as would consume its *natural wild Product* in their Caves or Thickets, 'tis plain that according to the usual increase of Mankind in Peace, the next Generation could not subsist without *Labour,* and vigorous *Agriculture.* 'Tis certain also that many Diseases and Deaths are occasioned by the Labours of Husbandry: Is it therefore for the publick Good that a thousand should barely subsist as *Hottentots* without Labour, rather than the double Number by Agriculture, tho a small Number should die by that means? When our Minds are dejected with old Age, or sudden apprehensions of Death or its consequences, we may prefer a few Days or Hours to all things else: But what Man of good Understanding, in sound Health, would not prefer a Life of sixty or seventy Years with good Accommodation, and a numerous Offspring, to eighty or ninety Years as a *Hottentot* or worse? What Man of com<380>mon Sense would refuse to cross the Channel for a considerable Advantage to his Family, tho they had the bare Necessaries? And yet even this Voyage hazards Life more than staying at home. If the Agriculture of three fourths can support the whole, the other fourth, by applying themselves wholly to mechanick Arts, will produce more Conveniences or Pleasures than could be hoped from a fourth of the Labours of each Man; since by confining their Thoughts to a particular Subject, the Artificers acquire greater Knowledge and Dexterity in their Work. Again, if Navigation and foreign Trade will support more Men than domestick Industry and Barter, it may really tend to the good of the whole, tho it endangers many Lives. Five Millions subsisting in any Country by help of foreign Trade, is a greater Advantage in the whole than four Millions without Trade, tho in each Age twenty Thousand should perish by Shipwrecks. The Rates of *Insurance* will teach us that the Losses at Sea are not even in this proportion to the Number supported by Trade, many of whom go not abroad at all, and others escape when the Goods are lost. Either then the Propagation of Mankind must be diminished, or Men must endure even the hazardous Labours of the Sea. But how few are there in the World who would not, even without any constraint, hazard a Voyage ra<381>ther than die childless: nay, rather than want any conveniences and pleasures of Life above Necessity for themselves or Families? The increase therefore of Trade does plainly tend to the good of the whole, notwithstanding all its hazards, which we see Men voluntarily submit to every day.[54]

Now if any own that the *Increase of Trade* promotes the present Happiness of human Life in the whole, and yet maintain that it is *vitious*; the Debate will turn upon the Idea of Vice. It is certain that almost all the Heathen Moralists agreed with him *who spake as never Man spake*,[55] that Virtue consists in *Love, Gratitude, and Submission* to the Deity, and in *kind Affections* towards our Fellows, and study of their greatest Good. All Sects, except the *Epicureans,* owned that kind Affections were natural to Men; and that consulting the greatest publick Good of the whole, as it was the surest way for each Individual to be happy, so it was *vita secundum naturam,* or *secundum rectam rationem.*[56] The *Epicureans* of the better sort, however they denied any Affection distinct from *Self-Love,* yet taught the same way to private Happiness, by Reasons like to those used by *Pufendorf,* only without consideration of the Providence of the Deity,

---

54. Mandeville had argued that the various risks and calamities that attend shipping and navigation contribute to the benefits to society that follow from these activities, in "A Search into the Nature of Society," in *The Fable of the Bees,* (1924), 1:359ff.

55. John, 7:46: "Never man spake like this man."

56. In the *Inquiry* Hutcheson declared that "If any Opinions deserve Opposition" they are the opinions of Epicurus and his modern followers: (1726), pp. 208–9; (2008), p. 143. "*Vita secundum naturam,*" or "life according to nature," and "*secundum rectam rationem,*" or "according to right reason" were maxims of the Stoics for a good and happy life: see Cicero, *De Finibus,* Book III, and *Tusculan Disputations,* Book IV. See also *The Meditations of Marcus Aurelius Antoninus,* Books I and XII.

or a future State.[57] If Vice be the Opposite to Virtue, *viz.* Those Affections or Actions which tend to the publick Detri<382>ment, or evidence Ingratitude or Contumacy towards the Deity, we may easily conclude that the utmost Improvement of Arts, Manufactures, or Trade, is so far from being necessarily vicious, that it must rather argue good and virtuous Dispositions; since 'tis certain that Men of the best and most generous Tempers would desire it for the publick Good.

But this Subject will require farther Consideration.

I am, Sir, yours, &c.[58]

P. M.

5.

No 46. *Saturday, February* 12, 1725/6.

To HIBERNICUS.[59]

> *Cui non conveniet sua res, ut calceus olim,*
> *Si pede major erit, subvertet; si minor, uret.*—HOR.[60]

SIR,

The only Arguments brought to prove that Vice tends to the publick Happiness of Society in this World, are these, "That the Power and Grandeur of any Nation depends much upon the Numbers of People and their Industry, which cannot be procured unless there be Consumption of <383> Manufactures: Now the *Intemperance, Luxury,* and *Pride* of Men

---

57. See "On the Natural Sociability of Mankind," in *Logic, Metaphysics, and the Natural Sociability of Mankind*, p. 202: "Pufendorf and most recent writers teach the doctrine of human nature which had been that of the Epicureans, that is that self-love (*philautia*) alone . . . is the spring of all actions. . . . Despite this they insist that social life is natural to man."

58. *DWJ*: "*Your humble Servant.*"

59. *DWJ*: "To the Author of the *Dublin Weekly Journal.*"

60. "When a man's fortune will not fit him, 'tis as oftimes with a shoe—if too big for the foot, it will trip him; if too small, will chafe" (Horace, *Epistles*, I.x.42–43, pp. 316–17).

consume Manufactures, and promote Industry." In like manner it is asserted, "That in Fact all wealthy and powerful States abound with these Vices, and that their Industry is owing to them."[61]

But if it can be made appear that there may be an equal *Consumption* of Manufactures without these Vices, and the Evils which flow from them; that Wealth and Power do not naturally tend to Vice, or necessarily produce it; then, tho we allow that these Vices do consume Manufactures and encourage Industry in the present Corruption of Manners, and that these Vices often attend Wealth and Power, yet it will be unjust to conclude, either that *Vices naturally tend to publick Prosperity, or are necessary to it; or that publick Happiness does necessarily occasion them.*

Intemperance is that Use of Meat and Drink which is pernicious to the Health and Vigour of any Person in the discharge of the Offices of Life. *Luxury* is the using more curious and expensive Habitation, Dress, Table, Equipage, than the Person's Wealth will bear, so as to discharge his Duty to his Family, his Friends, his Country, or the Indigent. *Pride* is having an Opinion of our own Virtues, Abilities, or Perfection of any kind, in comparison of others, as greater than what they really are; arrogating to ourselves <384> either Obedience, Service, or external Marks of Honour, to which we have no Right; and with this View desiring to equal those of higher Stations in our whole manner of Living. There is no sort of Food, Architecture, Dress, or Furniture, the Use of which can be called evil of itself. *Intemperance* and *Luxury* are plainly Terms relative to the *Bodily Constitution,* and Wealth of the Person. *Pride,* as it affects our Expences, is also relative to the *Station* and *Fortune* of the Person; so that it is impossible to fix one invariable *Quantity* of Food, one *fixed Sum* in Expences, the surpassing of which should be called *Intemperance, Luxury,* or *Pride.* Every one's own Knowledge, and Experience of his *Constitution* and *Fortune,* will suggest to him what is suitable to his own Circumstances. It is ridiculous to say, "That using any thing above the bare Necessaries of Life is *Intemperance, Pride,* or *Luxury*; and that no other universal Boundaries can be fixed; because what in one Station or Fortune is bare *Study* of

61. In Remark M of *The Fable,* (1724), p. 126; (1924), 1:124, Mandeville argued that "Pride and Luxury are the great Promoters of Trade."

Decency, or *Conveniency,* would be *Extravagence* in another."[62] As if *Temperance, Frugality,* or *Moderation,* denoted fixed Weights or Measures or Sums, which all were to observe, and not a *Proportion* to Men's *Circumstances. Great* and *Little* are relative to a Species or Kind. Those Dimensions are great in a Deer which are small in a Horse: What is great in a House would be small in a Mountain. Will any one <385> thence argue, that there can be no adapting one Form to another, so that it shall neither be too big nor little? Cannot a Coat suit a middle Stature, because the same Dimensions would be too great for a Dwarf, and too little for a Giant? If then in each *Constitution, Station,* or *Degree* of Wealth, a Man of good Sense may know how far he may go in Eating and Drinking, or any other Expences, without impairing his *Health* or *Fortune,* or hindering any *Offices* of Religion or Humanity, he has found the *Bounds* of Temperance, Frugality, and Moderation for himself; and any other who keeps the same Proportion, is equally temperate, tho he eats and drinks, or spends more than the other.

That these are the Ideas of *Temperance, Frugality,* and *Moderation,* given by all Moralists antient and modern, except a few *Cynicks* of old, and some Popish *Hermits,* is plain to all who read them. All Sects, as well as *Stoicks,* recommended the *Correction* of our *Opinions* and *Imaginations* about the Pleasures above Necessity; and yet the Use of them they all allow, when it is not inconsistent with the Offices of Life: In such Circumstances they were always looked upon as preferable to their Contraries. The Christian Law suggests nothing contrary to this; it has set before us, beside the present Pleasures of Virtue, which it represents as superior to all others, the Hopes of eternal Happiness; yet it frequently recommends <386> Diligence and Industry in providing for ourselves and Families, and for a Fund of good Offices toward others: It no where condemns the Rich or Powerful for being so, or for desiring high Stations, unless when these Desires are so violent as to counteract our Duty. The requiring some to part with their Possessions, was only a candid *forewarning* of the first Disciples, what their Profession of Christianity would probably cost

62. This is not a quotation but rather a paraphrase of Mandeville's concept of luxury, as expressed in Remark M of *The Fable,* (1924), 1:128–29; (1724), p. 132.

them in those Days of Persecution. A Community of Goods is no where commanded; tho Men who knew the approaching Persecution did wisely sell their Possessions, to turn them to the only valuable Purpose then in their power, and conveyed them to Persons who could possess them.

Since then *Intemperance,* or *Pride,* were scarce ever understood to denote all Use of any thing above bare Necessaries, all Conveniency of Life above *Hottentots*; why any one should affect to change their Meaning, is not easily guessed, unless it be with this View. *Luxury, Intemperance,* and *Pride,* in their common meaning, are *Vices*; but in this *new Meaning* are often innocent, nay *virtuous*; and without them, in this new Sense, there can be no *Consumption* of *Manufactures.* Common Readers however will still imagine that these Sounds denote *Vices*; and finding that what they confusedly imagine as vitious is *necessary to publick Good,* they will lose their Aversion to *moral Evil* in general, <387> and imagine it well compensated by some of its Advantages.

But let us retain the common Meaning of these Words. 'Tis certain, *Luxury, Intemperance,* and *Pride,* tend to consume Manufactures; but the Luxurious, Intemperate, or Proud, are not awhit the less odious, or free from *Inhumanity* and *Barbarity,* in the neglect of Families, Friends, the Indigent, or their Country, since their whole Intention is a poor selfish Pleasure. The Good arising to the Publick is no way owing to them, but to the Industrious, who must supply all Customers, and cannot examine whether their Expences are proportioned to their Fortunes or not. To illustrate this by an Instance in the manner of that notable Writer: "Suppose his *Decio,* or *Alcander,* or *Jack,* surfeited with Beef, falls into some light Distemper, and in hopes of attendance at low Rates, sends for a neighbouring Quack: The Quack imagines no Danger, but makes the Patient believe it; he talks much in the usual Cant of *Bilious Temperaments* and *Sanguine Complexions, of the Sinking of Spirits, and the Heart's feeling cold and condensed, and heavy as Lead, of Mists and Confusion about his Eyes;*" he promises, after some previous Preparations, "which the Quack finds necessary to prolong the Disorder, by some powerful Medicines, *to swell his Spirits, restore them to their Strength, Elasticity, and due Contexture, that they may fan the arterial* <388> *Blood again, and make him so light that he may tread upon Air.* The Patient grows worse, fears

Death, thinks on his past Life, and sends for an honest Parson, who instructs him in true Principles of Virtue, and shews him wherein he has been deficient: The strength of his Constitution overcomes both the Drugs and the Disease, the Patient recovers, becomes a Man of Integrity and Religion, and ever after honours the *honest Clergy* as the most useful Men in any State."[63] Now are these Effects to be ascribed to the Quacks? Are such Pretenders the less odious? Is Quackery the Cause of Religion or Virtue, or necessary to it? Does the Honour of the Clergy depend upon the Practice of Quacks? 'Tis best in such Affairs to go no farther than confused Apothegms: *Private Quackery, Publick Virtue: Medicinal Nonsense, Patients Repentance: Quacks Prescriptions, Honours to the Clergy.*

But let us in the next place examine if an *equal Consumption of Manufactures,* and *Incouragement of Trade,* may be without these Vices. Any given Number in a small time, will certainly consume more Wine by being Drunkards, than by being sober Men; will consume more Manufactures by being luxurious or proud (if their Pride turn upon Expences) than by being frugal and moderate. But it may be justly questioned, whether that same Number would not have consumed more in their whole Lives, by being temperate and <389> frugal: since all allow that they would probably live longer, and with better Health and Digestion; and Temperance makes a Country *populous,* were it only by prolonging Life.

Again, would there not be the same Consumption of the same Products, if inferior People contracted their Drinking and Dress within the Bounds of Temperance and Frugality, and allow'd poor Wives and Children what might be necessary to exhilerate and strengthen them for Labour, and to defend them from the Cold, or make their Lives easier? Would there be a less Consumption, if those of greater Wealth kept themselves within the bounds of Temperance; and reserved the Money thus

---

63. Hutcheson's illustration is a parody of Mandeville's Remark D of *The Fable,* (1924), 1:61–63 (1724), pp. 49–53: "These were call'd Knaves, But bar the Name, / The Grave industrious were the same." In Mandeville's story, two merchants, Decio and Alcander, attempt to best one another in trade. It will be evident that Hutcheson also took the opportunity to satirize Mandeville's practice of medicine, which included treatment of hysteric diseases. In Hutcheson's diagnosis of these diseases, they might be better treated by "an honest clergyman."

sav'd to supply the Interest of Money lent *gratis* to a Friend, who may be thereby enabled, consistently with Temperance, to drink as much Wine, as, had it been added to the Quantity drunk by the Lender, would have taken away his Senses? Or, if all Men drink too much, and Families too; what if they retrenched? The Money sav'd might improve their Dress, Habitation, or Studies; or might enable a poorer Friend to consume the same, or other Manufactures, with equal advantage to the Publick; or might preserve the same Persons longer in Life, and Health and good Circumstances, so as in their whole Lives to consume more.

In general, if the single Luxury of the Master of a Family consumes Manufactures, might not an equal Quantity be consumed by <390> retrenching his own Expences, and allowing Conveniences to his Family? If a whole Family be luxurious in Dress, Furniture, Equipage; suppose this retrenched, the increase of Wealth to the Family may soon enable younger Children in their Families to consume among them frugally, as much as would have been consumed luxuriously by the Ancestor; or the frugal Consumption of fifty Years, in the condition of a wise Gentleman, may be as great, as the luxurious Consumption of twenty Years, succeeded by thirty Years of Pinching, Remorse or Beggary. If a Man of Wealth has no Children, his own moderate enjoyment, with what he may enable worthy Friends to consume in their own Houses, or what he may spend temperately at a hospitable Table, and genteel Equipage, may amount to as much as the squandering of a luxurious *Epicure,* or vain Fool, upon his own Person, in the short time his Life or fortune will last.

Unless therefore all Mankind are fully provided not only with all Necessaries, but all innocent Conveniences and Pleasures of Life, it is still possible, without any Vice, by an honest care of Families, Relations, or some worthy Persons in Distress, to make the greatest Consumption. Two or three plain Suits becoming Gentlemen, worn by younger Brothers or Friends, will employ as many Hands as a foppish one worn by a vain Heir. The same may be said of Furniture of <391> Houses, Equipage, or Table. If there be sufficient Wealth to furnish the most sumptuous Dress, Habitation, Equipage, and Table to the Proprietor, and discharge all Offices of Humanity, after a proportionable rate, why should this be called Vice? It plainly tends to publick Good, and injures no Man. 'Tis indeed the business of a wise Man to look before him, and to be armed against those Hazards or Accidents which may reduce the highest Fortunes: All Men should correct their Imaginations, and avoid any Habit of Body or Mind, which might be pernicious upon a change of Fortune, or unfit them for any Duty of Life: But this may be done without reducing Men to a *Cynical* Tub, or Frize Coats. Wherein then the Virtue of this Retrenchment should consist, or the Vice of a more pleasant cheerful Way of Life, is not easy to tell; unless it lies in the confused use of ambiguous Words, *Temperance*, and *Frugality*, and *Humility*.

Who needs be surprized that *Luxury* or *Pride* are made necessary to publick Good, when even *Theft* and *Robbery* are suppossed by the same Author to be subservient to it,[64] by employing Locksmiths? Not to repeat again, that all the good Effect is plainly owing to the *Industrious*, and not to the *Robber*; were there no occasion for Locks, had all Children and Servants discretion enough never to go into Chambers unseasonably, this would make no Diminution of Manufactures; the Money saved to the House-keeper would <392> afford either better Dress, or other Conveniences to a Family, which would equally support Artificers: Even Smiths themselves might have equal Employment. Unless all Men be already so well provided with all sorts of convenient Utensils, or Furniture, that nothing can be added, a *necessity* or constant *usefulness* of Robbers can never be pretended, any more than the publick Advantages of *Shipwrecks* and *Fires,* which are not a little admired by the Author of the *Fable.*

'Tis probable indeed we shall never see a wealthy State without Vice. But what then? 'Tis not impossible: And the less any Nation has of it, so much the happier it is. Wise Governors will *force* some publick Good out of Vices if they cannot *prevent* them: And yet much greater publick Good would have slowed from opposite Virtues. The *Excise* is now increased by the Drunkenness of some poor Masters of Families: But sharing their Drink with their poor Families might make equal Consumption of the same kind; or if they retrenched this Article, they might consume[65] other

---

64. *DWJ*: "to tend to it."

65. In the 1729 text, the passage "if they retrenched this Article, they might consume" replaced *DWJ*'s "of."

Kinds of Goods, paying equal Duty to the Publick. The Persons themselves would avoid many *Diseases,* be more capable of *Labour,* live longer, in all probability, in Contentment and good Temper, without foolish *Contention, Quarrels,* and *Dissatisfaction* both in their Families and among their Neighbours. The like would be the Effect of a sober and temperate Deportment in better Stations. <393>

As to the Question of Fact in this Matter: Perhaps whoever looks into all the Ranks of Men, will find it is but a small part of our Consumptions which is owing to our Vices. If we find too splendid Dress at *Court,* or at *Lucas's,** or at *publick Meetings* for Diversion; we shall find plain Dresses at the *Exchange,* at the *Custom-House,* at *Churches.* The expensive Gaiety continues but a few Years of most Peoples Lives, during their Amours, or expectation of Preferment: Nor would a good-natur'd Man call this Gaiety always vitious. Our Gentlemen in the Country seldom suffer in their Fortunes by their Dress. The Consumption in Tables would not be much diminished, tho Men would never run into Surfeiting and Drunkenness: 'Tis not one in a hundred who is frequently guilty of these Vices, and yet all are every day consuming. The extraordinary Consumption of *Revels* occasions generally Abstinence for some time following; so that in a sober Week as much may be consumed as in the Week one has had a *Debauch.* Did we examine our own Manufactures, either Linen or Woollen, we should find that coarse Cloths and Stuff, the wearing of which none count extravagant, employ ten times as many Hands as the fine. And of the *fine Cloths* which are bought, not one of the Buyers in ten can be called extravagant. Were even this Ex<394>travagance removed, the Consumption of the same Persons during their Lives might be as great, as by the Vanity of a few Years with the Poverty of the Remainder.

Thus we may see with how little reason Vices are either counted necessary, or actually subservient to the publick Happiness, even in our present Corruption.

I am, Sir, Yours, &c.[66]

P.M.

---

* The gayest Coffee-House in *Dublin.* [Note added in 1729.]
66. *DWJ*: *"Your humble Servant."*

6.

No 47. *Saturday, February* 19, 1725/6

To HIBERNICUS.[67]

> *—Cujus velut agri somnia, vanae*
> *Finguntur species, ut nec pes nec caput uni*
> *Reddatur formae*   —HOR.[68]

SIR,

Mr. *Addison* in his fourth *Whig Examiner* has given an excellent Description of a certain way of Writing which is absolutely *Unanswerable;* and he has pointed out the secret Strength by which it is made so.[69] That the *Fable of the Bees* is a Performance of this kind, may be easily shewn, <395> not by general Encomiums, but by pointing out its particular Excellencies.

There is one Outwork of this sort of Authors, which, tho it be not their main Strength, yet is often of great consequence to terrify the timorous Reader, or Adversary; I mean *open Vanity,* and Pretences to the deepest Knowledge.—*Hic murus aheneus esto.*[70]

How formidable must that Writer be, who lets us know* "he has observed so much above the short-sighted Vulgar, and has given himself

---

67. *DWJ*: "To the Author of the *Dublin Weekly Journal.*"

68. "whose idle fancies shall be shaped like a sick man's dreams, so that neither head nor foot can be assigned to a single shape": Horace, "The Art of Poetry," lines 7–9, in *Satires, Epistles and Ars Poetica*, p. 451. These lines follow directly upon the lines quoted in Hutcheson's letter to *The Dublin Weekly Journal* for Saturday, June 12, 1725, above p. 203.

69. In *The Whig-Examiner*, no. 4, for Thursday, October 5, 1710, Addison remarked of nonsense that "it is incapable of being either answered or contradicted. . . . Its questions admit of no reply, and its assertions are not to be invalidated" (*The Works*, 3:265).

70. "*Hic murus aheneus esto, nil conscire sibi*": "Be this our wall of bronze, to have no guilt at heart": Horace, *Epistles*, I.i.60–61, in *Satires, Epistles and Ars Poetica*, pp. 254–55. This phrase had been used by Addison in a headnote to an essay in *The Guardian*, no. 123, for Saturday, August 1, 1710, in which he castigated men of rank who debauch innocent women of lower station.

* P. 89. [In 1729, Hutcheson provided page numbers for many of the quotations from Mandeville that follow, using the third edition (London, 1724) of *The Fable of*

Leisure to gaze upon the Prospect of concatenated Events, and seen Good spring and pullulate from Evil as naturally" (so condescending is he to the meanest of his Readers) "as Chickens do from Eggs?" How does he raise Admiration in the first Paragraph of his Preface, letting us know that he has seen the "Chief Organs and nicest Springs of our Machine," which are yet but "trifling Films, and little Pipes, not such gross strong things as Nerves, Bone, or Skin?" Nay, he has no doubt seen* "the very Strength, Elasticity, and due Contexture of Spirits which constitute the Fear of Shame, and Anger, or Courage"; and also all the other Qualities of Spirits which constitute the other Passions: These Passions "along with Skin, Flesh, and Bone, make the Compound Man." But this is not <396> all his Knowledge; he has† "Anatomised the invisible part, has seen the gentle Strokes, and slight Touches of the Passions."

This Author can‡ "swagger about Fortitude and Poverty as well as *Seneca,* and shew the way to *Summum Bonum* as easily as his way home.§ He has searched thro' every degree of Life; and foresees Opposition only from those who have lost Publick Spirit, and are narrow-souled, incapable of thinking of things of uncommon Extent, which are noble and sublime. He cries‖ *Apage Vulgus* to every Opposer, and¶ writes only for the few who think abstractly, and are elevated above the Vulgar."

He tells us "he has pleased Men of unquestionable Sense; will always live, and be esteemed while such read him."

---

the Bees. Hutcheson's references (in italics) will be followed by references in F. B. Kaye's edition, here volume 1, p. 91.]

* P. 234 [1:211].

† P. 153 [1:145].

‡ P. 162 [1:152].

§ Pp. 163 and 366, 367 [1:152 and pp. 319, 320].

‖ P. 232 [1:209–10; the reference was to the matter contained in the following note].

¶ *See the Journal subjoined to the Fable.* [Hutcheson was referring to *A Vindication of the Book, etc.* where Mandeville explained that his writing was not intended for the vulgar: "I have not said a Word to please or engage them, and the greatest Compliment I have made them has been *Apage vulgus* [Rabble be gone]": *Fable,* (1724), p. 470; (1924), 1:406].

Who will not stand in awe of that Author, "who* describes the Nature and Symptoms of Human Passions; detects their Force and Disguises; and traces Self-Love in its darkest Recess beyond any other System of Ethicks?" Who, after all this, and much more, and *Egotisms,* and Affectations in every Page, needs be told by the Author that *his Vanity he could never conquer?* <397>

Another useful Secret of *Invincible Authors* is to intersperse a contempt of *Pedantry* and of the *Clergy.* These damned Pedants have got a trick of reading many Authors, observing the Sentiments of the greatest Men in all Ages; and acquire an impertinent Facility of discerning Nonsense in the Writings of your *easy genteel Authors,* who are above perplexing themselves with the *Sourness* and Intricacies of Thought. Without some Defiances and Contempt of Pedants and Clergy, Readers would never have so much as dreamed that some of our Authors were *witty and easy Writers.* When this Point is obtained, then we may fall upon our Readers like Thunder, with all the little Learning we are Masters of, in Season and out of Season: About *Greek and Roman Religions, Egyptian Worship of Onions* (tho long ago laughed at by a *pedantick* Clergyman in a Brother-Easy-Writer on *Freethinking*)[71] *Trophys, Monuments, Arches, Military Crowns, Alexander, Lorenzo Gratian, Hydaspes,*[72] *Ostracisms;*[73] *The Laconick Spirit of our Nation appearing in the Word Gin: That fiery Lake, the Lethe, the*

---

* Pp. 467, 472. [1:404, 408. In his *Vindication,* Mandeville reprinted "an injurious, abusive letter" from *The London Journal* for July 27, 1723, addressed to "My Lord," whom Mandeville took to be Lord Carteret: *The Fable,* (1924), 1:386–401 and p. 15, n. 1.]

71. "An Enquiry into the Origin of Moral Virtue," *Fable,* (1924), 1:50. The "Brother-Easy-Writer on Freethinking," was Mandeville himself. See *Free Thoughts on Religion, the Church, and National Happiness,* p. 50; and F. B. Kaye, as above, p. 50, n. 1.

72. In "An Enquiry into the Origin of Moral Virtue," Mandeville argued that what had inspired the ancients in general, and Alexander in particular, to excel in virtue was the prospect of their "Monuments and Arches; their Trophies, Statues and Inscriptions": *Fable* (1724), pp. 36, 41; (1924), 1:51, 55.

73. In Remark N, *Fable* (1724), p. 147; (1924), 1:140, Mandeville had described "the Ostracism of the Greeks" as "a Sacrifice of valuable Men made to Epidemick Envy."

Stygian and Circean Cup, from whence pullulate Leucophlegmacies:[74] We
may talk of *Stoicks, Epicureans, Seneca's Estate*;[75] nay, even cite *Ovid,* and
transpose a Passage in *Juvenal: Si licet Exemplis*;[76] make double Entendres
upon the word *Enervate*;[77] *Trahat sua quemque Voluptas*:[78] a Latin Joke
from *Erasmus*:[79] Nay, <398> may make most Philosophico-Philological
Digressions about the *Essences of Hope, Inkerns, Ice, and Oak*;[80] we may
launch out into those profound Depths in Opticks, that *Air is not the
Object of Sight; that Bulk diminishes by Distance, is owing to our Imperfection; That the Sky might appear thro' a hole in a Wall as near as the Stones*;[81]

74. In Remark G, while explaining how "the worst of all the Multitude/Did something for the Common Good," Mandeville described how the sale of *"Gin"* (an abbreviation of "Geneva") is the cause of many vices and illnesses; among them, *"leucophlegmacies"* (a discharge of white phlegm) is a *"Stygian"* (hellish) comfort to those who drink from the *"Circean"* (the harlot's) cup; but those who are capable of following a more complicated chain of reasoning will recognize that the sale of gin provides a considerable source of public revenue. Thus, we "see *Good* spring up and 'pullulate' from *Evil*, as naturally as Chickens do from Eggs": *Fable*, (1724), pp. 86–89; (1924), 1:89–91.

75. In Remark O, Mandeville compared the attitudes of the *Epicureans* and the *Stoics* to "real pleasures, comforts, ease." He declared that he would be willing to write twice as much as Seneca in praise of poverty for a tenth of Seneca's estate: *Fable*, (1724), pp. 156–62; (1924), 1:147–52.

76. In Remark C, *Fable*, (1724), p. 66; (1924), 1:74, Mandeville cited lines from Ovid, *Amores*, I.v.7–8, to corroborate his (Mandeville's) opinion that modesty is not a virtue. In Remark G, *Fable*, (1724), p. 91; (1924), p. 93, he offered the very free translation of Juvenal's reminder: *"Dulcis odor lucri e re qualibet,"* *Satires*, xiv, 204–5: "The Smell of Gain was fragrant even to Night-Workers"; and, in Remark K, *Fable*, (1724), p. 106; (1924), p. 105, he compared the body politic to a bowl of punch, *"Si licet exemplis"* ("if one permits the simile"). He added "I confess the Simile is very low."

77. See *Fable*, Remark L, (1724), pp. 118–19; (1924), 1:118–19.

78. "Each man is led by his own taste": Virgil, *Eclogues*, II, 65, cited in Remark O, *Fable*, (1724), p. 157; (1924), 1:148.

79. Erasmus had entitled one of his colloquies *Cyclops Evangeliophorus*, after a character, one *Polyphemus*, who carried the gospels with him but did not live in accordance with them: Remark O, *Fable*, (1724), p. 165; (1924), 1:154.

80. It was Mandeville's view that simple things like *ice* and *oak* are much better understood by people in general than complex passions such as hope and fear: Remark N, *Fable*, (1724), p. 149; (1924), 1:141.

81. The passage "we may launch . . . near as the Stones" was added in 1729. In the course of his critique of Shaftesbury, in "A Search into the Nature of Society," Mandeville offered a digression on the origin of painting. It originated in an *imperfection* in the sense of sight, which typically presents objects to us as though they were flat: *Fable*, (1724), pp. 375–76; (1924), 1:326–27.

talk of *Pythagoras's abstaining from Flesh, Aesop's making Beasts to speak;*[82] *Ira furor brevis est;*[83] *Lucretia killed her self for fear of Shame.*[84] We may improve our Language by that easy Phrase, *Meliorating our Condition.*[85] We may use that most grammatical Epithet *Superlative;* talk of *Vannini, Bruno* and *Effendi as Martyrs*[86] (tho some of the Facts have been disproved long ago) That *Homer's Heroes talk as Porters; Lycurgus's Laws; Epaminondas, Leotychidas, Agis, the Polemarchi;*[87] *Saturnine Tempers,*[88] *Adoration of the Manes of the British Aesculapius;*[89] *Cicero's Vanity, he wrote O Fortunatam,* &c. *My Friend Horace:*[90] With many other most pert Evidences of *immense tritical Erudition;* which no Mortal could have known, without

82. Mandeville considered it a controversial indicator of improvement in the lives of the poor that they could now afford to eat meat. He remarked that *Pythagoras* "and many other Wise Men" had considered it barbarous to eat the flesh of animals. And he defended the theory (illustrated by *Aesop* in the character of a talking lion) that animals may have powers of reasoning superior to that of humans: Remark P, *Fable*, (1724), pp. 190–97; (1924), 1:176–81.

83. "Anger is short-lived madness": Horace, *Epistles*, I.ii.62, cited in Remark R, *Fable*, (1724), p. 230; (1924), 1:208.

84. *Lucretia* was moved to kill herself by a "*Superlative* Horror against Shame": Remark R, *Fable*, (1724), p. 232; (1924), 1:210.

85. This sentence was added in 1729. See Remark V, *Fable*, (1724), p. 274; (1924), 1:224.

86. See Remark R, *Fable*, (1724), p. 238; (1924), 1:214–15, where Mandeville remarked that atheists (*Bruno, Vanini, Effendi*) have been moved by the passion of honor to accept martyrdom; and *Fable*, (1724), p. 243; (1924), 1:219, for his opinion that it was because the Greeks and Romans did not engage in private duels but fought only for the honor of their cities that *Homer's heroes*, the rulers of those cities, expressed themselves so strongly in their exchanges with one another.

87. Mandeville was not an admirer of Spartan frugality. In Remark S, *Fable*, (1724), pp. 247–48; (1924), 1:223-24, he was sharply critical of the laws of Lycurgus, of the dinners served by *Epaminondas*, of the house of King *Leotichidas*. In Remark X, he noted that *Agis*, a Spartan monarch, was prevented by his own soldiers, the *Polemarchi*, from dining with his queen: *Fable*, (1724), p. 277; (1924), 1:245–46.

88. In Remark Y, *Fable*, (1724), p. 283; (1924), 1:250, Mandeville declared that a *Saturnine Temper*, or ill-nature, was often conducive to avarice, a vice Mandeville considered indispensable for prosperity.

89. "The British Aesculapius" (or God of medicine) was Dr. John Radcliffe (1650–1714), whom Mandeville held in scorn for many reasons, among them that he willed his fortune to charity: "An Essay on Charity and Charity-Schools," *Fable*, (1724), pp. 296–301; (1924), 1:262–66.

90. See "A Search into the Nature of Society," *Fable*, (1724), pp. 384 and 386; (1924), 1:335, 337, for Mandeville's complaint about Cicero's vanity and the description of Horace as Mandeville's friend.

having spent several Years at a Latin School, and reading *Plutarch's Lives Englished by several Hands.*[91]

When thus the Character of *Erudition* is secured, next comes *Knowledge of the World,* another essential Quality of an easy Writer. This may be displayed by a word or two of *French,* tho we have *English* <399> words exactly of the same meaning; by talking in the strain of Porters and Bauds, about *their* Affairs. Then the polite Gentleman of fine Genius will soon appear by a great deal of *Poetical Language,* mixed with Prose. What pity it had not all been in Rhyme, like the *Fable* it self? The Author's *Slaughter-House* and *Gin-Shop* would have been as renowned as the Cave of the *Cyclops,* or the Dwelling of *Circe: Ingenium par Materiae!*[92]

These are but additional Helps. The main Strength of the *Impregnable Writer* consists in *intricate Contradictions, and Inconsistencies; with some manifest Absurdities boldly asserted,* against which no Man can produce an Argument, any more than to prove that *twice Three are not Ten.* Thus his first Sentence is, that "All untaught Animals desire only to please themselves, and follow the bent of their Inclination, without regard to the good or harm of others":[93] But a* few Pages after we shall find that *Gratitude* is natural, or that Men "must with well to Benefactors: That Pity or Aversion to the Misery of others is a natural Passion; that Affection to Offspring, and desire of their Happiness, is natural: That Men may with well to any other in what they themselves cannot obtain." <400>

His very Definition of *Vice* is "† Gratifying Appetite without regard to the Publick": By [*without regard*] we may charitably understand him to have intended *pernicious to the Publick;* unless he can shew that all Men have agreed to call eating when one is hungry, or going to sleep when one is weary, vitious, whenever he does not think of a Community. Vice then here is "doing detriment to the Publick by gratifying Appetite." But go

91. See *Fable,* Remark S, (1724), p. 248; (1924), 1:224; and Remark X, (1724), pp. 277–78; (1924), 1:246 and notes 1 and 2.

92. "<unde> ingenium par materiae": "where will you find talent that matches your subject?" Juvenal, Satire I, 150–51, in *Juvenal and Persius,* pp. 142–43.

93. "An Enquiry into the Origin of Moral Virtue," *Fable,* (1724), p. 27; (1924), 1:41.

* P. 34, and p. 68, and 140. [1:47–48, 76, and 135. Hutcheson's representations of Mandeville's remarks are paraphrases, not literal quotations from the text.]

† P. 34 [1:48].

on, and you will find the whole strain of the Book to be, that "Vices are useful to the Publick, and necessary to its Happiness: The solid Comforts and Happiness of Life are the Gratifications of Appetite."

His Definition of Virtue is* "Endeavouring the Benefit of others contrary to the Impulse of Nature." Yet thro' the whole Book *Universal Virtue would be detrimental to Society;* that is, all Mens endeavouring to benefit others would be detrimental to all:† "The Moral Virtues are the Offspring of Flattery begot upon Pride"; yet in the very same *Page,* and many other places, "No Passion more natural or universal than Pride." Virtue then, which was before contrary to the Impulse of Nature, now is become following the strongest Impulse of Nature.

Again,‡ "Virtue is the Conquest of Passion out of the rational Ambition of being good"; but a few Pages after this, <401> "Doing worthy Actions from Love of Goodness has certain Signs of Pride, (which is the *strongest Passion)*": And yet, says the Author, "This is a sublimer Notion of Virtue than his own."

§"Heathen Religion could not influence Men to Virtue," says he: The direct contrary is asserted by all the Heathen Philosophers, Historians, Orators, Tragedians and Comedians. The wiser Men saw the Folly of their Theological Fables, but never denied a governing Mind: The Vulgar might believe the Fables of *Jupiter* and his Brothers; but imagining in the Gods a Right superior to that of Men, they might fear the Judgment of the Gods for like Facts to those done by *Jupiter,* and expect Rewards for Obedience to Laws given to Men, which yet did not bind Superior Natures. This Notion may make it probable that even very corrupt Religions may have in the whole much more good Effects than evil. But who will regard the Testimonies of poor *Heathens,* against this *Observer of concatenated Events?*

Presently we find‖ "The Seeds of all Virtue in the two Passions of Pride and Shame, which are most natural." In another place,[94] "Virtue was

* Ibid.
† P. 37 [1:51].
‡ P. 34 [1:48–49].
§ P. 36 [1:50–51].
‖ P. 56 [1:66–67].
94. *DWJ*: "Yet a while ago . . ."

contrary to the Impulse of Nature, and the Conquest of the Passions";
and soon after it will become what it was again,* "No Virtue in what is
de<402>signed to gratify Pride; the only recompence of Virtue is the
pleasure of doing good"; but even this pleasure of doing good, or acting
from Love of Goodness, was Pride.†

P. 59.⁹⁵ HE begins his *Anatomizing of Passions*; "The Passions concealed
from Modesty or good Manners, are Pride, Lust, and Selfishness." Either
then Pride and Lust is not *selfish,* but *disinterested*; or this division
amounts to these three Members, to wit, "one sort of Selfishness, another
sort of Selfishness, *and* Selfishness in general."

He asserts, that‡ "Ambassadors Debates about Precedency flow from
Pride concealed under shew of Virtue," that is, of *conquering the Passions
from the Ambition of being good.* It seems they all naturally desire to be
hindmost, but affect Precedency, that they may seem to conquer this
Passion.⁹⁶

§"Gratitude is a natural Motive of Inclination, and not Virtue: Returns
of good Offices are not from Gratitude but from Virtue, that is, opposition to the impulse of Nature; or Manners, that is, concealment of Pride,
Lust, and Selfishness, in order to gratify them."

‖"Luxury is the use of any thing above Necessity; nor can any other
bounds be fixed": and yet a few Pages after, "All Men ought to dress suitably to Condition." <403>

¶"Envy is a mixture of Sorrow and Anger. Sorrow arises from our want
of what we desire, and Anger is raised by us for our Ease." (A pleasing
Passion surely!) "Anger is the Passion arising when our Desire is crossed."
Thus Envy amounts to *Sorrow* for want of what we desire, compounded
with the *Passion arising when Desire is crossed.* This Composition is as art-

---

    * P. 68, and P. 246 [1:76, 222].
    † P. 43 [1:57].
  95. 1:68–69.
    ‡ P. 73 [1:79].
  96. *DWJ*: "but affect . . . this Passion" added in 1729.
    § P. 76 [1:82].
    ‖ P. 108, and 132 [1:107, 128–29].
    ¶ P. 140, and 221 [1:135–36 and 202].

ful as that of a merry Fellow's *Punch,* who liked to have it made of two Quarts of Brandy, and one Quart of Brandy; *Si licet Exemplis.*[97]

*"Self-Love bids us look on every satisfied Being as a Rival": And *yet nothing can excite any Being to oppose another but his being unsatisfied.*

†"Laughing at another's Fall, is either from Envy or Malice."

‡"Love signifies Affection, that is, liking or wishing well." The Object's Interest becomes our own in this wonderful manner. "Self Love makes us believe that the Sufferings we feel must lessen those of our Friend; and then a secret Pleasure arises from our grieving, because we imagine we are relieving him." How strangely does our *Self-Love* govern us! It first forms an Opinion so prodigiously secret, that never any Mortal believed it; and then makes us feel Pleasure, not in relieving *ourselves,* but another. Nay, what is it that Self-Love cannot <404> perform?§ "When a Man stands in the Street, and shrieks at another's Fall from a high Window or Scaffold,[98] he believes that he himself is flying thro' the Air: When a Man blushes, upon seeing another do a base Action, he believes he is doing it himself."

I have got yet no farther than the 150th Page, but with many Omissions: You may have when you please twice as many, rather greater Beauties of the same nature; but these may suffice at present. Only I cannot pass over two Passages more; the one is a wonderful *Composition,* so dearly does he love making a very *Dispensatory of Passions,* that rather than want Composition, he will take two pieces of the same thing for want of different Materials:‖ "Laziness is an Aversion to Business, generally attended with a Desire of being unactive." The other Passage is a most important Maxim; "That Man never exerts himself but when he is roused by Desire"; or never exerts himself but when he desires something or other. And he subjoins this sublime Simile, of *a Huge Windmill without a Breath of Air.*[99]

97. See p. 236, note 76 above.
* P. 145 [1:139].
† P. 146 [1:139].
‡ P. 149 [1:142].
§ P. 55 [1:66].
98. "from a high Window or Scaffold" added in 1729.
‖ P. 267 [1:239].
99. This sentence added in 1729.

Before any one pretends to answer this Book, he must know what the Author means by *good Opinion, high Value, Worth, Unworthiness, Merit, noble Actions, Overvaluing, Thinking well,*[100] or *having a Right* <405> *to do any thing.* But upon these Terms, all Mortals may despair of it.

We may make one general Observation on the Dexterity of this Author in confuting opposite Schemes. Suppose the Scheme of almost all Moralists, except *Epicureans,* to be true; "That we have in our Nature *kind Affections* in different degrees, that we have a *Moral Sense* determining us to approve them whenever they are observed, and all Actions which flow from them; that we are naturally bound together by *desire of Esteem* from each other, and by *Compassion*; and that withal we have *Self-Love* or desire of private Good." What would be the Consequence of this Constitution, or the *Appearances* in human Nature? All Men would call those Actions virtuous, which they imagine do tend to the Publick Good: Where Men differ in *Opinions of the natural Tendencies of Actions,* they must differ in Approbation or Condemnation: They will find Pleasure in contemplating or reflecting on their own kind Affections and Actions: They will delight in the Society of the kind, good-natured, and beneficent: They will be uneasy upon seeing or even hearing of the Misery of others, and be delighted with the Happiness of any Persons beloved: Men will have regard to private Good as well as publick; and when other Circumstances are equal, will prefer what tends most to private Advantage. Now these are the direct and necessary Con<406>sequences of this Supposition: And yet this penetrating *Swaggerer, who surpasses all Writers of Ethicks,* makes those very Appearances proofs against the Hypothesis. No proofs will please him but the contrary Appearances: If he saw "Men approving what is pernicious to the Publick; or Men agreeing to approve the same Action, tho one thought it useful to the Publick, and another thought it pernicious; or if Men had no manner of pleasure in good Actions, or in reflecting upon them, nor would value themselves more for Heroism than Villany; then indeed he would acknowledge a moral Sense independent of Interest and true Virtue."

100. *DWJ*: "Thinking well, *Ought, or having* . . ."

So also, "Men must delight in the Company of the proud, morose, revengeful and quarrelsome; they must be indifferent in beholding the most cruel Tortures, or the greatest Joy and Happiness of our Fellows, or even of our Offspring. Men must do mischief to themselves, or neglect their most innocent Pleasures, and Interest, by a tho-row *Self-denial*, without any Inclination to the good of others; and must have no more pleasure in Gratitude, Generosity, or Humanity, than in Malice and Revenge; otherwise this Author will never believe any other Affection than Self-Love: At present he sees all to be but Disguises of it, from his deep Reflections about *Fresh Herrings,* and the *Company* he would choose." <407>

He has probably been struck with some old *Fanatick* Sermon upon *Self-Denial* in his Youth, and can never get it out of his head since. 'Tis absolutely impossible upon his Scheme, that God himself can make a Being naturally disposed to Virtue: For Virtue is *Self-Denial, and acting against the Impulse of Nature.* What else then can we imagine concerning all the Works of God in their best State, but

> —*That they were intended,*
> *For nothing else but to be mended?* —Hud.[101]

Might we poor Vulgar make conjectures concerning the *Spirits of Nations,* we would be apt to conclude, that thro' incapacity for *Abstract Thinking,* the *Baeotick* Spirit of the *British* is much better discovered by a fourth Edition of this Book, than the *Laconick* by the Word *Gin.*

Thus may thine Enemies triumph, O *Virtue* and *Christianity*![102]

I am, Sir,
Your humble Servant,
P. M.

---

101. Samuel Butler, *Hudibras,* part 1, canto 1, lines 203–4.

102. When this letter was plagiarized in *The London Journal* for June 21, 1729, the words "and Christianity" were replaced with "O Morality." See the Introduction, p. xxiii above.

Letter to Samuel Card
in *Bibliothèque Angloise,* 1725

Letter of Francis Hutcheson to Samuel Card, October 1725[1]

J'ai vû il y a quelque temps, *dit* Mr. Hutcheson *à son ami,*[2] la derniere Partie de la *Bibliothèque Angloise*[3] de Mr. *Le Clerc,*[4] et trouvé dans ses *Nouvelles Litteraires* une Relation aussi ridicule que fausse de mon Livre, puis qu'on y insinue que dans ma premiere Partie j'ai prétendu être Inventeur, quoique j'aye pris, du *Traité du Beau* de Mr. *de Crousaz,* non seulement mon Plan général, mais aussi le détail des Preuves et des Eclaircissements, le tout, en un mot.[5] Mr. *Le Clerc* a la reputation d'un Homme trop franc et trop judicieux pour avoir été capable de donner cette idée de mon Ouvrage, après avoir lû les deux Livres. Cela me faire croire qu'il a écrit ceci sur les Memoires de quelque Correspondent auquel il ajoûte plus de foi que de raison. Je n'ai pas besoin de faire mon apologie pour me justifier aupres de vous, ni auprès d'aucune de mes Connoissances. Vous savez tous que, huit ans avant que je commencasse d'écrire, je reconnus avoir lû le Livre de Mr. *de Crousaz;*[6] que je le cherchai inutilement parmi les personnes que je connoissois, jusqu'à ce que mon Ouvrage eut paru pour la premiere fois; que j'ai déclaré avoir puisé dans quelques-uns des Anciens,

---

1. The original English text of this letter, now lost, was translated into French and printed in *Bibliothèque Angloise* 13, no. 2 (1726): 514–18. A modern retranslation follows the French text, pp. 248–51, below. The annotation to the text is to be found with the English translation.
2. See note 13, p. 248
3. See note 14, p. 248.
4. See note 15, p. 248.
5. See note 16, p. 248.
6. See note 17, p. 249.

et dans Mylord *Shaftesbury*,[7] toutes mes idées qui sont de quelque conséquence sur le sujet. Vous vîtes mon Livre croitre d'une demi-Feuille à vingt. Je ne me ressouvenois de rien plus du Traité de Mr *de Crousaz*, que de son idée générale de la Beauté, qui consiste en l'Unité variée, en quoi il est aussi peu original que moi, et que de la distinction qu'il met entre la *Beauté d'idée* et la *Beauté de sentiment*, laquelle je n'ai jamais goutée, et que j'ai même formellement combattue dans mon Livre, quoi qu'il s'y arrête fort dans le sien.[8] Il y a longtemps que j'ai ouï dire que l'on traduisoit a *Londres* en Anglois le Traité de Mr. *de Crousaz*. Cette Nouvelle m'épargne l'embarras de me defendre dans l'esprit de mes Compatriotes, ou même de qui que ce soit en Angleterre, qui lira les deux Livres. Il est surprenant que Mr *Le Clerc*, ou son Correspondent, s'ils ont lû ma Devise,[9] ou Mylord *Shaftesbury*, ayent pu croire que ma Définition a dû être copiée de Mr. *de Crousaz*; et quant aux Preuves et aux Eclaircissements, a peine y a-t-il rien de commun. Il y a environ une année que je lus le Livre de Mr. *de Crousaz*, et je fus surprise au contraire, de trouver si peu de choses qui nous fussent communes. Je suis assuré que de 100 Pages a quoi se monte mon livre dans la 2de Edition, il n'y a pas cinq qui nous soient communes, non pas même en pensée. Les sections V, VI, VII, et VIII, qui sont plus de la moitié de ce Traité, roulent sur des sujets que Mr. *de Crousaz* n'a presque point touchez; et les quatre premieres Sections sont réellements opposés en plusieurs choses au Système générale de Mr. *de Crousaz*, sans parler de la difference perpetuelle qu'il y a Presque à chaque Eclaircissement. Je ne sai ce que Mr. *Le Clerc* croit être, *tous ce qu'il y a de meilleur dans mon Livre*; mais il faut que ce soit peu de chose.

Je ne vois pas que j'eusse failli a ne faire aucune mention du Livre de Mr. *de Crousaz*, quand je l'auroit eu pendant que j'écrivois, puis que je m'en eloigne si fort dans les Points que je traite. En autre chose je l'approuve extrêmement, et sur tout à cause de les sentiments genereux et charitables envers les Religions differentes. Je ne vois pas en quoi consiste la modestie ou la prudence de quelques-uns de nos Auteurs, de même que des *Fran-*

---

7. See note 18, p. 249.
8. See note 19, p. 249.
9. See note 20, p. 250.

cois, qui, en écrivant sur quelque sujet que ce soit, se croyent obligez s'ériger, dans leurs Prefaces, en Maîtres de Cerémonies, et d'y regler le mérite et le pas de tous ceux qui ont traité la même matiere. Ce qui me paroit de plus incomprehensible dans les Nouvelles de Mr. *Le Clerc*, c'est que, quoique j'aye dit expréssement que j'avois tiré de quelques Anciens mes premieres idées, et de nouveaux Eclaircissements; quoi que je nomme Mylord Shaftesbury, pour insinuer, autant que je l'ai pu faire, sans irriter certaines bonnes gens, que ce Seigneur a bien écrit sur ce Sujet; Malgre tout cela, dis-je, Mr. *Le Clerc* dise, *il se debite hardiment pour l'Original. A l'entendre, il est le premier qui a débrouillé le chaos dans cette matiere philosophique*. Je ne vois pas dans mon Livre un seul endroit qui tende a cela, si ce n'est que je blâme nos Systèmes ordinaries de Philosophie, ou l'on omet cette partie de notre Sensation qui nous rend susceptibles du plaisir des Beaux Arts, et ou l'on se borne a quelques divisions, aussi leches qu'inutiles, de nos Sens.[10] Que cela soit ainsi, je m'imagine avoir l'aveu de tout honnetehomme, qui a vû quelques chose de plus dans la vie que les Murs du College. J'en appelle au Systeme même de Mr. *Le Clerc*. Je pourrais reponde aux Questions de Mr. *Le Clerc* par une autre. Quelle foi doit-on ajoûter a de semblables Nouvelles? Si je vois que le monde y ait le moindre egard, je pourrai bien faire la dépense d'une periode, sur cet Article, lors que je publierai quelque autre Pièce, don't vous avez vû le brouillon; et j'espere qu'il n y a point d'Etranger assez sot pour s'imaginer qu'il m'ait fallu emprunter d'autres Ecrivains que des *Anglois*, les petites allusions triviales aux Mathematiques, ou les éclaircissements tirez de cette Science, qu'il y a dans mon Livre.[11]

10. See note 21, p. 251.
11. See note 22, p. 251.

Translation of the Letter from Francis Hutcheson
to Samuel Card, October 1725[12]

Some time ago, *said* Mr. Hutcheson *to his Friend*,[13] I saw the last Part of the *Bibliothèque Angloise*[14] of Mr. *Le Clerc*.[15] And I find in his *Literary News* a report of my Book, which is as ridiculous as it is false. Moreover, it is there insinuated that in the first Part [of my Book] I have pretended to be an Inventer, as though I had taken from the *Treatise on Beauty* of Mr. *de Crousaz* not only my general Plan, but also the detail of the Proofs and the Illustrations, everything, in a word.[16] Mr. *Le Clerc* has the reputa-

12. The translation of the letter is by James Moore.

13. Samuel Card, an Irish student, eighteen years of age, was registered in the Faculty of Law at the University of Leiden on September 15, 1728: *Album Studiosorum Academiae Lugduno Batavae*, p. 901.

14. Hutcheson's letter was prompted by a notice of *An Inquiry into the Original of Our Ideas of Beauty and Virtue* (1725) in the section "Nouvelles Litteraires" of the *Bibliothèque Angloise*, vol. 13, part 1 (1725): 280–82. In that notice, Hutcheson was accused by Armand de la Chapelle (1676–1746) of having plagiarized his definition of beauty from Jean-Pierre Crousaz's (1663–1750) *Traité du Beau*.

15. Hutcheson believed mistakenly that Jean Le Clerc was the author of the notice in the *Bibliothèque Angloise*. Le Clerc had written a review of the first part of the *Inquiry* in the *Bibliothèque Ancienne et Moderne*, vol. 24, part 2 (1725): 421–37, and the second part of the *Inquiry* in the same journal in 1726, vol. 24, part 1, pp. 102–5. In his review of Hutcheson on Beauty, Le Clerc remarked: "Il y a ici diverse choses qui sont communes à cet Auteur et à Mr. de Crousaz qui dans la première Partie, Ch. III de son Traité du *Beau*, fait consister les caractères réel et naturels du Beau, dans la Varieté dans l'Unité, dans la Regularité, et dans la Proportion." ("There are diverse things that are common to this Author and to Mr. de Crousaz, who in the first part, Ch. III of his *Treatise of Beauty* makes the real and natural characteristics of Beauty consist in Variety, in Unity, in Regularity and in Proportion.") He added that the two authors had fallen into the same way of thinking, either in the course of their own meditations, or the later author had profited from the earlier, although the later author did not mention the earlier writer. Once he had made the point that the two authors had much in common, Le Clerc offered a long and respectful summary of Hutcheson's work.

16. Armand de la Chapelle put the matter more pungently and provocatively in the *Bibliothèque Angloise*: "Je puis dire qu'il m'a paru surprenant que l'Auteur, qui a pris de Mr. De Crousaz tout ce qu'il y a de meilleur dans sa première Partie, et qui n'a été que con Copiste dans la *définition* du Beau, n'ait pas daigne, en un seul endroit, nous indiquer les Sources ou il a puise. Il s'en faut bien qu'il ne le fasse. C'est tout le contraire. Il se debite hardiment sur l'Original. A l'entendre, il est le premièr qui a debrouillé le chaos qui regnoit dans cette matiere philosophique. . . . Si cet Anonyme n'a pas vu l'une ou l'autre des deux Editions du Traité du Beaux de Mr. de Crousaz, il est fort etrange qu'ils s'accordent si juste dans leur Système general, et dans le detail de leur preuves; et s'il les a vues, a quoi devons-nous imputer son silence? Au reste cet

tion of a Man who is too frank and too judicious to have been capable of offering this idea of my Work, after having read both books. That makes me believe that he has written this after the Memoirs of some Correspondent to which he has attached more faith than reason. I have no need to apologize to justify myself to you, nor to any of my Acquaintances. You all know that eight years before I began to write, I recalled having read the book of Mr. *de Crousaz*;[17] that I sought it in vain among the persons that I knew until my work had appeared for the first time; that I declared that I had drawn all my ideas of any consequence on the subject from some of the ancients and from my Lord *Shaftesbury*.[18] You saw my Book grow from a half-sheet to twenty. I remember nothing of the Treatise of Mr. *de Crousaz*, other than his general idea of Beauty, which consists in unity in variety, in which he is as unoriginal as I, and the distinction between Beauty as Idea and Beauty as sentiment is one I have never favored and have even formally attacked in my Book, although it is maintained strongly in his.[19] Some time ago I heard that Mr. *de Crousaz's*

Ouvrage Anglois est un petit 8 de 276 pages." ("I can say that it seems to me surprising that the author, who has taken, or at least seems to have taken from Mr. de Crousaz all that is best in the first Part, and who has been no more than his Copyist in the definition of Beauty, should not have deigned, if only in one place, to indicate the Sources from which he has drawn. It might be thought unnecessary that he should do so. It is quite the contrary. He is strongly indebted to the original. To listen to him he is the first who has disentangled the chaos that has prevailed hitherto in this philosophical matter. . . . If this anonymous author has not seen one or the other of the two editions of the Treatise on Beauty of Mr. de Crousaz, it is very strange that they correspond so exactly in their general System, and in the detail of their proofs; to what should we impute his silence? For the rest this English work is a little octavo of 276 pages.").

17. Jean Pierre de Crousaz, *Traité du Beau* was published in Amsterdam in 1715. It was revised and published in a second edition in Geneva, 1724.

18. See Shaftesbury, *Characteristics*, pp. 203, 351–52; and p. 450, n. 30, where Shaftesbury observed that Aristotle, in *On the Cosmos*, understood that harmony in music, painting, and in nature itself is achieved by bringing opposites together, "creating a single harmonious mixture . . . and so too is it under God's conducting the universe."

19. It was a central theme of Crousaz's logic and aesthetics that ideas must be distinguished from sentiments: "Nous sommes encore assez maitres de nos idées, nous les excitons nous-mêmes, elles naissent les unes devantres, ou, nous y arretons notre attention autant qu'il nous plait, et nous l'endetournous avec la meme facilité des que nous le voulons. Mais les sentiments dependent sur des objets externes, et des objets interieures qui ne sont pas en notre puissance" (*Traité du Beau*, p. 25). ("We are

Treatise was to be translated into English in *London*. This News spares me the embarrassment of having to defend myself in the minds of my compatriots or indeed of anyone in England who will read the two Books. It is surprising that Mr. *Le Clerc* or his Correspondent, if they had read my Epigram,[20] or my lord *Shaftesbury*, should have been capable of believing that my Definition must have been copied from Mr. *de Crousaz*; and as for Proofs and Illustrations, they have almost nothing in common. I am convinced that in the 100 pages at the beginning of the second Edition of my book, there are not five pages that we have in common, not even in thought. Section V, VI, VII, and VIII, which make up more than half of my Treatise, turn on subjects that Mr *de Crousaz* has scarcely touched upon; and the first four sections are really opposed in several respects to the general System of Mr. *de Crousaz*, without speaking of the perpetual difference that exists in Almost every Illustration. I do not know what Mr. *Le Clerc* believes to be *all that is best in my Book*; but it must be very little.

I do not see that I have erred in not mentioning the Book of Mr. *de Crousaz*, even if I had had it when I wrote, since I depart from it so widely in the points that I discuss. In other respects, I very much approve of him, above all for the generous and charitable sentiments towards different Religions. I do not see what the modesty or the prudence of some of our Authors or of French authors consists in, who believe themselves

---

sufficiently masters of our ideas, we arouse them in ourselves, they give birth to other ideas, and . . . we fix our attention on them as long as it pleases us, and we turn away from them as easily as we choose. But sentiments depend on external objects and on certain internal dispositions which are not in our power."). Cf. Syliane Matinowski-Charles, "Entre rationalisme et subjectivisme, l'esthétique de Jean–Pierre de Crousaz," *Revue de Theologie et de Philosophie* 136 (2004): 7–21. Hutcheson argued, contrary to Crousaz, that the idea of beauty is itself a sentiment or sensation brought to mind by an internal sense whenever we perceive objects or persons, compositions, or landscapes that exhibit unity in variety. It is also due to the providence of a benevolent God that we feel pleasure whenever we bring to mind an idea of beauty.

20. The epigram prefaced to Hutcheson's *Inquiry* was taken from Cicero, *De Officiis*, Book I, c. 4: "And so no other animal has a sense of beauty, loveliness, harmony in the visible world; and Nature and Reason, extending the analogy of this from the world of sense to the world of spirits, find that beauty, consistency, order are far more to be maintained in thought and deed."

obliged, when writing on any subject at all, to pose as critics or as Masters of Ceremonies in their Prefaces, and weigh the merit and the importance of all those who have treated the same subject matter. What appears most incomprehensible in the Literary News of Mr. *Le Clerc*, is that, although I said explicitly that I had drawn my basic ideas and some new Illustrations from the Ancients; although I name my lord Shaftesbury, to insinuate, so far as I was able to do so, without irritating certain good people, that this Lord has written well on this Subject; in Spite of that, I say, Mr. *Le Clerc* says *he boldly pronounces himself to be the Originator. To listen to him, he is the first who has brought order out of chaos in this philosophical matter.* I do not see a single passage in my Book which implies that, unless it is that I blame our ordinary Systems of Philosophy, either for omitting that part of our Sensation which renders us susceptible to the pleasure of the fine arts, or for limiting themselves to some divisions, as narrow as they are useless, of our Senses.[21] That this is so I imagine would be recognized by every honest man who has seen something more of life than the Walls of a College. I appeal even to the System of Mr. *Le Clerc*. I could reply to the Questions of Mr. *Le Clerc* by another question. What confidence should one place in News of this kind? If I perceived that the world paid it the least attention, I could trouble myself for a moment on this Head, when I publish another Piece, of which you have seen the draft; and I hope that there is no Foreigner so crazy as to imagine that it was necessary for me to borrow from writers other than some English authors, the little trivial allusions to Mathematics or illustrations drawn from that Science, that exists in my Book.[22]

21. Hutcheson, *An Inquiry into the Original of Our Ideas of Beauty and Virtue,* sec. 1, art. 8, p. 22: "The only Pleasure of Sense, which our Philosophers seem to consider, is that which accompanys the simple Ideas of Sensation: But there are vastly greater Pleasures in those complex Ideas of Objects, which obtain the Names of Beautiful, Regular, Harmonious."

22. The letter ends here. It is hard to imagine that Hutcheson would end the letter in this fashion without a personal aside to his young friend or an expression of good wishes. This letter may have been abbreviated or otherwise altered by the editor of the journal, Armand de la Chapelle, who indulged a mischievous habit of this kind on other occasions.

Letter to William Smith
in *Bibliothèque raisonée,* 1735

Letter of Francis Hutcheson to William Smith[1]

La Lettre suivante a été écrite en Anglais par Mr. François Hutcheson *Professeur en philosophie dans l'Université de Glasgow en Ecosse à G.* Smith *un des Imprimeurs de cette Bibliotheque, son ancien & intime Ami;*[2] *on l'a fait traduire en Français, & on croit faire plaisir aux Curieux en inserant ici.*

GLASGOW le 28 Fevrier 1734

11 Mars 1735

MONSIEUR,

Vous voulez que je vous rende compte du Traité que *Mr. Robert Simson* Professeur de Mathématique ici,[3] vient de donner au Public sur les Sections Coniques : il faut vous satisfaire. Je le puis d'autant plus aisément, que je me suis souvent entretenu avec l'Auteur sur cette matière, & qu'il m'a dit plusieurs choses dont il ne parle point dans sa Préface, & que vous trouverez ici.[4]

La méthode qu'ont suivie presque tous les Modernes qui ont traité des Sections Coniques, est le principal motif qui l'a porté à écrire ces Elémens. Il avoit remarqué qu'ils démontrent algébriquement les Propriétés de ces Sections, & écartent presque entièrement la méthode géométrique

---

1. This letter was published in French in the *Biblioteque raisonnée des ouvrages des savans de l'Europe* for April, May, and June 1735. An English retranslation of the letter follows below, pp. 259–66. The annotation is provided in full in the English translation. The original English text of this letter is no longer available, but see the draft printed below (pp. 267–71).

2. See note 29, p. 259.

3. See note 30, p. 259.

4. See note 31, p. 259.

employée par les Anciens : ce qui, joint à l'application que l'on fait mal à propos de l'Algèbre à d'autres sujets géométriques, (application que *Descartes* a le prémier introduite dans la Géométrie,[5] & que le Dr. *Wallis* a employée le prémier dans les Sections Coniques,)[6] est cause qu'on trouve aujourd'hui très peu de personnes qui sachent faire usage des méthodes soit *Analytique* soit *Synthétique* des Anciens dans la résolution des Problèmes, ou dans la démonstration des Théorèmes. Pour arrêter en quelque sorte le progrès de ce mal qui s'étend de jour en jour, l'Auteur a écrit ces Elémens selon la méthode des Anciens; quoiqu'il se soit servi des mêmes Descriptions des Sections *in plano*, que *Kepler*[7] le prémier, & Mr. *de la Hire*,[8] le Marquis de l'*Hôpital*[9] & beaucoup d'autres après lui, ont employées.

Dans les 3 prémiers Livres, les Propriétés élémentaires des Sections sont démontrées séparément, afin que le Lecteur ne soit pas obligé de considèrer toutes les Sections à la fois : mais dans les 2 autre Livres, pour éviter de répéter ou les mêmes Démonstrations, ou des Démonstrations fort semblables entre elles, les Propriétés des différentes Sections sont démontrées dans les même termes, par-tout où la chose a pu se faire. Une autre raison pour donner séparément les prémières Propriétés de chaque Section, est, que les Démonstrations des Propriétés de la Parabole sont généralement plus aisées & plus simples que celles des mêmes Propriétés des deux autres Sections. Et comme les Propriétés élémentaires du Cercle, qui est l'espèce la plus simple de l'*Ellipse*, sont déja démontrées dans *Euclide*, il a par leur moyen démontré quelques-unes des principales Propriétés de l'Ellipse : & dans l'Hyperbole, les Propriétés des Asymptotes contribuent à rendre les Démonstrations des Propriétés des Tangentes & des Diamètres plus aisées & plus simples; nouvelle raison pour les traiter séparément dans les 3 prémiers Livres. On en peut voir un exemple dans la 40. Proposition du 3. Livre, comparée avec la 20. du 2. Livre des Coniques d'*Apollonius*.[10]

L'Auteur a cherché la solution des Problèmes les plus difficiles par le moyen des *Data* d'Euclide, conformément à la méthode des Anciens, qui

est & plus commode & plus naturelle que celle des Modernes, & qui donne
des Constructions de Problèmes plus simples & plus élégantes, comme on
s'en appercevra sans peine en comparant la solution du Problème de la
Prop. 6, du Liv. 4. avec la solution algébrique du même Problème dans
la Prop. 12. Art. 66. Liv. 2. & dans l'Art. 431. Liv. 10. des Sections Coniques
du Marquis de l'*Hôpital*.[11] Voici le Problème : "Trouver deux Diamètres
conjugués d'une Ellipse, qui fassent entre eux un Angle égal à un Angle
donné, deux autres Diamètres conjugués étant donnés de position & de
grandeur". Il le propose dans le Corollaire de la Prop. 11. Art. 65. de son
second Livre, & il ajoute, que "comme la solution de ce Problème est assez
difficile, il la renvoie au 10. Livre".[12] Cependant il donne, dans la 12. Proposition, la solution du Cas de ce Problème où les deux Diamètres conjugués
sont les Axes, après avoir montré dans la Prop. 11. La manière de trouver
ces Axes : & dans le 10. Livre il donne la solution du Cas général où les
Diamètres ne sont point les Axes. Sur quoi il faut remarquer, que ce qui
lui fait trouver plus de difficulté dans ce Cas que dans celui où les Axes
sont donnés, c'est la méthode des solutions algébriques qu'il emploie, par
laquelle il est plus aisé de réduire un Problème à l'Equation lorsqu'il y a
un Angle droit parmi les choses cherchées ou données dans le Problème,
que lorsque l'Angle est oblique: car dans ce dernier cas ils sont obligés
d'abaisser une perpendiculaire, (du moins c'est leur pratique constante)
comme pour avoir un Triangle rectangle; & cela, quoique cette perpendiculaire n'ait nul rapport avec le Problème, sinon qu'elle sert à faire entrer
l'Angle oblique dans raisonnement : ce qui peut se faire plus aisément &
plus naturellement par les *Data* d'Euclide. C'est-là une des raisons gé-
nérales des solutions peu naturelles & peu élégantes des Problèmes géométriques par la méthode algébrique. Mais, qu'il n'y ait réellement pas plus
de difficulté à résoudre le Problème que j'ai rapporté, dans le Cas général,
lorsque l'Angle formé par les Diamètres donnés est oblique, que lorsque
les Diamètres sont les Axes & que l'Angle par conséquent est droit, c'est
ce qui paroîtra clairement si l'on compare les solutions de ces deux Cas
dans la Prop. 6. du 4. Liv. de ce nouveau Traité, dont le prémier est le Cas

11. See note 38, p. 262.
12. See note 39, p. 262.

des Axes, & le second celui de tous autres Diamètres conjugués.[13] Ils sont exposés l'un & l'autre fort au long, afin de montrer qu'il n'y a nulle différence dans leurs solutions, si ce n'est que dans le prémier on fait usage du 32. & du 31. des *Data* d'Euclide, au-lieu que dans l'autre on emploie le 44. & le 29. Outre cela, la recherche & la composition des deux Cas sont plus aisées & plus courtes que par la mèthode algébrique. Ce qui les fait paroître plus longues, c'est que la Démonstration de la solution du Cas général est entièrement omise dans le 10. Liv. du Marquis *de l'Hôpital*, de même que la recherche & la composition de la détermination du Problème, au-lieu que dans la 6. Prop. du Liv. 4. de Mr. *Simson*, elles sont données tout au long dans les deux Cas.[14]

Outre un grand nombre de nouvelles Démonstrations de Propositions, déja connues, on trouve dans cet Ouvrage plusieurs Propositions entièrement nouvelles. En particulier, cette Propriété des Sections Coniques plus générale qu'aucune autre de leurs Propriétés connues jusqu'ici, savoir celle qu'*Apollonius* démontre dans la Prop. 16. & les sept suivantes de son 3.[15] Livre, est rendue deux fois aussi général par Mr. *Simson* dans les Propp. 14. & 23. de son 4.[16] Livre, en l'étendant aux lignes qui ne rencontrent point du tout la Section, aussi bien qu'à celles qui la touchent ou la coupent, & cela par le moyen de la 12. de la 13. & de la 21. du même Livre.[17] La 18. & la 24. du 4. Livre, & la 12. du Liv. 5. qui en dépend, sont nouvelles[18] : & de cette dernière l'Auteur tire aisément, dans ses deux Corollaires, la solution du Problème qui consiste à "décrire une Section Conique qui passe par trois points donnés, & touche deux lignes droites données de position", solution qui n'avoit pas encore été faite comme il faut. De cette même Prop. 12, du 5. Liv. la solution de ce Problème plus difficile, "Décrire une Section Conique qui passe par deux points donnés, & touche trois lignes droites données de position", se peut déduire aisément, sans avoir recours aux ennuyeuses transmutations de la Section, dont le Chev. *Newton* s'est servi dans la 25. & la 26. Prop. du I. Liv. de ses *Principes*.[19] Voici la solution que l'Auteur m'a donnée de ce Problème.

13. See note 40, p. 263.
14. See note 41, p. 263.
15. See note 42, p. 263.

16. See note 43, p. 263.
17. See note 44, p. 263.

18. See note 45, p. 263.
19. See note 46, p. 264.

PROPOSITIO.

"Datis in Sectione Conica duobus punctis A, B, *datisque positione tribus rectis lineis* CD, CE, DE, *quae sectionem contingunt; dabuntur in ipsis puncta contactus,* F, G, H.*"*

Jungantur enim AB, FG, FH, HG, & occurrat AB *tribus reliquis in* K, L, M, *punctis. Quoniam igitur dantur duo puncta in sectione viz.* A, B, & *datae positione sunt duae rectae* CD, CE *Sectionem contingentes, dabitur (per Cor. I. Prop. 12. Lib. 5.)*[20] *punctum* K, *in quo recta* AB *occurrit rectae* FG *quae per contactus transit; & similiter dabuntur puncta* L. M. *Et quoniam quatuor rectae lineae sunt* LM, LF, KF, MG, & *dantur tria intesectionum puncta* L, K, M, *in una rectarum; alia vero duo* G, H, *tangunt rectas* CE, DE *positione datas, tanget reliqua intersectio* F *rectam positione datam (per Prop. in Transactionibus Philosophicis No. 337. pag. 330);*[21] *idem vero punctum* F *tangit aliam rectam* CD *positione datam: dabitur igitur punctum* F:& *similiter dabuntur puncta* G, H; *unde Sectio Conica facile describi poterit.*

Problema vero quo describenda est Sectio quae tangat quatuor rectas positione datas, & transeat per punctum datum, solvi poterit ope Prop. 7., ejusdem Lib. 5.[22]

La Scholie de la page 198, & les Propositions dont elle est déduite,[23] contiennent une Propriété des Sections très générale & d'un très grand usage, que l'Auteur a découverte à l'occasion que je vais dire. Mr. *MacLaurin*, savant Professeur de Mathématique à Edimbourg, étant sur son départ pour la France en 1723,[24] Mr. *Simson* lui communiqua une Proposition de *Pappus d'Alexandrie* qu'il avoit rétablie, savoir : *"Si a tribus punctis datis in recta linea, ducantur tres rectae lineae, & ipsarum intersectiones duae tangant rectas positione datas; tanget reliqua intersectio rectam lineam positione datam."* Cette Proposition a été imprimée ensuite dans les *Transactions*

---

20. See note 47, p. 264.   22. See note 49, p. 264.   24. See note 51, p. 265.
21. See note 48, p. 264.   23. See note 50, p. 265.

Philosophiques, comme elle vient d'être rapportée. A son retour, Mr. *Mac-Laurin* dit à Mr. *Simson*, "qu'il avoit trouvé que si les trois points donnés n'étoient point dans une ligne droite, tout le reste demeurant comme dans le cas précédent, alors le *Lieu* seroit une Section Conique, & que par le moyen de ce *Lieu* on pourroit décrire une Section Conique à travers cinq points donnés"; méthode qu'il montra à Mr. Simson, mais sans lui donner la démonstration ni *du* Lieu, ni de la méthode : il lui dit seulement, qu'il l'avoit faite par le moyen d'un Lemme qui se trouve les Principes du Chevalier *Newton*. Ce fut en cherchant ces Démonstrations, que Mr. *Simson* trouva les Propositions contenues dans sa Scholie, & celles dont elles dérivent : ce qu'il fit par la même méthode suivant laquelle elles sont rapportées dans son Livre, sans le secours d'aucune autre Proposition que de celles qui y sont citées.[25]

La 19. Prop. du Liv. 5. contient cette élégante Propriété de la Parabole, que Mr. *Fermat* propose à démontrer au Dr. *Wallis*, dans la pénultième Lettre du *Commercium Epistolicum*, page 859. vol. 2, des Oeuvres de ce Docteur.[26] Sur quoi il faut remarquer, que cette même Propriété a lieu dans l'Hyperbole & dans toute ligne parallèle à l'une de ses Asymptotes, savoir : "Si de deux points donnés l'Hyperbole ou dans des Hyperboles opposées, l'on tire deux lignes droites à un troisième point quelconque dans l'une des Courbes, elles couperont des segmens, d'une ligne parallèle quelconque à l'une des Asymptotes, & donnée de position, entre elles-mêmes & le point où la parallèle rencontre l'Hyperbole, lesquels auront une raison donnée." L'Auteur réserve pour une autre occasion la démonstration de cette Proposition.

A la fin du Livre on trouve une nouvelle Quadrature de la Parabole, de même que les Propositions & les Démonstrations d'*Archimède*, dans lesquelles il compare l'Ellipse avec le Cercle & avec d'autres Ellipses.[27]

Je suis & c.

F. H.

25. See note 52, p. 265.
26. See note 53, p. 266.
27. See note 54, p. 266.

Translation of the Letter from
Francis Hutcheson to William Smith[28]

The following Letter has been written in English by Mr. Francis Hutcheson, Professor of Philosophy in the University of Glasgow in Scotland to G. [Guillaume] Smith, one of the publishers of this Journal, his old and intimate Friend;[29] it has been translated into French & it is believed that it will please the Curious by inserting it here.

GLASGOW 28th of February 1734

11 March 1735

SIR,

You ask that I give you an account of the Treatise on Conic Sections that Mr. *Robert Simson* Professor of Mathematics here,[30] has recently given to the Public; it is necessary to satisfy you. I can do this more easily since I have often conversed with the Author on this matter, and he has told me several things that he has not spoken about in his Preface, and that you will find here.[31]

28. This translation is by James Moore.

29. William Smith (1698–1741) was born in Belfast. He had been a student at the University of Glasgow from 1711 to 1720, overlapping with Francis Hutcheson in 1710–18. He opened a bookseller's shop in Dublin in the early 1720s in partnership with John Smith, also a former student at Glasgow; together they published Hutcheson's *Inquiry into the Original of Our Ideas of Beauty and Virtue*. Smith went to London, then to Holland in 1725, where he became a partner with Rudolf and Jacob Wetstein, booksellers in Amsterdam. Smith was the effective editor of the *Bibliothèque raisonnée* from 1728 to 1741. See James Moore and M. A. Stewart, "A Scots-Irish Bookseller in Holland: William Smith of Amsterdam (1698–1741)," *Eighteenth-Century Scotland* 7 (1993): 8–11.

30. Robert Simson (1687–1768) was professor of mathematics at the University of Glasgow from 1711 to 1761. He had studied divinity under John Simson, his maternal uncle, and then distinguished himself as a student of classical texts before he turned to mathematics (*ODNB*). Simson devoted himself to the restoration of ancient geometry texts, a project in which he was strongly supported by Hutcheson. See the Private Correspondence: Letters 22 and 46.

31. In the composition of his letter, Hutcheson was indebted to Simson not only for conversation. Simson also composed for Hutcheson or edited a letter drafted by Hutcheson on the subject of Simson's book. This draft of a letter was found among Simson's papers by William Trail, the author of *Account of the Life and Writings of Robert Simson* (1812), who described the document as "without any signature, but it is in the Doctor's handwriting" (p. 84). In light of the close resemblance of this document and the letter published in the *Bibliothèque raisonnée*, it is appropriate that a copy of this document is attached below, pp. 267–71.

The method that has been followed by almost all the Moderns who have treated Conic Sections is the principal motive that has prompted him to write these Elements. It has been remarked that they demonstrate the Properties of these Sections Algebraically, and discard almost entirely the geometrical method employed by the Ancients: which along with the application that has been made improperly of Algebra to other geometrical subjects (application that *Descartes* first introduced in Geometry[32] and that Dr. *Wallis* first employed in Conic Sections)[33] is the reason that one finds today very few persons who know how to make use of the *Analytic* or *Synthetic* methods of the Ancients in the resolution of Problems, or in the demonstration of Theorems. To stop in some way the progress of this evil which increases from day to day, the Author has written these Elements according to the method of the Ancients; although he has used the same Descriptions of the Sections *in places* that *Kepler*[34] first, and Mr. *de la Hire*,[35] the Marquis *de l'Hôpital*[36] and many others after him, have employed.

32. *La Géométrie* of Rene Descartes (1596–1650) was published as an appendix to *Discours de la méthode pour bien conduire sa raison et chercher la vérité dans les sciences* (1637). Descartes' *Géométrie* is divided into three books: the first two treat of analytical geometry, and the third includes an analysis of the algebra then current: W. W. Rouse Ball, *A Short Account of the History of Mathematics*, p. 274.

33. John Wallis (1616–1703) has been described as the most influential English mathematician before Isaac Newton. In *Tractatus Sectionibus Conicis* (1655) "he described the curves that are obtained as cross sections by cutting a cone as properties of algebraic coordinates" (*Encyclopedia Britannica*, s.n.; and see *ODNB*).

34. Johannes Kepler (1571–1630), best known for his *Astronomia Nova* (1609), had written on conic sections in *Paralipomena* (1604): W. W. Rouse Ball, *Short Account of the History of Mathematics*, p. 256.

35. Philippe de la Hire (1640–1719) in *Nouveaux élémens des sections coniques* (1679) provided "the first real step toward solid analytic geometry" (Carl B. Boyer and Uta C. Merzbach, *A History of Mathematics*, p. 337).

36. The influential Marquis de l'Hôpital's (1661–1704) *Analyse des infiniment petits* (1696) has been described as "the first text-book on the differential calculus to appear in print." One of its postulates maintained "that a curve can be considered as made up of infinitely small straight line segments that determine, by the angles they make with each other, the curvature of the curve" (Boyer and Merzbach, *History of Mathematics*, 381 and 395). His *Traité analytique des sections coniques* (1707) was the text that Simson had principally in mind when he composed his treatise on conic sections. Trail, *Account of the Life and Writing of Robert Simson*, p. 27 and n.: "He had observed,

In the first 3 Books, the elementary Properties of the Sections are demonstrated separately, in order that the Reader would not be obliged to
consider all the Sections at the same time: but in the other Books, in order
to avoid repeating either the same Demonstrations, or Demonstrations
very much like them, the Properties of the different Sections are demonstrated in the same terms, everywhere the thing could be done. Another
reason for giving the Properties of each Section separately is that the
Demonstration of the Properties of the Parabola are generally easier and
simpler than those of the same Properties of the two other Sections. And
as the elementary Properties of the Circle, which is the simplest species of
the Ellipse, are already demonstrated in Euclid; he has by their means
demonstrated some of the principal Properties of the Ellipse: and in the
Hyperbola, the Properties of the Asymptotes contribute to render the
Demonstrations of the Properties of the Tangents and the Diameters easier and simpler; a new reason to treat them separately in the 3 first Books.
One can see an example of it in the 40th Proposition of the 3rd Book,
compared with 20th of the 2nd Book of the Conics of Appolonius.[37]

The Author has searched for the solution of the most difficult Problems
by means of the *Data* of Euclid; conforming to the method of the Ancients,
which is more commodious and more natural than that of the Moderns,
and offers simpler and more elegant Constructions of the Problems, as
may be seen without difficulty in comparing the solution of the Problem
in Prop. 6 of Book 4 with the algebraic solution of the same Problem in
the 12th Prop. Art. 66. Book 2 and the Art. 431. Book 10 of the Conick

---

in the first years of his study of mathematics, that the Treatises on Conic Sections,
then in most general use and estimation, were entirely algebraical; and the great merit
of the work, written in that stile by the Marquis de L'Hopital, contributed not a little
to the popularity of this mode of treating geometrical subjects. It occurred therefore
to Dr. Simson, that a treatise on Conic Sections, written on the purer model of antiquity, might have some influence in correcting the prevailing false taste, of introducing
algebraic calculation into those branches of geometry where it was not necessary. . . .
This I have frequently heard the doctor express."

37. Robert Simson, *Sectionum Conicorum*, book 3, proposition 40 (1735), pp. 86–88;
and in the English translation (Books 1–3 only): *Elements of the Conic Sections*, 2nd ed.
(Edinburgh, 1792), pp. 243–47. An advertisement to the translation states: "These
books contain as much of the doctrine as usually enters into an academical education." Apollonius of Perga, *Conics*, pp. 133–37.

Sections of the Marquis *de l'Hôpital*.[38] Here is the Problem: "Find two conjugate Diameters of an Ellipse, which make between them an Angle equal to a given Angle, two other conjugated Diameters, position and size being given." He proposes it in the Corollary of Prop. 11, Art. 65, of the second Book, and he adds that "as the solution of this problem is sufficiently difficult he will revisit it in the 10th Book."[39] However, he gives, in the 12th Proposition, the solution of the case of this Problem where the two Diameters conjugated are the Axes, after having shown in the 11th Prop. the manner of finding these Axes: and in the 10th Book he gives the solution of the general Case where the Diameters are not the Axes. On which it is necessary to remark that what makes it more difficult in this case than in that where the Axes are given, it is the method of algebraic solutions that he employs, by which it is easier to reduce a problem to the Equation when there is a right Angle among the things sought for or given in the Problem, than when the Angle is oblique: for in this last case they are obliged to lower a perpendicular (at least this is their constant practice) so as to have a right angle triangle; and that, although this perpendicular has no connection with the Problem, if only that it serves to bring the oblique Angle into their reasoning: which can be done more easily and more naturally by the *Data* of Euclid. Here then is one of the general reasons for the less natural and less elegant solutions of geometrical Problems by the algebraic method. But, that there is really no more difficulty in resolving the problem that I have described, in the general Case, where the Angle formed by the given Diameters are the Axes & the Angle consequently is right, it is what will clearly appear if one compares the solutions of these two Cases in the 6th Prop. of the 4th Book of this new Treatise, where the first is the Case of the Axes, and the second that of all other conjugated Diameters.[40] The one and the other are presented at

---

38. *Sectionum Conicorum* (1735), book 4, prop. 6, pp. 107–14; and *Traité analytique des sections coniques* (1775), book 2, prop. 12, art. 66, pp. 39–41, and book 10, art. 431, pp. 370–74.

39. *Traité analytique*, book 2, prop. 11, art. 65: "Mais comme la solution de ce Probleme est assez difficile, on l'a renvoyee dans le 10e Livre, & on a suivi ici une autre voye qui est plus simple" (p. 39).

40. *Sectionum Conicorum* (1735), book 4, prop. 6, pp. 107–14.

some length, in order to show that there is no difference in their solutions, if it is only in the first that makes use of the 32nd and the 31st of the *Data* of Euclid, while in the other one employs the 44th and the 29th. Apart from that, the inquiry and the composition of the two Cases are easier and shorter than by the algebraic method. What makes them appear longer is that the Demonstration of the solution of the general Case is entirely omitted in the 10th Book of the Marquis *de l'Hôpital*, even the inquiry and the composition of the determination of the Problem; whereas in the 6th Prop. of Book 4 of Mr. Simson, they are given at length in the two Cases.[41]

In addition to a great number of new Demonstrations of Propositions already known, one finds in this Work several Propositions entirely new. In particular, this Property of Conick Sections, more general than any other of their Properties known up until now [and] known to be that which Apolonius demonstrates in the 16th Prop. and the seven following of his 3rd Book,[42] is rendered twice as general by Mr. Simson in Propp. 14 and 23 of his 4th Book,[43] by extending it to lines which do not meet at all [in] the Section as well as those which touch or intersect it; and that by means of the 12th, of the 13th and the 21st of the same Book.[44] The 18th and the 24th of the 4th Book, & the 12th of Book 5 which depend on it, are new:[45] and from the last [Proposition] the Author derives easily, in his two Corollaries, the solution of the Problem which consists in "describing a Conic Section which passes by three given points, & touches two straight lines given in position," a solution which again has not been produced as it should have been. From this same Prop. 12 of the 5th Book the solution of this more difficult Problem, "to describe a Conic Section which passes by two given points and touches three straight lines given in position, can be deduced easily without having recourse to the annoying

41. Ibid.

42. Apollonius of Perga, *Conics*, book 3, props. 16–24, pp. 200–211.

43. *Sectionum Conicorum* (1735), book 4, prop. 14, pp. 124–27, and prop. 23, pp. 133–34.

44. *Sectionum Conicorum* (1735), book 4, props. 12, pp. 122–23, 13, pp. 123–24, and 21, pp. 131–32.

45. *Sectionum Conicorum* (1735), book 4, props. 18, p. 130, and 24; and book 5, prop. 12, pp. 159–60.

transmutations of the Section, which are employed by Sir Isaac Newton in the 25th and 26th Prop. of the 1st Book of his *Principles*.[46] Here is the solution that the Author has given me of this Problem.

PROPOSITION

In a Conic Section two points A and B are given, and three straight lines CD, CE, DE, are given, that also touch the section; they will give these contact points, F, G, H.

If AB, FG, FH, HG, are joined, then AB meets in three more points K, L, M. Since two points are given in the section, viz. A and B, then two straight lines are added to this position CD and CE. Point K is given where line AB meets line FG (by Corollary 1, Proposition 12, Book 5);[47] and similarly given are points L, M. And whereas four straight lines LM, LF, KF, MG create three intersecting points L, K, M, in one straight line; the other two G and H touch the section at F (according to Proposition No. 337 in Philosophical Transactions, p. 330);[48] *the same is true of point F which touches upon another straight line CD: and in a similar manner, so do points G, H; and so the Conic Section can be easily described.*

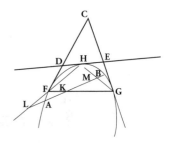

The problem truly is to describe the Section so that the four straight lines pass through a given point, and this can be solved by Prop. 7 of the same Book 5.[49]

46. Isaac Newton, *The Mathematical Principles of Natural Philosophy*, book 1, props. 25, pp. 124–25, and 26, pp. 126–30.

47. *Sectionum Conicorum* (1735), book 5, prop. 12, corollary 1, p. 160.

48. "Pappi Alexandrini Propositiones duae generales, . . . Restitutae a Viro Doctissimo Rob. Simson, Math. Prof. Glasc.," *Philosophical Transactions of the Royal Society* 32, no. 377 (1722–23): 330–40.

49. Book 5, prop. 7, p. 155: "If two straight lines are inscribed in a conic section, not parallel with each other and they terminate in a juncture with four straight lines; all intersecting, and two of the intersections connect with the others that have been drawn, all four will be in a straight line."

The Scholium on page 198, and the Propositions from which it is deduced,[50] contain a Property of the Sections that is very general and of very great use that the Author discovered on the occasion that I am going to relate. Mr. Mac-Laurin, learned Professor of Mathematics in Edinburgh, being about to leave for France in 1723,[51] Mr. Simson communicated to him a Proposition of *Pappus of Alexandria* that he had discovered, to wit: *"If from three given points in a straight line, three straight lines are drawn, and two of the same straight lines touch the given positions; then the remaining straight line will touch the given positions."*

This proposition has been printed subsequently in the *Philosophical Transactions,* as it came to be reported. On his return, Mr. Mac-Laurin said to Mr. Simson "that he had found that if three given points were not in a straight line, all the rest remaining as in the previous case, then the locus [*Lieu*] would be a Conic Section across five given points"; he showed the method to Mr. Simson, but without giving him the demonstration of the locus or the method; he said to him only that he had done it by means of a Lemma which may be found in the Principles of Sir [Isaac] *Newton*. It was in searching for these Demonstrations, that Mr. *Simson* found the Propositions contained in the Scholium, and those derived from it: which he found by the same method according to which they are recorded in his Book, without the aid of any other Proposition than those which are cited there.[52]

50. The Scholium on pages 198–99 recapitulates the propositions (44, 45, 46, and 47) that describe conic sections by straight lines that intersect at two, three, and four given points.

51. Colin MacLaurin (1698–1746) studied mathematics at the University of Glasgow with Robert Simson and was professor of mathematics at Marischal College, Aberdeen, 1719–25 and the University of Edinburgh 1725–46. He shared Simson's interest in ancient Greek geometry and enjoyed the esteem of Newton for his work in mathematics. In matters of religion and moral philosophy, MacLaurin thought like Hutcheson: see MacLaurin to Hutcheson, Private Correspondence, Letter 6 above.

52. MacLaurin had a personal interest in the story told by Hutcheson, following Simson, of his sojourn in France from 1722 to 1725. He claimed that his unpublished work on conic sections had been plagiarized in a letter published in *Philosophical Transactions* 39 (1735): 25–36. He replied with a letter of his own, in volume 39, pp. 143–65, citing work he had done in France prompted by "that very ingenious paper concerning *Pappus's* Porisms, communicated by Mr. Sympson, Professor of Mathematics at *Glasgow* published in the *Phil. Trans.* No. 377." This episode is noted by Charles Taylor,

The 19th Proposition of Book 5 contains the elegant Property of the Parabola that Mr. *Fermat* proposes to demonstrate to Dr. *Wallis*, in the penultimate Letter of the *Commercium Epistolicum,* page 859, Volume 2 of the Works of this Doctor.[53] On which it is necessary to remark that this same Property has a place in the Hyperbola & without any line parallel to one of the Asymptotes, to wit: "If of two points given in the Hyperbola or in opposed Hyperbolas, one draws two straight lines to any third point whatever in one of the curves, they will cut some segments of any line whatever to one of the Asymptotes, & given some position between themselves & the point where the parallel meets the Hyperbola, they will have a given ratio." The Author reserves the demonstration of this Proposition for another occasion.

At the end of the Book one finds a new Quadrature of the Parabola; the same as the Propositions and Demonstrations of Archimedes, in which he compares the Ellipse with the Circle & with other Ellipses.[54]

I am &c.

F. H.

An Introduction to the Ancient and Modern Geometry of Conics, p. 264n: Hutcheson was more concerned that MacLaurin had not replied to Berkeley's critique of Newton's and MacLaurin's method of fluxions or moments, which Berkeley considered indistinguishable from the method of "infinitesimals" employed by de l'Hôpital and other "foreign" mathematicians: *The Analyst* (1734), p. 14. See Hutcheson's letter to MacLaurin, Private Correspondence, Letter 16, above.

53. See the letter from Pierre de Fermat (1607–1665) to Wallis via Kenelm Digby in John Wallis, *Opera Mathematica*, 2:857–59.

54. The work of Archimedes, Pappus, and Apollonius on conics is discussed in J. L. Coolidge, *A History of the Conic Sections and Quadric Surfaces*, chapters 1 and 2.

Draft of the Letter to from Francis Hutcheson to William Smith[55]

De Sectionibus Conici Libri V &

Sir

At your desire I send you an Account of the Treatise of Conick Sections lately published in this Country, and shall take notice of Some things the Author did not think worth while to give Account at large in his preface, which I can do the better that I have had Occasion to discourse with him on that Subject.

The chief motive of writing these Elements was that he observed the late writers on the Conick Sections, a few excepted, demonstrated their properties Algebraically, almost entirely discarded Geometrical demonstrations after the method of the Ancients; by which together with the undue application of Algebra to other geometrical Subjects, which Descartes introduced and Dr. Wallis first made use of in demonstrating the properties of these Sections, it Has come to pass that very few at this time can make either use of the Analytical or Synthetical method of the antients in demonstrating Theorems or in resolving of Problems. To put a stop to this evil, he has wrote these Elements in the method of the Antients, tho he has made use of the Same definitions of the Sections in places that Kepler first and de la Hire & the Marquis de l'Hopital with many others have since made use of.

---

55. In *Account of the Life and Writings of Robert Simson, M.D.,* William Trail reported, "Among Dr. SIMSON's papers there is an account of his Conics, drawn up soon after the publication, in the form of a letter, and in the name of some friend of the Doctor's, apparently with the design of being transmitted to a distance, and perhaps for publication. It is a sort of enlargement of the preface, giving a more particular detail of the author's views in composing the treatise, and of the improvements which he had made in it." He added: "the copy of this letter, found among Dr. SIMSON's papers, is without any signature, but it is in the Doctor's handwriting" (pp. 83 and 84). In a note, p. 83, he added: "Since writing this account," he was directed to "a letter from the celebrated Professor HUTCHESON of Glasgow, on Dr. Simson's *Conic Sections* . . . in the *Bibliothèque raisonée* for April, May, and June 1735, and which, on comparison, I ascertained to be the very letter here alluded to. In that journal it is translated into French, and Professor HUTCHESON is mentioned as an old friend of M. Smith, one of the publishers, at Amsterdam. The letter is dated Glasgow, 28 Feb. 1734." The manuscript of the letter, drafted by Simson and published over the signature of Hutcheson, is transcribed here.

In the first 3 books the Elementary properties of the 3 Sections are Separately demonstrated, that the learner might not have all the three Sections to consider in each propertie which would be too hard for him at the first, but in the two other books, to Avoid repeating the same or very like demonstration the properties of the different Sections are where it could be done, demonstrated in the same words. The properties of the Parabola are placed in the first book because they are easier to demonstrate than the other two; And because the elementary properties of the Circle, which is the most Simple Species of the Ellipse, are also demonstrated in Euclid's Elements he has by help of them demonstrated some of the chief properties of the Ellipse. In the 3rd book the properties of the asymptotes of the hyperbola are made use of in demonstrating some Propositions such as the 40th of the 3rd book, which could not have been so well done by help of the properties of the ordinates to the diameters, as will appear by comparing that proposition with the 20th Lib. 2 of Appoll-Conicks, where the same thing is more tediously demonstrated, tho' as Elegantly as can be by the medium Appolonius makes use of. And this is another reason of the treating of the 3 Sections Separately in the first 3 books.

The solutions of the more difficult Problems are investigated by the help of Euclid's book of the Data according to the method of the Ancients, which is both more easy and Natural than the Algebraic method of the Moderns, and affords more Simple and Elegant constructions of the Problems, as will easily appear by comparing the Solution of the Problem in Prop. 6 Lib. 4 with the algebraic Solution of the same given by the Marquis de l'Hopital in Prop. 12 art 66 of Lib. 2 & Example 3 art 431 of Lib. 10 of his Conick Sections. The problem is, to find two conjugate diameters of an Ellipse which shall make with one Another an angle equal to a given angle, from having two other conjugate diameters given; this he proposes in the Cor. of Prop. 11 art. 65 of his 2d book & adds, That as the Solution of this problem est assez difficile he remits it to the 10th book and in the mean time gives in Prop. 12 the solution of that Case of it where the two diameters given are the Axes, which he had shown how to find in the preceding prop. 11 and then in book 10th gives the solution of the general case where the given diameters are not the Axes. And here it is to be observed that his reckoning the general case more difficult than that where the Axes are given arises from the method used in Algebraic Solutions by which method it is easier to bring problems to and equation where a right angle is among the things given or sought in the problem viz. by the 47.1. Eucl. than where the angle is oblique, for in this case they are obliged (at least it is their constant practice) to let fall a perpendicular so as to have a triangle whose angles & consequently the proportions of the sides are known, and that even where the declining of this perpendicular has no connexion with anything in the problem further than to help them to make the oblique Angle enter into their reasoning which can be done in a much more natural and easie method by Euclids data. And this is one general reason of the Unnatural & inelegant Solutions of geometrical problems by the algebraic method. But that there is in reality no greater difficulty in Solving the above mentioned problem in the general case, than in that where the axes are given, will plainly appear by comparing the Solutions of the 1st & 2d Cases of Prop. 6. Lib. 4 of this treatise the 1st being the case of the Axes & the 2nd that of any other conjugate diameter, and they are set down both at large on purpose to show there is no manner of difference in their Solutions but that in the first the 32 & 31 of Euclids data are made use of where the 44th & 29 are used in the other, and the Investigation there & composition of both cases are easier and shorter than those done in the classical way; that they appear longer proceeds from this that the demonstration of the solution of the general case in the Marquis de L'Hopital's 10th book is entirely left out, as also both the Investigation & composition of the determination of the problem, which in the above named 6th prop. of Lib. 4th are given at large in both cases.

There are a great many new demonstrations of propositions formerly known, and several new propositions particularly the most general properties of the Conick Sections known to the Antients Viz.: that which is Demonstrated in the 16th Prop. Lib. 3 of Apollonius Conicks is here in the 14th & 23rd Prop. of book 4th rendered twice as general, by Extending it to lines which do not at all meet the Section as well as to those which touch or cut it; by help of the 12th, 13th and 21st of the same book. Also the 18th and 24th of book 4th & and the 12th of the 5th & several others are new and from the last of these 3 is easily derived in Corollaries given the Analysis of the Problem to describe a Conick Section which shall touch two straight lines given in position & pass through 3 given points. And from the same 12th lib. 5 the Analysis and composition of the Problem to describe a Conick Section that shall touch 3 lines given in position & pass thro 2 given points may with the like ease be given, without having recourse to the transformation of the Conick Section which Sir Isaac Newton makes use of in the 25th & 26th Prop. of the 1st book of his Principles. The Analysis (from which the composition easily flows) the Author gives is thus.

Propositio

Datis in Sectione Conica duobus punctis A, B, datisque positione tribus rectis lineis CD, CE, DE, quae Sectionem contingentibus: dabuntur in ipsis puncta contactus, F, G, H.

Jungantur AB, FG, FH, HG, et occurat AB tribus reliquis in K, L, M, punctis, Quoniam igitur dantur duo puncta in Sectione viz: A, B, et datae positione Sunt duae rectae CD, CE Sectionem contingentes; dabitur (per Cor. 1 Prop. 12. Lib. 5) punctum K, in quo recta AB occurit rectae FG quae per contactus transit; et similiter dabuntur puncta L, M. Et quoniam quatuor rectae lineae sunt LM, LF, KF, MG, et dantur tria intersectionum puncta L, K, M, in una rectarum, alia vero duo G, H,[56] tangunt rectas CE, DE, positione datas tanget reliqua intersectio E rectam positione Datam per propositionem in Transactionibus Philosophicis No. 337 pag. 330. Idem vero punctum F tangit aliam rectam CD positione datam. Dabitur igitur punctum F: et similiter dabuntur puncta G, H Q.E.D.

Problema vero quo describenda est Sectio Conica quae tanget quator rectas positione datas, et transeat per punctum datum, solvi poterit ope Prop. 7 ejusd. Lib. 5. Sect. con.

The Scholium in pag.198 and the Propp. it flows from, contain a very general & useful propertie of the Sections which the Author discovered upon this Occasion. When Mr. Mac Laurin the learned professor of

---

56. Here the manuscript has the diagram as printed in the *Bibliothèque raisonnée*, April, May, and June 1735, p. 481, and reprinted above, p. 257.

Mathematics in the University of Edinburgh was going to France in the year 1723, Mr. Simson communicated to him a Locus of Pappus ~ Alexandria which he had restored Viz: " Si a tribus datis in recta linea, ducantur tres recta lineae, et ipsarum intersections duae tangant rectas positione datas; tanget reliqua intersectio rectam lineam positione data" which was afterwards printed in the above cited place in the Philosophical Transactions. When Mr. Mac Laurin had come home from France, he told Mr. Simson that he found, when the 3 given points were not in a streight line, all the rest remaining as in the former case, that the Locus described would be a Conick Section, and by help of this locus he could easily describe a Conick Section through 5 given points, this locus method of description he gave Mr Simson without any demonstration which he said he had made by help of a lemma in Sir Isaac Newton's Principles; And it was in Searching for the demonstration of them that Mr Simson found out the propositions in the Scholium & those they flow from, which he did in the same method they are now printed in his book.

Prop.19th of Book 5 Contains that elegant propertie of the Parabola which Mr Fermat proposed to Dr Wallis to demonstrate in the last letter save one of the Commercium Epistolicum in p. 859 of the 2nd Vol. of the Doctors works and which no demonstration has hitherto been given but a confused one in the last leaf of De La Hire's Conicks.

It is to be observed that the Same propertie holds of the Hyperbola. And any line parallel to one of the asymptotes Viz.: If from 2 given points in the hyperbola or Opp. There be 2 straight lines to any 3rd^{d} point of that Curve they shall cut off Segments of any line parallel to an asymptote given in position betwixt themselves at any value which shall have a given ratio.

*Considerations on Patronages Addressed
to the Gentlemen of Scotland,* 1735

CONSIDERATIONS

ON

PATRONAGES

Addressed to the
GENTLEMEN of SCOTLAND[1]

LONDON:

Printed for J. ROBERTS, near the *Oxford-Arms* in
Warwick-Lane. MDCC XXXV.

(Price 4 d.)

1. *Considerations on Patronages* was written to persuade gentlemen in Scotland to support an Act of the General Assembly of the Church of Scotland in which it was proposed that the calling or nomination of ministers in the Church should be made by "Heritors and elders of the vacant Parish, in presence of the Congregation": *The Principal Acts of the General Assembly of the Church of Scotland Conveened at Edinburgh the 4th Day of May 1732* (Edinburgh, 1732), Act VIII, 22. It was an Act designed to relieve the Church of the grievance of patronage or the calling of ministers by the Crown and noble lords.

CONSIDERATIONS

ON

Patronages, &c.

When the Settlement of the Churches in *Scotland* are occasioning such heat and contention, 'tis surprizing to find so many of the Gentlemen of *Scotland* standing as idle Spectators of the Flame, when it does not actually touch themselves, in the immediate Settlement of their own Parish-Churches, taking no steps to prevent the Disorder in general, by a new Law. The Matter is left almost wholly to the Clergy, and a few Gentlemen who happen to be much under their influence, as if this were an Affair in which the Clergy alone are concerned: while yet 'tis manifest that the Interest of the Gentlemen of *Scotland* is much more concerned than that of the Clergy: and they are generally sensible of it when it is represented to them.

<4> The rash imprudent Schemes pursued by some weak Zealots of the Church,[2] have contributed not a little to make wise Men averse from concurring with them: but this should not hinder their contributing what they can for obtaining a wise Regulation of this matter, different from that pursued by the Zealots. I apprehend that many of the Gentlemen are not yet fully apprized of the miserable State of this matter, according to the present Laws; and of the fatal Consequences to be apprehended, if these Laws continue unrepealed. Others lie still in this affair from a base Indifference about the Interests of their Country, or from a servile Caution of offending those in Power, by taking any Steps to which they are not previously commanded; lest they should lose any little Places or Pensions they hold, or lose their distant Hopes of such Advantages: While yet they won't do the ingenuous friendly office of representing faithfully to

---

2. This Act of the General Assembly was vehemently opposed by the Reverend Ebenezer Erskine (1680–1754) and three other ministers, described by Hutcheson as "weak zealots," who maintained that the calling of ministers should not be confined to heritors and elders but should involve all members of the parish. Erskine and his supporters were censured and suspended from their ministries, and in 1733 withdrew from the General Assembly to form the Associate Presbytery. In 1739 the Associate Presbytery seceded from the Church of Scotland (J. M'Kerrow, *History of the Secession Church*; *ODNB*).

Men in Power, what the Nation in general expects from them; the granting of which, would really settle their Interest in the hearts of a great Majority of the Gentry, as well as of the Clergy, and Populace.

The following Considerations are humbly offered to the Gentlemen of *Scotland;* first, on the present State of Patronages, and the Consequences to be apprehended, if the Laws continue as they are; and next are offered some Thoughts upon the Importance of those Rights, which the Gentlemen of *Scotland* have lost by these Laws.[3]

<5> I. To apprehend well the present State of Patronages, we must resume this matter from the Reformation. At that remarkable Period, the whole *Temporalities* of the Church were resumed by the Crown and Parliament:[4] and soon after, a new Maintenance was settled for Ministers, in about 960 Parish-Churches. Yet in that irregular hasty Settlement the *Patronages* were not abolished by Law: The Patrons therefore of the old, splendid, Popish Livings, still claimed a Patronage in the new-settled, poor Stipends for Parish-Ministers.[5] The Lords, or Gentlemen, who got from the Crown Grants of the Superiorities and Lands of old Abbeys, claimed

---

3. Authorship of *Considerations on Patronages* was never publicly acknowledged by Hutcheson or attributed to him during his lifetime. The earliest ascription to Hutcheson appears to have been made in *Tracts concerning Patronage* (1770). In the Preface to that collection, the editor, the Reverend Thomas Randall of Stirling, declared that a "bosom friend" of Hutcheson, the Reverend Robert Patoun of Renfrew, had informed him that Hutcheson was the author of *Considerations on Patronages*. He was told by the same informant that Hutcheson, by his own account, had been assisted in the first part of the pamphlet, which addressed historical and legal matters, by William Grant (1700/1–1764), the clerk of the General Assembly. William Grant, later Lord Prestongrange, was the author of *The Present State of the Church of Scotland, with respect to PATRONAGES; and the Bill Now Depending before the Parliament* (1736). It will be apparent from the notes that follow that *The Present State of the Church of Scotland*, although it was published a year later, must have been available to Hutcheson when he composed *Considerations on Patronages*. Many of the observations and turns of phrase are more fully documented in *The Present State of the Church of Scotland*. The two tracts were complementary but addressed to different groups of readers: Hutcheson was attempting to enlist support from landed gentlemen; Grant was appealing to politicians in London.

4. Compare *The Present State of the Church of Scotland*, p. 1: "The whole Temporalities or Revenues of the Church were resumed and vested in the Crown."

5. Ibid., p. 3: "those who had been Patrons of the more splendid Popish Livings still claimed the Patronage of these poor ones."

also the Patronage of all the Churches which were in the Gifts of those *Abbeys*, during Popery. The King too claimed the old Patronage of the Crown, and those of any *Ecclesiastick Corporations* not granted away. The *Scotch Bishops*, whensoever they came in, claimed the Patronages belonging in times of Popery to the Popish Sees. But upon the Reformation, the Ecclesiastick Laws, or Acts of Assembly, Confirmed also in Parliament, required, in order to a Settlement of a Minister, some Concurrence of the Congregation, of the Heretors and Kirk-Session, before a Presbytery could regularly ordain or install the Minister presented. Frequent Confusions, no doubt, were occasioned by the jarring of the Patrons with the Presbyteries, or Heretors; But the final Decision of all such Debates in the Settlement of Churches, was by Act of Parliament, *James* VI. *Anno* 1567, committed to the General Assembly.

Thus Matters continued to the Year 1649, when by Act of Parliament Patronages were abo<6>lished entirely, and the Election or Nomination of Ministers was committed to the *Kirk-Sessions*, or Elders; who, in those days of universal Sobriety, and, outward Appearance at least, of Religion among the Presbyterians, were generally the Gentlemen or Heretors of best Condition in the Parishes, who were in Communion with the Church.[6] After the Restoration of King *Charles* II, along with Episcopacy Patronages returned, yet under the old Laws; and all Debates were finally determinable by the *General Assemblies*, which, even under Episcopacy, were the Supreme Ecclesiastick Court. Thus they continued 'till the Revolution, when the Presbyterian Model was restored by Act of Parliament.

The Presbyterian Parliament after the Revolution, *An.* 1690, Act 23 did first abrogate all Laws establishing the Right of Patronage, and "*cass, annul, and make void*, that Power altogether"; committing to the *Heretors and* Elders in the Country, and to Magistrates, Town-Council, and Elders, in Burroughs, the Right of electing the Ministers.[7] And then by a

---

6. Ibid., p. 5: "In 1649 the Right of nominating or calling Ministers was lodged in the Kirk-Sessions or Consistory of Elders in the Parish; who, in those Days of outward Sobriety and Regularity at least, were the most considerable Laymen in the Parish who communicated with the Church."

7. Ibid., p. 6: "With the Restoration returned Episcopacy and Patronages, and continued till the Revolution, and then by Act of Parliament the Presbyterian model

subsequent Act, viz. the 29th of the same Session, vested all the Superiorities and Rights of the Scotch Bishops, in the Crown. Sure they never intended to include among them that Right of Patronage, which by a former Act was abolished altogether.[8] There must be some other Foundation for this Claim of the Crown, if there be any at all. The Patronages of the Bishops, were they to subsist at all, should more naturally have gone, with their other Ecclesiastick Powers, to the several Presbyteries; as that Right now devolves, by any neglect of any Patron, to the Presbytery.

<7> Thus Matters continued in a very peaceable easy manner till the Year 1711; when the late Queen's Ministry, intending to defeat the *Hanover* Succession, took all methods to harrass such as were firmly attach'd to it, which the Presbyterian Gentry and Clergy ever were, both from Principle and Interest. An Act therefore was obtained, restoring Patrons to their Power, tho' in the most direct Opposition to the *Articles of Union*,[9] and the publick Faith of the Nation then given, in that sacred Treaty, upon which is founded his Majesty's Title to the Crown of *Scotland*, and the very Parliament of *Great-Britain* itself. This Treaty, as sacredly and solemnly secured to the Church of *Scotland* all its Rights and Privileges, and all the Laws, as they then were, in its favour, to continue unalterable for ever, as it secured any thing else whatsoever.

By this Act, however, in 1711, the King is now in possession of the Patronage of above 550 Churches, out of 950: having not only the old Patronage of the Crown, but many Patronages acquired at the Reformation, not yet alienated; all the Patronages of the fourteen Bishops; and all the Patronages of the Lords forfeited in 1715; and these Patronages may all be used for any such purposes as the Ministers of State shall advise. Of

---

of Church-Government was restored, in King William's first Parliament. Another Act in the year 1690 abolished Patronage altogether . . . and committed the Power of nominating or calling the Minister, to the Heretors or Freeholders and elders."

8. Ibid., p. 8: "altho' by a prior Act of the same Session, viz. Act 23d, the same Parliament had wholly 'discharged, cassed, annulled and made void that Power of Patronage, . . .' the 29th afterwards investing the Crown with the Superiorities and Rights of the Bishops, can be understood to vest a Power previously annulled altogether."

9. Grant and Hutcheson perceived the restoration of patronage in 1711 as an attempt to subvert "the Hanover Succession, to which the Church of Scotland was always firmly attached in Interest and Principles" and "in open Violation of the Union" (Grant, *Present State*, p. 7).

the remaining Churches not in the King's Gift, there are near 200 in the Patronage of some Lords, who sometimes have not one foot of Land in the Parishes, nor any Rents or Interest whatsoever in them, or at best, but some trifling few Duty, or free Tiends; and this by virtue of some old Grant to their Ancestors, of the Superiorities of some Abbeys or Convents; or by their retaining this, among some other little <8> Superiorities over Lands, which their Ancestors have squandered away some Ages ago. The Magistrates of some few Burroughs are Patrons of some of their Churches. But there are not 150 Parishes in *Scotland,* where the Patronage is in any Gentleman of considerable Estate, or natural Interest in the Parishes, to whom it is of any real consequence, as to himself, whether the Minister be a Person of Sobriety, Diligence, or good Abilities in his Office, or not.

The Mischiefs of Patronage are but beginning to appear. The Patrons cannot yet successfully present Men of bad Morals, or make *Simoniacal Bargains,* tho' some Attempts of this kind are talked of. The Presbyteries, and some Heretors, are not yet tame enough to quit their Rights altogether; Settlements upon Presentations are often retarded, and sometimes defeated: The Presentations are not yet current saleable Goods; a silly, vicious, or grossly imprudent Presentee, may be defeated. The Gentry, tho' too indolent about the Affair in general, or about the obtaining a new Law, yet when a Settlement, contrary to their Inclinations, is a forcing upon them in their own Parishes, shew abundant Zeal in the particular Case. 'Tis deplorable that the Populace, who have little Judgment about the Abilities of Men, generally pitch upon as weak Candidates as the Patrons do, nay, sometimes upon worse: And the Gentlemen who oppose the Patron must join them, and allow them greater Power than in proportion to their Abilities of discernment. Men must not subdivide into Parties, who are opposing a superior Power. The Presbyteries generally too oppose a Presentation, unless they can bring a tolerable Concurrence of <9> the Parish; sometimes chiefly regarding the Heretors, and sometimes the Elders also and People. There are generally yet great Struggles in this Matter. But if the Humour increases among the Gentry of despising their own Right in this Matter; and if along with their Rights, those of the Presbyteries, and other Church-Judicatories, tho' confirmed by Acts of Parliament, must be given up to gratify the Patrons, the Presbyteries and Elders thus deserted by the Gentlemen, will soon be wearied out, especially if Decisions of the Lords of the Session run against them: Then at last every Presentation will pass current, and take effect, without Opposition; and when this happens the natural Effects of such a Settlement of Patronage will appear deplorable.

Instead of studying Sobriety of Manners, Piety, Diligence or Literature, one or other of which Qualities are now necessary to recommend the Candidates to the Favour of Heretors, Elders, or Presbytery, the Candidates sole study will be to stand right in *Politicks,* to make his Zeal for the *Ministry of State* conspicuous, or by all servile compliance with the Humour of some great Lord who has many Churches in his Gift, whether that Humour be virtuous or vicious, to secure a Presentation from him.

When a Patron, or one much in favour with a Patron, or with a Minister of State happens to be mercenary and covetous there will be *Bribes* and *Purchases* in the case. A Man of Literature of a Gentlemanly Education, can afford nothing for a small Stipend, the whole of which cannot maintain him in the way of Life he must lead, or provide him with Books for his further Improvement. The poor illiterate Wretch, <10> who never was accustomed to a better way of Life than a Plough-man, who desires no Books, or learned Conversation, or Society with Gentlemen, he is the sure Purchaser; he can subsist on twenty or thirty Pounds *per annum*; to him this is a sufficient Living, nay his Condition is raised; he can allow the other half of his Stipend to run on for eight or ten Years to discharge the *Simoniacal Debt.* In better Livings of 90 or 100 *l. per annum* the Bargain may be better: the Price may be three or four hundred Pounds Sterling; a Sum not despicable to some very honourable Families in *Scotland,* or great Court-Favourites. One must expect, whenever Presentations take effect without obstruction, that this will be the case ordinarily in this Country, where there is so much Indigence; and then the *Scotch* Clergy will be the most despicable Set of Church-men in *Christendom.*

Many of the Gentry who depend on the present Ministers of State, and have their Favour, are very keen in the Cause of Patronages: 'tis the Power of their Patrons they are supporting. Little do they think of the Inconstancy of Power, or Favour at Court, what they now are building up, may hereafter be the Support and Defence of their Enemies, upon a Change of Favour. The Enemies to the present Ministry, however many of them appear keen for the Repeal of the Patronage Act, yet would be grieved if it succeeded under the present Ministry; they well know how popular an Act it would be to restore so valuable a Right to the Body of the Gentry in *Scotland*: they know that the whole Odium of the Refusal will still fall upon those in Power and those only. No Artifice the Ministers of State can use will <11> screen them from it; if the Bill is defeated it is by their means, however they may allow a Friend or two to vote for it. They could easily carry the Bill without Expense or Trouble if they pleased, when so many of the State-Opposition are moving for it. A Lord or two may desire to be heard by their Lawyers against the Bill, but 'tis well known that if the Court were hearty for it these very Lords, rather than lose their *Places* or *Pensions,* would be the first Movers for the Repeal. The Repeal indeed would diminish a little, and but a very little, the Power of the present Ministry to oblige Friends by a Presentation from the Crown now and then. But till the Heretors, Elders, People, and Clergy have forgotten more thoroughly their ancient Right this Power is not so very considerable. It may indeed hereafter become pretty great, and obtain to some future Ministers perhaps four or five Years Purchase of near two thirds of the Church-Revenues of *Scotland* as they fall vacant.

'Tis submitted to all impartial Men whether that Act in 1711 was not the most direct Breach of the most solemn publick Faith in the Articles of Union? And whether it can be very glorious in the Ministers or Friends of a Protestant Prince of the *Hanover-Line,* to retain that Claim, so oppressive to the Church of *Scotland,* which was introduced by the Enemies of that illustrious Family, on purpose to distress and raise Dissensions in the Church of *Scotland,* because of their steady Adherence to their Succession, when it was in great Danger.

II. As to the *Importance* of those Rights the Gentlemen of *Scotland* are deprived of by that <11> Law restoring Patronages: Rights are of importance, according to Men's Notions of Life: what affects Religion is of Importance to the Religious: but to all Men it is of Importance to have some Power to serve their Friends, or the Men they esteem and love.[10]

---

10. The idea of rights as the power to exercise benevolence to friends and to mankind in general was maintained by Hutcheson in all of the statements of his moral philosophy. The idea that rights can be justified in abstraction from "all religious considerations" is consistent with *An Inquiry concerning . . . Moral Good*, sec. 7, art. 1,

Suppose a Man of Fortune void of all Religion or regard to Piety and Virtue, yet he must desire such Power of every kind. Would not any Gentleman think himself highly injured, were he deprived of his Right of voting in the Meetings of the Shire, about choosing the Collectors of the Sess, or any other civil Matters? And yet this is but one Vote among 50 or 60 Votes, or perhaps 90 or 100, in chusing to Places of small Profit. What is it then when the whole Gentry of a Nation, or at last ninety-nine in a hundred, lose their Votes, and all Influence in Elections to Places of greater Value, in Elections where each one had a Vote among eighteen or twenty Voters, nay, sometimes among far fewer? This is the case as to Elections of Parish-Ministers. What is it to have the Votes of almost all who have any natural Concern in such Matters struck off; to have near two thirds of such Places disposed of by a Minister of State, or some Favourite of his, while the best Gentlemen in the Country are mere Cyphers in this Matter which so nearly concerns them; and the remaining third part of such Places in the Gift of a few Lords and Gentlemen who often have no Estate or Interest in the Parishes? The most disagreeable Man, who has perhaps affronted a Gentleman, may be settled under his Nose as a Spy upon him, by a Court Interest; or by some disaffected Lord, because of the Gentleman's good Affection to the King and his Ministry. 'Tis sur<13>prizing that the Gentry of *Scotland* are not more aware of the Consequences of all this, as a civil Matter, abstracted from all religious Considerations.

As to those who have some Regards for Religion, they cannot be at a loss in seeing the Mischiefs which must arise in a little time from the present Laws. Let Divines insist on Arguments from Scripture, and the innumerable severe Canons in the early and less corrupt Ages of the Church: I suggest only Thoughts of common Prudence.[11]

Can a Minister of State at *London* know the Characters of our Probationers for the Ministry in the Church? Is it to be expected that his De-

---

but not with *A Short Introduction to Moral Philosophy* or *A System of Moral Philosophy*, texts prepared, in part, for the use of students where rights are deduced not only from the moral sense but also from duties to God, self, and others.

11. See Hutcheson to his father, Private Correspondence, Letter 4, above, on the subject of church government: "I will own to you what I scarce ever own'd to any body else, that it seems to me wholly a point of Prudence" (p. 8).

pendents and Favourites, in soliciting by his means for a regal Presentation, will ordinarily regard conscientiously the moral Characters and Abilities of the Candidates? Is there no danger of *secret Contracts* of a very infamous nature? If a Candidate is related to one who has some Votes in the Shire for Members of Parliament, or has great Interest in a Burrough, mayn't he generally obtain a regal Presentation from a Minister of State without any regard to Merit? nay may not Men of Interest in Shires or Burroughs make conditional Sales of such Presentations? 'Tis certain there may be some Abuse made, some Mistakes may happen upon the best Schemes of Church-Settlements: But let any Man of common Candour consider whether the Dangers of Presentation of worthless, immoral, or weak mean Men be not incomparably greater according to the present State of Patronages, than in almost any Scheme which was ever devised. If Ministers are to be chosen by the Men of Property in the seve<14>ral Parishes, in conjunction with the Elders as Representatives of the People, is there any such Hope of Success to a vicious or despicable Creature? How hardly will a number of Persons someway concerned in the Character of their Minister, be either unacquainted with it or concur in electing an infamous Candidate? Can Ministers of State or great Lords living at *London,* or in remote parts of *Scotland,* have such Opportunities of Information, or such Interest in settling agreeable diligent wise Men? Can a *Simoniacal Bargain* be a Secret which is contracted with ten or a dozen of Electors? There's no Comparison in these points. Would Heretors, Elders, Presbytery, or People, ever have chosen that *Fornication-Hero*[12] who is lately excommunicated? 'Tis well known that Kirk-Session, Presbytery, Synod, and People, long opposed his Settlement, 'till at last the want of legal Proof of relevant Immoralities, and the great Deference to that truly noble and great Lord the Patron, brought them to a sort of unwilling Compliance. When such an Instance happened by the Presentation of that most noble Lord, whose hereditary Good-will and Affection to the Church of *Scotland,* whose Superiority to all base Temptations of Money

12. The "fornication-hero" was most likely James Adam of Hallhill, who was charged with not having insisted "in his Appeal against a Sentence of the synod of Glasgow and Ayr, in a Process of Scandal against him and Jean Stapleton, his servitrix, and the said Appeal declared fallen from": *The Principal Acts of the General Assembly of the Church of Scotland, Conveen'd at Edinburgh the 8. Day of May, 1735,* p. 38.

are so well known, what may be dreaded from many other Patrons of very different Characters?

Is it nothing to the Gentlemen of *Scotland* to transmit, along with their Lands, to their Heirs a *natural hereditary Influence* among their Neighbours, by which they can reward any wise ingenious sober Scholar, who by faithful Diligence as a Tutor, has formed the Minds of their Heirs to Knowledge and Virtue? What when a worthy Kinsman takes to that way of Life in the Church? <15> If a Gentleman's Relations are unworthy or vicious, unfit for that sacred Office, Men of Estates won't get the Concurrence of other Heretors and Elders or the Presbytery. But when the Kinsman is really worthy and pious, is it nothing to have some Influence in obtaining to him a comfortable Support? Must this whole Power be confined to the King and seven or eight Lords? As to the few Burroughs where Magistrates and Council are now Patrons of their own Churches, or of some of them, they have their own Friends to take care of: Country Gentlemen cannot have any Expectation from them. Is it the true *Scotch* Spirit to love to be Suppliants for every thing, to cringe to Men in Power rather than to have a natural Power of their own, a few *Beneficia Populi*, to be obtained by their Favour?

Is it to be expected that Men of Fortune, thus deprived of what was established to them as their Right by the most solemn Faith of the most solemn Treaty incorporating two Nations, will think themselves concerned to regard or to support the Credit and Influence of Preachers forced upon them without their Consent? And when Ministers are thus neglected by Men of Fortune in the Parish, and perhaps affronted (as the Passions of Men in a just Cause may often lead them farther than they ought) is it to be expected that Ministers won't soon too be despised by the Populace, and lose all Influence with them as to any thing of Piety or Virtue in their Manners? I need not enlarge upon these Mischiefs; they are abundantly known in some Places already; and all who have any regard to Religion must think it a Matter of Consequence to prevent them for the future.

<16> In whatever light we consider this Matter, it can't appear as a thing indifferent. Is it not of some Importance to Gentlemen to have a Minister capable of entertaining them agreeably in publick with rational and edifying Discourses? Is it nothing to Gentlemen particularly to such

as reside in the Country, to have a Minister they could make a Friend of, a Man of Letters and good Sense one of social virtuous Dispositions of Mind, who hath had the Advantage of a liberal Education and not only knows Books but Men and good Company? Would not a Gentleman also value one who understands and teaches the true Principles of Religion and Morality to his Children his Family his Tenants and all his Neighbourhood, and who does what he can by his Life and Doctrine to form their Tempers and Lives in the most effectual Manner for promoting their own Happiness, and being good Members of Society; one who is capable of giving wise Advices, reconciling Variances, promoting Peace and Love, and hath a just Influence for advancing these good Ends? Abstracting even from Christianity and a future State, don't these things well deserve the Care and Attention of any Gentleman of Thought and Conduct. And is it not therefore of some Consequence to have some Influence in their Parishes in the Choice of a right Minister? And if we suppose that Gentlemen have a real Regard to Piety and our holy Christian Religion, as God be thanked there are still many such in *Scotland,* they have still much more Reason to be solicitous in this Matter.

I shall not say much of the present Bill in dependence, or other Schemes proposed. 'Tis plain the Bill proposed would effectually prevent many <17> of these Evils which arise from Patronage. If it took place Settlements would generally be according to the Inclinations of the principal Men of Interest in each Parish, who could give most Credit and Influence to the Minister, and contribute most to his Encouragement in his Work, and these Men of Interest generally speaking would bring the Tenants and inferior People along with them, so that unhappy Debates and Divisions about Settlements would be in a great measure prevented. There are few Parishes in which there would not be ten or twelve Electors; there generally would be three times that number. The People would be represented by the Elders, and hold a like Ecclesiastick Liberty to that they have in civil Matters. Simony would be generally impracticable. Immoral or weak Men could have small hopes of Admission.

If that Bill passed I should not doubt of seeing a great Improvement among the *Scotch* Clergy in a few Years. More of the younger Sons of Gentlemen would study Divinity, and such would have better Hopes of being soon admitted into Livings. Their better Education and Interest, with their Patrimonies, would obtain more Esteem and Influence among the Gentry as well as among the People. They might be improving Companions, Instructors, Advisers to the better sort in general, particularly to young Gentlemen in their Education and Conduct in Life.

Nor would the Sons of Gentlemen have any reason to despise this way of Life. To every wise and virtuous Man this Office must appear to be of the most useful Tendency, wherein a Man may at least propose to do as much Good to his Fellow-Creatures, as in any other of the middle <18> Stations of Life whatsoever; and therefore it has the justest Claim to Esteem and Respect among Mankind. And it may be said in general that bad as we are it must be owing to the present Misbehaviour of Clergymen themselves if they want as much Regard (among People at least of ordinary Thought and Discretion) as they ought reasonably to desire. And though indeed their Livings be but small in comparison of those in the neighbouring Countries, or rather that they are more equally divided and no very great Benefices among them, yet such as they are they don't seem to be below, even in a civil Account, Gentlemen's younger Sons, or even the eldest Sons of many of them. At a moderate Computation one with another including Glebes and Manses they may be reckoned about Eighty Pounds *per annum.* Pray how few Gentlemen's Sons make more in their different Ways of Life, even those of our other learned Professions, Lawyers, Attorneys, Physicians, Surgeons, how few of them would not cheerfully give their yearly Profits by their Business for Eighty Pounds? Where one makes more in *Scotland,* I believe I may venture to say three make less. And what is a great Advantage to Ministers is that what they have is sure, at least not exposed to such terrible Vicissitudes or such precarious Circumstances as the Fortunes of most other People are. Besides much depends upon that Sobriety and Regularity of Life both at home and abroad which their Character in a particular manner requires, and enables them to live better upon their Stipends, than most other People in a different Way, upon the like Sum and a good deal more.

<19> If Gentlemen's Sons were educated this way a stop would naturally be put to Lads of mean Parentage and Circumstances directing their

Views to the Ministry,[13] none of whom indeed should be encouraged or recommended by Gentlemen or Ministers and push'd through Schools and Colleges as too many since the Revolution have been, unless there be evidently something uncommonly bright and promising in their Genius. For the Interests of Religion and Virtue and the reasonable Credit and Influence of the Clergy for doing Good, I wish that much more Caution may be used this way for the future. For this Reason it is to be desired that some Regulation were made about Bursaries, that some were suppressed altogether, and two, three, or four others were joined in one, to be a handsome Encouragement not below any young Man of real Merit. Some Method I hope will be fallen upon for this. But in the mean time it is one thing indeed that very much recommends this Bill to me, that by putting Settlements chiefly into the hands of the principal Men of Interest in the Parishes, it will encourage a greater number of virtuous and studious young Gentlemen to take to this way of Life, which is contemptible upon no account, if it be not perhaps thought so by reason of so many People of very mean Birth and Fortune having got into it. And this is what I think very well deserves the Consideration of the *Scotch* Gentry, those particularly of the middle kind, and should also excite the Concern of all those who wish well to the Advancement of all valuable and useful Improvements among the Clergy.

<20> There have been many other Schemes proposed about the Settlement of Churches, every one of which is liable to Inconveniences, and I am far from thinking the one proposed in the Bill is altogether free of them. Yet I would prefer it to the most I have seen, particularly to such as put it wholly or chiefly in the hands of the Populace. Instead of many Reasons I shall only name one why I would do so, *viz.* that the Populace are by no means the fittest and best Judges of ministerial Qualifications. Preaching for instance is one main thing to be noticed in a right Choice. Now what kind of Preachers are they whom the Vulgar chiefly admire?

13. Hutcheson also thought that more caution should be exercised in the award of bursaries. Coincidentally, the student author of *Shaftsbury's Ghost Conjur'd* was awarded a bursary on October 15, 1733 (GUA 26647, p. 129). Hutcheson was absent from that meeting of the faculty. See note 8, p. 294.

Why chiefly those who strike their outward Senses in the strongest manner, such as have the most noisy and strange Vociferation, use the most violent Action and Gestures; or such as declaim most against Superiors in Church and State, and shew the warmest Zeal about little things. They may live well enough with Ministers of another Character. But such Clergymen as these now described will be generally the greatest Idols of the Populace, though they are possessed of little Learning, Sense, or Moderation, or any other good Qualities. Now if the Choice of Ministers were chiefly in the Vulgar, I would be much afraid this would be one bad Effect among others, that it would be too violent a Temptation to Preachers in order to gain the Applause of the Electors to suit themselves to their mean and depraved Taste. A Habit of this kind is soon contracted, and the Effect of it very charming to many Minds, and indeed it is a much more easy Task than to gain the rational Approbation of Gentlemen of Virtue and Discernment. But <21> alas need I say of what vast Prejudice this would be to all elegant and valuable Studies? and what is much more to be considered a very great Loss to the Interests of true Religion and Virtue?

But not to argue upon other Schemes, it may be of more use to notice that by Men's disagreeing about the different Schemes in any good Design, the whole is often defeated. It were heartily to be wished that all would unite in the one already proposed in Parliament, even though they don't think it the best possible. No Scheme will prevent all Inconveniences; and none will ever succeed which does not allow a great Influence to the Gentlemen of Estates. 'Tis a grand Advance to remove once the old inveterate Evil of *Patronage*; Amendments may perhaps be more easily obtained hereafter, if they are found necessary. 'Tis strange Folly to be contriving varieties of Schemes, while it is yet so uncertain whether any Alteration is really intended by those who alone can accomplish it. I can't but suspect all as Enemies in their hearts to this Repeal who are not willing to accept that Bill with all Gratitude to God and our Civil Governours, whatever better Plans they may fancy: and setting a-foot unpracticable Schemes, such as cannot be expected from the *Legislature,* must be a Stratagem of the secret Enemies of the whole Design, by which weak honest Men are to be defeated of the Advantage desired.

Honest Men who wish well to the Country and King, and to the Church of *Scotland,* should not upon any Delay of their Requests run violently against the King, or those he thinks fit to employ. Enemies of the Church may instigate them to this Conduct, on purpose to de<22>feat the Repeal of Patronages. This Conduct oftner flows from a *factious ambitious Spirit,* than from real Love to our Country. But 'tis hoped the Friends of the Administration will seriously consider the Danger to the Country from such continual Ferments; the terrible Evils to be feared from the Patronages when they come to take effect without Opposition; the Corruptions of the Clergy, and the neglect of Religion and Sobriety of Manners among the People, when unrestrained by a Clergy, grown despicable or hateful to them: and the Advantages which would accrue to the body of the Gentry from obtaining their old Right again; while yet the Patrons if they are Men of Estates in the Parishes would still have an Influence almost equal to Patronage, of a more neighbourly and gainly sort. If these things be well considered and represented to the Ministry by those who stand well with them, such Applications could not well want Success.

At the Quarterly Meetings of the Shires are there none on the Court-Side, who have such Regard for their Country and Church, as to concert proper Representations, or Petitions about this Matter? Must every thing Popular, every Motion in favour of the Country, of the Body of the Gentry, of the Church, ever take its rise among Gentlemen disaffected to the Administration?

I might mention many other Considerations to shew that 'tis of consequence to Gentlemen to countenance the Clergy of *Scotland* more than they do; to improve their Condition; to choose Men of Learning and Manners. Most Gentlemen are solicitous to have their Sons sober and <23> virtuous, and yet where Religion, and those employed in religious Offices, are so generally neglected and despised, the young Gentry will ever look upon Sobriety, and Virtue, and Piety, as Qualities necessary only in the Mob, or the Teachers of the mean Populace.

Were Clergymen pleading for more Power, or great Augmentations of their Livings by burdening further the Gentlemen's Estates, the Laity should be on their guard. But when the point aimed at is the enlarging the Power of the body of the Landed-Gentlemen, 'tis strange that any of the Gentry should oppose them, or refuse their Concurrence, except those few who have great Patronage themselves.

The direct pleading for Patronages in *Scotland* is so odious to all Men of Piety, that not one of the Clergy, not a King's Chaplain, or *Politician-Clergyman* among them dared to open his mouth in favour of them in their Assemblies or Synods, how much so ever some such are suspected to favour them secretly, through Confidence in their Court-Favour; in hopes to get regal Presentations to Cousins and Tools of their own. All honest Men among the Clergy abhor them; though the high Spirit (I call it so rather than Pride) of some of them makes them lie by, out of Indignation that some weak hot Men have got a greater Following among the Populace, and greater Influence in Synods and Assemblies. I hope good and wise Men will conquer this low Resentment, and be no longer inactive in so good a Cause, the Success of which is their hearts desire and Prayer to God; though they should not have the Glory among the Populace of any Success which may <24> ensue, or of any honest Efforts whether they succeed or not. A faithful Representation from some of the wiser and calmer Men in the Church would contribute much more to advance the Design than the Clamours of Multitudes.[14]

FINIS.

14. The bill to abolish patronages was brought before the House of Commons on April 18, 1736, but did not pass: *The History of the Proceedings of the House of Commons from the Restoration to the Present Time* (London, 1742), p. viii. On May 22, 1736, the General Assembly of the Church of Scotland passed a resolution declaring the intention of the Church "to persist in using her best Endeavours, from time to time, to be relieved from the grievance of Patronage, until the same shall, by the Blessing of God, prove successful": *The Principal Acts of the General Assembly of the Church of Scotland Conveen'd at Edinburgh the 13. Day of May 1736* (Edinburgh, 1736), p. 45. There was a recurring initiative in eighteenth-century Scotland to confer upon heritors and elders the right to present ministers to their parishes, but these initiatives were unsuccessful. See Richard Sher and Alexander Murdoch, "Patronage and Party in the Church of Scotland, 1750–1800." In his subsequent writings and pronouncements on this subject Hutcheson considered it prudent to leave the calling of ministers to the "Chief Magistrate" and "officers of the state": *A Short Introduction to Moral Philosophy*, (1747), p. 319; (2007), pp. 266–67; and *A System of Moral Philosophy*, p. 312. It was a system that offered at least the assurance that ministers would not be chosen by "the populace"—that is, by men who might well have been, in his opinion, weak zealots.

Shaftesbury's Ghost conjur'd: or, A Letter to Mr. Francis Hutcheson, 1738

Shaftsbury's *Ghost conjur'd:*

OR, A

LETTER

TO

Mr. Francis Hutcheson[1]

Professor of Moral Philosophy
in the University of *Glasgow.*

WHEREIN

Several gross and dangerous Errors, vented by him in the Course
of his Teaching, are brought to Light, and refuted.

Titus i.13. *This Witness is true: Wherefore rebuke them sharply, that
they may be sound in the Faith.*[2]

Printed in the Year M.DCC.XXXVIII.

---

1. The author of this letter was Hugh Heugh. His father, Reverend John Heugh (1688–1731), minister of the Church of Scotland in Kingoldrum, was deeply opposed to "enemies of the church" such as the Reverend John Simson: Hamilton Macgill, *The Life of Hugh Heugh, D.D.*, p. 14.

2. This letter consists, for the most part, of citations from the Holy Bible in the King James translation. The citations were printed in italics, without further identification.

SIR,

Tho' the World has in all Ages abounded with *Men of corrupt Minds, resisting the Truth*[3] *as it is in Jesus,* and establishing in the Room thereof the Wisdom of this World; yet I am firmly persuaded, that, if we compare the present State of the Church with the Revolutions that have happened in it since Christianity first began to dawn among the Nations, it will easily appear, that the Father of Lies never had mo<re> Hands at Work in advancing his Interest, by venting Errors and Heresies of every Kind, than in these latter Ages wherein our Lot is cast: And we will find it lamentably accomplished (which the Spirit expressly foretold) *That in the latter Times some should depart from the Faith, giving Heed to seducing Spirits and Doctrines of Devils, speaking Lies in Hypocrisy, having their Consciences seared with a hot Iron;*[4] And that in these *perilous Times Men should be Blasphemers, Unholy,*[5] &c. The Scriptures of Truth, and the several Doctrines of our holy Religion therein-contained, have been openly impugned by our modern Deists, who have publickly maintained the Religion of Nature in direct Opposition to the Religion of Jesus; and these we may reckon the avowed Enemies of the Truth. There are others again, who, without a professed Opposition to Christianity, but with Hearts full of Enmity against it, have more cunningly attempted its Ruin, by laying down such Principles, and promoting such Schemes, as have a direct Tendency to subvert and undermine it; of which Sort I have always thought my Lord *Shaftsbury* one, who, I am persuaded, has been more instrumental by his Writings in propagating Infidelity and Deism, than *Collings, Woolston, Tindal,* and all the rest of the acknowledged Adversaries of Christianity:[6] He was a Man of better Morals, Parts and Education than any of them, and so much the fitter for promoting the Kingdom of Darkness; for 'tis a common Proverb, *The Devil has more Wit than to employ a Fool.* But,

---

3. 2 Timothy 3:8.

4. 1 Timothy 4:1–2.

5. 2 Timothy 3:1–2.

6. Shaftesbury, *Characteristicks of Men* (1711); Anthony Collins, *A Discourse of Free-Thinking* (1713) and *A Discourse of the Grounds and Reasons of the Christian Religion* (1724); Thomas Woolston, *Discourses on the Miracles of Our Saviour* (1727–29); and Matthew Tindal, *Christianity as Old as the Creation* (1730).

besides these, there is yet another Sett of Adversaries, <4> by whom the Christian Religion has suffered more than by all the former, and who are therefore most of all odious in the Eyes of every true Christian; I mean, such as publickly own their Subjection to the Gospel, and their Belief of the Truths thereof, while at the same Time they espouse and propagate such Tenets and Opinions as are contrary to it, and inconsistent with it: They take upon them the Name of Christians, yea, they profess their Faith in the peculiar Doctrines of Christianity, and yet are not ashamed to say A Confederacy with Infidels and Deists, and to lend them their helping Hand in fighting against the God of Truth, by venting and propagating the most gross and scandalous Errors: They put on a Cloke of Friendship, that they may be admitted into publick Offices in the Church; and, when this Banner is given them, they don't display it for the Truth, but against the Truth, exerting their utmost Abilities for advancing *Satan*'s Kingdom, and joining Issue with him in *blinding Mens Minds, lest the Light of the Knowledge of Christ, and of the Truth as it is in him, should shine into them:*[7] These, as I said before, are the most dangerous Adversaries of our holy Religion; and therefore it is the Duty of all true Christians, who sincerely love the Truth and desire to walk in it, to endeavour by all possible Means to convince such Gainsayers, and reclaim them from the Error of their Way, and to open Men's Eyes who are ready to be led astray by their vain Delusions from the Paths of Truth and Godliness. And this, I think, may be sufficient to excuse me for the Freedom I have used in the following Paper; to which I shall now very quickly introduce myself, leaving it to the World to judge, whether there is not too just Ground to number you among this last Sort, and to ascribe the above-mentioned Characters unto you.

I had Occasion, *Sir,* some Years ago to hear your Lectures of *Natural Theology* and *Moral Philosophy* in the University of *Glasgow* for two Sessions successively:[8] I own, when your Scheme of Principles was first pre-

---

7. 2 Corinthians 4:4.

8. Hugh Heugh would have heard Hutcheson's lectures on moral philosophy for the first time in 1734–35, in his third year at the University of Glasgow. In his second year at the university he was awarded the bursary noted above, p. 287, note 13.

sented to my View, I was in Danger of falling in with the most Part of it, finding it exceedingly agreeable to the Dictates of corrupt Reason; my Fancy was tickled with your chimerical Ideas of Virtue and a Moral Sense, and depraved Nature was not a little pleased to hear of a God *altogether such an one as ourselves.* Thus I was almost carried down the Stream, and my Feet had well nigh slipt: But I desire to <5> bless the Lord, who afterward put it into my Heart to go *to the Law and to the Testimony,*[9] that I might examine whether you *spake according to these,* and thence might judge of the Truth and Solidity of your Doctrines. Accordingly, during my second Attendance upon your Class, I made it my Business, when I heard any Thing that I was not fully satisfied about, to write it down as soon as I returned to my Room; and, when my Conveniency allowed, I endeavoured to compare the Propositions I heard you advance with the Principles of our holy Religion, as contained in the Scriptures of Truth, and agreeably thereto summed up in our excellent *Confession of Faith*:[10] Which I was the rather inclined to do, because I knew you was solemnly engaged, before your Admission to your present Office, to assert, maintain and defend all the Truths contained in the said *Confession,* at least to teach nothing directly opposite to them.[11] And now, understanding, to my great Grief, the vast Number of Proselytes you have made, several of whom are already Office-bearers in the Church, and so in a Capacity of spreading your Opinions; and considering the quick Progress your Principles are daily making among these who have an Eye to that sacred Office; I thought the Remarks I had formerly made upon them might possibly be of some Use, if not for your Conviction, at least for undeceiving the Minds of others, and so suppressing in some Measure the further Progress of your dangerous Tenets: And, if the Lord shall be pleased in the

9. Isaiah 8:20.

10. *The Confession of Faith, Larger and Shorter Catechisms: First Agreed upon by the Assembly of Divines at Westminster: And now appointed by the General Assembly of the Church of Scotland to be a Part of Uniformity in religion between the Kirks of Christ in the Three Kingdoms* (Glasgow, 1732).

11. See "Documents relating to Hutcheson's Appointment at the University of Glasgow," above, p. 127.

least Degree to bless my weak Endeavours for this Purpose, the End which I desire to have in View will be gained. In the several Propositions which contain your Opinions, I have kept your own Words as near as I could: And tho' I shall not positively affirm, that there is no Variation; yet I am confident that in the main your own Expressions are used, and am very sure I have charged you with nothing but what I heard you advance. As for the Remarks, I doubt not but I have sometimes omitted Arguments which would be of greater Weight than any of these I have adduced; only I can say, that these which I insist on, being the first that occurred to my View, are such as fully satisfied my own Judgment that the Propositions are false. Perhaps you will object, That, since the Character you bear as a *Professor of Philosophy* confines you to what *the Light of Nature* teaches, it is not just to attack you with Arguments from *Revelation*.[12] To which I answer, That, by *the Light <6> of Nature,* I understand the faint Remains of that original Knowledge wherewith Man was endowed at his first Creation, that are yet to be found in our Minds in this fallen State; and, as this Knowledge had God for its Author, it can reach nothing inconsistent with any Revelation he should at any Time make: Wherefore, when I prove any of your Tenets to be contrary to the Word of God, I justly conclude, that they are not the Dictates of the Light of Nature, as above-described, but the Product of that gross Ignorance and thick Darkness that prevails in the natural Man. In a Word, I think no Man that professes to be a Christian, should, upon any Pretence whatsoever, so far divest himself of that Character, as to give loose Reins to his blinded Understanding to dictate any Thing contrary to the Revelation God hath given us. I shall now proceed to what I intend; and, that I may be the more distinct, I shall first give you the Proposition containing your Opinion, and then subjoin my Remarks upon it.

---

12. In 1695, at a meeting held to draft a syllabus for philosophy courses in the four Scottish universities, William Law, of the University of Edinburgh, expressed the consensus of his colleagues when he argued that to find a foundation or ground for "rules of Morality and other Ethick conclusions . . . no other ways than by quotations of Scripture . . . is not at all to philosophize" (EUL MS MC 1.4TT, 1695).

PROPOSITION I.

We could have the Knowledge of Moral Good and Evil, altho' we knew nothing of the Being of a God.

The Knowledge of God is one of the principal Duties required in the first Commandment: And indeed it is very justly put in the first; for it is the Basis and Foundation of all Religion, which principally consists in *knowing God, whom to know is Life eternal.*[13] And I don't know if a better Reason can be assigned for the innumerable Errors that Mankind are liable to both in Judgment and Practice, than the gross Ignorance of God and Spiritual Things, which is so rooted in our Natures, that nothing but supernatural Illumination can overcome it. Some represent God as moved from a Principle of *Self-love* (as they blasphemously call it) in all his Actions, and hence they make *Self* the supreme Standard of Good and Evil: while others again have feigned a Deity performing all his Works with an ultimate View to the Good of his Creatures, whence they form quite contrary Notions of Good and Evil: But in both Cases the fundamental Error lies in their <7> Ignorance of God. Now then, if right Notions of God are necessary to the Knowledge of Good and Evil, and if mistaken Apprehensions of the Divine Nature do constantly produce Mistakes about Sin and Duty; What do ye think would be Case, if we should suppose one so stupidly ignorant as not to have the least Notion even of the Being of God? (tho' I doubt very much if you can produce any such Instance) Would such a one be a whit *wiser than the Fowls of Heaven?*[14] Would he have any more Knowledge of Good and Evil, of Virtue or Vice, than *the Beasts that perish?*[15] For my Part, I think *our foolish Minds are so much darkned,*[16] that, till once we be made *Light in the Lord,*[17] we can have no right Notions either of Good or Evil, of Sin or Duty: Until this *Light shine into our Souls,* we'll *call Evil Good, and Good Evil;* we'll *put Darkness for Light, and Light for Darkness.*[18] Since then *it is God that teacheth Men this Wisdom,* since *the Fear of the Lord is the Beginning of Knowledge,*[19] How is

13. John 17:3.
14. Job 35:11.
15. Psalms 49:20.

16. Romans 1:21.
17. Ephesians 5:8.

18. Isaiah 5:20.
19. Proverbs 1:7.

it possible that Knowledge can be attained without knowing that there is a God? I own that unregenerate Men may have some very imperfect Knowledge of Good and Evil; for all Men, even the Heathens themselves, have *Consciences bearing Witness within them, and Thoughts which accuse or else excuse one another.*[20] But, pray what does that make for your Point? It only shows that they *have the Works of the Law written in their Hearts,*[21] and consequently they must have some faint Knowledge of the Lawgiver; at least they know that there is a God, and they generally believe that he is possessed of infinite Perfections, whatever Errors they may fall into about his Nature and Providence: *For the invisible Things of God from the Creation of the World are clearly seen, being understood by the Things that are made, even his eternal Power and Godhead.*[22] Moral Good and Moral Evil are still to be considered with a Regard to the Divine Law; that is to say, if we have no Knowledge of the Law, neither by Revelation, nor by having it written on our Hearts, we can have no Knowledge of Moral Good and Evil: And, since the Knowledge of the Law must be presupposed, 'tis plain that the Knowledge of the Lawgiver is necessary likewise. But I find this leads me forward to the second Proposition, which is very near a-Kin to the first: And it is this. <8>

PROPOSITION II.

Tendency to promote the Happiness of others, is the Standard of Moral Goodness.

That this is your Opinion, is evident from the Definition you give of a good Action, in your *Essay on the Passions* (Sect. 2. Art. 3. Def. 12.) *viz.* "That *an Action is good in a Moral Sense, when it flows from benevolent Affections, or Intention of absolute Good to others.*"[23] And from what you say in your *Enquiry* (Sect. 3. Art. 10.) "That *that Action is the most perfectly*

20. Romans 2:15.
21. Romans 2:15.
22. Romans 1:20.
23. *Essay on the Nature and Conduct of the Passions and Affections*, (1728), p. 37; (2002), p. 36.

virtuous, which appears to have the most universal unlimited Tendency to the greatest and most extensive Happiness of all the rational Agents to whom our Influence can reach."[24] Contrary to which, I join with the *Westminster Assembly,* who tell us, That *the Moral Law, contained in the Ten Commandments, is the perfect Rule of Righteousness, and a comprehensive Summary of our Duties, both towards God and Man* (Conf. of Faith, Chap. 19. Sect. 2 & 6).[25] If this Law is not a Rule of Life, informing us of the Will of God and of our Duty, and binding us to walk accordingly, pray what Purpose does it serve for? Why was it so solemnly delivered from Mount *Sinai,* and written twice upon Tables of Stone with the Finger of God? Why was our Lord at so much Pains to inculcate the Precepts of it upon his Followers, and to persuade them of its immutable Obligation? Why did he, to remove all Ground of Doubting in this Matter, tell them expressly, *That he came not to destroy the Law, but to fulfil it; And that one Jot or one Title shall in no wise pass from the Law, till all be fulfilled?*[26] In a Word, Why have the Saints in all Ages *delighted in the Law of God, and loved his Commandments above Gold, yea, above fine Gold?*[27] Shall we not from all these conclude, that Persons and Actions are to be accounted morally good or bad, according to their Conformity or Contrariety to the Law and Will of God? I think the Apostle is abundantly plain on this Head, when he tells us, That *he had not known Sin but by the Law.*[28] And again, That *he was alive without the Law once; but when the Commandment came, Sin revived:*[29] For (says he in another Place) *by the Law is the Knowledge of Sin:*[30] Might not one very justly infer from such Expressions as these, that the Divine Law is the Rule of our <9> Faith and Obedience, by which we are to judge of Righteousness and Sin? But, besides these, I might mention other Texts of Scripture still more manifest, which are sufficient to convince any one that will not stop his Eyes when, he meets with any Thing contrary to his own Opinion. For Example, the Prophet *Micah* tells us, that God *hath shewed us what is good,*[31] or what he requires of us; that is, he has revealed to us the Moral Law, which contains his

---

24. *Inquiry,* (1725), p. 165; (2008), p. 126.
25. *The Confession of Faith,* p. 42.
26. Matthew 5:17–18.
27. Psalms 119:127.

28. Romans 7:7.
29. Romans 7:9.
30. Romans 3:20.
31. Micah 6:8.

Will concerning our Actions; which plainly proves that the Divine Law is the Standard of Moral Goodness. And then the Apostle *John* gives us an express Definition of Sin, *viz.* that it is *the Transgression of the Law*;[32] and therefore Righteousness or Moral Goodness must consist in Conformity to it. 'Tis needless to multiply Scriptures; every Man that reads his Bible must know that both the Old and New Testament are full of Texts which tend very much to establish this Definition of Goodness: But I don't remember to have seen any Thing in either of them that seems in the least to favour yours; nor did I ever hear you pretend any Argument from Revelation for confirming your Notion on this Head, save only one Text, wherein you mightily triumph as an insuperable Difficulty, which presses the common Opinion, as you call it: Your Objection in its full Force is this, "If Goodness consists in Conformity to a Law, is it not a poor Elogium of that Law, when it said to be *holy, just and good,* that is, to be conform to itself? And what Perfection does it argue in the Nature of God, that it is agreeable to his own Law? If the Devil, say you, should make a Law, both he and it might be morally good in this Sense."[33] But I am surprised that you should build your Dissent from an Opinion that has so universally prevailed, on such a weak Foundation: You still speak of Goodness, as if it were always to be understood in a certain determined Sense; whereas it is abundantly plain that that Word is used very ambiguously, and is capable of various Meanings; sometimes it has a particular Sense, sometimes a more general One. And, when we are speaking of a Law, I don't know if it is strictly proper to ascribe Moral Goodness to it; that, one would think, is rather applicable to Persons and Actions: And I am sure, the Text you speak of may very easily be explained otherwise; for the Law of God is justly called Good, inasmuch as it is the Transcript of his Will, and tends to promote Moral Goodness in these that observe it. As for the Goodness of God again, you reckon your<10>self obliged in order to have any distinct Notion of it, to make it consist in a strong Disposition to promote the Happiness of his Creatures: For, if Moral Goodness in the Creature is referred to God, you think we lose our Notion of

---

32. 1 John 3:4.
33. *Inquiry,* (1725), pp. 253–54; (2008), pp. 181–82.

his Goodness altogether, or at least have but a very trifling Idea of it. According to this Scheme, the Goodness of God seems to be entirely dependent upon his Creatures. You'll allow me therefore to ask you, Whether God would have been properly and strictly good in a Moral Sense, if he had not thought fit to create any Being beside himself or rather, if you please, I shall ask you, Whether God was truly morally good before the Existence of any other Being? If you say he was, I refer it to any Man to judge, which of these two is the most trifling Idea of the Divine Goodness, supposing it to consist in a Disposition to make these Beings happy who were not to exist till a certain Period of Time infinitely distant, which must be your Notion of it; or placing it in the Possession of inexhaustible Blessedness and infinite Perfection, together with an unspeakable Complacence and Delight in the Contemplation of his own Nature from all Eternity, which is mine? To be sure, a fixed Disposition to promote Happiness, is a relative Way of conceiving the Goodness of God (or rather his Mercy, as these two are distinguished in Scripture): But it is equally certain, that there is an absolute independent Goodness, which did as properly belong to him from all Eternity, as it does now. I shall only add one Difficulty that occurs to me, with respect to this Proposition, *viz.* That I am afraid, some Actions may tend to the external Good of Society, which are expressly prohibited in the Divine Law; and it seems hard to admit of a Dispensation in all these Cases. I know your Way of speaking is, That in general every good Action is agreeable to the Divine Law: But then you say, that is only like a secondary Property of it. The grand Criterion, by which we judge of our own and other Mens Actions, is their Tendency to the publick Good; and therefore, when that is at the Stake, you make no Scruple to dispense with a Divine Commandment. However, I must take the Freedom think,[34] that that derogates not a little from the Honour and Dignity of the Law, and consequently of the Lawgiver also. And I wish, *Sir,* you would seriously propose to yourself the following Question: Suppose a Civil Magistrate should command you to transgress the Law of God, for the external Benefit of your Country, <11> and suppose you were firmly persuaded that the Action you were to do would really tend to the

34. Presumably the intention was "freedom to think."

publick Good, at the same Time that you knew it to be directly contrary to a Divine Commandment, from which there is no Exception mentioned in Scripture: I say, if this Case should happen (and I doubt not but it is possible) *whether would you think it right in the Sight of God, to hearken unto Man more than unto God?*[35] For my Part, I heartily agree with Bishop *Sanderson,* that every Transgression of the Divine Law is Sin, tho' it were to procure the Salvation of the whole World;[36] and I was sorry to hear you mention that as an Instance of superstitious Bigotry. I shall now proceed to consider some of the particular Precepts of the Law, from which you admit of a Dispensation in order to promote the publick Good.

PROPOSITION III.

Self-murder is in some Cases lawful.

Our Saviour sums up all the Commands of the second Table of the Law in that one Precept, *Thou shalt love thy Neighbour as thyself;*[37] which seems manifestly to import, that we owe the same Duties to ourselves which we owe to our Neighbour: And consequently, if it be a Sin to take away the Life of others, or to do any Thing that may have a Tendency thereto, the same must hold with respect to our own Life; therefore I think Self-murder is in no Case lawful. And, besides the general Prohibition, I have very good Authority for it in the Case of the Jaylor; for, *when he drew out his Sword, and would have killed himself,* Paul *cried with a loud Voice, Do thyself no Harm.*[38] It is true, Men may sometimes meet with very strong Temptations to prevent the violent Torments they are threatened with, by taking away their own Lives in the easiest Way they can; and I believe it was Fear of the Magistrates of *Philippi* that influenced the Keeper of the Prison in the Case just now mentioned: But, when a Thing is manifestly

35. Acts 4:19.
36. Robert Sanderson (1587–1683), bishop of Lincoln, *Sermons* (1689). See Peter Lake, "Serving God and the Times: The Calvinist Conformity of Robert Sanderson."
37. Matthew 19:19.
38. Acts 16:28.

prohibited in the Divine Law, I think *we are not to fear them which kill the Body, and are not able to kill the Soul; but ought rather to fear him who is able to destroy both soul and body in Hell.*[39] An Instance of Self-murder which I have <12> heard you justify, is that of *T. Pomponius Atticus,* who starved himself to Death, to put an End to the violent Disease he was ceased with, as it is related by *Cornelius Nepos.*[40] But I am surprised you should mention this as a Case of Necessity, since you pretend to allow of Exceptions from the ordinary Rules only when the publick Good requires it. For one would think, if *Atticus* had acted for the publick Good, he would rather have endeavoured to preserve his Life; it seems to have been *Self-love,* and not *Benevolence,* that was his Principle; and I never thought that a Disciple of *Shaftsbury's* would have approven any Action arising from that Spring. I know you alledge, "That his Physicians thought there was no Probability of his Recovery, that he was dreadfully tormented; and besides, that he had no Prospect of doing any more Good to Mankind all the Time he could live." To which I answer, That no Man can certainly know *the Times and Seasons, which the Father hath put in his own Power.*[41] But, abstracting from this, and granting all that you alledge; yea, suppose one were assured that his Disease would against a certain Time issue in Death, by a Message from God, like that sent to *Hezekiah*; yet I doubt very much if even this would justify a Man either in actually putting an End to his Life, or in neglecting to use the Means necessary for preserving it. And accordingly we see *Hezekiah* did neither of these, tho' *he was sick unto Death*: On the contrary, he betook himself to Prayer, *and the Lord added unto his Days Fifteen Years.*[42] Nor was this the Practice of *Job,* who suffered as much Affliction, both in Body and Mind, as the Cunning and Malice of *Satan* could invent. His Wife indeed suggested

---

39. Matthew 10:28.

40. Cornelius Nepos, *A Selection Including the Lives of Cato and Atticus* (Oxford: Clarendon Press, 1989). See *A Vindication of Mr. Hutcheson,* p. 346 below, for a vehement denial that Hutcheson ever taught that suicide was justified.

41. Acts 1:7.

42. Kings 20:1–6 and Isaiah 38:1–6.

this Remedy to him, when she advised him to *curse God and die*:[43] But he rejected the Temptation with so much Disdain, that one may very easily see that he reckoned Self-murder absolutely unlawful, whatever Calamities might be involved in: It was no Wonder tho' he longed for an End of his insupportable Agonies; yet it was his Endeavour (and ought to be the Endeavour of every good Man, in Imitation of this noble Pattern) to *wait patiently all the Days of his appointed Time, till his Change come.*[44] I have heard another imaginary Case proposed, which I own is a little more consistent with your Scheme than the former namely, "If some important Secret were to be extorted from a Man by violent Tortures, the Discovery of which might tend exceedingly to the Detriment of Society, and <13> perhaps expose the Lives of some valuable Members of it, then you think it would be highly laudable in such a Man to put an End to his Life, and thus effectually to conceal that which otherwise, thro his own Weakness and the Violence of the Torments, he might be tempted to discover."[45] But, on the contrary, I think we ought rather to submit ourselves to any Injury from others, which is their Sin, than to lay violent Hands on ourselves, and so die in a Sin after which there is no Time nor Place for Repentance. If we look into, *the Cloud of Witnesses,* who are recorded in Scripture for our Imitation, we'll find that *thro' Faith they subdued Kingdoms, quenched the Violence of Fire, and escaped the Edge of the Sword; Others of them were tortured, not accepting Deliverance; And others had Trial of cruel Mockings and Scourgings, yea, of Bonds and Imprisonment: They were stoned, they were sawn asunder, and slain with the Sword; and in all these they obtained a good Report thro' Faith:*[46] But we never see Self-murder recommended or approven of as a Remedy in the greatest Distress. Altho' *David* was many Times in the utmost Danger of becoming a Prey to his Enemies, he never took *Saul's* Method to deliver himself from

---

43. Job 2:9–10.

44. Job 14:14.

45. Jean Barbeyrac (1674–1744) offered a similar opinion in a note to Pufendorf, *Of the Law of Nature and Nations*, book 4, chap. 1, sec. 7, pp. 314–15. In *A Vindication of Mr. Hutcheson,* p. 350, it is remarked that Hutcheson criticized the lax morals of Pufendorf and Barbeyrac on this and other matters.

46. Hebrews 11:33–39.

their Insults, but *trusted in God, and was not afraid what Man could do unto him:* And he records it to the Glory of Divine Grace, that in his greatest Extremities *the Lord was his Defence, and his God was the Rock of his Refuge.*[47] On these Considerations then, it would seem to be the Duty of one in the Circumstances you here suppose, to *cast his Burden upon the Lord, and he will sustain him; for he will never suffer the Righteous to be moved.*[48] I am surprised that you should make his Unbelief an Argument for his breaking a Divine Law; on the contrary, if he be conscious of his own Weakness, he ought the rather to cry earnestly to the Lord, that *his Grace may be sufficient for him,* and that he may *make his Strength perfect in Weakness;*[49] *what Time he is afraid, let him call upon God, he will be with him in Trouble, and will deliver him:*[50] And, if he be a sincere Christian, he may be assured that Providence will order Matters so as will tend most to the Glory of God and to his real Happiness; *For all Things work together for Good to them that love God.*[51] But I proceed now to <14>

PROPOSITION IV.

It is sometimes lawful to make a Lie.

I Have frequently thought it strange, when I heard this Principle vented, how it was possible for any Man to get over innumerable Texts of Scripture, wherein maintaining the Truth is pressed with the strongest Motives, and the least Violation of it prohibited on our highest Peril: *Thus saith the Lord of Hosts—Speak ye every Man the Truth to his Neighbour, execute the Judgment of Truth in your Gates, and love no false Oaths, for these are Things that I hate, saith the Lord.*[52] The Apostle bids us *put away Lying, and speak every Man the Truth with his Neighbour, for we are Members one of another.*[53] And again, *Lie not to another, seeing ye have put off the old Man with his Deeds,*[54] David declares, that it is *he that walketh uprightly, and speaketh the Truth in his Heart, that shall abide in*

---

47. 2 Samuel 22:2–3.
48. Psalms 55:22.
49. 2 Corinthians 12:9.
50. Psalms 18:2.
51. Romans 8:20.
52. Zechariah 8:16–17.
53. Ephesians 4:25.
54. Colossians 3:9.

the Tabernacle of the Lord, and dwell in his holy Hill.[55] In a Word, he who is *the faithful and true Witness* hath assured us, that *all Liars shall have their Part in the Lake that burneth with Fire and Brimstone*;[56] *for whatsoever maketh a Lie shall in no wise enter within the Gates*[57] of the New Jerusalem. If these awful Scriptures be duly considered, I think all the Arguments that can be adduced for justifying a Lie, whether from its Tendency to the publick Good, or the Necessity of it for Self-preservation, or on any other Account whatsoever, will be of very little Moment. However (that I may mention some Things which you alledge on this Head) I find your Dispensations from our Obligation to Veracity (as in the former Proposition) are for the most Part founded upon their Necessity for promoting the Good of Society; and, in order to illustrate this, I have heard Tullus Hostilius a *Roman* General highly commended for encouraging his Soldiers by telling them a Lie, and thus gaining a compleat Victory over the Enemy:[58] But there is one Thing I cannot miss to observe here, and that is, the vast Difference betwixt the Practice of your *Hero,* and that of the *Worthies* mentioned under the foregoing Proposition; for whereas these took *the Shield of Faith,* and thereby *waxed valiant in Fight, and turned to Flight the Armies of the aliens*;[59] the Weapon he overcame with, was the genuine Offspring of its Father the Devil: And therefore, however <15> you may commend the Conduct of this General, as the Fruit of a very ready Invention, and highly serviceable to his Country; yet I shall never approve of it, since it is neither consistent with the Word of God, nor with the Practice of his Saints in former Ages; for the Divine Law is the Touch-stone by which we are to examine every Word and Action, and to pronounce of them accordingly: *To the Law, and to the Testi-*

---

55. Psalms 15:1–2.
56. Revelation 21:8.
57. Revelation 21:27.
58. Livy, *Early History of Rome* 1:27. In *A Short Introduction to Moral Philosophy,* (1747), p. 244; (2007), p. 208, Hutcheson declared that "Tullus Hostilius is renowned to all ages for presence of mind in delivering a false account by which the Roman people were preserved." In *A System of Moral Philosophy*, book 2, chap. 17, art. 5, vol. 2, p. 126 Hutcheson denounced "some divines" who "have denied all these extraordinary rights of necessity."
59. Hebrews 11:34.

mony, if they speak not according to this Word, it is because there is no Light in them.[60] If we may dispense with a Divine Commandment whenever our Country, our Friend, or ourselves are reduced to any dangerous Extremity, and if our corrupt Reason is to be the sovereign Judge in these Cases, as you would make it, truly I know very little Use the Law serves for; our Reason, it seems, might have determined what is Sin, and what is Duty, well enough without it. *David* however has had another View of it, when he found it to be *a Light to his Feet, and a Lamp to his Path*;[61] when *it made him wiser than his Enemies, and gave him more Understanding than all his Teachers*;[62] he made it his *Meditation all the Day,* and yet he cries out in his fervent Devotion, *I have seen an End of all Perfection, but thy Commandment is exceeding broad.*[63] It is further alledged in Vindication of this Proposition, "That *Rahab* was saved for preserving the Spies by Means of a Lie; and thence you conclude, that it is lawful to make a Lie in order to preserve the Life of any valuable Member of Society, if no other Thing will do it."[64] To which I answer, That *Rahab* was by no Means saved because of her Lie, which was manifestly her Sin, and deserved eternal Punishment; it was her Faith that saved her, for the Apostle tells us plainly, that *by Faith the Harlot* Rahab *perished not with them that believed not, when she had received the Spies with Peace:*[65] And, when *Jericho* was destroyed, *Joshua* commanded the Spies to *go into her House and bring her forth*; not because of her Lie, but because *they had sworn that they would deal kindly with her.*[66] And, to add no more upon this Head, my Opinion is, that the Life of the best and most useful Man in the

60. Isaiah 8:20.
61. Psalms 119:105.
62. Psalms 119:99.
63. Psalms 119:96.
64. Grotius had used the story of Rahab to illustrate an exception to the divine command to the Jews that the nations who opposed them should be destroyed: *The Rights of War and Peace*, book 2, chap. 13, art. 4, p. 776. Barbeyrac thought it "no wonder if the Hebrews, to whom she [Rahab] had done so considerable a piece of Service, spared her"; Barbeyrac's note 2 in Pufendorf, *Of the Law of Nature and Nations*, book 4, chap. 2, art. 7, p. 340. Hutcheson did not address the case of Rahab in *A Short Introduction* or in *A System of Moral Philosophy*.
65. Hebrews 11:31.
66. Joshua 6:31.

World, is too dear bought at the Price of the least Sin, which could not be atoned for but by the Death of the eternal Son of God; therefore, in our greatest Extremities, let us *call upon the Lord most High, and make our Refuge in the Shadow of his Wings till these Calamities be overpast:*[67] David did so, and see with what a holy Gloriation he is allowed to triumph <16> over his Enemies; *Those* (says he) *that seek my Soul to destroy it, shall go into the lower Parts of the Earth, they shall fall by the Sword, they shall be a Portion for Foxes: But the King shall rejoice in God, every one that sweareth by him shall glory, but the Mouth of them that speak Lies shall be stopped.*[68]

Before I proceed to the next Proposition, there is another Subject that natively falls in under this, namely, the Obligation of Promises and Oaths. I am obliged to mention it, because your Opinion in this Matter is very unaccountable, *viz.* "That a Promise, tho' in itself lawful, if it be extorted by Fraud or by unjust Violence (such as these made to Robbers) is not in the least obligatory, even tho' it be confirmed with an Oath."[69] The contrary of this has always been maintained by our greatest Divines, and the venerable Assembly at *Westminster* have determined in these Cases, That *an Oath in any Thing not sinful, binds to Performance, altho' to a Man's own Hurt;*[70] and I think they had very good Reason for saying so, since it is given as a Character of the Righteous, that *he sweareth to his own Hurt and changeth not.* There is a great Debate among the Writers on this Subject,[71] whether the *Israelites* were obliged by the Oath that they made to the *Gibeonites,* since they were brought over to it by Fraud and Deceit: It is generally acknowledged that it was lawful for *Joshua* to make a League with them, had their Pretence been true; But the Question is, Whether, in Consequence of his Oath thus fraudulently extorted, he was bound to preserve them? And there are two Considerations which make it pretty evident to me that he was: One is, That the Reason which the Children of *Israel* gave for their not destroying them was, that *the Princes of the Congregation had sworn unto them by the Lord God of* Israel; *and*

---

67. Psalms 57:1–2.
68. Psalms 63:9–11.
69. See *A Short Introduction to Moral Philosophy,* (1747), p. 190; (2007), p. 164.
70. *Confession of Faith,* chap.24, art. 4.
71. See note 64 above.

when the People murmured against the Princes, the Princes said unto all the Congregation, We have sworn unto them by the Lord God of Israel, now therefore we may not touch them.[72] But then, what makes it still more evident is, that when there was a Famine three Years in the Days of *David,* and *David* enquired of the Lord; the Lord answered, *It is for* Saul *and for his bloody House, because he slew the* Gibeonites, *notwithstanding that* Saul *sought to slay them in his Zeal to the Children of* Israel *and* Judah[73] (which by the Way shews us, that it will never excuse a Man for sinning against God, that he did it out of Zeal for the Good of his Country). From these and such like Reasons I think, it is evident, that, if <17> a Promise or Oath may otherwise be lawfully performed, it will by no Means destroy its Obligation, that it was occasioned by the Fraud or unjust Violence of the Person who required it; for this is the Thing which the Lord hath commanded in the strictest Manner, that, *If a Man swear an Oath to bind his Soul with a Bond, he shall not break his Word, he shall do according to all that proceedeth out of his Mouth.*[74] I shall only observe one Thing further which you advance on this Head, *viz.* "That it is sometimes necessary to make a Promise without any Design to perform it; and in some very extraordinary Cases of Necessity, you say, it may be lawful even to give an Oath with direct Intention to break it"[75] To this I might oppose the Words of our Confession, wherein it is expressly asserted, *That no Man may bind himself by Oath to any Thing but what he is resolved to perform.*[76] And truly it seems so dreadfully impious for a Man deliberately to invoke the Divine Vengeance upon his own Head, that, if we had the least Sense of the Solemnity of the Act, I dare say it would fill us with Horror; it would be *swearing deceitfully* with a Witness, and a horrid Profanation of *the glorious and fearful Name of God,* which certainly would

72. Joshua 9:18–19.

73. 2 Samuel 21:1–2.

74. Numbers 30:2.

75. *A System of Moral Philosophy*, book 2, chap. 12, art. 1, vol. 2, p. 45: "'Tis a monstrous abuse too to employ oaths where they can give little or no security. Such are those required in declaring our assent to long systems of disputable and sometimes unnecessary opinions in matters of religion and promising to adhere to them." See also *A Short Introduction to Moral Philosophy*, (1747), p. 204; (2007), p. 176.

76. *Confession of Faith*, chap. 24, art. 4.

not go unpunished; *for the Lord will not hold him guiltless that taketh his Name in vain.*[77] When *Zechariah* saw the flying Roll, then the Lord said unto him, *This is the Curse that goeth forth over the Face of the whole Earth;—and every one that sweareth shall be cut off according to it: I will bring it forth, saith the Lord of Hosts, and it shall enter into the House of him that sweareth falsely by my Name, and it shall remain in the Midst of his House, and shall consume it with the Timber thereof and the Stones thereof.*[78] I shall only add, that the making of a lawful Promise or Oath and not performing it, especially if it be made with that Design, is manifestly contrary to the third Commandment, which requires *the holy and reverend Use of the Name of God;* and particularly when we swear, that we do it *in Truth, in Judgment, and in Righteousness:*[79] And whatever you may think of that, *Sir,* our Saviour declares, that *whosoever shall break one of these least Commandments,* AND SHALL TEACH MEN SO, *shall be called the least in the Kingdom of Heaven.*[80] < 18>

PROPOSITION V.

It is ridiculous to speak of the Sinfulness of Cards and Dice, or any such Diversion wherein Lottery is practiced.

The Solemnity with which the casting of Lots was wont to be practiced, according to Scripture-History, particularly in the Choice of the twelfth Apostle, seems plainly to prove that it is an Ordinance of God for determining Cases of Difficulty, for causing *Contentions to cease,* and for *parting between the Mighty:*[81] And therefore it ought not to be used but upon grave and important Occasions; and, since the whole *disposing of it is of the Lord,*[82] it should be performed with a holy Reverence, and a humble Submission to the Decision of his Providence. Now then, since in Cards and Dice, and other such Diversions, the Event of the Game cannot possibly be determined by any Art or Skill in the Player, it must be owing either to Chance, or to the Disposal of Providence: I suppose you won't

---

77. Exodus 20:7.
78. Zechariah 5:3–4.

79. Psalms 111:7–9.
80. Matthew 5–19.

81. Proverbs 18:18.
82. Proverbs 16:33.

alledge the former of these; and, if you allow the latter, it necessarily follows, that these Games contain in them all that is meant by the casting of a Lot, *viz.* an Appeal unto God for his Determination; and do you think, *Sir,* that the Nature of a Diversion is consistent with these pious Dispositions we were just now speaking of? Is it not a Profanation of an Ordinance of God, to turn it into a childish Game, wherein we dare not pray for the Divine Conduct and Direction, as we see the Apostles did in the Case above-mentioned? I know you pretend, "That the Event of a Lot depends upon certain mechanical Causes, tho' unknown to us, in the same Manner as the Direction of a Bullet to a particular Mark, when it is projected from a Machine, or any such Thing as that."[83] But, in my Opinion, there is a vast Difference: For, in Lottery, it is absolutely impossible to attain to the least Probability with respect to the Event, and the greatest Art is of no Manner of Service; whereas, in the other Case, every Body knows that a Man of Skill and Experience can not only have the highest Probability, but even a moral Certainty, that he will hit the Mark. And then, as for the Event's depending upon certain mechanical Causes, you must say the same with respect to the Lots mentioned in <19> Scripture; and with equal Reason you may infer that they were nothing but a Jest, tho' gone about with the greatest Solemnity; and, because the pronouncing of an Oath depends upon the Mechanism of the Body, you may conclude that there is no Evil in taking the Name of God in vain. If you say that an Oath is a great deal more solemn than a Lot, because the Name of God is expressly mentioned in it; I answer, That they are both appointed by God for *putting an End to all Strife*;[84] and, if a Regard unto him be expressly included in the one, it is as necessarily supposed in the other; for none of them ought to be done but in a reverend Manner, with a sincere View to the Glory of God. Thus I have laid before you what is to me a

83. Hutcheson was critical of lotteries, public or private; "they should be everywhere under the restraint of laws; lest that wealth, were it employed in manufactures or commerce would be adding new strength to the state, should be turned into this useless and dishonorable channel": *A Short Introduction to Moral Philosophy*, (1747), p. 220–21; (2007), p. 190.

84. Hebrews 6:16: "For men verily swear by the greater; and an oath for confirmation is to them an end of all strife."

sufficient Proof of the Sinfulness of these Diversions; and, however learned and good Men have been of a different Opinion, I doubt if any of them has gone your Length, to treat the opposite Side (even in a disputable Point) with Scorn and Ridicule: When the Question is stated about Sin and Duty, I think the Debate ought to be managed with Gravity and Concern.

PROPOSITON VI.

It is wrong to say that God acts for his own Glory, or that we ought to have that End always in View.

It is needless to tell you that this Proposition is contrary to our established Principles: If you please to look into our *Larger Catechism,* you will see it peremptorily affirmed, that *God did decree and create, and does constantly preserve and govern, all Things for his own Glory;* and that therefore *it is the chief and highest End of Man to glorify him.*[85] And these are not bare groundless Assertions, but are founded on express Texts of Scripture, which are so many plain Demonstrations of the Falsehood of this Proposition. *Solomon* tells us, that *God hath made all Things for himself, and even the Wicked for the Day of Evil;*[86] and, if that be true, I don't see how he can be said to do all for the Good of his Creatures. I know you give a particular Criticism upon the Translation of this Verse, as if the overturning of it would make all this Doctrine fall to the <20> Ground; but you are quite mistaken: For there is abundance of other Texts which establish it beyond all Dispute, and at the same Time show that this Translation does not involve so great Absurdities as you would alledge. The Words of the Apostle with respect to our Saviour are pretty much to the same Purpose; *By him,* says he, *were all Things created that are in Heaven and that are in Earth, visible and invisible, whether they be Thrones, or Dominions, or Principalities, or Powers; all Things were created by him and for him.*[87] And the same Apostle tells us very plainly in another Place, that the Manifestation of the Glory

85. See Larger Catechism, Q. 18.
86. Proverbs 16:4.
87. Colossians 1:16.

of God was the End of Election and Reprobation: *What,* says he, *if God willing to shew his Wrath, and to make his Power known, endured with much Long-suffering the Vessels of Wrath fitted to Destruction? and that he might make known the Riches of his Glory on the Vessels of Mercy which he had before prepared unto Glory.*[88] *For* (says he in another Place) *he hath predestinated us unto the Adoption of Children, by Jesus Christ to himself, to the Praise of the Glory of his Grace.*[89] And, speaking of the People of God, he says, *They are a chosen Generation . . . that they may shew forth the Praises of him who called them out of Darkness into his marvellous Light.*[90] And Isaiah calls them *a People whom God hath formed for himself, that they might shew forth his Praise.*[91] Besides these, I might mention a great many special Dispensations of the Providence of God, wherein he is expressly said to have acted for his own Glory: Thus God raised up *Pharaoh* for this very Purpose, *that he might shew his Power in him, and that his Name might be declared throughout all the Earth;*[92] and *he divided the* Red-sea, *that he might get him Honour upon* Pharaoh *and upon all his Host.*[93] Our Saviour likewise tells us, that *the Sickness of* Lazarus *was not unto Death, but for the Glory of God, that the Son of God might be glorified thereby.*[94] I shall only add one further Instance of *the Zeal God hath for his own Glory,* in his Conduct toward the Children of *Israel; For my Name's Sake,* says he, *will I defer mine Anger, and for my Praise will I refrain for thee, that I cut thee not off. . . . For mine own Sake, even for mine own Sake will I do it, and I will not give my Glory unto another.*[95] The only Argument I heard you advance in Defence of this Proposition is, "That it is reckoned a Vice in Men to act for their own Glory; and therefore it must be much more unworthy of God to propose such a mean End to himself."[96] And indeed, <21> if God were *altogether such an one as ourselves,* this Argument might be of some

88. Romans 9:22–23.
89. Ephesians 1:5–6.
90. 1 Peter 2:9.
91. Isaiah 43:62.
92. Romans 9:17.
93. Exodus 14:17.
94. John 11:4.
95. Isaiah 48:9–11.
96. Cf. *A Vindication of Mr. Hutcheson,* pp. 351–52 below.

Weight; but since *his Ways are not as our Ways, nor his Thoughts as our Thoughts,*[97] it is too presumptuous to make the least Comparison. *For Men to search their own Glory, is not Glory:*[98] But with God it is quite otherwise; for *his Name alone is excellent, and his Glory is above the Earth and Heaven:* [99] And therefore, as *he swears by himself because there is no greater,*[100] so it is his eminent Excellency to act for his own Glory, because he can have no higher nor nobler End in View. Now, from the same Reasons it will appear, that it is the chief End of Man to glorify God; for, since that is the highest End, it most becomes his rational Nature to aim at it: Besides, he is bound to do so in Point of Gratitude; *For in him we live and move and have our Being:* [101] And his Happiness is inseparably connected with it; for *thus saith the Lord God of* Israel, *Them that honour me, I will honour.*[102] Our blessed Saviour, when he came into the World, *sought not his own Glory, but the Glory of him that sent him;*[103] and therefore, in Imitation of this perfect Pattern, we must *give unto the Lord the Glory due unto his Name:*[104] For *he is the* Alpha *and* Omega, *the Beginning and the End; of whom, and through whom, and to whom are all Things.*[105] From this Proposition you natively infer, "That an Action may be good in the Sight of God, tho' it be not ultimately referred to his Glory."[106] To which I shall only oppose the Words of the Apostle, *Whether ye eat or drink, or whatsoever you do, do all to the Glory of God:*[107] Whence it is evident, that when we do any Action with an ultimate View either to our own Good, or the Good of others, overlooking the Glory of God, which ought to be our chief End, we rob him of what is his Due, we *worship and serve the Creature more than the Creator,*[108] and therefore cannot be approven of him; for

97. Isaiah 55:8.
98. Proverbs 25:27.
99. Psalms 55:8.
100. Hebrews 6:13.
101. Acts 17:28.
102. Samuel 2:30.
103. John 7:18.
104. Psalms 29:2.
105. Revelation 1:8 and 22:13.
106. See *Illustrations upon the Moral Sense*, sec. 6, (1728), pp. 301–33; (2002), pp. 187–204.
107. 1 Corinthians 10:31.
108. Romans 1:25.

he is a jealous God,[109] *and will by no Means give his Glory unto another.*[110] <22>

PROPOSITION VII.

There is a Superiority of Moral Good in the World.

If our Eyes were opened to see the original Corruption of our Natures, whereby we are utterly indisposed, disabled and made opposite to all Good, and wholly inclined to all Evil, we would readily agree with our Saviour, that *a corrupt Tree cannot bring forth good Fruit*:[111] But, since it is one of the fatal Effects of this universal Depravation, that *our Eyes are shut* and *our Understandings darkened*,[112] it is no Wonder that *every Way of a Man is right in his own Eyes.*[113] We are not however to regard this blind Testimony (which is itself an Evidence that the Judgment is corrupt) we must appeal to the Oracles of God, *who searcheth the Heart, and trieth the Reins*;[114] and there we will find, that all Mankind are by Nature *dead in Trespasses and Sins*;[115] that *the Heart of Man is deceitful above all Things, and desperately wicked,*[116] and that *every Imagination of his Thoughts is only Evil continually;* in a Word, that *there is none that doth Good, no not one.*[117] These, and a great many other Scriptures to the same Purpose, are to me a sufficient Evidence of the Falsehood of this Proposition: However, I shall under this Head take Notice of some other Tenets which you think necessary to be maintained, in order to account for your Superiority of Moral Goodness.

First of all then, you maintain, "That a wicked Man is capable of doing good Actions."[118] I cannot express myself in this Matter better than

109. Exodus 1:14.
110. Isaiah 42:8.
111. Matthew 7:8.
112. Ephesians 4:18.
113. Proverbs 211:2.
114. Jeremiah 17:10.
115. Ephesians 2:1.
116. Jeremiah 17:9.
117. Romans 3:10.
118. This assertion seems to contradict the spirit of Hutcheson's philosophy that good actions are recognized as evidence of a good character.

in the Words of our *Confession of Faith* (Chap. xviii Art. 7.) That *Works done by unregenerate Men, although for the Matter of them they may be Things which God commands; yet, because they proceed not from an Heart purified by Faith, nor are done in a right Manner according to the Word, nor to a right End, the Glory of God, they are therefore sinful, and cannot please God.*[119] *Goodness*, Sir, *is a Fruit of the Spirit*;[120] and *the natural Man receiveth not the Things of the Spirit of God*;[121] he is *all as an unclean Thing*,[122] and *who can bring a clean Thing out of an unclean? Not one.*[123] Even these that are regenerated, they still acknowledge, that *they are not sufficient of themselves to think any Thing as of themselves, but their Sufficiency is of God*,[124] *who worketh in them both to will and to do of his own Pleasure; they can do* <23> *all Things through Christ strengthening them*,[125] *and without him they can do nothing.*[126] You need not think it strange when you hear, that *these who are in the Flesh cannot please God*;[127] for *Solomon* assures us, that their religious Actions (which have the greatest Shew of Righteousness) are *an Abomination to the Lord*,[128] and that *the* very *Plowing of the Wicked is Sin*;[129] the Reason is, that the Heart is corrupted, and thereby every Thing that proceedeth out of it is defiled, and rendered abominable in the Sight of God: Which was very clearly represented under the Law by him that was unclean by a dead Body, who made every Thing that he touched unclean; and is plainly applied to this Purpose by the Prophet *Haggai*, in his Answer to the Priests, *So is this People, and so is this Nation before me, saith the Lord, and so is every Work of their Hands, and that which they offer there is unclean.*[130]

Another of the Principles upon which you build this Proposition is, "That the Number of good Men is superior to that of the Wicked,"[131] *i.e.* that the greatest Part of Mankind will be saved. But, as this is one of the *secret Things* that *belong unto the Lord*,[132] I doubt if it is lawful to pry too

---

119. *The Confession of Faith* (1732), p. 38.
120. Galatians 5:22–23.
121. 1 Corinthians 2:14.
122. Isaiah 64:6.
123. Job 14:4.
124. 2 Corinthians 3:5.
125. Philippians 4:13.
126. John 15:5.
127. Romans 8:8.
128. Proverbs 12:22.
129. Proverbs 2:4.
130. Haggai 2:14.
131. See *Vindication*, p. 352–54.
132. Deuteronomy 29:29.

curiously into it: If our Saviour had thought it one of these Things that belong to our Peace, he would not have shifted the Question when one said unto him, *Lord, are there few that be saved?*[133] We should therefore follow the Advice which he gave to his Followers on this Occasion, *Strive,* says he, *to enter in at the strait Gate; for many, I say unto you, will seek to enter in, and shall not be able:*[134] And, instead of searching into the hidden Counsels of God, which is equally foolish and sinful, we ought rather to *give all Diligence to make our Calling and Election sure; for many are called, but few are chosen.*[135] There is as much revealed, as is sufficient to convince us that it is no easy Matter to attain to Salvation: *The Righteous themselves are scarcely saved;*[136] *for wide is the Gate and broad is the Way that leadeth to Destruction, and many there be which go in thereat; but strait is the Gate and narrow is the Way which leadeth unto Life, and few there be that find it.*[137]

I shall here also take Notice of some particular Considerations, whereby you prove that a Plurality will be saved. One is, "That, since Infants are capable of no Sin, we must in Charity believe, that all that die before they come to the Years of Discretion will be saved."[138] But sure I am, there is no Ground for such an extensive Cha<24>rity given in Scripture; altho' Infants are not guilty of any actual Transgression, yet, as they are of the Posterity of *Adam,* they are guilty of his first Sin, and are therefore *by Nature the Children of Wrath, even as others:*[139] If Men came into the World perfectly innocent, you would have some Ground for what you alledge; but, if you make the Bible the Rule of your Faith, you must acknowledge that the Case is quite otherwise; for *what is Man that he should be clean, and he which is born of a Woman that he should be righteous?*[140] *We are shapen in Iniquity, and in Sin do our Mothers conceive us;*[141] and, by this original Guilt, all Mankind, as soon as they enter into the World, are bound over to the Wrath of God by the Curse of his Law, and are justly liable to all Misery in this World and in that which is to come: The Death of Infants, which is the Wages of their Sin, is a manifest Proof that they

133. Luke 13:23.
134. Luke 13:24.
135. 2 Peter 1:10.
136. 1 Peter 4:18.
137. Matthew 7:13–14.

138. See *Vindication,* below, pp. 352–54.
139. Ephesians 2:3.
140. Job 15:14.
141. Psalms 51:5.

are guilty; for *by one Man Sin entered into the World, and Death by Sin, and so Death passed upon all Men, for that all have sinned.*[142] Since then the Transgression of our first Parents is conveyed to all their Posterity; and since the Scripture gives us no Ground to believe that Infants are exeemed from the Guilt of this Sin, because they are free from actual Transgression, but on the contrary, in the Destruction of the old World, in the Overthrow of *Sodom* and *Gomorrah,* and in a great many other Instances, it includes the Children as well as the Fathers, the Young as well as the Old, and *sets them all forth for an Example as suffering the Vengeance of eternal Fire;*[143] I say, since this is the Case, I see no Reason why we should suppose that all Infants must be saved, far less that it would be an unrighteous Thing for God to execute the just Sentence of his broken Covenant upon them: We must by no means *limit the holy One of* Israel;[144] *he doth according to his Will in the Army of Heaven, and among the Inhabitants of the Earth; and he will have Mercy on whom he will have Mercy.*[145]

Again, in order to show that a Plurality will be saved, you maintain the Sufficiency of the Light of Nature to lead Men to Happiness. If Salvation were confined to the visible Christian Church, 'tis hardly possible your Hypothesis could stand, so that you are obliged to extend it likewise to the heathen Nations: And, for the former Establishment of this Doctrine, you pretend to prove it from several Passages of Scripture; particularly, I have heard a mighty Stress laid upon the Words of the Apostle, <25> that as to these that live *without the Law, their Uncircumcision should be counted for Circumcision.*[146] But, in my Opinion, this makes very little for your Purpose; for it depends entirely upon this Supposition, that *the Uncircumcision keeps the Righteousness of the Law*: And it is not a general observing of it that will do the Business, as you seem to understand it; by no Means: The Terms are, *Cursed is every one that continueth not in all Things which are written in the Book of the Law, to do them;*[147] *for he that offendeth*

---

142. Romans 5:12.
143. Jude 1:7.
144. 2 Kings 19:22; Psalms 71:22; Isaiah 1:4; etc.
145. Romans 9:18.
146. Romans 2:26.
147. Galatians 3:10.

in one Point, is guilty of all.[148] No doubt *the Man who doth these Things shall live by them*;[149] but the Question is, Whether any Man is able to attain, or even to come near to, that absolute Perfection that the Law requires? And indeed it is, in my Opinion, very easily answered; for the Scripture plainly proves *both* Jews *and* Gentiles *to be all under Sin*,[150] and declares at the same Time that as *these who have sinned in the Law shall be judged by the Law*, so *these who have sinned without the Law shall also perish without the Law.*[151] And we may observe further, that, seeing there is a twofold Debt of Satisfaction and Obedience owing to the Law, suppose we should henceforth live up to the highest Perfection required, we are utterly incapable of atoning for our former Offences. Another Scripture which I have heard very much insisted upon is the Words of *Peter,* when he came to *Cornelius; Of a Truth,* says he, *I perceive that God is no Respecter of Persons, but in every Nation be that feareth him and worketh Righteousness is accepted with him.*[152] But truly this proves no more than the former; all that is intended here is, that the Wall of Partition betwixt the *Jews* and *Gentiles* was broke down by the Coming of our Saviour: It would be absurd to infer from this, that Works of Righteousness could be the Ground of our Acceptance with God; for the contrary is many Times asserted in the strongest Terms; That *by Grace we are saved through Faith, and that not of ourselves, it is the Gift of God;*[153] It is *not by Works of Righteousness which we have done, but according to his Mercy that he saveth us.*[154] I shall only mention another of your Arguments for the Salvation of Heathens, which you take from the *Revelation,* where *a great Multitude, which no Man could number, of all Nations, and Kindreds, and People, and Tongues,* are represented *standing before the Throne of God.*[155] But it plainly appears that this has a Respect to the general Conversion of all Nations to the Christian Religion, which is to be before the End of the World: That these <26> were saved by the Merits of Christ, is abundantly evident from the Song that is put in their Mouths, wherein they ascribe their *Salvation to God who sitteth upon the Throne, and unto the Lamb;*[156] and

---

148. James 2:10.
149. Romans 10:5.
150. Romans 3:9.

151. Romans 2:12.
152. Acts 10:34.
153. Ephesians 2:8.

154. Titus 3:5–7.
155. Revelation 7:9.
156. Revelation 7:10.

from their *having wasten their Robes, and made them white in the Blood of the Lamb*:[157] And it likewise appears from other express Scriptures, that *there is no Salvation in any other; for there is none other Name under Heaven, given among Men, whereby me* [we] *must be saved.*[158] I remember you use to shift the Force of this Argument by telling us, "That Men may be saved by the Merits of Christ, tho' they never heard of him."[159] But we are expressly told, that *without Faith it is impossible to please God*;[160] *He that believeth shall be saved, but he that believeth not shall be damned*;[161] *And how shall Men believe in him of whom they have not heard? And how shall they hear without a Preacher? And how shall they preach except they be sent?*[162] If the Knowledge of Christ is so small an Affair, how came the Apostle to represent these who want it as *Aliens from the Commonwealth of* Israel, *and Strangers from the Covenant of Promise, having no Hope, and without God in the World?*[163] And, if *the Wisdom of this World*[164] has such a mighty Influence upon our Happiness, why did it please God to *destroy it, and by the Foolishness of Preaching to save them that believe?*[165] Allow me only to add the Opinion of the *Westminster Assembly* in this Matter, *That they who, having never heard the Gospel, know not Jesus Christ, and believe not in him, cannot be saved, be they never so diligent to frame their Lives according to the Light of Nature, and the Law of that Religion which they profess; neither is there Salvation in any other but in Christ alone, who is the Saviour only of his Body the Church.*[166]

Thus I have gone through a Chain of Principles you maintain, which are all connected with the above Proposition. I have only one Thing to observe further, and that is, That, granting a Plurality were to be saved, yet you would find it difficult, even on this Supposition, to prove a Superiority of Moral Goodness in the World, and that for two Reasons; one is, That severals of the People of God spend a great Part of their Lives wholly in the Service of Sin, before a saving Change is wrought upon them: And then, After they are born again, you are not to imagine that every

157. Revelation 7:14.
158. Acts 4:12.
159. See *Vindication*, p. 353.
160. Hebrews 11:6.
161. Mark 16:6.

162. Romans 10:14–15.
163. Ephesians 2:12.
164. 1 Corinthians 3:19.
165. 1 Corinthians 2:12.
166. *Confession of Faith*, 10:60.

Thing they do is morally Good; no, they themselves can testify the contrary to their woful Experience: *If they say that they have no Sin, they make God <27> a Liar, and his Word is not in them;*[167] for, as long as they are in the Body, *the Flesh lusteth against the Spirit, so that they cannot do the Things that they would;*[168] *there is a Law in their Members warring against the Law of their Minds, and bringing them into Captivity to Sin:*[169] And therefore, notwithstanding that they are *renewed in the Spirits of their Minds,*[170] still *Iniquities prevail against them;*[171] and *in many Things they offend all.*[172] I shall now proceed to some others of your Tenets, and shall say as little on them as possible; for I am afraid you will think I have been too tedious, both on this, and on some of the former Propositions.

PROPOSITION VIII.

It is not probable that the same Bodies that are laid in the Grave,
will be raised again at the Resurrection.

This is directly contrary to the Words of our Confession of Faith, that *all the Dead shall be raised up with the self-same Bodies that are laid in the Grave, and none other:*[173] And, however little regard you may pay unto it, I think you are bound to notice with more Reverence the Scriptures upon which this Opinion is founded; particularly, I would have you to consider the Words with which *Job* comforted himself upon the Thoughts of his Dissolution, wherein he expressly declares, that notwithstanding that his Body should rot in the Grave, yet he would behold his Redeemer at the latter Day with these very same Eyes with which he then saw; *I know,* says he, *that my Redeemer liveth, and that he shall stand at the latter Day upon the Earth; and tho' after my Skin Worms destroy this Body, yet in my Flesh shall I see God; whom I shall see for myself, and mine Eyes shall behold, and not another, tho' my Reins be consumed within me.*[174] If you turn over again to the History of our Saviour, you'll find him declaring to his Followers,

---

167. 1 John 1:10.
168. Galatians 5:17.
169. Romans 7:23.
170. Ephesians 4:23.

171. Psalms 65:3.
172. James 3:2.
173. *Confession of Faith*, chap. 34, art. 2.
174. Job 19:25–27.

that *the Hour is coming in which all that are in their Graves shall hear the Voice of the Son of Man, and shall come forth;*[175] and, if this does not signify that the Dust of the Bodies that are laid in the Grave shall be at the last Day again adapted to the Service of the same Souls to which they were formerly united, I know no other Meaning <28> it can have. It would be endless to go through all the Texts of Scripture that might be adduced on this Head: Wherever you read of the Resurrection from the Dead, you have an invincible Argument that the same Body will be raised; for the very Word *Resurrection,* or *Rising again,* manifestly presupposes that the Dust that shall be raised did formerly subsist in a human Body; else I see no Reason why *Adam* may not be as properly said to have risen from the Dead, when his Body was formed out of the Dust of the Earth, as the Dead may be said to rise, when departed Souls are furnished with new Bodies at the last Day. I remember to have heard one very subtle Argument against this Doctrine, "That it would be ridiculous to suppose that these Bodies, which are swoln or extenuated at their Death, shall be raised again in the same State at the last Day."[176] But pray, is it not an easy Matter with God, to raise such Bodies out of the Dust that is laid in the Grave as shall be abundantly subservient for all the Purposes of Happiness or Misery, for which they are designed in their future Existence? And, as for his Saints, it is a Promise left upon Record, that *he will change their vile Bodies, that they may be fashioned like unto his glorious Body, according to the Working whereby he is able even to subdue all Things unto himself.*[177] Paul obviates an Objection pretty much of the same Kind, in his Epistle to the *Corinthians; But some Man* (says he) *will say, How are the Dead raised up, and with what Bodies do they come?*[178] And, in Answer to that, he first compares Death and the Resurrection to the Sowing and Growing up of Seed, and then he adds, *So also is the Resurrection of the Dead; it is sown in Corruption, it is raised in Incorruption; it is sown in Dishonour, it is raised in Glory; it is sown in Weakness, it is raised in Power; it is sown a natural Body, it is raised a spiritual Body.*[179] In a Word, it no more follows from the

175. John 5:28.
176. See *Vindication*, below, pp. 353–54.
177. Philippians 3:21.
178. 1 Corinthians 15:35.
179. 1 Corinthians 15:42–44.

Resurrection of the same Body that Mens Bodies will have the same Qualities in Heaven which they had at their Death, than that the Diseases of which they die will continue with them through all Eternity. There is another Objection here too, that I am well enough aware of, "That by this Means we restrict the Providence of God to a ridiculous and useless Nicety; and that another Body may serve all the Purposes of the Soul in another State, as well as that which was laid in the Grave." But, is it any more unworthy of God to be employed about *the Dust of his Saints*;[180] or to *number the very Hairs of* <29> *their Heads,*[181] *so as nothing of them should be lost, but all raised up again at the last Day*;[182] I say, Is this more unworthy of the Majesty of God, than his extending his Providence to the most insignificant of the Brute-creation, so that *a Sparrow does not fall to the Ground without him?*[183] Yea, is it not highly reasonable, that these Members, which have been *Instruments of Righteousness unto God,* should likewise share in the Reward? And, for the same Reason, that the Bodies of the Wicked, which have been *Instruments of Unrighteousness unto Sin,*[184] should also partake in the Punishment? But altho' no such Reason could be assigned, why the same Body should be raised more than any other Dust; yet, since a God of infinite Wisdom has told us that this is his Purpose with respect to all Mankind, *What are we that we should reply against him? For he giveth not Account of any of his Matters.*[185]

PROPOSITION IX.

The Divine Right to Dominion over the Creatures is not properly founded upon Creation, nor upon their absolute Dependence, nor upon Benefits received.

The Creature is under so strong Obligations to serve his Creator, *in whom he lives and moves and has his Being,*[186] that the very Light of Nature seems to teach us, that Creation founds a Right to Dominion over the Creatures. But besides, if we take into our Consideration a great many Texts of

180. Job 14:13.	183. Matthew 10:29.	185. Job 33:13.
181. Matthew 10:29.	184. Romans 6:13.	186. Acts 17:28.
182. John 5:40.		

Scripture, wherein our Obligation to serve our Maker is inferred from his having created us, I think there will scarcely be any Room left for Dispute in this Matter. How frequently does the holy Psalmist stir up himself, and exhort others, to worship and praise the Lord, for this very Reason, that he is their Maker, and they the Workmanship of his Hands? *O come,* says he, *let us worship and bow down, let us kneel before the Lord our Maker; for he is our God, and we are the People of his Pasture, and the Sheep of his Hand.*[187] And, in another Place, *Serve the Lord with Gladness, come before his Presence with Singing: Know ye that the Lord he is God; it is he that hath made us, and not we ourselves; we are his People, and the Sheep* <30> *of his Pasture.*[188] When he is adoring the Majesty of God, he says, *All Nations whom thou hast made shall come and worship before thee, and shall glorify thy Name;*[189] and he exhorts *Israel* to *rejoice in him that made him; and the Children of* Zion *to be joyful in their King.*[190] In a Word, he summons the Angels, and even the inanimate Creation, to praise the Lord, because he created them; *Praise ye him all his Angels, praise ye him all his Hosts; Praise ye him Sun and Moon; praise him all ye Stars of Light; Praise him ye Heavens of Heavens, and ye Waters that be above the Heavens: Let them praise the Name of the Lord, for he commanded and they were created.*[191] *Isaiah* frequently chides the Children of *Israel* for contending with the Lord, from this Consideration, that they were in his Hand as the Clay in the Hand of the Potter; *Surely,* says he, *your turning of Things upside down shall be esteemed as the Potter's Clay; for shall the Work say of him that made it, He made me not? or shall the Thing framed say of him that framed it, He had no Understanding?*[192] He pronounces a Wo against these who strive with their Maker; *shall the Clay say to him that fashioneth it, What makest thou? or thy Work, He hath no Hands? Thus saith the Lord, the holy One of* Israel, *and his Maker, I have made the Earth, and created Man upon it; I, even my Hands have stretched out the Heavens, and all their Host have I commanded; I have raised him up in Righteousness, and I will direct all his Ways.*[193] *Jeremiah* was sent down to the Potter's House, and *the Word of the Lord came*

---

187. Psalms 95:6–7.
188. Psalms 100:2–3.
189. Psalms 86:9.

190. Psalms 149:2.
191. Psalms 148:2–5.

192. Isaiah 29:16.
193. Isaiah 45:9, 11–13.

to him, saying *O House of* Israel, *cannot I do with you as this Potter? saith the Lord: Behold; as the Clay is in the Potter's Hand, so are ye in mine Hand, O House of* Israel![194] And the Apostle uses the same Comparison, in his Epistle to the *Romans; Shall the Thing formed say to him that formed it, Why hast thou made me thus? Hath not the Potter Power over the Clay?*[195] I shall only add this one Text, which I think it is impossible for you to get over; you'll find it in the *Revelation,* where the Four and twenty Elders are represented casting their Crowns before the Throne, and saying, *Thou art worthy, O Lord, to receive Glory and Honour and Power; for thou hast created all Things, and for thy pleasure they are and were created.*[196] I know you alledge (according to your Principles) "That nothing can found One's Right to govern, unless it show that his Governing will tend to the publick Good; whence you argue, That it does not follow from God's having created <31> us, that it will tend to our Good that he should likewise govern us; and therefore Creation does not found a Right to Dominion."[197] In Answer to which, I desire you to look back to what was formerly advanced concerning the Definition of Righteousness; to which I shall only add, That it must be acknowledged on all Hands, that Men as well as other Creatures are obliged to aim at that End to which their Natures are adapted, and for which they were created: And since none can be supposed more capable of directing their Actions, so as they may obtain this End, than their Creator himself; I think it is evident that Creation founds a Right to Dominion, even upon your own Scheme. There is another very singular Argument you make use of, in refuting the established Opinion; "You suppose with the *Manicheans,* that an evil Being created us, and a good Being rescued us out of his Hands; in which Case (you say) we would be obliged to obey our Deliverer, not our Creator; and therefore Creation will in no Case found a Right to Dominion."[198] This deserves no better Answer than

---

194. Jeremiah 18:5–6.

195. Romans 9:20–21.

196. Revelation 4:11.

197. This is a summary of Hutcheson, *Inquiry concerning . . . Moral Good,* (1725), p. 273; (2008), p. 196. Here and in the following it is impossible to tell the extent to which Heugh quoted and paraphrased what he had heard in Hutcheson's lectures.

198. Ibid.

merely to tell you, *Ex quolibet supposito sequitur quolibet;* Suppose an Absurdity, and you'll prove an Absurdity. However, I cannot forbear asking you, what Idea you can have of a malicious Demon creating an Order of Beings whose Dispositions naturally lead them to pursue Happiness of one Kind or another, and who, according to you, enjoy a Superiority of natural Good? Or, how can you conceive that such Beings as these depend absolutely upon the Will of their Creator both for their Being and Preservation, and yet that another rescues them out of his Hands, and puts them beyond the Reach of his powerful and tyrannical Influence? In a Word, How can you imagine the Existence of two uncreated Beings, one infinitely perfect, and the other limited to a certain Degree of Perfection? These Things appear to me to be manifest Contradictions. But further, I might shew you something in this Hypothesis manifestly inconsistent with your own Proposition: You deny that Benefits bestowed can found any Right to the Benefactor, and yet you maintain the Deliverer's Right to govern these whom he rescued from Slavery; which certainly is the greatest Benefit that he could possibly bestow upon them. I know you maintain, "That it is his Goodness and Wisdom, not his rescuing them, that shews his Right to govern";[199] and thus you must found it on abstract Good-will, without any Re<32>gard to beneficent Actions. But, in my Opinion, these cannot justly be separated: For, when Benefits are conferred, we are obliged to conclude there is Good-will; and, when they are not if an Opportunity is offered, we can have no sure Evidence of a Person's Benevolence. And I presume you are so much of my Opinion in this Matter, that altho' one had abundance of Wisdom, and pretended the greatest Good-will to you, if he never evidenced these by any wise or good Action, I doubt very much if you would heartily subject yourself to him as having a sufficient Right to govern you. All that you have to alledge against the Validity of Benefits for founding a Right of Dominion, is, "That, if every Benefit that a Man receives immediately enslaved him to his Benefactor, Beneficence would be the most dangerous Thing in the World."[200] But pray, *Sir,* is it not too

199. *Inquiry,* (1725), pp. 270–72; (2008), pp. 195–96.
200. Heugh is applying a crude version of Hutcheson's argument about human governance to the idea of divine governance (ibid.).

great Presumption to compare any insignificant Benefactor on Earth with him *who giveth unto all Life and Breath and all Things?* [201] I am sure, if any little trifling Benefit among Men lays an Obligation upon the Receiver to make considerable Returns of Gratitude, and if the Obligation heightens in Proportion to the Greatness of the Benefit (which no Man can deny) it will be abundantly evident that the Benefits we have received from our Maker lay us under the highest Obligation to subject ourselves to his Dominion, since he is the *Father of all our Mercies, from whom we receive every good and perfect Gift,* [202] and seeing our greatest Happiness lies in submitting ourselves to his Government. I shall only observe further with respect to your *Manichean* Supposition, that I am afraid it is scarcely consistent with that holy Reverence with which we should speak of God and of his mighty Works: These are Subjects which must not be abused according to our profane Fancies and vain Imaginations, and it would be a miserable Case if Truth could not be supported without the Help of such gross and blasphemous Suppositions. After what is said, I need not add any Thing with respect to absolute Dependence (which is a Part of the above Proposition) that being necessarily included in Creation: I shall therefore proceed to <33>

PROPOSITION X.

Sin is not aggravated from the Consideration of the infinite Majesty of God against whom it is committed.

This Proposition is designed for overturning what you comtemptibly call the Theological Way of speaking, That there is an infinite Evil in Sin, because it is committed against a God of infinite Purity and Perfection. A great many Considerations might be advanced in Defence of this Opinion, but I shall only mention two: One is, That it affords us a considerable Argument for justifying the Eternity of Hell-torments; for, unless we supposed a Kind of infinite Evil in Sin, it might possibly be thought that

201. Acts 17:25.
202. 2 Corinthians 1:3 and James 1:17.

Divine Justice would be satisfied with a determined finite Time of Suffering: And, since this Notion of Sin tends to illustrate and confirm the Scripture-Doctrine of Punishments, that is no small Argument to me that the Opinion is just; however I shall not say it is *argumentum ad hominem:* For you seem to propose it as a disputable Question, Whether the Punishments of Hell will be eternal or not? And therefore you are no doubt very easy whether that Doctrine be established, or fall to the Ground. But there is another Argument showing that there is an infinite Evil in Sin, which you cannot so easily get over: Daily Experience teaches us, that an Injury done to a Prince is reckoned vastly more heinous than the same Injury done to a Subject; and, in general, that the Highness and Dignity of the Person is one of these Circumstances which tend exceedingly to aggravate any Crime that is committed against him. Does it not then necessarily follow, that such Sins as are committed against One who is infinitely exalted above the highest Angels, may be said in the most proper Sense to be infinitely sinful? And seeing every Sin, being a Breach of the Law of God, is committed against God, therefore every Sin is infinitely Evil. It is impossible for you to deny the Consequence; and therefore, to support your beloved Thesis, you bring in another Opinion, which is fully as unreasonable, and most evidently contrary to the whole Strain of the Bible: "No Man, say you, can properly be said to sin against God; for he is a Madman who thinks that by any Action of his he can hurt <34> God, or in the least disturb him in his Government:[203] You think Men may want a due Degree of good Affections toward God, but you don't believe that it is possible for any Man to hate a Being *who is good to all, and whose Mercies are over all his Works.*"[204] And really, *Sir,* for my Part, I heartily wish that these Opinions were true; but, since ever I read my Bible, I could not allow myself to believe that they are so: Either you are mistaken, or *David* must have been deceiving himself, and mocking God, when he prayed, *That the Lord might heal his Soul, because he had sinned against him*;[205] and when he mentions it as the greatest Aggravation of his

203. See *Vindication,* below, pp. 355–56.
204. Psalms 145:9.
205. Psalms 41:4.

Sin, that it was done against God, and in his Sight; *Against thee, thee only have I sinned, and done this Evil in thy Sight.*[206] If it is impossible for any Man to hate God, it was a very foolish Question, *Wherefore do the Wicked contemn God?*[207] And, for as wise a Man as *Solomon* was under the Conduct of the unerring Spirit of Truth, you condemn both him and his Leader, when he tells us, that *he that is perverse in his Ways despiseth the Lord;*[208] yea, our Lord himself must get the Lie, when he declares to his Disciples that the Wicked *hated both him and his Father.*[209] You must score out the *Haters of God*[210] out of the Apostle's Catalogue; and you may tell your Scholars, according to your usual Manner, that his Words are unjustly translated, or that there is a Debate about the Reading in the Original, and the most judicious Cricks think the common Reading wrong: Either of these will be good enough for *deceiving the Hearts of the Simple.*[211] And when the same Apostle declares that *the carnal Mind is Enmity against God,*[212] you need never mention that: Perhaps your Hearers won't notice it; or, if you are afraid they do, you may fortify them against its Influence by your Catholick Observation, "That Divines wrest the Scriptures according to their own whimsical Fancies, and that they dwell continually upon the black Side of human Nature, never noticing these beautiful, virtuous, and lovely Dispositions with which every Man is naturally endued."[213] But, however these Things may take with some, your pretending to lay the Blame upon others will never in Reality take it off yourself: And therefore I would have you to remember, that, *if any Man shall take away from the Things that are written, God shall take away his Part out of the Book of Life;*[214] and whoever *wrests the Scriptures,* it is *to his own Destruction.*[215] Sinning against God, and particu<35>larly hating him, are so frequently and expressly mentioned in Scripture, that, if I had not heard you with my Ears, I could not believe that any Man would presume to call the Reality of it in question: And, since your Opinion itself is so absurd and unscriptural, 'tis no Wonder tho' the Reason upon which you build it be very weak and insufficient. All that you pretend to

206. Psalms 51:4.
207. Psalms 10:13.
208. Proverbs 14:2.
209. John 15:23.

210. Romans 1:30.
211. Romans 16:18.
212. Romans 8:7.

213. See *Vindication*, p. 352.
214. Revelation 22:19.
215. 2 Peter 3:16.

say for it is, "That human Nature is not capable of hating a Being of infinite Goodness." And indeed, if God were entirely made up of Goodness, if he were destitute of every other Perfection (with Reverence be it spoken) I should be very ready to agree with you: And, even when we consider him as he has revealed himself in his Word, I believe no Body will say that any Man hates God on the direct View of his Goodness; but then, when a guilty and polluted Sinner considers him as possessed of spotless Purity and inflexible Justice, I think it is not only possible for him to hate such a Being, but it is really impossible that it should be otherwise: These who *delight in Sin, and rejoice in doing Evil,*[216] must necessarily hate him *who is of purer Eyes than to behold Evil, and cannot look on Iniquity;*[217] *who is not a God that hath Pleasure in Wickedness.*[218] They hate the Goodness of God, in as far as they know they can never enjoy the Fruits of it: And, in a Word, they hate his very Being, and wish *in their Hearts that there were no God.*[219]

PROPOSITION XI.

The Government of the Church belongs to the Civil Magistrate.

I heartily approve of your zealous Appearances against the spiritual Tyranny of the Church of *Rome,* and her abominable Usurpations in Matters of Civil Concern, which belong allenarly[220] to the Civil Magistrate: But, as *the Officers of the Church are not to handle or conclude any Thing but that which is Ecclesiastical, and are not to intermeddle with Civil Affairs which concern the Commonwealth;* so neither are *Magistrates to judge or determine in any Thing but that which is Civil, and must by no Means assume to themselves the Power of the Keys of the Kingdom of Heaven.* (*Confes<36>sion of Faith*, Ch. 23, Sect. 3 and Chap. 31, Sect. 5) And therefore I am apt to think, that your political Zeal carries you too great a Length, when you look upon the Authority which the Church of *Scotland* justly assumes, in inflicting their Censures, as so much of the Remains of that Popish Policy

216. Proverbs 2:8.
217. Habakkuk 1:13.
218. Psalms 5:4.

219. Psalms 14:1.
220. only, solely.

which once prevailed among us: And I am firmly persuaded that you deprive the Ministers of Christ of *the Liberties wherewith* their Master *hath made them free*,[221] when you take the Power of Church-government (which *is not of this World*)[222] entirely out of their Hands, and give it to the Civil Magistrate, as an Affair wholly subservient to the temporal Good of the State, which is to be managed by him any Way that will best conduce to that End.[223] 'Tis true indeed, the publick Good of any State is best promoted when sincere Piety is cultivated among all its Members; but at the same Time I am very far from thinking that the Happiness of this World is the principal End and Design of the Christian Religion, or that it is lawful for the Governor of a State to do any Thing that may obstruct the Success of the Gospel, and ruin the Souls of his Subjects, with a pretended View to advance the publick Trade and Prosperity of the Nation. Neither do I agree with you, "That it would tend to the real Good of any People, if Errors in Practice were made the sole Matter of Punishment, and all Heresies in Principle were passed without any Censure"; *i.e.* if there were an absolute unlimited Toleration of all Manner of Doctrines that are not directly inconsistent with the publick Tranquility. Our *Confession of Faith* (Ch. 23, Sect. 3) mentions it as a Duty of the Civil Magistrate, *To take Order that the Truth of God be kept pure and entire, that all Blasphemies and Heresies be suppressed, and that all Corruptions and Abuses in Worship and Discipline be prevented or reformed:* And that this is really incumbent upon them, is abundantly evident from the Apostle's charge to *Titus, A Man that is an Heretick, after the first and second Admonition, reject;*[224] and from his solemn Command to the *Thessalonians, Now,* says he, *we command you, Brethren, in the Name of our Lord Jesus Christ, that ye withdraw yourselves from every Brother that walketh disorderly, and not after the Tradition which he received of us.*[225] All the Advantage you propose by tolerating Hereticks is the Increase of the Number of Subjects, which, I own, might tend considerably both to the enriching and strengthening of the Nation; but then I'm <37> afraid these temporal Advantages would be more than

---

221. Galatians 5:1.
222. E.g., John 15:19, 22:24.
223. See *Vindication*, below, pp. 354–55.

224. Titus 3:10.
225. 2 Thessalonians 3:16.

over-balanced by the Hazard that Men would run in another Respect. When People have erred concerning the Faith themselves, it seldom happens but they overthrow the Faith of some others also, especially if they are in any publick Station of preaching the Word, or *instructing Youth:* And 'tis dangerous, particularly for weak Christians, to be too much in the Company of Hereticks, who generally reckon it both their Duty and Honour to make as many Proselytes to their own Way of thinking as they can; for (as *Solomon* observes in another Case) *can a Man take Fire in his Bosom, and his Clothes not be burnt?*[226] I have heard another Direction which you lay down to the Civil Magistrate for the more happy Constitution of your political Church-Government; and that is, "That, in the Admission of Teachers to instruct the People, nothing should be made an Article of Faith, save only some general Propositions about the moral Perfections of God, and the mutual Duties of Christians; and that, in all other Points, every Man should be allowed to enjoy and to teach his own Opinion": That is to say, That subscribing a Confession of Faith should be banished out of the Church, as a Thing pernicious to human Society. "That Confessions of Faith do harm to a State, you think, is very easily proven; because (say you) a great many pretty Men, who might be very useful in the Church, are by this Means kept out of it, being unwilling to bind up their Freedom of Thought in Matters which in their Opinion are not essential to real Goodness; whereas others, tho' they come under the Engagements to qualify them for a Post, will endeavour to evade the Obligation, by putting remote, strained Meanings on the Words of the *Confession,* by mental Reservations, or even by Perjury itself, rather than confine themselves to so narrow Bounds as are therein prescribed." In Answer to the first to these Arguments, I shall only inform you, that it was always my Opinion, that it would tend much more to the Advancement of Religion, if the People were under the Direction of pious and godly Pastors, who would teach them the Doctrines of the Gospel *in the Demonstration of the Spirit and of Power;*[227] than if the Church were filled with Men of greater Learning, but of unsound and corrupt Principles, who

226. Proverbs 6:27.
227. 1 Corinthians 2:4.

would *teach for Doctrines the Commandments of Men,*[228] and be ready *to corrupt the Minds of their Hearers* <38> *from the Simplicity that is in Christ.*[229] 'Tis dangerous for a People, when *these that lead them cause them to err;*[230] for the ordinary Consequence is, that *they who are led of them are destroyed:*[231] And a Pretence to singular Learning is so far from being a sufficient Reason for admitting a Heretick into the Church, that it is really in my Opinion the strongest Argument against it; for his excelling others in natural or acquired Parts only renders him the fitter for gaining a greater Following, and for spreading his poisonous Doctrines with more Success than otherwise he could do. As for your second Argument, I am very ready to agree with you, that a great many even in our own Church are guilty of very heinous Sins in subscribing our Confession of Faith; for when Men entertain in their Minds, *and much more when they teach others,* such Opinions as are manifestly contrary to the *Confession of Faith* to which they have solemnly adhered, I think in that Case we may very safely conclude that these Men have either perjured themselves, or at least have been guilty of some very base Equivocations in their pretended Adherence; and, this being your own Practice, you are no doubt the more ready to judge that others dissemble the same Way.[232] But pray, at whose Door do these Sins ly? Whether is the Society that requires this Profession to be blamed, or are not these rather guilty who deal falsely and treacherously both with God and them? I am sure, no Body is forced to think as they do, contrary to the Light of his Conscience; only, if he professes himself to be of another Opinion, they won't admit him as a Member of their Church: And must not every one acknowledge that this is highly reasonable? If it is wrong for a Church to take her Members under so strict Engagements, because some Men will have Impudence enough to break them, you may with as much Reason alledge that 'tis wrong to administer an Oath in any Case, because some abandon'd Wretches will despise it; and that no Laws should be enacted, because wicked Men will transgress

228. Mark 7:7; Mathew 15:9.
229. 2 Corinthians 11:30.
230. Isaiah 9:16.
231. Ibid.
232. See *Vindication*, p. 357, on "the good-natured charge of perjury."

them. 'Tis the Danger that the Church is exposed to from erroneous and corrupt Teachers, that makes it necessary to be established as a standing Rule, That all that enter upon any of these publick Offices should make a solemn and publick Profession of their Faith; for *the Law is not made for the righteous Man, but for the Lawless and Disobedient . . . for Liars, for perjured Persons, and against every Thing that is contrary to sound Doctrine*:[233] And if a great many transgress <39> notwithstanding of the Law, if unsound Doctrines are taught notwithstanding of the Bar that is put in their Way by an established Confession of Faith, surely the Danger would be still greater, if this Bar were removed, and every Man left at full Liberty to think and teach whatever he pleased. I might insist at greater Length upon this Proposition, and endeavour to refute the unscriptural Principles advanced by *Tindal* in his *Rights of the Christian Church,* which you are at so much Pains to recommend.[234] I might likewise show you, that Christ is the sole Head of the Church, and that the Church, as his Body, is subject to him alone as its supreme Lord and Law-giver; and at the same Time show, that these Doctrines are not pernicious to Society, nor inconsistent with the Sovereignty of a State, as you alledge: And then I might prove from Scripture, that the Lord Jesus, as King and Head of his Church, hath therein appointed a Government in the Hand of Church-Officers distinct from the Civil Magistrate; and that to these Officers the Keys of the Kingdom of Heaven are committed, by virtue whereof they have Power to inflict such Censures as are necessary for the reclaiming and gaining of offending Brethren, and for deterring others from the like Offences. But since these Things are plainly contained in our Confession of Faith,[235] and undeniably proven by several Texts of Scripture therein adduced, I shall not add any more upon them, but conclude my Remarks on this Proposition with one general Observation upon the whole, That a Church is never in greater Danger of being ruined, than when her Youth are early instructed in such Principles as have a direct Tendency to overturn both her Doctrine and Discipline.

233. Timothy 1:9–10.

234. It is interesting to learn that Hutcheson recommended Matthew Tindal's *Rights of the Christian Church Asserted* (1706) to his students.

235. *Confession of Faith*, chap. 23, art. 3, pp. 124–25.

I shall now conclude this Letter, after noticing two or three Texts of Scripture, which you explain in a very odd Manner, because they are manifestly inconsistent with some of the above Propositions. The first is in the *Proverbs* (Chap. xvi. V. 4.) and it is contrary to Proposition sixth, where you may see it mentioned: The Words, as they stand in our Translation, are these; *The Lord hath made all Things for himself, and even the Wicked for the Day of Evil*: But, according to you, they ought to be translated thus; *The Lord hath adapted one Thing to another, and Misery to Wickedness.* Whereon you found this Translation, indeed I know not: For the original Word is very fairly translated in our Text according to its plain and obvious Meaning, <40> and agreeable to the most learned and judicious Interpreters; and it has a very emphatical Signification, which, if it were fully expressed in our Language, might justly be rendered, *for his own very self.* And then this Passage is explained, and our Translation of it supported by several other Texts of Scripture wherein the same Things are asserted. *God's making all Things for himself* was proven by a great many Scriptures under the above-mentioned Proposition; and it is no less evident that *the Wicked are made for the Day of Evil,* if we consider the Words of the Psalmist, that, *when the Wicked spring as Grass, and when all the Workers of Iniquity flourish, it is that they shall be destroyed for ever.*[236] Another of your ingenious Criticisms falls upon a Passage in the Epistle to the *Romans* (Chap. iii. V. 8.) *And not rather, as we be slanderously reported, and as some affirm that we say, Let us do Evil, that Good may come; whose Damnation is just.* This Verse contains an invincible Argument against the third and fourth Propositions; and therefore you give it as your Opinion, "That the Rule here mentioned is of no Manner of Use in Morals, and that it is only to be understood as an Answer to those who reproached the Apostles, as if they preached up the Lawfulness of Sin, that the Grace of God might abound the more."[237] But, for my Part, if this Precept is of no Manner of Use in Morals, if it is lawful *to do Evil that Good may come*; I cannot understand why the Apostle should in so solemn a Manner pronounce *their Damnation to be just,* who charged him

236. Psalms 92:7.
237. This is not a quotation from Hutcheson's writings.

and his Fellow-Apostles with the Breach of this Rule. There is another Text in the same Epistle (Chap. xii. V.11.) which you endeavoured to pervert, where the Apostle exhorts the *Romans* to be *fervent in Spirit, serving the Lord:*[238] This you correct, by changing the *Greek* Word Κύριον into Καιρο; as if the Apostle had exhorted us to be *fervent in Spirit, serving the Time:* And the Reason of your doing so is very manifest; for *tempori purendum esse* was a Maxim of the ancient Heathen Philosophy:[239] And therefore you take this Opportunity of degrading the Scriptures of Truth, and exalting the Wisdom of this World; slyly insinuating to your Hearers, that the inspired Apostles derived their Knowledge from the Heathen Philosophers, and not from the Spirit of God. The last Scripture I shall mention is in the first Epistle to the *Corinthians* (Chap. x. V. 31.) where the Apostle resolves some Doubts of the primitive Christians with respect to their <41> eating and drinking with them that believed not, and then adds this general Proposition, *Whether therefore ye eat or drink, or whatever ye do, do all to the Glory of God.* Now, every Body sees that this Text does manifestly overturn the sixth Proposition; and therefore you endeavour to evade the Force of it, by telling your Scholars, "That it is only to be understood of eating and drinking Things offered to Idols, and that it does not at all prove it to be our Duty in every Thing we do to glorify God." And indeed, if the Apostle had bid the *Corinthians* glorify God *only* in their Eating and Drinking, you might have had some Shew of Reason for saying so; but when he tells them plainly (as if he had foreseen your Objection) that, *whatever they did,* they were to do it for the Glory of God, I see not the least Ground for a Pretence to restrict it; and I am sure no Body that reads the Verse with the least Attention will join with you. I shall only mention other two parallel Texts wherein the same Thing is asserted, and which therefore do confirm the plain and obvious Meaning of this Verse; the first is contained in *Paul's* Advice to the *Colossians* (Chap. iii. V. 17.) *Whatsoever ye do in Word or Deed, do all in the Name of the Lord Jesus, giving Thanks to God and the Father by him:* The other is in the first Epistle of *Peter* (Chap. iv. V. 11.) where he commands *them that speak, to speak as the Oracles of God; and them that minister, to do it as of*

---

238. Romans 12:11.
239. Presumably Heugh intended "parendum": One must keep up with the times.

the Ability which God giveth; that God in all Things may be glorified through Jesus Christ.

Thus, *Sir,* I have laid before you a Specimen of the Doctrines you teach: And I assure you the Eyes of a great many are already upon you, and their Hearts are grieved at the Success of your Labours; but you may depend upon it, if you continue *to resist the Truth, your Folly shall* in due Time *be manifest unto all Men*:[240] For *the Eyes of the Lord are upon the Truth*;[241] and, altho' none should plead for it, he will not suffer it to fall to the Ground, but will *arise and plead his own Cause,*[242] to *the swift Destruction of all these false Teachers who have brought in damnable Heresies, and have changed the Truth of God into a Lie.*[243] In the mean Time, I heartily pity the Youth that are under your Charge; they have much Need of *the Spirit of Truth to guide them into all Truth*:[244] And I earnestly wish that the Lord may preserve them from these dreadful and dangerous Errors, and enable them to *hold fast the Form of sound Words,*[245] lest you should *spoil them through Philosophy and vain Deceit.*[246] As for your<42>self, I pray the Lord may forgive you wherein you have already dishonoured his Name, grieved the Spirit of Truth, and born down the Interest of Religion, by venting these Principles; that he may in his Mercy prevent you, by *inlightning your Darkness,*[247] and *convincing you of the Error of your Way, opening the Eyes of your Understanding, and shining into your Heart, to give you the Light of the Knowledge of his Glory in the Face of Jesus.*[248] And, notwithstanding the grand Sentiments which you now entertain of corrupt Nature, I am sure, if you get a Sight of the infinite Glory and Perfection of God, and of the natural Corruption and Wickedness of Man, by the powerful Illumination of the Holy Ghost, *You'll abhor* human Nature, and *your own Nature* in particular, *and repent* of your former Tenets *in Dust and Ashes*:[249] Which is the earnest Desire of

Your real Well-wisher,

EUZELUS PHILALETHES.

240. 2 Timothy 3:9.
241. Jeremiah 5:3.
242. Psalms 74:22.
243. 2 Peter 2:1.

244. John 16:1.
245. 2 Timothy 1:13.
246. Colossians 2:8.

247. Psalms 18:28.
248. 2 Corinthians 4:6.
249. Job 42:6.

*A Vindication of Mr. Hutcheson
from the Calumnious Aspersions
of a Late Pamphlet, 1738*

A
VINDICATION

OF

Mr. *HUTCHESON*

FROM

The Calumnious Aspersions
OF A LATE
PAMPHLET.

By Several of his SCHOLARS.[1]

EXOD. Chap. xx. V. 16. *Thou shalt not bear false witness against thy neighbour.*
MATTH. Chap. vii. V. 15, 16. *Beware of false Prophets, who come to you in sheeps cloathing; But inwardly they are ravening wolves. Ye shall know them by their fruits.*

Artificer of Fraud! and was the first,
That practis'd Falsehood, under saintly Shew,
Deep Malice to conceal, couch'd with Revenge,
Yet not enough had practis'd to Deceive.—Milton.[2]

— *Fragili quærens illidere dentem*
Offendet solido —HOR.[3]

Printed in the Year, M.DCC.XXXVIII.

---

1. Concerning the authorship of this pamphlet, see the Introduction, p. xxv.
2. John Milton, "Paradise Lost," book 4, lines 121–24, in *Paradise Lost and Selected Poetry and Prose*, p. 83.
3. Horace, "Satires," II.i.77–78, in *Satires, Epistles and Ars Poetica*: "trying to strike her tooth against something soft will dash upon what is solid."

THE
PREFACE.

Whereas about the Beginning of this Session of the College, a Paper was printed and published by One who pretends to be a Student, or to have been one lately in this University, without signing his true Name, charging Professor Hutcheson *with teaching many dangerous Errors, by which some weak People are prejudiced against him and the University. We who have also been his Scholars for several Years, thought ourselves obliged in Charity to any good People, who may be imposed upon by the Author's Pretences of Zeal for Religion, to represent to the World what Mr.* Hutcheson *really taught on these Heads, by which the Falsehood, Ignorance, and unchristian Malice of that Author will appear to all honest Men; and they will at the same Time know what to think of the Honesty, Knowledge, Learning and Christianity of his Abettors, let them be in what Stations they please. As we hear that some in better Stations knew of his Design, perused his Paper in Manuscript, encouraged the Design privately, sent the <4> printed Paper to their Correspondents at a Distance, with their Recommendation; nay, could not conceal, from good Women they visited, their Hopes, before it was printed, of the Hurt would soon be done to Mr.* Hutcheson's *Character.*

We cannot allow ourselves to imagine, that any Member of the Faculty could be capable of such Malice and Stupidity; or be so grossly ignorant of the Scriptures, as to relish such a Paper. But good People, to whom this Paper has been recommended, will from what follows, know how to judge of its Author and his Abettors.

In the first Place, every good Christian would have followed the plain Rule of, First speaking privately to a Brother who offended him; *Matth.* xviii. 15, 16. *This was never done, but the Charge blazed abroad at once, at that Time when it could most have hurt Mr.* Hutcheson, *if he could have been hurt by such an Adversary.*

Again, all who know any Thing of the University, know there are proper Superiors, to whom regular Application should have been made, upon the Misdemeanour of any Member: Particularly, the Dean of Faculty, as to Matters of Faith. No such regular Step was taken. The Design was to give a Stab in the dark, and to vent Malice and Calumny with Impunity, and this Design premeditated a long Time. But this will better appear by the whole

Strain of the Paper; which we shall take notice of, by setting what Mr. Hutcheson *really taught over against each Proposition of our Author's, with a few Notes on them; by which any One may judge both of his Malice, Disingenuity, and ignorant Abuse of the holy Scriptures to serve his base Purposes.*

We disregard the general Cant in the Preface. Let the World judge whether it was the Spirit of Truth, Charity and Love; *or* the Father of Lies and Hypocrisy *(our Author's charitable Words) who inspired him. All Sides can charge their Adversaries in Scripture Language, if they are profane enough to apply these Writings to their malicious Purposes, with any Crimes, Heresy, Deism and all.* The Devil can employ Fools in doing Mischief;[4] *this sometimes needs neither Learning nor Ability, tho' it may require considerable Abilities to do any important Good. We leave it to all who have heard Mr.* Hutcheson's *Lectures, to judge whether he is any confederate with Deists, or any Way serves their Cause. We know very well that ignorant malicious Zealots have <5> done as much Hurt to the Christian Religion, as any Enemies secret or open, by dressing it up in such a Manner, as every Man of Understanding must despise it. This is to be seen in Popery, and others still retain many of the most odious Parts of Popery: A blind Bigotry, an implicit Faith without impartial Inquiry, and Rage against all who differ from them, with a Spirit of Persecution. But it is below Christians to render Railing for Railing, tho' it be vented in Scripture Language with great Professions of Piety. With what Sincerity or Piety our Author could hope God would bless such Endeavours so directly contrary to the Gospel, and the Method prescribed by it, upon any Offence taken, let himself account. <6>*

---

4. Proverbs 10:23.

The Author'*s Propositions, with Remarks on them.*[5]

PROPOSITION I.

"We could have the Knowledge of Moral Good and Evil, altho' we knew nothing of the Being of God."

REMARK.

He speaks here indefinitely, as if Mr. HUTCHESON had taught, That we could have Notions of all Sorts of Moral Good without any Knowledge of God: And then calls it blasphemous, to say, God acts from Love of himself; tho' presently we will find, in his Paper, That He did all Things for himself, and his own Glory.

Mr. *HUTCHESON*'s Propositions.

PROPOSITION I.

We may approve or condemn some Sorts of Virtues and Vices, even tho' we had not known GOD, or had any Persuasion, that, by his Laws, he required the one, and prohibited the other: We should, for Instance, approve humane, friendly, grateful Actions toward our Fellows, and condemn the contrary; the very *Epicureans* did so, who believed no Providence or Laws of God.

Again, we have a Notion of Moral Goodness, prior, in the Order of Knowledge, to any Notion of the Will or Law of God; altho' the Moral Perfections of God are prior, in Nature, to all our Faculties.[6]

---

5. In the original printing of this item, in 1738, The Author's Propositions, with 'remarks' were printed verso on pages 6, 8, 10, 12, 14, 16, and the top of page 18, while "Mr. Hutcheson's Propositions" were printed recto on the facing pages 7, 9, 11, 13, 15, 17, and the top of page 19. This format suggests that "Mr. Hutcheson's Propositions" were composed separately and then juxtaposed to focus both responses on the succession of the arguments of Hutcheson's former pupil and critic.

6. See *A Synopsis of Metaphysics*, in *Logic, Metaphysics and the Natural Sociability of Mankind*, part 2, chap. 4, sec. 2, pp. 174–78, where the goodness of God is inferred from human perceptions of goodness, benevolence, and happiness and from the benevolent design of the world. See also *A Short Introduction to Moral Philosophy*, (1747), p. 72; (2007), p. 76.

The Author'*s Propositions, with Remarks on them.*

PROP. II

"Tendency to promote the Happiness of others is the Standard of Moral Goodness."

REMARKS.

To prove this to be Mr. HUTCHESON's Tenet, you cite two Passages from his Books, nothing to the Purpose; and some Passages from the Confession and the Scriptures, not opposite to this Tenet, even as you express it: Only asserting, That the Law of God is *the Rule, or chief Rule of our Actions;* or, *That Sin is a Transgression of his Law;* which Mr. HUTCHESON never denied.

Next follow fine Reasons, to shew, That the Moral Goodness of God is different from Benignity; otherways, his Moral Goodness commenced only at the Creation, and he was void of it from Eternity, even unto a Period at an infinite Distance: I suppose you mean, from the Commencement of Eternity, for otherways the Creation was not at any Distance from Eternity, or any Part of it, since it is supposed to have no Parts. Now, Is not a firm, constant Purpose in the Divine Mind, from all Eternity, to create a World, an equal Evidence of eternal Goodness, as the present Existence is a Proof of present Goodness? <8>

His Notion of Moral Goodness is *Possession of Blessedness and Perfection.* Is *Blessedness* Happiness of any Kind, or is it only Happiness of a moral Kind. Then Moral Goodness is defined by Moral Happiness, (no clearer than the Thing defined) and *Perfection:* Is this any natural Perfection, such as *Eternity, Omnipresence, Simplicity?* the Possession of these imports no Moral Goodness. 'Tis then the Possession of moral Perfection or moral Goodness; *i.e.* the Definition of moral Goodness is moral Perfection. Again the same is defined by the same, and nothing clearer. The *contemplating his Nature with Delight* argues no Moral Goodness, unless the Qualities contemplated be previously known to be good, and this Goodness is explain'd by loving Goodness.

Mr. *HUTCHESON*'s Propositions.

PROP. II.

Benevolent Affections toward others are our primary Notion of Moral Goodness, or the primary Object of our Approbation. But, as there are different Sorts of benevolent Affections, so there are different Degrees of Moral Goodness: We count God morally Good, on this Account, that we justly conclude, he has essential Dispositions to communicate Happiness and Perfection to his Creatures with most perfect Wisdom, and raised above all mean Views, opposite to it: That we must have another Notion of moral Goodness, prior to any Relation to Law, or Will, or even to essential Rectitude, or Conformity to Divine Perfection: Otherways, when we say, *God's Laws are good,* we make no valuable Encomium on them; and only say, God's Laws are conformable to his Laws, or, his Will is conformable to his Will. He would not then command Actions, because they are good; or, prohibit them, because they are evil. So, when we say *God is morally good,* or, *excellent,* we would only mean, he is conformable to himself; which would be no Praise, unless he were previously known to be good.[7] <9>

Mr. Hutcheson ever maintains, That the Observation of the Divine Laws tends to the greatest Good of Mankind; tho' 'tis disingenuously alledged, that he speaks only of Tendency to external Good. He even speaks of it as an impossible Supposition, contradictory in Terms, That any Sin or Violation of God's Law can tend to the absolute Good of Mankind; tho' he teaches, with all Moralists ancient and modern, That many of the ordinary Precepts admit of exceptions, in Cases of singular Necessity.

The Author's Representations of this Doctrine shew, either gross Disingenuity, or Ignorance. None ever taught, That Necessity made Sin, or the breaking of God's Laws lawful.

---

7. *Inquiry concerning the Original of Our Ideas of Virtue or Moral Good,* (1725), pp. 253–54; (2008), pp. 181–82: "to call the Laws of the supreme Deity good, or holy, or just, if all Goodness, Holiness, and Justice be constituted by Laws, or the Will of a Superior anyway reveal'd, must be an insignificant Tautology, amounting to no more than this, "That God wills what he wills.""

The Author'*s Propositions, with Remarks on them.*

PROP. III

"Selfmurder is in some Cases lawful."

REMARKS.

The Impertinence of the Scripture Proofs here is amazing; as if Mr. HUTCHESON had taught that Men might kill themselves when they pleased, under any Evil, even while they had further Prospects of doing good in Life, and express Commands of God to endure these Afflictions, with Promises of his Support, and the Assistance of his Spirit. Whereas Mr. HUTCHESON ever taught that in these Cases all Suicide was unlawful.[8] When he mentioned the Excuses, alledged by some for the Heathens, as They had no other Guide but the Light of Nature, and were left to judge by the Probabilities they had, without any special Promises of Support, or revealed Commands to endure these Afflictions; he only did, as in other controverted Cases, candidly represent what is said on both Sides. But we assert, He never approved of any, even, the most celebrated Instances of Suicide among them, which Christians have since looked on as the most excusable: For Example, he condemned those of *Lucretia, Cato,* and *Brutus.* He shewed, that *Atticus* would have acted a far more virtuous and glorious Part, by continuing in Life, and giving an Example to all about him of Fortitude, Patience, and Resignation to the Divine Will; and, as he did not, was so far deficient in Virtue.

As for the imaginary Case mentioned by this Author, in which, he says, Mr. HUTCHESON thinks Suicide highly <10> laudable; he has grossly confounded and misrepresented it with his usual Calumny and Absurdity. Mr. HUTCHESON is so far from the Opinion he is here charged with, That he represented the Want of Resolution to stand all Tortures for so noble a Cause, as a Weakness of Mind, and a Want of a sufficient Force of

---

8. See *A Short Introduction to Moral Philosophy*, (1747), p. 246; (2007), p. 210; and *A System of Moral Philosophy*, book 2, chap. 2, art. 16, vol. 2, pp. 105–6: "Human society has a right by force to prevent attempts of *suicide* from any unreasonable dejection, or melancholy, or chagrin; and these general rights of all, each one as he has opportunity, by what assistance he can obtain, may justly execute."

Virtue. He always spoke of those, who had rather chosen to undergo the severest Torments in such a Case, as Heroes worthy of the highest Admiration, and Applause.

Never did any Man of Gravity say *Selfmurder* was lawful in any Case. But our Author knew this was an odious Word, always importing Guilt. He taught it lawful to kill Men in a just War. Our Author might as justly have charged him with teaching the Lawfulness of *Murther*. But he knew the Word *Selfmurther* was fit to raise a *Popular Odium and Clamour*.

Mr. *HUTCHESON*'s Propositions.

PROP. III.

As Mr. HUTCHESON's Doctrine on this Point is sufficiently plain, from what we have said in the Animadversions on this Proposition in the Author; we have only to observe here, that Mr. HUTCHESON's grand Aim, in his Explications of the *5th* Chapter of *Puffendorf,* where this Question occurs, was to inspire into his Scholars a noble Contempt of Danger, and a generous Readiness to expose our Lives, were it to the most certain Death, whenever the Cause of our Country, or the Good of Mankind requir'd it.[9]

He told us, at great length, the plausible Arguments of a great Number of Writers, in Defence of the Doctrine and Practice of many Ancients: And the Arguments on the other Side, in the most plausible Cases. But we never heard him decide, as our Author alledges. <11>

---

9. Samuel Pufendorf, *On the Duty of Man and Citizen*, book 1, chap. 5, (1991), pp. 46–55; Samuel Pufendorf, *The Whole Duty of Man, According to the Law of Nature*, book 1, chap. 5, (2003), pp. 69–94; *A Short Introduction to Moral Philosophy*, (1747), pp. 79–86; (2007), pp. 81–86; and ibid., (1747), p. 142; (2007), p. 129: every man has "a right over [his own] life, so far that each one, in any honourable services to society or his friends, may expose himself not only to dangers, but to certain death, when such public good is in view as overballances the value of his life. This our conscience or moral sense, and love of virtue will strongly recommend in many cases."

The Author'*s Propositions, with Remarks on them.*

PROP. IV

"'Tis sometimes lawful to make a Lie."

REMARKS.

Mr. Hutcheson never spoke such Words, or any equivalent to them. *Lying* is a Word always importing a Crime. He might as justly have charged him with teaching Murder and Theft. The Scriptures are as wisely cited, as if One heaped together all the Texts against Murder and Theft, and all the solemn Commands to the *Hebrews* in *Deuteronomy,* to observe the Laws of God; and thence concluded that all our Divines, Moralists and Cricks, were guilty of gross Heresy and Deism, for saying, "That a Man perishing by Hunger, when he could not, by any Intreaty or Offers of Service, get Food to preserve Life by Consent of One who had superfluous Stores, might justly take secretly, or by Force, what might preserve Life": and "that in an overloaded Boat, 'tis lawful to cast Lots who should be thrown over": and "that it was lawful in *David* to take the shew Bread".

Our Author is such a deep Moralist and Casuist that he ventures like a Hero to encounter the whole World in denying that the *Fraud* or *unjust Violence of the Party is a just Exception against a contract, especially if confirmed by Oath.* "He maintains the Validity and Obligation of the Contract obtained <12> "thro' Fraud by the *Gibeonites,* because confirmed by Oath", tho' the Matter of it was contrary to an express Command of God, to cut off that People. Oaths are, it seems, easy Engines of eluding God's Laws, when we please; easier than Mr. HUTCHESON's Cases of great Necessity. He proves this first by the Judgment of the Princes of *Israel,* the very Judgment in Question, whether just or not; and then by a Proof which no Man of common Sense could use; the Punishment inflicted on *Saul's* Sons, for their Father's Breach of this Covenant: whence he proves it obligatory. Did not our deep Author know, that all Writers say, it became obligatory by the subsequent Ratification, after the Fraud was known to the *Israelites,* and not in Virtue of what was obtained by Fraud? The Difficulty however is not at all removed, as he might see, if he looked into any good Writer on this Case. He has Learning enough to assert strongly against his Adversary, which is enough for a Man of Zeal.

Mr. *HUTCHESON*'s Propositions.

PROP. IV.

Mr. Hutcheson ever taught, That the Law of Veracity was as sacred a Precept of the Law of Nature, as, *Thou shalt not kill: Thou shalt not steal.* Tho' he has also told us, Almost all Writers on Morals plead, that all these Laws are understood to admit Exceptions, in Cases of great Extremity; but still without deciding this Debate.

Nothing can be a more malicious Calumny, than the Aspersion on Mr. HUTCHESON in this Place. Whoever understands any Thing of the Business of a Professor of Moral Philosophy, must know, he is obliged, in all controverted Points, to represent what is said on both Sides, in a fair and just Light. The Author could not but know this; and was guilty of base Disingenuity, to represent, as a Man's own Opinion, what he delivered in that Manner. We assert, He never taught, as his own Sentiments, any of the Arguments he mentioned on this Head, for submitting Veracity to the Public Good in Cases of urgent Necessity: But, on the Contrary, confuted, at great length, the loose Tenets of *Barbyrac*, as well as *Puffendorf,* in Opposition to what he is here charged with.[10] He dwelt long, and warmly on the high Importance of inculcating, in the strongest Manner, into the Minds of Youth, an universal regard to *Veracity* and *Sincerity,* in all Cases. He constantly taught That the Heart has the same ultimate Feeling of the native Beauty and Loveliness of Veracity and Sincerity, as of any of the other Virtues.

Mr. Hutcheson teaches, with all Moralists and Civilians, That the Fraud or unjust Force of one Party in a Contract, makes void the

---

10. Cicero, *De Officiis,* I.X.32; Pufendorf, *On the Duty of Man and Citizen,* book 1, chap. 10, pp. 77–79; *The Whole Duty of Man,* pp. 119–23; *Of the Law of Nature and Nations,* book 4, chap. 1, esp. pp. 314–15, the note of Barbeyrac; Hutcheson, *Short Introduction to Moral Philosophy,* (1747), pp. 195–208; (2007), pp. 169–79; and *System of Moral Philosophy,* book 2, chaps. 10 and 11, pp. 28–53.

Obligation of the other, even tho' it had been confirmed by an Oath given during the Error occasioned by the Fraud, or during the Terror occasioned by <13> the unjust Force: But limited this to such avowed unjust Force as is used by Pyrates and Robbers, so as not to extend to the Force used in Publick Solemn Wars, upon specious Allegations of Right. He told, what seemed to him the Opinion not only of *Cicero,* but of *Puffendorf* and *Barbeyrac,* That, as Pyrates, Robbers, and manifest Tyrants had renounced a Social Life, and all the Laws of Nature, we were free from all Bonds toward them in the Use of Speech;[11] and might use Forms of Swearing, without Intention of performing. This last Article he directly opposed, every Time he mentioned it; and used this very Expression, *That to die, rather than use the Name of God with Intention to violate the Oath, would be as much Martyrdom, as dying rather than renounce Christianity.* The Author's Charge here is directly false Calumny; and yet, on this Occasion too, he can cite the Holy Scriptures.

The Author's *Propositions, with Remarks on them.*

PROP. V

"'Tis ridiculous to speak of the Sinfulness of Cards and Dice, or any such Diversion in which Lottery is practiced."

REMARK.

He proves this to be false, because we find Lots solemnly used in Scripture on a grand Occasion. So was Bread and Wine, and he should thence infer it to be unlawful to use them on any other Occasion.

---

11. *Short Introduction to Moral Philosophy,* (1747), p. 190; (2007), pp. 164–65; *System of Moral Philosophy,* book 2, chap. 9, art. 11, sec. 5, pp. 20–22. Adam Smith, who attended Hutcheson's lectures on moral philosophy in 1738–39, described Hutcheson's position on this matter in the same terms in *The Theory of Moral Sentiments,* p. 331. Smith thought that promises made under duress would not oblige only if the matter was treated as a point of jurisprudence; as a matter of moral casuistry, he thought that such promises must oblige, at least in some degree.

Mr. *HUTCHESON*'s Propositions.

PROP. V.

Mr. Hutcheson said Words to this Effect often, particularly in his warm Exhortations to his Scholars to abstain from any Diversions which might too much waste their Time by their being agreeable: And when he was shewing the Sin of hazarding our Fortunes, without an important Cause, or of being covetous to obtain the Wealth of others by Gaming. Let the World judge of the Wisdom of the Charge here brought.[12]

The Author's *Propositions, with Remarks on them.*

PROP. VI

"'Tis wrong to say, God always acts for his own Glory, or that we ought to have that End always in view."

REMARKS.

He hath subjoined here Heaps of Texts, without any Explication of their Meaning; Whether God's sole and ultimate End in all his Actions, is promoting his *essential* Glory, or his *declarative*? or, Whether we should, in each Action, aim at promoting the Essential, or the Declarative? <14> Whether promoting the Declarative means any Thing else, than making the Perfections of God known to Men? which must flow from Gratitude and Love to God, and Goodwill to them, and natively tend to their Increase in Virtue and Perfection.

---

12. *Short Introduction to Moral Philosophy*, (1747), pp. 220–21; (2007), p. 190; *System of Moral Philosophy*, book 2, chap. 14, art. 9, p. 76: "'Tis most inhumane, as well as foolish, to expose the fortune which should support a family, our friends, or the poor, or even assist our country, to such unnecessary hazard."

Mr. *HUTCHESON*'s Propositions.

PROP. VI.

Mr. Hutcheson never taught these Words. But at great Length shewed the Ambiguity of the Expression, and explain'd in what Sense God might be said to act for his own Glory, and in what Sense Men should act for it.[13]

He never arrogated to himself some Criticisms the Author refers to. If he had had as much Inclination to reading, as he had to vent his good Nature in Print, he might have found these Criticisms in known approved Authors. This was a fine Topick however for a popular Clamour. <15>

The Author's *Propositions, with Remarks on them.*

PROP. VII

"There is a Superiority of Moral Good in the World."

REMARKS.

The following Reasoning of the Author leads the Reader to conceive, that Mr. HUTCHESON said there was a Superiority of Moral Good among the Adult of Mankind in this Earth.

A wicked Man is capable of doing good Actions. This is said here indefinitely, without any of the usual Distinctions of *Material* and *Formal, Natural* and *Spiritual.* And then Heaps of Citations from the Confession and Scriptures about spiritual Good, and about the Actions of profligate Persons.

The Number of the Saved is greater than that of the Damned, because all who die in Infancy are saved: And then by an Heap of Scriptures, some of them very impertinently used, he insinuates as if Mr. HUTCHESON denied original Sin.

The Light of Nature sufficient to Salvation. This confuted too by many Texts of Scripture, proving that no Man can observe the whole Law fully,

---

13. *A System of Moral Philosophy*, book 1, chap. 9, art. 16, p. 207: "*God* cannot be conceived as ultimately studious of glory from creatures infinitely below himself. . . . *God* displays his perfections to make his creatures happy in the knowledge and love of them; and not to derive new happiness to himself from their praises, or admiration."

and that all Salvation must be thro' Christ: None of those Points did ever Mr. HUTCHESON deny.

Mr. *HUTCHESON*'s Propositions.

PROP. VII

Mr. Hutcheson taught that in the whole of a good God's Works, or the Universe in all its Duration, there must be a great Superiority of Good:[14] He never confined this Assertion to the Adult of Mankind.

He maintained, as every Moralist in teaching the Law of Nature must, that many actions of Heathens were morally good.

In answering *Bayle*'s Manichean Objections against the Goodness of God, from the vast Superiority of the Number of Damned to that of the Saved, he denied that any could prove the Fact to be so, and that from a probable Judgment that all the Children of the Heathens are not damned. This is called prying into the Counsels of God, but to damn them all, is modest Humility, and no Prying at all, it seems.

He never said there was any Salvation to any of fallen Mankind, except by the Merits of Christ, but often said, he saw no proof, that none could reap the Benefits of his Merits, but those who actually knew him; Nor do we see it yet, either from the Scriptures cited by this Author, or the Confession.

The Author's *Propositions, with Remarks on them.*

PROP. VIII

"It is not probable that the same Bodies that are laid in the Grave, shall be raised again at the Resurrection."

---

14. In *A Synopsis of Metaphysics,* part 3, chap. 4, sec. 2, Hutcheson listed among the "Arguments which show that God is good," "the preponderance of happiness in the world" and added: "All these things have that much greater weight because we see that there are far, far more good and happy things in life than there are sad and gloomy things" (*Logic, Metaphysics and the Natural Sociability of Mankind,* pp. 174–75).

Then are subjoined such Reasoning and Texts, as if Mr. Hutcheson had denied that any of that Matter laid in the Grave, should be raised again: And this with great Ostentations of Wisdom and Piety. <16>

Mr. *HUTCHESON*'s Propositions.

PROP. VIII.

Mr. Hutcheson teaches, That the same Body shall rise again; but, to *Sameness of Body*, he does not make it necessary, that all the same Particles should be raised, without any Addition or Deduction; otherways our Bodies would not be the same from Morning to Night. One must have been very keen to find Heresy, who looked for it here. The Author says as much himself on this Head.[15] <17>

The Author's *Propositions, with Remarks on them.*

PROP. IX

"The Divine Right of Dominion over the Creatures is not properly founded upon Creation, nor upon absolute Dependence, nor upon Benefits received."

REMARKS.

Here follow Heaps of Scriptures, as if Mr. Hutcheson had said, that from Creation, or Benefits conferr'd, we were under no Obligations of Duty or Gratitude, or had no Motives to Obedience; which is a base Misrepresentation.

---

15. Whether or not "the same body shall rise again" was not a question that Hutcheson addressed in his natural theology. His concern was to defend the proposition that we "have a probable expectation that the soul will survive the dissolution of the body"; for "we cannot infer from the death of the body that a thing which is completely different from it will also perish": *A Synopsis of Metaphysics,* part 2, chap. 4, sec. 3, in *Logic, Metaphysics and the Natural Sociability of Mankind,* pp. 147–49.

And then because he argued upon the bare Supposition of two opposite Principles, there follows a silly Confutation of the Supposition, as if Mr. HUTCHESON had believed it fact, or thought it a possible or probable Scheme.

Mr. *HUTCHESON*'s Propositions.

PROP. IX.

Mr. Hutcheson taught, That, from the Moral Perfections of God, we could deduce his Right of Governing his Creatures, in the most proper Manner: Tho', at the same Time, he ever subjoined, that Creation and Benefits were strong Motives to Gratitude and Love; and, that this Question was only a speculative Nicety, since all that ever was alledged, as a Foundation of Dominion, by any one, was found in the only True God.[16] This Tenet is taught by many zealous Calvinists, in their Systems, It must therefore be a higher, or a very different Sort of Zeal, which could find Heresy in it.

The Author's *Propositions, with Remarks on them.*

PROP. X

"Sin is not aggravated by the infinite Majesty of God against whom it is committed." And "'tis a disputable Point, whether the Punishments of the Wicked are eternal. No Man can be said properly to sin against God." And the Author heartily wishes these Opinions were true, if his Bible would let him, and then such Heaps of Texts and Reasonings as on former Articles. <18>

---

16. Hutcheson had argued in *An Inquiry concerning . . . Moral Good* that creation cannot be the ground of our obligation to God, since "supposing our *Creator Malicious,* and a *good Being* condescending to rescue us, or govern us better, . . . his *Right* to govern would be perfectly good" (1725, p. 273; 2008, pp. 196–97). He added that "this is rather matter of curious Speculation than Use; since both Titles of *Benevolence* and *Property* concur in the *one only true* Deity, as far as we can know."

Mr. *HUTCHESON*'s Propositions.

PROP. X.

The Charge against Mr. HUTCHESON is here directly false and calumni-ous, in these three Points and some more, in this Article. He argued di-rectly, That Crimes, or Sins, are aggravated by the Dignity of the Object against whom they are committed: He taught this in Print. He expressly taught too, That however the Platonists, and *Origen* and some others, to vindicate the Goodness of God, seemed to look for a universal Restora-tion of all; yet the express Words of Scripture would allow no Christian to make that Defence. He offered several Reasons in Defence of Eternal Punishments.

He ever said, That Men could sin against God, as well as Men; tho' they could not hurt him.[17] Indeed he often said, He knew not how any actual Quality of a finite Being could be called infinite; that Hatred of God must be the highest Guilt possible; but, to call all Sin infinitely evil, when the Guilt of one Sin may surpass another so exceedingly, must be a very disputable Expression, as it supposes one Infinite much greater than another, in the very Respect in which the other is infinite. <19>

The Author's *Propositions, with Remarks on them.*

PROP. XI

"The Government of the Church belongs to the Civil Magistrate." Here he subjoins, as if Mr. HUTCHESON asserted, that all the Powers in the Church of Preaching, Administrating the Sacraments, Rebuking, Cen-suring, were derived from the Magistrate, with gross Disingenuity: So he

---

17. See *A Short Introduction to Moral Philosophy*, (1747), pp. 74–75; (2007), p. 77; and *A System of Moral Philosophy*, book 1, chap. 10, art. 2, pp. 210–11: "Due attention to the moral attributes must excite the highest possible esteem, and love, and grati-tude. . . . When we are conscious of having offended him, they [the moral attributes of God] must fill our souls, not only with fears of punishment, but with inward re-morse, ingenuous shame, and sorrow, and desire of reformation."

charges him with teaching, *That all Heresies in Opinion, should pass without any Censure.* That *Subscribing a Confession should be banished out of the Church.* To this are subjoined, in Mr. HUTCHESON's Name, some Reasonings the Author has made for him, that he might have an Opportunity for the good-natured Charge of Perjury on him, and many Ministers of the Church, who, he says, are preaching against the Confession.

Mr. *HUTCHESON*'s Propositions.

PROP. XI.

Mr. Hutcheson maintains, that there are Powers of a religious Kind belonging to every Minister, and even some to every Christian, not derived from the Magistrate: But that it belongs to the Magistrate to take Care of the religious Notions of the People, to appoint proper Teachers, and to support them.[18] This Scheme he seemed to approve most, when mentioning two other different ones, One of the Papists, the Other of Independents; we cannot directly charge him with it, let it be good or bad. He also pleaded for universal Toleration by the State, toward all peaceable Subjects of whatever Religion, Let the Church censure their Opinions as it pleases: And shewed how this is reconcilable with the Magistrate's Care of Religion.[19]

18. Hutcheson thought that individuals have a "sacred right of judging for themselves" in matters of religion, but also that "the far greater part of every people will not use this right, that they will incautiously give themselves up to be led" by "designing men." Hence, "it must plainly be the business of the magistrate to get the *leading* into his own hands; by appointing men of character and learning to teach the just sentiments of religion and virtue": *A Short Introduction to Moral Philosophy*, (1747), pp. 318–19; (2007), pp. 266–67. Concerning rights and prudence in Hutcheson's philosophy, see Knud Haakonssen, "Natural Rights or Political Prudence? Francis Hutcheson on Toleration"; and James Moore, "Presbyterianism and the Right of Private Judgment: Church Government in Ireland and Scotland in the Age of Francis Hutcheson."

19. Here the parallel printing of opposing propositions ends, and continuous text resumes.

We must also observe what follows upon these Propositions, A Charge of perverting Texts of Scripture, in which the Author both shews his Malice and Ignorance. Any Man who will look into *Pool*'s Synopsis, a Book to which any Scholar can have Access,[20] will find that, *Prov.* xvi. 4. is interpreted by many great Men, as Mr. HUTCHESON does. *God fitted each Thing for itself, or its own Business*; Our Author has made indeed a new Interpretation of his own in Mr. HUTCHESON's Name, different from all those in the Criticks. So *Rom.* xii. 11. That Reading is known to all Men of Letters to be common in the Greek Manuscripts, and was followed by many Fathers, as well as several modern Criticks, among the *Calvinists* too; and yet this Author ignorantly or maliciously ascribes this to Mr. HUTCHESON as a Perversion, who told us of it without espousing it.

Mr. Hutcheson said that the Rule used by some, as a great leading Maxim, *We must not do evil, that good may come of it,* was not taught by the Apostles as a Rule, nor could be of any Service to decide any debated Point in Morals. For often for a good End, we may do what would have been criminal without a View to such an End, as in Amputations, ha<19>zarding Life in War, delivering Money to a Robber to save our Lives, or putting Men to Death for Defence of our Country. In other Cases there are some Evils we should not do, even to obtain these Ends, such as Blasphemy, Perjury, Abjuring the Faith. Now this Rule does not tell us what we are to do for a good End, and what not.[21]

Mr. Hutcheson never said that the Rule, 1 *Cor.* x. 31. was to be restricted only to the Case of Eating or not eating Meats offered to Idols, or prohibited among the Jews. So all his fine Triumphs are lost.

As our Author takes upon him to direct and admonish others, we shall only suggest to him and all our Fellow-students, to examine Matters well, before they charge Men in Print with Heresies, to consult Men of more Wisdom, Learning and Experience than themselves, and to follow the

---

20. Matthew Poole, *Synopsis criticorum aliorumque Sacrae Scripturae interpretum et commentatorum* (1669–76). This was a vast synopsis of commentaries on the Bible.

21. *A Short Introduction to Moral Philosophy,* (1747), pp. 242–46; (2007), pp. 207–10; *A System of Moral Philosophy,* book 2, chap. 2, sec. 17, arts. 3–9, pp. 120–40.

charitable Precepts of the Gospel. If he was instigated or patronized by Men of any Character or Station, let them consider what a fine Example is set. Other Students may fall a writing and printing against themselves or their Favourites, in Church or in Colleges, and how can they complain, if others follow the Example set before them. What the Effects of such Paper-war may be, 'tis easy to foresee. Mr. <20> HUTCHESON is almost a Stranger in this Country, they thought fewer perhaps would espouse his Quarrel. But the same Practice may be turned against any Man, and considering our present Animosities about religious Matters, no Man is safe from such insidious Attacks upon his Character; and enew will be found ready to receive Aspersions against any of the opposite Party. And with what Face can the Beginners of such Attacks complain of them?

We have only to add further, that we had never thought of writing against this Author, had it not been at the Desire of some good Men, who informed us a few Days ago, that they were afraid, the Mask of Piety he has put on, and the Assurance with which he vents his Falsehoods, might influence some who were Strangers to Mr. HUTCHESON and Him.

As to the Truth of the whole of this Account of what Mr. HUTCHESON teaches, we appeal to all his Scholars in general, many of whom are now Men of the best Characters in all Ranks of Life: And in particular we take the Liberty to mention the Names of a few who are nearest at Hand, and may immediately vouch for us to any who inquire at them.

The Reverend Mr. HENRY MILLER, Minister of the Gospel at *Neilston.*

The Reverend Mr. JOHN HAMILTON Minister of the *Barony.*

Mr. GEORGE ROSSE Professor of Humanity in the University of *Glasgow.*

Mr. GERSHOM CARMICHALL Library-Keeper.

Mr. ROBERT HALL Preacher of the Gospel.

Mr. THOMAS CLELAND Preacher of the Gospel.

Mr. ROBERT MARSHAL Elder of the High-church Parish.

Mr. ROBERT FOULIS.

Mr. ANDREW FOULIS.

Mr. GEORGE MUIRHEAD.

Mr. JAMES MOOR.

Mr. ALEXANDER DUNLOP Jun.
Mr. MATTHEW BRISBANE.
Mr. WILLIAM BROUN Merchant in *Glasgow.*

We could have mentioned many more.

FINIS.[22]

22. Later in the same year, 1738, *A Vindication* was reinforced by a rough satire on *Shaftsbury's Ghost conjur'd* and the preaching of evangelical Calvinists: *A Letter to the Valiant and Undaunted Champion of our Broken Covenants, the Reverend Mr. Ebenezer Erskine, in Relation to the Present Heresies, Backslidings, Defections, and Lukewarmness of the Times and His Apostolical Testimonies against them* (London, 1738). The title page declared it to be "By a bold young Soldier under his Banner, Euzelus Philalethes, Author of Shaftsbury's Ghost conjur'd." But the content of the letter makes it evident that it was not the work of Hugh Heugh, but of Hutcheson's students and friends. Concerning further repercussions of the controversy, see Private Correspondence, Letter 25. See James Moore, "Evangelical Calvinists versus the Hutcheson Circle: Debating the Faith in Scotland, 1738–1739."

Preface to *Divine Dialogues*
by Henry More, 1743

DIVINE DIALOGUES,

Containing DISQUISITIONS

Concerning the ATTRIBUTES

AND PROVIDENCE of GOD.

IN THREE VOLUMES.

By *HENRY MORE,* D. D.

Thy wisdom, O Lord, reacheth from one end to another
mightily; and sweetly doth she order all things.
—*Wisdom* viii. 1.[1]

GLASGOW.

Printed by ROBERT FOULIS, and sold by him there; at *Edinburgh,*
by Mess. HAMILTON and BALFOUR and John Paton. MDCCXLIII

---

1. "The Book of Wisdom of Solomon" 8:1, one of the deuterocanonical or apocry-
phal books of the Catholic Bible, in *The Jerusalem Bible,* p. 884.

The EDITOR to the READER.[2]

The high reputation Dr. HENRY MORE *obtained for eminent learning and piety, in that religious age in which he flourished, gave the editor ground to hope, that this new edition of his* Divine Dialogues *would be very acceptable to the better sort of readers in this age, and could give offence to none. He was justly renowned for great piety, and purity of manners, during the whole course of his life.[3] He was fellow of Christ's College in* Cambridge *during the civil wars, and after the restoration: and his works continued in such high reputation, long after his decease, that certain gentlemen of great piety and liberality generously contributed to have a collection of his Theological and Philosophical works translated into* English, *and printed in two volumes in folio, in the reign of Queen* ANNE;[4] *and were thought to have by this means done great service to religion. His Dialogues are deemed not inferior to any of his works, either in the goodness of the design, or the justness of reasoning, or the pleasantry of the composition.*

The design is to establish the grand foundations of all religion, the being, and moral perfections of GOD, and to vindicate his Providence in the permission of evil natural and moral. The reasonings are much the same with those insisted on by the greatest authors, both ancient and modern; and the agreeable manner of delivering them is in a very natural dialogue, managed by a variety of characters, very well maintained thro' the whole conversation; mixed with abundant humour and pleasantry, such as, however now a little

---

2. Hutcheson was identified as the author of the "recommendatory preface" by James Fletcher, an Oxford bookseller, in a list of books published by the Foulis Press that was printed at the back of Edward Bentham, *An Introduction to Moral Philosophy*. Caroline Robbins also attributed the preface to Hutcheson in *The Eighteenth-Century Commonwealthman*, p. 421.

3. In More's account of his own life, quoted in English translation in Richard Ward, *The Life of the Learned and Pious Dr. Henry More* (London, 1710), pp. 6–8, he recorded that while still a boy at school he experienced a "deep Aversion" to "*Calvinistick Predestination*." He attributed his "Perswasion of the Divine Justice and Goodness" to "an *inward Sense* of the *Divine Presence*"; for "since no distinct Reason, Philosophy, or Instruction taught it me at that Age; but only an *internal Sensation* urg'd it upon me; I think it is very evident, that this was an *innate Sense* or *Notion* in me, contrary to some witless and sordid *Philosophasters* of our present Age."

4. *The Theological Works of the Most Pious and Learned Henry More, D.D.* (1708).

antiquated, will please all that can relish the manners of other ages as well as their own, and have some other standard of politeness than the usual chat and wit of our modern drawing-rooms, coffee-houses, or play-houses. 'Tis enough to justify the editor, that our author is never mentioned without expressions of esteem and reverence by men of piety and learning, in their defences of religion and virtue; and that even the ingenious Earl of Shafts\<iii\>bury *has done the highest honour to this author's* Enchiridion Ethicum, *or, his* Summary of Morals.[5]

As to such readers who are acquainted with the controversies of the learned, no apology is necessary for any part of these dialogues: they know the indulgence due to inquisitive minds, in their peculiar sentiments about some abstruse metaphysical questions relating to the immensity and eternity of God:[6] and that no meaner names than Sir Isaac Newton *and Dr.* Clarke *seem to have embraced the same sentiments with Dr.* MORE; *nor will such readers be surprized, that, in the infancy of true natural philosophy among us in* Britain, *there are some reasonings of our author's not conclusive against the whimsical fictions of* Cartesius.[7] *Few men of that age knew more of these things than our author; but the honour of grand improvements in natural knowledge was reserved by Providence to the subsequent generation.*

As to other readers of good judgment, if they can excuse some little dif\<iv\>ficulties of metaphysicks in the first dialogue, they will find interspersed some beautiful just reasonings, easy to be apprehended; and, in the second and third dialogues, 'tis hoped, they will find abundant pleasure and entertainment, as well as useful instruction. They will easily see the constant friendly intention toward Christianity, to warn men against the corruptions,

5. In *Philosophiae Moralis/Short Introduction,* book 1, chap. 6, art. 3, p. 95n, Hutcheson noted: "Very useful observations have been collected by Henry More, a most virtuous man, in his *Enchiridion Ethicum,* and by the Earl of Shaftesbury, a man not less noble in capacity than in birth, in his *Inquiry on Virtue* and in his *Philosophical Rhapsody.*"

6. In *A Synopsis of Metaphysics,* in *Logic Metaphysics, and the Natural Sociability of Mankind,* part 3, chap. 2, sec. 7, pp. 165–66, Hutcheson considered the "difficult question" whether God is immeasurable and eternal to be one "which altogether surpasses the power of the human mind." See also ibid., p. 83n.

7. On More's differences with Descartes and the influence of his theory of space on Newton, see Ernst Cassirer, *The Platonic Renaissance in England* (Edinburgh: Thomas Nelson, 1953), pp. 146ff.

depravations, and abuses of that divine institution, and to remove, as far as 'tis possible for our weak understandings, the objections which have given the greatest perplexity to inquisitive and serious minds in all ages.

To some editions of these three dialogues, a fourth and fifth are subjoined; but, as these were separately published by the author, and are upon subjects quite different, viz. the explication of some obscure parts of the prophetick books, particularly, the Revelation; *it was not thought proper to subjoin them.*[8] *The editor sincerely wishes these dialogues he has re-published may continue to serve the pious and worthy intention of the author, in promoting true* Religion *and* Virtue.

8. *The Two Last Dialogues, Treating of the Kingdome of God within Us and without Us, and of the Especial Providence through Christ over His Church from the Beginning to the End of Things* (London 1668) was published posthumously as a companion volume to the first three dialogues, and all five were published together in 1713.

BIBLIOGRAPHY

The following bibliography has been divided into three sections: modern sources, ancient sources, and secondary literature.

Modern sources

Abernethy, John. *Scarce and Valuable Tracts and Sermons*, 1–5. London and Dublin, 1751.

Abernethy, John, and William Bruce. *The Nature and Consequences of the Sacramental Test with Reasons for the Repeal of it*. Dublin, 1731.

Addison, Joseph. *The Works*. New York, 1837.

[Allestree, Richard?]. *The Practice of Christian Grace. Or the Whole Duty of Man*. London, 1658.

Anonymous. *A Serious Address to the Church of Scotland, with Relation to the Growth of Deism and Immorality: Examining Some Parts of Their Discipline and Constitution*. London, 1739.

Balguy, John. *The Foundation of Moral Goodness*. London, 1728.

Bayle, Pierre. *Pensées diverses sur la comète* (1680). Translated as *Miscellaneous Reflections, occasion'd by the Comet*. 2 vols. London, 1708.

Benson, George. *History of the First Planting the Christian Religion: Taken from the Acts of the Apostles, and Their Epistles*. 2 vols. London, 1735.

Bentham, Edward. *An Introduction to Moral Philosophy*. Oxford, 1745.

Berkeley, George. *The Analyst; or, A Discourse Addressed to an Infidel Mathematician*. London, 1734.

———. *Passive Obedience; or, The Christian Doctrine of Not Resisting the Supreme Power, Proved and Vindicated upon the Principles of the Law of Nature*. Dublin, 1712.

Blackburne, Francis. *Memoirs of Thomas Hollis, Esq*. 2 vols. London, 1780.

Blackwood, John. *Dissertatio philosophica de imperii civilis origine et causis*. Glasgow, 1741.

Bruce, William. *See* Abernethy.

Bruyère, Jean de la. *Les caractères, ou Les moeurs de siècle* (1688). Translated in *The Works of Monsieur de la Bruyère*. 2 vols. London, 1713.

Butler, Joseph. *Fifteen Sermons Preached at the Rolls Chapel*. London, 1726.

Butler, Samuel. *Hudibras* (1663). Edited by John Wilders. Oxford: Clarendon Press, 1967.

Carlyle, Alexander. *Anecdotes and Characters of the Times*. Edited by James Kinsley. London: Oxford University Press, 1973.

Carmichael, Gershom. *Breviuscula introductio ad logicam*. Glasgow, 1720; 2nd ed. Edinburgh, 1722. English translation in *Natural Rights on the Threshold of the Scottish Enlightenment*, pp. 287–317. Indianapolis: Liberty Fund, 2002.

———. *Natural Rights on the Threshold of the Scottish Enlightenment. The Writings of Gershom Carmichael*. Translated by Michael Silverthorne. Edited by James Moore and Michael Silverthorne. Indianapolis: Liberty Fund, 2002.

Clarke, Samuel. *A Discourse Concerning the Unchangeable Obligations of Natural Religion, and the Truth and Certainty of the Christian Revelation*. London, 1706.

———. *The Scripture-Doctrine of the Trinity*. London, 1712.

The Confession of Faith, Larger and Shorter Catechisms: First Agreed upon by the Assembly of Divines at Westminster: And Now appointed by the General Assembly of the Church of Scotland to be a Part of Uniformity in Religion between the Kirks of Christ in the Three Kingdoms. Glasgow, 1732.

Collins, Anthony. *A Discourse of Free–Thinking*. London, 1713.

———. *A Discourse of the Grounds and Reasons of the Christian Religion*. London, 1724.

Cotton, Charles. *Scarronides, or Virgil Travesty, on the First and Fourth Books of the Aeneid*. London, 1665.

Crousaz, Jean-Pierre. *Traité du Beau*. 2nd ed. Tours, France: Libraire Artheme Fayard, 1985.

Cumberland, Richard. *De Legibus Naturae* [1672]. Translated by John Maxwell (1727), *A Treatise of the Law of Nature*. Edited by Jon Parkin. Indianapolis: Liberty Fund, 2005.

[Defoe, Daniel?]. *Merry Andrew's Epistle to His Old Master, Benjamin, a Mountebank at Bangor-Bridge, on the River Dee, near Wales*. London, 1719.

Duchal, James. *Sermon on the Occasion of the Death of Dr. Arbuckle*. Dublin, 1747.

Eustachius a Sancto Paulo. *Ethica, sive summa moralis disciplinae*. London, 1693.

Fiddes, Richard. *A General Treatise of Morality, Form'd upon the Principles of Natural Reason Only. With a Preface in Answer to Two Essays Lately Published in "The Fable of the Bees."* London, 1724.

Fordyce, David. *Dialogues concerning Education*. 2 vols. London, 1745–48.

———. *The Elements of Moral Philosophy* [1754]. Edited by Thomas D. Kennedy. Indianapolis: Liberty Fund, 2003.

Grant, William. *The Present State of the Church of Scotland, with Respect to Patronages; and the Bill Now Depending before the Parliament*. London, 1736.

Grotius, Hugo. *The Rights of War and Peace* [1738]. Edited by Richard Tuck. 3 vols. Indianapolis: Liberty Fund, 2005.

Harrington, James. *The Prerogative of Popular Government. A Political Discourse in Two Books. The Former Containing the First Preliminary of Oceana . . . The Second concerning Ordination, against Dr. H. Hammond, Dr. L. Seaman*. London, 1658.

Hoadly, Benjamin. *The Nature of the Kingdom, or Church, of Christ: A Sermon Preach'd before the King, at the Royal Chapel of St. James's, on Sunday March 31, 1717*. London, 1717.

———. *The Works of Benjamin Hoadly, D.D.* 3 vols. London, 1773.

Hobbes, Thomas. *The Elements of Law*. Edited by J. C. A. Gaskin. Oxford: Oxford University Press, 1994.

l'Hôpital, Guillaume François Antoine, Marquis de. *Traité analytique des sections coniques* [1707]. Paris, 1775.

Hume, David. *A Treatise of Human Nature: Being an Attempt to Introduce the Experimental Method of Reasoning into Moral Subjects*. 3 vols. London, 1739–40.

Hutcheson, Francis. *An Essay on the Nature and Conduct of the Passions and Affections with Illustrations on the Moral Sense*. [1728; 3rd ed. 1742]. Edited by Aaron Garrett. Indianapolis: Liberty Fund, 2002.

———. *An Inquiry into the Original of Our Ideas of Beauty and Virtue*. [1725; 2nd ed. 1726]. Edited by Wolfgang Leidhold. Indianapolis: Liberty Fund, rev. ed., 2008.

———. *De Naturali Hominum Socialitate* [1730]. Translated in *Logic, Metaphysics, and the Natural Sociability of Mankind*, pp. 189–216. Indianapolis: Liberty Fund, 2006.

———. *Logic, Metaphysics, and the Natural Sociability of Mankind.* Translated by Michael Silverthorne. Edited by James Moore and Michael Silverthorne. Indianapolis: Liberty Fund, 2006.

———. *Logicae compendium* [1756]. Translated in *Logic, Metaphysics, and the Natural Sociability of Mankind*, pp. 1–56. Indianapolis: Liberty Fund, 2006.

———. *The Meditations of the Emperor Marcus Aurelius Antoninus* [1742]. Translated by Francis Hutcheson and James Moor. Edited by James Moore and Michael Silverthorne. Indianapolis: Liberty Fund, 2008.

———. *Metaphysicae synopsis.* [1742; 2nd ed. 1744]. Translated in *Logic, Metaphysics, and the Natural Sociability of Mankind*, pp. 57–187. Indianapolis: Liberty Fund, 2006.

———. *On Human Nature. Reflections on Our Common System of Morality. On the Social Nature of Man.* Edited by Thomas Mautner. Cambridge: Cambridge University Press, 1993.

———. *Philosophiae moralis institutio compendiaria.* [1742; 2nd ed. 1745]. *A Short Introduction to Moral Philosophy.* Translated by anonymous [1747]. Edited by Luigi Turco. Indianapolis: Liberty Fund, 2007.

———. *A System of Moral Philosophy* [1755]. Edited by Knud Haakonssen and Christian Maurer. Carmel, IN: Liberty Fund, forthcoming.

King, William. *De origine mali.* London, 1702.

———. *An Essay on the Origin of Evil.* [Translated by Edmund Law]. London, 1731.

[Kirkpatrick, James]. *An Historical Essay upon the Loyalty of Presbyterians in Great-Britain and Ireland from the Reformation to this Present Year 1713.* [Belfast], 1713.

Law, William. *Remarks upon a Late Book, Entituled "The Fable of the Bees; or Private Vices, Public Benefits." In a Letter to the Author. To Which Is Added, a Postscript, containing an Observation or Two upon Mr. Bayle.* London, 1724.

Le Clerc, Jean. *Bibliothèque Ancienne et Moderne, pour server de suite aux Bibliothéques Universelles et Choisie*, vol. 24. Amsterdam, 1725.

Leechman, William. "The Preface Giving some Account of the Life, Writings, and Character of the Author," in Francis Hutcheson, *A System of Moral Philosophy*. Carmel, IN: Liberty Fund, forthcoming.

————. *The Temper, Character, and Duty of a Minister of the Gospel: A Sermon Preached before the Synod of Glasgow and Air, at Glasgow, April 7th, 1741*. Glasgow, [1741].

MacLaurin, Colin. *A Treatise of Fluxions. In Two Books*. 2 vols. Edinburgh, 1742.

Malebranche, Nicholas. *The Search after Truth* [1674]. Translated by Thomas M. Lennon and Paul J. Olscamp. Columbus: Ohio State University Press, 1980.

————. *Treatise concerning the Search after Truth*. Translated Thomas Taylor. London, 1700.

Mandeville, Bernard. *The Fable of the Bees; or, Private Vices, Public Benefits*. 3rd ed. London, 1724. Edited by F. B. Kaye. Oxford: Clarendon Press, 1924; Indianapolis: Liberty Fund, 1988.

————. *Free Thoughts on Religion, the Church, and National Happiness*. London, 1720.

Milton, John. *Paradise Lost and Selected Poetry and Prose*. Edited by Northrop Frye. New York: Rinehart, 1951.

More, Henry. *An Account of Virtue*. London, 1690.

————. *Divine Dialogues. Containing Disquisitions Concerning the Attributes and Providence of God*. Glasgow, 1743.

————. *The Theological Works of the Most Pious and Learned Henry More, D.D.* London, 1708.

Nettleton, Thomas. *Treatise on Virtue and Happiness*. London, 1736.

Newton, Isaac. *The Mathematical Principles of Natural Philosophy*. 2 vols. London, 1729.

Patoun (or Paton), Robert. *The Main Duty of Bishops*. Edinburgh, 1739.

"Philasthenes." *A Letter from a Gentleman in Town to His Friend in the Country, relating to the Royal Infirmary of Edinburgh*. Edinburgh, 1739.

[Pitcairne, Archibald]. *The Assembly, a Comedy, by a Scots Gentleman*. London, 1722.

Poole, Matthew. *Synopsis criticorum aliorumque Sacrae Scripturae interpretum et commentatorum*. London, 1669–76.

Pope, Alexander. *An Essay on Criticism*. London, 1711.

Pufendorf, Samuel. *De Officio Hominis et Civis juxta Legem Naturalem Libri Duo* [1673]. Edited by Gershom Carmichael [1718]. Edinburgh, 2nd ed., 1724.

————. *Of the Law of Nature and Nations* [1672]. Translated by Basil Kennet. London, 4th ed., 1729.

———. *On the Duty of Man and Citizen* [1673]. Translated by Michael Silverthorne. Edited by James Tully. Cambridge: Cambridge University Press, 1991.

———. *The Whole Duty of Man, According to the Law of Nature* [1673]. Translated by Andrew Tooke [1691]. Edited by Ian Hunter and David Saunders. Indianapolis: Liberty Fund, 2003.

Randall, Thomas, ed. *Tracts Concerning Patronage*. Edinburgh, 1770.

Rapin-Thoyras, Paul de. *History of England*. 15 vols. London, 1726–31.

Sanderson, Robert. *Sermons*. 8th ed. London, 1689.

Shaftsbury, Anthony Ashley Cooper, third Earl of. *Characteristicks of Men, Manners, Opinions, Times* [1711]. Edited by Lawrence E. Klein. Cambridge: Cambridge University Press, 1999.

Simson, Robert. *Elements of the Conic Sections*. 2nd ed. Edinburgh, 1792.

———. "Pappi Alexandrini Propositiones duae generales, . . . Restitutae a Viro Doctissimo Rob. Simson, Math. Prof. Glasc." *Philosophical Transactions of the Royal Society* 32, no. 377 (1722–23): 330–40.

———. *Sectionum Conicarum. Libri V*. Edinburgh, 1735.

Smith, Adam. *The Theory of Moral Sentiments*. [1759; 6th ed. 1790]. Edited by D. D. Raphael and A. L. Macfie. Indianapolis: Liberty Fund, 1984.

Steward, Thomas. *Fifteen Sermons upon Several Practical Subjects*. London, 1734.

Swift, Jonathan. *Poetical Works*. Edited by Herbert Davis. London: Oxford University Press, 1967.

Tindal, Matthew. *Christianity as Old as the Creation*. London, 1730.

Trail, William. *Account of the Life and Writings of Robert Simson, M.D.* London, 1812.

Vries, Gerard de. *De natura Dei et humanae mentis*. 4th ed. Edinburgh, 1703.

Wallis, John. *Opera Mathematica*, vol. 2. Oxford, 1693.

Ward, Richard. *The Life of the Learned and Pious Dr. Henry More*. London, 1710.

Watson, John. *The Gentleman and Citizen's Almanack*. Dublin, 1737.

[White, Jeremiah]. *A Persuasive to Mutual Love and Charity among Christians Who Differ in Opinion. Drawn from the Motives of the Gospel, and Proper for Healing the Present Divisions among us*. Glasgow, 1739.

Wodrow, Robert. *Analecta: or Materials for a History of Remarkable Providences*. 4 vols. Edinburgh: Maitland Club, 1842–43.

Wollaston, William. *The Religion of Nature Delineated*. London, 1724.

Woolston, Thomas. *Discourses on the Miracles of Our Saviour*. London, 1727–29.

Ancient sources

Apollonius of Perga, *Conics*. Translated by R. Catesby Taliaferro. Edited by Dana Densmore. Santa Fe: Green Lion Press, 2000.

Cicero, Marcus Tullius. *De finibus bonorum et malorum*. Translated by H. Rackham. Cambridge, MA: Harvard University Press, 1971.

———. *De Officiis*, I.x.32. Translated by Walter Miller. London: William Heinemann, 1913.

Diogenes Laertius. *Lives of Eminent Philosophers*. Translated by R. D. Hicks. Cambridge, MA: Harvard University Press, 1965.

Homer. *The Iliad of Homer*. Translated by Richmond Lattimore. Chicago: University of Chicago Press, 1951.

———. *The Odyssey*. Translated by E. V. Rieu. Harmondsworth, Middlesex, NJ: Penguin Books, 1959.

Horace. *Odes and Epodes*. Translated by Niall Rudd. Cambridge, MA: Harvard University Press, 2014.

———. *Satires*. Translated by H. Rushton Fairclough. London: William Heinemann, 1966.

———. *Satires, Epistles and the Art of Poetry*. Translated by H. Rushton Fairclough. London: William Heinemann, 1926.

The Jerusalem Bible. Edited by Alexander Jones. London: Darton, Longman and Todd, 1966.

Juvenal. *Satires*, in *Juvenal and Persius*. Translated by Susanna Morton Braund. Cambridge, MA: Harvard University Press, 2004.

Livy. *Ab Urbe Condita* (*From the Founding of the City*). Translated by Frank Gardner Moore. 13 vols. London: William Heinemann, 1943.

Longinus. *On the Sublime*. In Aristotle, *The Poetics*; "Longinus," *On the Sublime*; Demetrius, *On Style*. Translated by W. Hamilton Fyfe. London: William Heinemann, 1953.

Lucretius. *De Rerum Naturae*. Translated by W. H. D. Rouse. London: William Heinemann, 1947.

Nepos, Cornelius. *A Selection Including the Lives of Cato and Atticus*. Oxford: Oxford University Press, 1990.

Virgil. *Aeneid*. Translated by H. Rushton Fairclough. Revised by
    G. P. Goold. 2 vols. Cambridge, MA: Harvard University Press, 2014.

Secondary sources

Agnew, Jean. *Belfast Merchant Families in the Seventeenth Century*. Dublin:
    Four Courts Press, 1996.

Album Studiosorum Academiae Lugduno Batavae MDLXXV–MDSCCCLXXV
    Accedunt Nomina Curatorum et Professorum Per Eadem Secula. The Hague:
    Martin Nijhof, 1875.

Ball, W. W. Rouse. *A Short Account of the History of Mathematics*. London:
    Macmillan, 1893.

Barnard, Toby. *A New Anatomy of Ireland: The Irish Protestants, 1649–1770*.
    New Haven, CT: Yale University Press, 2003.

Boyer, Carl B., and Uta C. Merzbach. *A History of Mathematics*. Hoboken,
    NJ: John Wiley and Sons, 2011.

Cassirer, Ernst. *The Platonic Renaissance in England*. Edinburgh: Thomas
    Nelson, 1953.

Coolidge, J. L. *A History of the Conic Sections and Quadric Surfaces*. Oxford:
    Oxford University Press, 1945.

Grote, Simon W. *The Emergence of Modern Aesthetic Theory: Religion and
    Morality in Enlightenment Germany and Scotland*. Cambridge: Cambridge
    University Press, 2017.

Haakonssen, Knud. "Natural Jurisprudence and the Identity of the Scottish
    Enlightenment." In *Philosophy and Religion in Enlightenment Britain*.
    Edited by Ruth Savage, pp. 258–71. Oxford: Oxford University Press, 2012.

———. "Natural Rights or Political Prudence? Francis Hutcheson on
    Toleration." In *Natural Law and Toleration in the Early Enlightenment*.
    Edited by Jon Parkin and Timothy Stanton, pp. 183–200. Oxford: Oxford
    University Press, 2013.

Hochstrasser, Timothy J. *Natural Law Theories in the Early Enlightenment*.
    Cambridge: Cambridge University Press, 2000.

Lake, Peter. "Serving God and the Times: the Calvinist Conformity of
    Robert Sanderson." *Journal of British Studies* 27 (1988): 81–116.

Macgill, Hamilton. *The Life of Hugh Heugh, D.D.* Edinburgh, 1850.

Mackay, Angus. *The Book of Mackay*. Edinburgh, 1906.

M'Kerrow, John. *History of the Secession Church*. Edinburgh: William Oliphant and Son, 1849.

McLachlan, H. "Thomas Nettleton, M.D." *Transactions of the Unitarian Historical Society* 9, no. 1 (October 1947): 21–27.

Malcolm, Noel. "Charles Cotton, Translator of Hobbes's De Cive." *Huntington Library Quarterly* 61 (1998): 259–87.

Matinowski-Charles, Syliane. "Entre rationalisme et subjectivism, l'esthétique de Jean-Pierre de Crousaz." *Revue de Theologie et de Philosophie* 136 (2004): 7–21.

Moore, James. "Evangelical Calvinists versus the Hutcheson Circle: Debating the Faith in Scotland, 1738–1739." In *Debating the Faith: Religion and Letter Writing in Great Britain, 1550–1800*, pp. 177–93. Dordrecht: Springer, 2013.

———. "Natural Rights in the Scottish Enlightenment." In *The Cambridge History of Eighteenth-Century Political Thought*. Edited by Mark Goldie and Robert Wokler, pp. 291–316. Cambridge: Cambridge University Press, 2006.

———. "Presbyterianism and the Right of Private Judgment: Church Government in Ireland and Scotland in the Age of Francis Hutcheson." In *Philosophy and Religion in Enlightenment Britain*. Edited by Ruth Savage, pp. 141–68. Oxford: Oxford University Press, 2012.

Moore, James, and Michael Silverthorne. "Hutcheson's LL.D." *Eighteenth-Century Scotland* 20 (2006): 10–12.

Moore, James, and M. A. Stewart. "A Scots-Irish Bookseller in Holland: William Smith of Amsterdam (1698–1741)." *Eighteenth-Century Scotland* 7 (1993): 8–11.

Nobbs, Douglas. "The Political Ideas of William Cleghorn, Hume's Academic Rival." *Journal of the History of Ideas* 24 (1965): 575–86.

Nuttall, Geoffrey. *Calendar of the Correspondence of Philip Doddridge DD (1702–1751)*. London: HMSO, 1979.

Robbins, Caroline. *The Eighteenth-Century Commonwealthman*. Cambridge, MA: Harvard University Press, 1959.

Scott, W. R. "James Arbuckle and His Relation to the Molesworth-Shaftesbury School." *Mind*, n.s., 30 (1899): 194–215.

Sher, Richard, and Alexander Murdoch. "Patronage and Party in the Church of Scotland, 1750–1800." In *Church, Politics and Society in Scotland*

1408–1929. Edited by Norman McDougall, pp. 197–220. Edinburgh: John Donald, 1983.

Stephen, Leslie. *English Thought in the Eighteenth Century*. London: Smith, Elder, 1876.

Stewart, M. A. "John Smith and the Molesworth Circle." *Eighteenth-Century Ireland* 2 (1987): 89–102.

———. *The Kirk and the Infidel*. Lancaster: Lancaster University, 1995.

Stewart, M. A., and James Moore. "William Smith (1698–1741) and the Dissenters' Book Trade." *Bulletin of the Presbyterian Historical Society of Ireland* 22 (1993): 20–27.

Taylor, Charles. *An Introduction to the Ancient and Modern Geometry of Conics*. Cambridge: Deighton, Bell, 1881.

INDEX

Francis Hutcheson is indicated by "FH" in index subentries. Correspondence with Francis Hutcheson is indexed by the name of the correspondent.

388 INDEX

Joshua 6:31, 307n66
Joshua 9:18–19, 309n72
1 Samuel 2:30, 314n102
2 Samuel 21:1–2, 309n73
2 Samuel 22:2–3, 305n47
1 Kings 18:27, 213n41
1 Kings 20:1–6, 303n41
2 Kings 19:22, 318n144
Job 2:9–10, 304n43
Job 14:4, 316n123
Job 14:13, 323n180
Job 14:14, 304n44
Job 15:14, 317n140
Job 19:25–27, 321n174
Job 33:13, 323n185
Job 35:11, 297n14
Job 42:6, 337n249
Psalms 5:4, 330n218
Psalms 10:13, 329n207
Psalms 14:1, 330n219
Psalms 15:1–2, 306n55
Psalms 18:2, 305n50
Psalms 18:28, 337n247
Psalms 29:2, 314n104
Psalms 41:4, 328n205
Psalms 49:20, 297n15
Psalms 51:4, 329n206
Psalms 51:5, 317n141
Psalms 55:8, 314n99
Psalms 55:22, 305n48
Psalms 57:1–2, 308n67
Psalms 63:9–11, 308n68
Psalms 65:3, 321n171
Psalms 71:22, 318n144
Psalms 74:22, 337n242
Psalms 92:7, 335n236
Psalms 95:6–7, 324n188
Psalms 100:2–3, 324n189
Psalms 111:7–9, 310n79
Psalms 119:96, 307n63
Psalms 119:99, 307n62
Psalms 119:105, 307n61
Psalms 119:127, 299n27
Psalms 145:9, 328n204
Psalms 148:2–5, 324n191

Psalms 149:2, 324n190
Proverbs 1:7, 297n19
Proverbs 2:4, 316n129
Proverbs 2:8, 330n216
Proverbs 6:27, 332n226
Proverbs 10:23, 342n4
Proverbs 12:22, 316n128
Proverbs 14:2, 329n208
Proverbs 16:4, 312n86
Proverbs 16:33, 310n82
Proverbs 18:18, 310n81
Proverbs 25:27, 314n98
Proverbs 211:2, 315n113
Isaiah 1:4, 318n144
Isaiah 5:20, 297n18
Isaiah 8:20, 295n9, 307n60
Isaiah 9:16, 333n230
Isaiah 29:16, 324n192
Isaiah 38:1–6, 303n41
Isaiah 42:8, 315n110
Isaiah 43:62, 313n91
Isaiah 45:9, 324n193
Isaiah 45:11–13, 324n193
Isaiah 48:9–11, 313n95
Isaiah 55:8, 314n97
Isaiah 64:6, 316n122
Jeremiah 5:3, 337n241
Jeremiah 17:9, 315n116
Jeremiah 17:10, 315n114
Jeremiah 18:5–6, 325n194
Micah 6:8, 299n31
Habakkuk 1:13, 330n217
Haggai 2:14, 316n130
Zechariah 5:3–4, 310n78
Zechariah 8:16–17, 305n52
Matthew 5–19, 310n80
Matthew 5:17–18, 299n26
Matthew 7:8, 315n111
Matthew 7:13–14, 317n137
Matthew 8:5–13, 29n46
Matthew 10:28, 303n39
Matthew 10:29, 323n181, 323n183
Matthew 15:9, 333n228
Matthew 19:19, 302n37
Matthew 22:37–39, 137n5
Mark 7:7, 333n228

This book is set in Adobe Garamond, a modern adaptation by
Robert Slimbach of the typeface originally cut around 1540 by the
French typographer and printer Claude Garamond. The Garamond
face, with its small lowercase height and restrained contrast between
thick and thin strokes, is a classic "old-style" face and has long been
one of the most influential and widely used typefaces.

This paper meets the requirements of ANSI/NISO z39.48-1992
(Permanence of Paper). ♾

Book design by Louise OFarrell, Gainesville, Florida
Typography by Westchester Publishing Services, Danbury, Connecticut
Index by Indexing Partners LLC, Rehoboth Beach, Delaware
Printed and bound by Sheridan Books, Inc., Chelsea, Michigan